Sharing the Eucharistic Bread

The Witness of the New Testament

by
Xavier Léon-Dufour, S.J.

Translated by
Matthew J. O'Connell

PAULIST PRESS
New York/Mahwah

This English edition contains a few slight modifications from the original French edition.

Library of Congress Cataloging-in-Publication Data

Léon-Dufour, Xavier.
    Sharing the Eucharistic bread.

    Translation of: Le partage du pain eucharistique selon le Nouveau Testament.
    Bibliography: p.
    Includes index.
    1. Lord's Supper—Biblical teaching.   2. Bible.
N.T.—Criticism, interpretation, etc.   I. Title.
BV823.L4313   1986   264'.36'09015   86–25368
ISBN 0–8091–2865–9 (pbk.)

Published by Paulist Press
997 Macarthur Boulevard
Mahwah, New Jersey 07430

Printed and bound in the
United States of America

Contents

iii

Part III
The Presentations

Part IV
Overture

Preface

My first reason for undertaking a book on the Eucharist is that I myself have grown as a believer through the deepening of my faith. The celebration of the Eucharist is still an essential part of my Christian life, but I now have what I regard as a more profound understanding of it. My second reason, inseparable from the first, is that, being a member of the Christian people, I share with my contemporaries the questions which our historical conjuncture poses for the understanding and preaching of the faith. I would therefore like also to share with others the study of the New Testament which my profession as an exegete has enabled me to carry on, and in this way to enter into dialogue with my believing brothers and sisters and those who reflect on sacramental practice.

Jean-Marie Tézé, an artist, recently undertook a comparison of Raphael's celebrated painting, *The Disputation on the Blessed Sacrament,* with a Byzantine mosaic. In Raphael's painting, an arch of clouds divides the picture into two parts. In the upper part Christ is enthroned with the angels around him; above him is the Father and above the latter in turn a dove which symbolizes the Spirit. Below the arch, at the center, there is a monstrance on an altar; on either side are the figures of numerous theologians, philosophers, or bishops, most of them turned toward the host as they carry on their learned discussion.

The attitude exemplified in this painting is far removed from that of the Eastern Church, if we may judge by the splendid mosaic in the apse of Hagia Sophia in Kiev. Here, on either side of an altar that is framed by two angels, Jesus is shown in the act of distributing, on the one side, the bread and, on the other, the cup to the disciples who advance toward him. In the upper part of the painting there is a tall female figure who stands in the traditional posture of the orant and is turned toward the Pantocrator in the dome; she is Mary, who symbolizes the entire Church.

1

These two works of art exemplify two complementary ways of looking at the Eucharist: on the one hand, as a difficult speculative problem which faith must face and which is reserved for the learned; and, on the other, as the distribution of the eucharistic gifts by Jesus to all his disciples within the great prayer celebrated by the welcoming Church.

The latter approach—"bread broken for a new world"—has been felicitously highlighted by the recent International Eucharistic Congress of Lourdes (1980). Moreover, theologians are now better able to appreciate the "symbolic" perspective adopted by the Fathers of the Church. As a result, these scholars have moved toward a more authentic presentation of the mystery, such as we find in the Kiev icon.

The present book seeks to contribute to this movement by reexamining the scriptural foundations of the Eucharist. My aim is not a dogmatic synthesis but a biblico-theological approach that takes into account all the inspired texts on the subject. Its results will facilitate dialogue with the dogmatic theologians of the various Christian confessions. Faith will thereby acquire an improved expression that remains faithful to the New Testament message and draws inspiration from authentic tradition.

Finally, my dearest wish is that this work might contribute, directly or indirectly, to a renewed understanding of faith in the eucharistic mystery. Such a renewal, of course, requires of the reader, as it did of me, a real effort to enter into the labyrinth of exegesis. My experience has been that the results are well worth the effort.

This book has been in the making for over thirty years, ever since I wrote an article on the passion narratives for the *Supplément* to the *Dictionnaire de la Bible*. At that time I developed a hypothesis which was gradually consolidated through contacts with my colleagues as well as with my students, Jesuits and others, and with those attending biblical sessions which I directed. Finally, the expert collaboration of Renza Arrighi has led to many clarifications during the three years actually spent on the writing of the book. I am deeply grateful to all these individuals.

May this book enlighten and strengthen my brothers and sisters in the faith, as it has me!

Xavier Léon-Dufour
Paris, November 13, 1981

Introduction

Different though they are among themselves, the liturgies of the various Christian confessions are all connected with the "breaking of bread" and the "Lord's Supper" and, through these, with the last meal of Jesus. They are the outcome of lengthy traditions; in the course of time they have gradually transformed the original practice by integrating into it elements added by successive communities. These changes in the manner of celebrating one and the same mystery are fully understandable and justified, since living tradition is not satisfied to repeat exactly what was said and done in the past. Rather, in its effort to express the faith of a particular people it takes into account the cultural currents affecting that people as they encounter new situations and develop new sensibilities. The early Christians themselves were not afraid to let differently situated communities vary their practice even within one and the same period of time. We shall see this to be so as we read the eucharistic texts of the New Testament.

Amid all this variety and development, however, the New Testament data have always remained *the* point of reference for the liturgical expressions adopted by the Churches over the centuries. This fact justifies the work of the exegetes as they constantly seek to manifest anew the meaning of the foundational texts, as understood in their time and by the means available to them.

I would like, by way of introduction, to lay my cards on the table and tell the reader what my own presuppositions are, what method I am using, and what route I shall be following.

PRESUPPOSITIONS OF MY READING

Readers would be naive were they to believe that I, as a scientific worker, could eliminate all presuppositions from my reading of the Bible. They would be no less naive were they to imagine that the scriptures can be read purely in the light of "common sense." All human beings are conditioned by their environment, their previous history, and their temperament. I myself am a man and not a woman, a monotheist and not a Buddhist, a Christian and not a Jew, a Catholic and not a Protestant, a priest and not a layperson, a Jesuit and not a Dominican. Need I add more? All these facts condition my viewpoint, and I must therefore compensate for the inclinations my condition sets up in me by having recourse to the viewpoints of others who are different from me. I have given up thinking of myself as "the man who states the meaning of the Bible"; I adopt other "points of view," but I continue nonetheless to say how I read the text. The statements I make may at times seem peremptory; they are in fact meant as invitations to a dialogue—all the more so since I am inseparably linked to those who have written on the subject and instructed me. But why should not these others in turn dialogue now with me?

A principle of totality

The first group with whom I wish to engage in dialogue are the dogmatic theologians, since they and the exegetes together form a team that seeks to explain the biblical message in a satisfying way. Let me say a few words, therefore, on how I see myself in relation to them.

Dogmatic theologians endeavor to explain the meaning of revelation with the help of the thinking proper to their own time, while also taking account of the scriptures *as read down through the centuries.* That is to say, in their interpretation of revelation they draw light directly from what is known as "tradition," because in the various currents that have appeared in the course of history they see the Holy Spirit at work, enabling Christians to understand divine revelation not only in its radical thrust but also in relation to the vital questions and thinking of this or that period. In trying to present the content of Christ's vital message to the men and women of today, these theologians seek to discern and express a meaning that will be useful to them.

The dogmatic theologians, no less than the exegetes, regard the scriptures as the foundation of their work and understand them to have an authority far beyond that of the successive interpretations which ecclesial thought has elaborated down the centuries and which derive from that thinking. Admittedly, the canonical writings date from the first century and already reflect

various traditions regarding the event of Jesus Christ. But that
does not make them simply the first in a series that continues
through the centuries to today. They are not number one of any
"series" but the point in which any subsequent series originates;
they are the zero that cannot be counted with the numbers that
follow.

For dogmatic theologians, then, the Bible remains the main
point of reference. For exegetes, however, it is the sole point of
reference. Exegetes are, of course, conditioned personally by the
tradition which has transmitted the faith to them and by which
they live, but they do not use that tradition in order to shed light
directly on the text. In their reading of the Bible they methodically
refuse to let even the most authentic contributions of Tradition
(with a capital "T") play a part in their interpretations. They look
to the texts alone, as these are in themselves, and try to read them
as though they had just been written. In consequence, the results
which the exegetes reach are limited, and in the final analysis it is
the dogmatic theologians who must supply the full meaning of the
texts; in doing so, the latter use the results furnished by the exegetes, in the measure in which it is appropriate to do so.

Since dogmatic theologians take the work of the exegetes into
account, I want them to know, as part of our dialogue, what I
mean by an "exegete." The principle of totality plays a part in the
work of exegesis. Some people think that the meaning of a given
text is to be found in the earliest formulation of it that can be
reached. Others, on the contrary, see in the final formulations of a
text the authentic expression that was struggling to emerge in the
initial stammerings. Each group thus sticks to one or other formulation and as a result runs the risk of downplaying the formulation which it regards as too recent or too confused. In response
to both groups it must be said that the object of exegetical work is
by definition not this or that text removed from its context in the
Bible as a whole and declared to be more accurate than any other.
The object is the total biblical datum that we call "canonical." Exegetes must think of themselves as "biblical theologians," or they
will not do justice to the revealed datum as it really is.

Back to the dialogue between dogmatic theologians and exegetes. Dogmatic theologians have unfortunately tended to think
of exegetes as people who supply the meaning of this or that
incomplete text; as a result, they consider it their own task to create a synthesis from the analyses offered by the exegetes. If, however, the exegetes refuse to be simply interpreters of a given pas-

sage, a particular book, or even a group of books, the dialogue takes a different turn. The dogmatic theologians now converse with "theologians of the Bible," who use the scientific means at their disposal to show the overall meaning of the canonical books in all their diversity. It is obvious that this ideal is rarely realized, since the individual exegete would have to be able to do justice to all the books of the Bible, even in dealing with a limited subject. It is clear, moreover, that all of our interpretations are based on hypotheses. But, this being admitted, exegetes, while modestly conscious of the provisional nature of their conclusions, must nonetheless attempt a comprehensive interpretation.

In this book, then, my aim is to produce a "biblical theology" of the Eucharist and thereby offer dogmatic theologians a synthesis that will serve them as point of reference for the comprehensive interpretation they must provide on the basis of tradition. That is why I have been anxious to examine here *all* the texts that speak of the Eucharist. There are indeed not very many of them, but they must be interrelated, and this is not always an easy task.

The principle of totality comes into play once again at the level of a synthesis which I presuppose here. By reason of my studies and my situation a broad conception of the "plan of God" has become part of me. It would be naive to think that this more or less developed synthesis has not influenced my understanding of the eucharistic texts. Moreover, readers of this book will perhaps have their appetites stimulated by my brief explanation of this presupposed synthesis. I do not say this as though granting that I am locked into a circle and content to rediscover what I already know. The point is rather that, as Poincaré used to say, the relation between knowledge and hypothesis controls every inquiry. Here, then, is a preview of the way in which I locate the Eucharist in the history of God's dealings with humankind.

My relation to the Eucharist was distorted due to an excessive concentration on the nature of the change that takes place in the bread and wine. It is odd that instead of attending to the mystery of the new presence of Jesus Christ who gives himself in the Eucharist, people should be concerned with how the bread and wine are changed into his body and blood. This shift of problematic introduced all kinds of questions which in the final analysis show that a wrong approach is being taken to the mystery. The eucharistic mystery is even isolated thereby from the other mysteries of faith, so that instead of being a part of the history of

God's plan, it is considered separately, in itself, and independently of the relation between God and human beings, which alone is a source of meaning. Let me try, then, to locate the eucharistic mystery within the movement of biblical revelation.

I take as the starting point of my thinking the Prologue of the fourth gospel. God expresses himself through his Logos, who is life and light for human beings. Down the ages and in all places, God seeks to enter into dialogue with his creatures and in particular with his chosen people. He accompanies the patriarchs on their wanderings and makes himself known to them through mysterious personal encounters. In the wilderness of Sinai he manifests himself in thunder and lightning; a few centuries later, however, the prophet Elijah rejects these crude images and hears his God speak in the gentle murmur of the breeze. Little by little the presence of God takes more refined forms. YHWH is indeed present at the ark, in a precisely defined place, but on an empty throne, and the wings of the cherubim bracket a space that opens into infinity. The whole story of the ark shows human beings trying to reconcile transcendence and the human need of representations. A purified conception of the presence of God (in Hebrew: *Shekinah*) is being developed, although at the same period others turn the "presence" into something intermediary between God and human beings, and still others make a kind of idol of it.

In all this history the darkness muffles the word of God that is trying to make itself heard in the hearts of human beings. Thus even the Jewish law, which is an expression of the divine will, does not produce the results hoped from it.

Then the Logos takes full human form in Jesus of Nazareth. He thus expresses himself in a more definite way in accordance with the human condition, which has its advantages (intelligible, communicable words . . .) and its drawbacks (limitation, weakness, conceptual language . . .). In this way God concretizes his word. In order to do so, he accepts the limitations and, more particularly, the death which the incarnate Son undergoes. At this point the problem has become acute: without a human form the Logos has not made himself heard; but when he takes a human form he is not accepted. God nonetheless goes on willing to overcome all barriers and be present to human beings, and he accomplishes his purpose by a gift that transcends all other gifts.

This ultimate intervention is the gift of the Spirit, because the Spirit penetrates the depths of hearts, as the prophet had foretold. If the Spirit was to be given, the Logos had to become flesh as

mediator of the Spirit. A successful giving of the Spirit presupposed this "incarnation" and the death and resurrection. Through
the Spirit who is poured out in the hearts of human beings God is
able at last to express himself in the innermost recesses of individuals and turn these individuals into authentic human beings. We
may apply here a comparison made by St. Cyril of Jerusalem: the
rain that falls from heaven is always the same but it becomes white
in the lily, green in the hyacinth, and rose or violet or any other
color as it adapts itself to each plant and makes it yield the color
and perfume which delight the flowerbed of God. So too God at
last expresses himself in a personal way in each human being.

But in addition to this ultimate presence that is both universal
and particular there is another mode of presence that is adapted to
our kind of knowledge. Between the bodily presence of Jesus of
Nazareth and his "spiritual" presence, there is an intermediate
kind of presence that is attuned to sense knowledge and at the
same time gives a grasp of the mystery. Such an intermediate presence, if verified, would indeed be provisional, but it would also be
indispensable to us in our human condition. Its existence would
make the "spiritual" presence of Jesus less likely to become
debased and disappear. As a first remedy, then, the word of Jesus
became a "written letter" in the New Testament, which exists to
prevent the subtle impoverishment and "inevitable" humaniza-
tion of the word of Jesus. As a result the word of Jesus is still communicated through ecclesial tradition. But the risk of distortion is
also still present: the word can be buried in the book.

A second remedy, even more sensory in character and even
more "symbolic," was therefore found: the sacramental mode of
the presence of Jesus Christ. As he was about to depart in the body
from his disciples Jesus chose to continue a mode of presence
based on nourishment. No longer does God take a human form;
he takes the form now of bread. Human beings must eat if they
are to live; believers too must eat if they are to live in a Christian
way. God therefore chooses the symbol which best expresses both
the profound closeness and the effect of the relation uniting God
and human beings. That, after all, was what he was seeking when
he gave himself through a book or took human form; in becoming
food he adapts himself to the universal necessity of eating in order
to live. The God who gave manna from heaven to the Hebrews in
the wilderness now gives *himself* in Jesus, under the "appearances" of bread and wine: "presence" becomes "gift."

By the power of his word this food becomes himself; Jesus

continues to be present in the form of a fraternal meal celebrated in his memory. He focuses his attention on the reality of the bread and by his word—which is infinitely more powerful than mine when I create a "metaphor" and change the meaning of a word by giving it a different reference—really transforms it into his body; in so doing, he expresses himself in a manner which we call "sacramental." This presence in turn communicates the Spirit and is a pledge of the banquet at the end of time.

Is it proper to give a name to the force that urges God to go out of himself, to express himself, to be all in all? I find no other word for it except love. Seen in this light, the Eucharist is God's crowning act of love for us.

In the medium of language

The principle of totality thus comes into play in defining my place among all those—dogmatic theologians and exegetes—who investigate the meaning of the scriptures. It comes into play again in situating the Eucharist within an overall understanding of revelation. This principle is the first presupposition that I must bring into the open.

There is a second and no less important presupposition. Whether or not I like it, I use a language which takes its character from usage. This usage, however, does not necessarily capture the meaning which this word or that representation has in the texts; after all, the meaning of words changes and we can be mistaken in our reading. For example: while the idea that the human being is a composite of body and soul is certainly no longer fashionable in contemporary philosophy, it continues to exist in many minds. Yet this idea is hardly consonant with biblical anthropology, according to which a human being in its entirety is a single entity, an animated body, and for which, in addition, a human being exists only in virtue of its relation to God, the Living One par excellence, and of its relation to the community to which it belongs. I shall have occasion later on to stress the importance of these facts for an understanding of the texts.

Another example: "epistemology," or the science of how we know. We are all habituated to the conceptual mode of knowing, in which we determine the meaning of words and define the possibilities of interpretation. But there is another mode of knowing, the "symbolic" mode. The prophets practiced it, and the language of Jesus is consistently symbolic. Since the term "symbolic" is both complex and indispensable, I shall define it when the time comes. But one point should be stressed even here: despite the way the word is often used today, "symbolic" is not opposed to "real"; on the contrary, the symbolic is the depth-dimension of the real.

QUESTIONS OF METHOD

Any book claiming to be scientific must make clear the method it is applying. In dealing with biblical texts several methods have proved fruitful.

A first source of light is a comparison of the eucharistic texts with the data provided by the history of religions. Other religions too used to have their cultic meals, and sacrifices were common. It is obvious that the activities of the early Christians had analogues in the practices of their non-Christian contemporaries. What must be avoided, however, is too quick an assertion of Christian "dependence" on this or that other religion. As the Germans used to say: "Analogy is not genealogy."

In the past, scholars did not always avoid this pitfall, especially when they adopted the "analytical" perspective of a Reitzenstein who "barraged" each New Testament text with parallels from Iranian documents (which, moreover, could not be dated). On the other hand, the practices followed in the monastery of Qumran are very important and enable us today to look at the texts objectively. I shall use this vantage point in dealing with the Lord's Supper of which Paul speaks and with the breaking of bread; in these instances we will have reliable contexts with which to work. It will also be essential to compare the Supper with the Jewish Passover feast in order to recapture the outlook of Jesus as he celebrated his final meal.

The second method that will be used, following the major authors, will be the method of literary criticism. In its classic form this method operates "diachronically," that is, by studying the history of a text. For example: Did Matthew copy Mark, while also altering him? The criteria used are admittedly often subjective, as when, for example, an author claims that this or that idea was not common in the period when the texts were composed. These criteria do, nonetheless, allow scholars modestly to set forth hypotheses.

Literary criticism can be practiced in another way, using the "synchronic" method. Instead of trying to describe the genesis of the text, the exegete strives to see it as it is, taking into account the relations between its constitutive elements. The ideal goal is to discover the structure which the text retains through its various recensions. The student would then be able to grasp the invariant element that explains the very essence of the text.

Finally, there is the historical method, which is concerned with establishing the events of which the text speaks. It should not be regarded as a competitor of the literary method, since its purpose is different. Literary criticism attempts to determine *what* the text is saying; historical criticism attempts to determine that *about which* it speaks. Consequently, the analogies offered by the history of religion and the forms brought to light by literary criticism do not in any way settle the question of the historical character of the passage under consideration.

THE ROUTE TO BE FOLLOWED

This book continues my personal journey. After having attempted, in my *Resurrection and the Message of Easter*, to see how the mystery of what followed the death of Jesus could be better presented, I ventured into the problems raised by the language we use in speaking of the death of Jesus. What exactly is meant by "expiation," "ransom," and many other such terms? What is the redemptive significance of the death of Jesus? In my book *Face à la mort: Jésus et Paul* (Confronting Death: Jesus and Paul) I sought to show the attitude of Jesus to the death that threatened him, and how Paul used several vocabularies to express his faith in Jesus as Savior of humankind. Readers of the present book should be familiar with the conclusions reached in those earlier works, since they are presupposed here. In particular, they should keep in mind the sense in which the death of Jesus is a sacrifice. The reason is that the eucharistic mystery is closely connected with the death and resurrection of Jesus.

The route followed here also depends on the insights which gave rise to the work. The important thing in my view is not the problem of transubstantiation or the problem of the assembly. Two positive insights are at the origin of the present book.

Some twenty-five years ago, in an article for the *Supplément* to the *Dictionnaire de la Bible*, I proposed a hypothesis that would explain the texts of the institution in a more precise way. I realized that there were two kinds of tradition about the final meal of Jesus: one tradition had for its purpose to ground eucharistic practice, and I called it the "cultic tradition"; the other tradition was

content to convey understanding of the final hours of Jesus by telling of them in a kind of "farewell discourse." This discovery had
very important consequences when it came to situating worship
more accurately in its relation to life. It emerged that worship is
not the only means of remaining in contact with him who has left
our earth; there is also service of the brethren, as the fourth gospel
makes amply clear. This is the first basic hypothesis behind the
present book.

The second insight has to do with taking into consideration
the account in its entirety. Instead of focusing my attention on the
elements, that is, the bread and wine, as is too often done, I realized that if the account is read as a narrative of action and dialogue, these elements find their proper place, which is a secondary
one in the liturgical action of Jesus and the early Christians.

What route shall I follow in presenting the various eucharistic
texts? The answer is not easy. I could have organized the development in function of my primary insight and therefore emphasized the constitutive relationship of the two traditions, the cultic
and the testamentary. But such a distribution of the material
would in practice have seemed overly directed toward a demon-
stration of the hypothesis, whereas what I want is that the hypothesis should be seen as arising out of the texts themselves.

Should I therefore have divided the material as I might in a
course, by examining all the scriptural passages in order? Such an
analytical method would enable me to present in a satisfactory
way the perspectives peculiar to each recension, but it would also
entail extensive repetitions and, more importantly, would ignore
the gradual formation of the texts. The end result would be a series
of "theologies"—of Matthew, Luke, Paul, and so on—but not a
comprehensive presentation aimed at a New Testament theology
of the Eucharist.

I have therefore chosen to proceed in a "circular" fashion by
considering the texts at the various stages of their production.
This requires attention, first of all (Part One), to the eucharistic
practice of the early Christians as expressed in the breaking of
bread (I), the "Lord's Supper" (II), and the gospel texts on the institution (III). The second part of the book deals with the eucharistic
traditions which are studied according to the methods of literary
criticism. The "synchronic" examination of them in Chapter III is
followed by a lengthy "diachronic" study aimed at finding out
how the texts as we know them were formed. There are two tra-

ditions regarding the final meal of Jesus, one cultic, the other "testamentary" (IV); the cultic tradition in turn shows two main directions (V). At this point I shall be in a position to examine the three fundamental words in the accounts of institution: memory (VI), bread (VII), and cup (VIII). On the basis of this analysis I shall venture to pinpoint the event that stands behind these traditions, in order then to sketch out the development of the traditions themselves (IX). In the third part of the book I shall continue to discuss the event and the traditions about it, but now as found in the various authors: Mark (X), Paul (XI), Luke (XII), and John (XIII).

How should the book end? I might have chosen a "conclusion" that would gather up the main results in synthetic form and provide dogmatic theologians with the elements of a biblical theology of the Eucharist according to the New Testament. I did not dare to attempt such a reconstruction, however, and have chosen instead, in the form of a fourth part, to offer an "overture" (XIV) which brings together some of the points established in the course of the book. In this final part I try to situate my approach in relation to the terms traditional in discussion of the Eucharist, especially "sacrament," "sacrifice," and "real presence." At the very end of the book I add an appendix on the relation of the Supper to the Jewish Passover meal.

The route followed inevitably entails repetitions. These, however, may be only seemingly repetitions, since the level at which statements are made differs in each section; the movement is spiral. Each section of the exposition is part of a circle, and therefore there are repetitions; but there is also a vertical movement given by changing perspective.

Here is an example. In my reading of the account of institution in Chapter III I explain the whole group of texts and in so doing make numerous remarks that will be fully justified only later on when the various traditions are analyzed. This chapter, then, gives readers a broad contact with the literary data before guiding them into the labyrinth of analytical study. The chapter thus follows a method that I would like to see practiced more often in literary study: the synchronic method.

In the overall movement of the work I advance first from the actual practice of the early Christians to the account of it that was developed: from life to narrative. I pass next from the account to the underlying traditions and from these traditions in turn to the event that gave rise to them. Finally, I move forward again from the event to the traditions in order to discuss the various presentations by the evangelists and Paul. The movement does not in fact stop at this point, but it is the role of the historian of tradition, and not of the exegete, to follow it further. The movement continues in the mind of the reader and in the life of the Church.

One of the problems under discussion today is the structure of the "Mass." Under what conditions can we say that a Mass is authentically celebrated in memory of Jesus? I would like readers to keep in mind the questions that concern them but not to try to answer them immediately. The route I follow here involves an advance, a gradual introduction of the various elements of the problem. Let us not forget, too, that we are always dealing with the eucharistic "mystery" and that we must therefore give the various problematics their proper place in relation to the central vision and not subordinate what is essential to peripheral problems.

PART I

Eucharistic Practice

Many surprises are in store for twentieth-century believers who go back to the original New Testament data in order to ground their faith in the Church's eucharistic practice.

The texts which speak of this practice among the early Christians are not very many: three or four brief mentions by Luke in the Acts of the Apostles, and two reminders by Paul in a letter, one of these reminders including the account of institution that is also given by the first three evangelists. Our surprise will lessen if we recall that except for the gospels and Acts, the New Testament writers have left only letters written with an eye on the particular situations of their addressees. Except in the Letter to the Romans and, to some extent, in the Letter to the Ephesians, there is no dogmatic synthesis. If the communities did not have problems with the Eucharist, why should the writers bring the matter up? That is the nature of occasional writings.

Another surprise: Contrary to their expectations modern Christians will not find the word *eucharistia* used for the eucharistic liturgy: when the word occurs it designates a recommended kind of prayer, the "thanksgiving."[1] Only in the second century will it be found clearly referring to the celebration of the Eucharist: in about 110 in Ignatius of Antioch[2] and in about 150 in Justin.[3] Perhaps even earlier, in the *Didache* (which dates from the end of the first century or the beginning of the second) the "Eucharist" is mentioned as a current liturgical practice.[4]

The only two names given to the Eucharist in the New Testament are "the breaking of bread" and "the Lord's Supper." I shall therefore begin by establishing the historical bases of these names (I) and explaining their background (II). Then, because Paul, in speaking of the Lord's Supper, brings in the account of its institution by Jesus, I shall attempt a first reading of the Supper story

15

(III). By turning to this last subject only after having dealt with the first two (the breaking of bread and the Lord's Supper) I am making clear the difference between Christian eucharistic practice and the final meal of Jesus; we must not think of the "Mass" as completely resembling the meal celebrated by Jesus at the Last Supper.

I
The Eucharistic Assemblies of the Early Christians

The name "Eucharist" refers first and foremost to a liturgical celebration and thereby calls to mind a specific living community. In this chapter I shall not offer a theory about the rite itself but simply the evidence about how it was designated and practiced in the first years of Christianity.

Historians have several good sources at their disposal for learning about the behavior of the early communities. The letters of Paul are full of allusions to the recently founded churches; among these the First Letter to the Corinthians, like a current news-report, takes us into the life of believers who regularly celebrated *the Lord's Supper.* The other source is the New Testament writer Luke: in the Acts of the Apostles he sketches a portrait of the Jerusalem community in the apostolic age.[1] His work dates from the eighties of the first century and has often been suspected of idealizing the reality; it is impossible, however, to cast doubt on what he says about *the breaking of bread.*

What was the contemporary reality behind these two names? I shall limit myself here to presenting the textual data; in Chapter II a discussion of the symbolism of meals will lead the reader into the question of the content and origin of the Church's early practice.

A first glance at the texts makes two points evident. First, the Eucharist presupposes that the community is not only gathered together (convoked by the Lord Jesus who bade his followers do this in his memory) but also united. Second, it is linked to a call for, or effective practice of, brotherhood in the form of a sharing of possessions.

17

I. THE LORD'S SUPPER

As early as 50 A.D., the year of Paul's first stay in Corinth, the faithful were familiar with what the apostle, in a letter of 55/56, calls "the Lord's Supper."[2] He speaks of this in connection with conflicts that had surfaced in the community, not about the value of the Lord's Supper for the life of faith, but about the way it was being practiced. Because of these dissensions among brothers and sisters and also because of the inequalities that led to the dissensions, Paul intervenes to criticize the behavior of the Corinthians and to make clear not only the meaning of the celebration but the requirements of unity and mutual respect that flow from the celebration.

To this end Paul introduces into his admonition the traditional account of the Supper. In addition, he provides us with information on the main lines of the celebration as ordinarily carried out.

The Lord's Supper is first and foremost an action of the entire community: whatever their social status the faithful gather regularly for a *fraternal* meal. This meal, however, is not simply a meeting of brothers and sisters who are united by a common faith; it is also marked by what we today call *the eucharistic rite*. Paul has recalled this rite earlier in the same letter and supposes it to be well known: "The cup of blessing which we bless, is it not a communion in the blood of Christ? The bread which we break, is it not a communion in the body of Christ?" (1 Cor 10:16).

Gathering and meal

It is not surprising that when the community of Corinthian believers gathered it should be for a meal. Both among the Jews and in the Hellenistic world communal meals were a regular and frequent part of religious and social life.

Both in Palestine and in the Jewish diaspora these meals were of many kinds.[3] They were connected with religious feasts (Passover, Pentecost . . .) or the practice of public worship (communal meals on the temple square after a sacrifice) or the observance of the law (the eve of the sabbath . . .) or special occasions in domestic life (circumcision of newborn sons, weddings, funerals . . .). In addition there were special meals of one or other group, as for example the Pharisees and Essenes.[4] Outside of Palestine we find mention of other festive meals, for example those of the Therapeutae,[5] or those held when a young pagan girl engaged to a Jew became a Jewish convert: she was renewed by the "bread of life" and the "cup of blessing."[6]

The Jewish practice of communal meals was so widespread that according to the historian Josephus they were specially authorized by the emperor: "When Caius Caesar . . . prohibited by decree the formation of associations *(thiases)* at Rome, the Jews were the only ones he did not forbid to collect money and hold communal meals *(syndeipna poiein)*" *(Ant.* 14, 214–16). Although the authorities looked with suspicion upon gatherings of any kind as likely to foster revolutionary intrigues, they made an exception for Jewish meals, thus showing that they regarded these as essentially religious in nature. The point of interest here is that "the diaspora Jews felt it necessary to gather not only in a house of prayer but at a common table."[7]

The fact that Jews gathered in this way would not be surprising to their contemporaries. The pagans of the Hellenistic world had for centuries been forming associations for religious purposes or to deal with economic concerns of various kinds. These associations were variously called *orgaia, eranoi,* and *thiasoi.*[8] Originally, people gathered to celebrate a boisterous festival, as, for example, in the Bacchic associations. Later on, the same names were given to brotherhoods that wished to honor a god or hero at a meal. Finally, there were cultic meals in which worshipers, having offered sacrifice, consumed the remains of the sacrificial victim. We can hardly fail to recall here the food sacrificed to idols, of which St. Paul speaks.[9]

It seemed only natural, then, that the Christian community of Corinth, made up as it was of believers who had come from Judaism and other religious environments, should express and strengthen their cohesiveness by means of communal meals. The meals were probably eaten in the home of one of the more affluent brethren[10] who, together with other guests of the same economic class, would furnish the food. Paul likes to mention in his letters the names of believers whose homes were thrown open to receive the brethren. Of interest to us here are two connected facts that emerge clearly from the data: the mingling of guests from different social classes, and the direct help given through the sharing of food with the most disadvantaged.[11]

The disparate social status of those present immediately distinguished the Lord's Supper from the meals taken in Jewish or Hellenistic associations. In group meals, for example among the Pharisees, the guests included only persons of the same kind; in the case of Jews this reflected a need for exclusiveness (probably for reasons of legal cleanness) rather than a positive desire to strengthen unity among the guests.[12]

Concern for the poor, on the other hand, while unknown in the cosmopolitan atmosphere of Corinth, was by no means alien to Judaism. In Jerusalem, as Charles Perrot has clearly shown, there existed

> the familiar Jewish customs of the "poor bowl," distributed daily, and the "poor basket," handed out each week on Friday, just before the sabbath. The Christian meal is to be seen as in part a charitable meal served on the *trapeza*, the table-counter of Acts 6:2; these meals were an exercise of *diakonia*, a serving of food that was also an act of charity. . . . The meal was connected with the distribution of gifts to the poor.[13]

In Corinth there was no longer question of two practices, one eucharistic and the other charitable. There was but a single occasion which derived its character from the fact that rich and poor were mingled in the assembly.

Lord's Supper and Eucharist

Considered abstractly, then, the communal meal of the Corinthian Christians already had a value in itself; its function was to have believers share their lives and thus strengthen their sense of identity and their cohesiveness. In addition, it provided an opportunity to feed the hungry, not only for humanitarian reasons but also in order to let the concrete Church express itself.

In practice, however, this twofold purpose was achieved only because of the indissoluble link between the meal and the properly liturgical action celebrated during it. The meal would have been simply a fraternal agape or love-feast if it had not been wholly motivated by and directed toward the eucharistic meeting with him who was the very reason for the community's existence. The bread broken and the cup blessed are a sharing in the body and blood of Christ (10:16). This belief is explicitly reaffirmed later on in the letter: the bread and cup *of the Lord* (11:27). The Lord Jesus is the real host, and this is why Paul gives the name "Lord's Supper" to the entire meal.

The Pauline text provides no details on the organization of

this liturgy.[14] It can be said, however, that at this period the Eucharist was celebrated conjointly with a meal, and we are given Paul's reaction: if the spirit of brotherhood is missing, the meal cannot be the *Lord's* Supper.

> When you gather in common, it is not the Lord's Supper that you eat. For when the eating begins each person goes ahead with his or her own meal, and one person is hungry while another gets drunk. Do you not, then, have houses in which to eat and drink? Or do you scorn the Church of God and intend to shame those who have nothing? (1 Cor 11:20–22).

> Each time that you eat this bread and drink this cup, you proclaim the death of the Lord until he comes. Therefore whoever eats the bread or drinks the cup of the Lord unworthily will be guilty in regard to the body and blood of the Lord. Let each person examine himself and then eat of this bread and drink of this cup, for those who eat and drink without recognizing the body, eat and drink their own condemnation (1 Cor 11:26–29).

V. 26 of this passage reveals a new dimension of the eucharistic assembly. The community that celebrates in Jesus the Savior is gathered in expectation of his return; it pleads with him: "Our Lord, come!" (*Maranatha:* 1 Cor 16:22; see Rev 22:20). The present of cult is located between the past of the cross and the future of the return. The food which the faithful receive at his table keeps them in communion with him who lives through all ages. Their existence, in mystery, as a community is henceforth inseparable from his existence in God. As they wait for their union with him to be fully revealed on the last day, only authentic fellowship guarantees the reality that is already there.

II. THE BREAKING OF BREAD

The Acts of the Apostles mentions several times an activity that was characteristic of the Christian community from the very beginning of the apostolic age. The activity is not described in detail; the author speaks of it as something quite familiar to his readers, referring to it simply by the noun "the breaking of bread" (Acts 2:42) or the verb "to break [the] bread." Only one further detail is given: the activity took place "in their houses" (Acts 2:46). The context, however, shows in addition that the breaking of bread presupposed a gathering of the community and that it occurred frequently. The breaking of bread is mentioned again in Acts 20:7; the scene now is not Jerusalem but Troas, a small town on the northwest coast of present-day Turkey.

The expression "breaking of bread" was not used in the Greek world and refers first and foremost to a Jewish custom. Though the gesture of breaking bread is mentioned only once in the Old Testament,[15] frequent references to it are to be found in rabbinical literature.[16]

Jewish rite and Christian Eucharist

Among the Jews the action of "breaking bread" was the central one in a "domestic" rite that marked the beginning of a family meal, whether ordinary or festive. The rite as a whole had three steps: after seating himself, the head of the family took the bread and said a blessing; he then broke the bread with his hands (he did not cut it with a knife); finally, he gave the pieces to the others at table.

The *blessing* was essential: it showed that those present were receiving from God the food needed for their life; the food was thereby drawn into the current of divine power. The others at table responded with an "Amen." The *bread to be broken* was made of barley or wheat flour and was usually round and flat in shape. The *sharing* of the pieces effectively established a table fellowship;[17] those at table henceforth formed a single body, and God the giver was considered to be present. This twofold belief is behind what Paul says to the Corinthians about the Eucharist: "As there is one loaf, so we, although there are many of us, are one single body, because we all share in the one loaf" (1 Cor 10:17).

In the gospels, the successive gestures of this rite that begins a meal are always listed; the rite is not described simply by mentioning one of its parts. This is the case in the accounts of the multiplication of loaves,[18] in the accounts of the Supper, and in the story of the appearance of the risen Jesus to the disciples at Emmaus.[19]

What, then, is the meaning of the unqualified expression "breaking of bread" or "to break [the] bread" which the Acts of the Apostles uses in an ecclesial context? The meaning cannot be simply "to take a meal together," since in Acts 2:46 the action of breaking bread and the action of taking food are mentioned one after the other and are therefore distinct. Furthermore, in Jewish documents the "breaking of bread" never signifies the entire meal but only the complete introductory rite.[20]

The expression is therefore clearly ritual. Does it refer to the eucharistic action, as we spontaneously tend to think? There are scholars who doubt it.[21] However, the eucharistic reference seems more than probable if we take into account another passage of Acts in which Luke relates an incident he claims to have witnessed[22] when traveling with Paul on the latter's last great missionary journey. The incident occurred at Troas on a Saturday evening at the hour when the solemn "Lord's day" was beginning[23] and the brethren had gathered to commemorate the resurrection of Jesus:[24] "On the first day of the week when we were gathered together *(synēgmenōn)* to break bread *(klasai arton)*, Paul talked with them, intending to depart on the morrow; and he prolonged his speech until midnight. There were many lights in the upper chamber where we were gathered" (Acts 20:7–8). Paul was not destined to finish his sermon. A young man sitting on the windowsill was overcome by sleep and fell from the third story to the ground, but Paul went down and brought him back to life. The passage then continues: "And when Paul had gone up and broken bread and eaten, he addressed them a long while, until daybreak, and so departed" (Acts 20:11).

The account is of interest not because of the miracle of resuscitation but because of what it tells us about the gathering over which Paul is presiding: the gathering is liturgical, as can be seen from the verb *synagō*, the day of the week, and the many lamps. The purpose of the assembly is the breaking of the bread, an action framed by the sermon.[25] Elsewhere, when Paul reminds the Corinthians of the true meaning of the practice he had taught them, he confirms Luke's story by speaking of "bread which we break" and expressly adding that this bread is "a communion in the body of Christ" (1 Cor 10:16).

It is therefore permissible to think that Luke, or the tradition before him, created a name for the Eucharist out of one of the gestures in the rite that began Jewish meals.[26] While referring to the sacramental rite as a whole, the term "breaking of bread" emphasizes the element of sharing, within unity, that characterizes the Christian celebration, an emphasis all the more justified since according to Luke the community's daily life reflected that unity and sharing. There is no doubt that Christians applied an idea inherited from Judaism and saw the breaking of the bread as a symbol of the unity Christ had in mind in bringing the faithful together. It is possible, in addition, that in Jerusalem the presence of the absent master was felt more intensely by the disciples as they gathered at the very moment of the meals in which at one time Jesus of Nazareth himself had broken bread for them.

 In any event, the choice of another name besides the Pauline "Lord's Supper" shows the diversity that could exist in the churches from the very beginning of Christianity.

In their houses

The gatherings for celebration take place, according to Acts 2:46, "in their houses," as I have already pointed out. The disciples undoubtedly remain faithful to their Jewish tradition by also faithfully attending the temple (as v. 46 explicitly says), but they go there only in order to share in the public prayers, for example, the prayer at the ninth hour (3:1). They are never shown taking part in any cultic sacrifice. In this respect they follow the lead of their Master[27] whom the gospels nowhere describe as taking part in a sacrificial ceremony. Whenever Jesus speaks of this form of cult he does so in order to assert the superiority of mercy that is inspired by fraternal or sisterly feeling; more than that, he criticizes the observance of the sabbath and the regulations governing legal cleanness. Jesus does of course continue vigorously to confess the oneness of God and the respect due to God's house, but his message is concerned with the eschatologically new way in which his Father is now acting, thereby invalidating what has preceded. Jesus does go to the temple, but in order to teach, engage in controversy, and sometimes to work a sign; the "new thing" that he proclaims is not a break with the old but an incredible fulfillment of it. According to Luke, the apostles, like Jesus, teach in the temple and proclaim the good news there (Acts 5:42), but the Christian assembly as such is held not in a sacred place but where the faithful reside.

Christian practice at this point represents a significant change from Jewish custom, since these "houses" cannot be identified with the Jewish synagogues in which the sabbath service was held. It is in private dwellings belonging to various of the faithful[28] that the community gathers for the breaking of the bread. It is noteworthy that the first Christians, remembering perhaps that their ancestors celebrated the Passover meal in the family circle, felt no need of providing themselves with places reserved for cultic activity.[29] The veil of the temple had been torn at the death of Christ; God can henceforth be present in every place and manifest himself there. The hitherto fundamental distinction between sacred space and profane space is now blurred. A prediction of Jesus had already suggested as much, for, as John the evangelist makes clear in the words addressed to the Samaritan woman, "the hour is coming, and now is, when true worshipers will worship the Father in spirit and truth" (Jn 4:23).

Such was the eschatological freedom which the early Church already enjoyed. The temple was still venerated as a place for prayer and preaching, but the rite of the breaking of bread was independent. It was celebrated outside any sacred place, just as the appearances of the risen Jesus and the event of Pentecost had taken place outside such places.

Was the breaking of bread accompanied by a communal meal, as it was at Corinth? The passages in Acts do not tell us, although it is said in 2:46 that the Christians of Jerusalem "took their food with joy and simplicity of heart." It was the usual thing in a Jewish milieu (as I pointed out earlier) for a community to gather for a fraternal meal which in itself already had a religious character.[30] It is therefore likely that the breaking of bread was celebrated in Christian homes in conjunction with a meal proper, that is, a meal intended to allay hunger. At the same time, however, it must be said, with H. Schürmann,[31] that the practice of eating at a common table had a different origin than the eucharistic rite. The very name of the latter, "breaking of [the] bread," implies that it was looked upon as an action independent of the common meal.

I shall now try to take a further step by situating the rite of breaking bread in the overall life of the Church as presented to us in Acts.

Place in the community's life

It is difficult for us today to understand completely the situation of Jesus' disciples in the period after Easter and Pentecost. An extraordinary "joy"[32] pervaded them: God had brought to fulfillment in Jesus the promises he had made to Israel; he had fulfilled the prophecies by giving the Holy Spirit and forming a new people for himself through the covenant which had been sealed by the fidelity of his Christ.

As they awaited the final day, these Jews who acknowledged

the crucified and risen Jesus as their Messiah remained quite naturally attached to the religion of their forebears, for it had given
them knowledge of the one God and his merciful plan. At the
same time, however, they had present and dwelling in them henceforth the Spirit who enabled them to understand and put into practice the message of the Nazarene whom God had glorified and
thereby shown to be truthful. The behavior of the faithful would
reflect a completely new freedom, as though the end of time had
already come. But this freedom did not degenerate into the enthu-
siasm of visionaries; the subjective liberation experienced by individuals did not lead to divergent types of behavior, still less to a
splitting of the community. On the contrary, the cohesiveness of
the baptized and their practice of mutual service impressed those
around them.[33] Their ecclesial life took everyday form; it acquired
concrete   foundations   and   manifestations: "They   devoted
themselves[34] to the apostles' teaching *(didache)* and fellowship
(koinonia), to the breaking of bread and the prayers" (Acts 2:42).

    This Lukan "summary" probably does not describe "the
sequence of an early Christian service: first the teaching of the
apostles and the (table) fellowship, then the breaking of bread and
the prayers."[35] Rather it lists in two groups of two each the activities characteristic of the early community: the teaching of the
apostles and fraternal communion describe the relationships internal to the young Church, while the breaking of bread and the prayers describe its immediate links with its Lord. I shall discuss these
two aspects in a little more detail, taking into account the pairing
of the components. This will locate the breaking of bread more
clearly in the overall life of the first Christians. I shall begin with
the community's relationship to its Lord.

(a) The breaking of bread and the prayers

    The community's relationship with the Lord is expressed in
two ways. The breaking of the bread, which brings down God's
blessing, links the community to Jesus of Nazareth and more particularly to Jesus at the moment of his final meal. Here as in the
upper room there is always an acceptance of the word of Jesus; but
here and today there must also be an action in which life is
received and the union of the assembly with its Savior is thereby
renewed.

    This liturgical activity takes place in a context of "prayers"
which, it may be supposed, found expression as in the ancestral
tradition, chiefly in the recitation of the psalms.[36] We may think

also of the Christian confessions of faith and hymns exemplified in the Pauline letters and of the Our Father.

Taken together, the breaking of bread and the prayers point to a community that lives out its new faith in union with Jesus.

(b) Apostolic teaching and fraternal communion

Christians are united with Christ not only by their liturgical action but also by their diligent attention to the apostles, who are the authoritative witnesses to Jesus of Nazareth, and by their concern for living as brothers and sisters.

Peter and the other apostles have proclaimed Christ, their preaching being confirmed by miracles, and have urged their listeners to believe in him whom God has sent. After this initial proclamation they continue to instruct the baptized. By communicating their own faith experience they become the link that connects the community with Christ. The present of the community has its roots in the past; it is the culmination of a "tradition" or handing on: the word of Jesus Christ continues to be transmitted, thus ensuring the existence of a community that draws its life from the dead and risen Christ.

It is likely, then, that the *didachē* mentioned in the summary in Acts 2:42 signifies not the first proclamation of the gospel (the word of God descending vertically upon human beings) but the further instructions (a horizontal phenomenon, to continue the image) needed by the community.

Where and how was this *didachē* given? Luke tells us the place: "Every day in the temple and at home they did not cease teaching and preaching Jesus as the Christ" (Acts 5:42). As we saw, when the apostles taught in the temple they were acting like Jesus who had so often preached his message there. It would seem, on the other hand, that the instruction given to the faithful in private homes was a ministry of the word which took place during liturgical assemblies and therefore during the breaking of the bread.

The account of the liturgy at Troas, which I mentioned above, confirms this interpretation. It was while the faithful were gathered in order to break the bread that Paul conversed with them (*dielegeto*), prolonged his sermon (*logos*), and gave them a discourse (*homilēsas*). The reference is clearly to a lengthy homily of Paul and perhaps also to dialogue among the brothers and sisters.[37]

Any information we have regarding the words spoken at the gatherings of the faithful is indirect. But if we keep in mind that they were spoken by the heirs of the Jewish synagogal liturgy, there can be no doubt about their tenor. In the synagogue service on the morning of the sabbath the scriptures were regularly read and commented on in a targumic version[38] in order to make the word of God relevant to its hearers. Among Christians the text of the Torah was no longer read; instead the teaching had to do with the life and work of the risen Lord.

The scriptures nonetheless continued to provide the needed light: the apostles made it their business to present the events involving Jesus of Nazareth by locating these in the divine plan, with the help, for example, of the prophecy of the Servant of God in Isaiah 53.[39] A clear indication of the part played by the word of God in Christian worship is given in the account of the risen Lord's appearance to the disciples at Emmaus, an account which, like the other appearance stories, has its place in a liturgical setting.[40] The travelers have just recognized the Lord "at[41] the breaking of bread," and they say to one another: "Did not our hearts burn within us while he talked to us on the road, while he opened to us the scriptures?" (Lk 24:32). So too when Christ appeared to the disciples gathered in the upper room he "opened their minds to understand the scriptures" (Lk 24:45).

The conclusion is unavoidable: the word of God was always joined to the shared bread.

Luke joins *koinōnia* with *didachē* as another characteristic of the new community. *Koinōnia* has a wide range of meanings. I cannot agree with those who translate it in the present context as "communal gatherings"[42] nor with those who understand it as meaning the meals that took place during the liturgical assembly[43] or as referring exclusively to the bond uniting the faithful to the apostles.[44] Nor can the term be limited to the sharing of material goods,[45] since the gift of the Holy Spirit which is mentioned in this context gives it a spiritual dimension. What Luke has in mind is the union of all the members of the community with one another in the same faith and the same salvation; this union leads them to share their goods. This interpretation is confirmed by the various references to the unanimity of the faithful, a trait mentioned in another summary: "The company of those who believed were of one heart and soul" (Acts 4:32).

The gatherings of the faithful bear witness to this unanimity: "All the believers were together."[46] The many converts did not live together, of course, but they formed a community that met faithfully in the temple and in private houses.[47] The ideal harmony described by Luke was therefore grounded in a shared faith, but it found concrete expression in the sharing of material goods. Luke makes this point in two other summaries in the same sections of Acts: "And all who believed were together and had all things in common *(eichon apanta koina)*; and they sold their possessions and goods and distributed them to all, as any had need" (Acts 2:44–45); "No one said that any of the things he possessed was his own *(elegen idion einai)*, but they had everything in common *(ēn autois apanta koina)*" (Acts 4:32).

When Luke gives examples of goods being sold as the needs of the community required, he insists that the gesture was entirely voluntary. He congratulates Barnabas for having made it (thus indicating that the case was exceptional), while Ananias is punished not for having refused to sell his field but for having lied to the apostles about the price he received for it.[48] It would therefore be wrong to see in Luke's description an invitation to surrender all of one's possessions and contribute them to a common store; he speaks explicitly of what individuals "possessed" while emphasizing the point that they could no longer speak of it as "their own" *(idion)*, since everything was placed at the disposal of all. Thus Mary, the mother of John Mark, had kept the house which belonged to her, but she made it available for the use of the faithful.[49]

So too, without waiting for Paul to take the initiative on the collection (which is called *diakonia, koinōnia, leitourgia*[50]), the first Christians immediately tried to translate their faith and their life in Christ into action by sharing their goods with their brothers and sisters and helping those who lacked these goods.[51]

The present life of the community was rooted in the past through the instruction of the apostles. Meanwhile the community now living looked to the future: They had "favor with all the people. And the Lord added to their number day by day those who were being saved" (Acts 2:47). The communion among brothers and sisters was already the "spiritual worship" which, according to Paul, is co-extensive with the entire life of Christians. The breaking of bread was as it were the heart and hidden source of this fraternal service. The community lived its new life in union with the Lord, thanks to the gift he had made of himself.

CONCLUSION

Lord's Supper and breaking of bread—the two names used for the Christian assembly at the beginning—are as it were the symbolic expression of a communal life of faith. But the rite to which they refer never appears in isolation. It is accompanied by the word, which obviates the danger of a bogus ritualism and spurs it on to constant renewal. It is also inseparable from the call to mutual service in justice and love.

Furthermore, the two early names have convergent meanings. The breaking of bread, which directly names a rite, also signifies the "sharing" of the bread and thus looks to the social dimension of the Eucharist. On the other hand, "Lord's Supper," which directly refers to a communal gathering in which class distinctions play no part, signifies first and foremost that this gathering is convoked by the Lord and thus has for its focus the presence of God himself at the meal. In whichever direction one looks, the Eucharist closely links cult and life.

In the next chapter I shall examine this aspect of the "Supper" in detail. Meanwhile I prefer to translate *klasis tou artou* more expressively as "the sharing of bread," which has the advantage of referring not only to the eucharistic rite but also to the fraternal kind of life that is the normal expression of participation in the rite.

"Sharing of bread" aptly describes the situation of Christians, whether in their everyday lives when they look upon the goods at their disposal as ordered to the human community, or in their private lives when they symbolically celebrate the mystery of Jesus Christ giving himself for the salvation of the human race, or, finally, when they receive the word of faith or pronounce it in their turn. These are the three areas in which believers must share "bread" in the joy given them by their Christian convictions.

The sharing of bread expresses what the risen Lord expects of his disciples, as the appearance stories make clear.[52] Having taken the initiative in the encounter, he requires a "recognition" of him who was alive ("It is I!"), that is, Jesus of Nazareth; by giving a mission ("Go!"), he bids his disciples broaden the Church to include the entire community of peoples. The breaking of bread in the special sense of this phrase is done on the initiative of the risen Jesus; it serves to unite us ever anew both to his past life and to his present existence in God. Recognition takes place through the *didachē* received from the apostles, and the mission is to share our goods, both material and spiritual.

In addressing his disciples as he does, the risen Lord makes them adopt the attitude proper to every creature. I mean the attitude and outlook of "dialoguers," which all human beings are by their nature, since they are dependent on the living God and have unbreakable ties to all others of their kind.

Here we have the reason why in the days of the first Christians the liturgy was not separated from a fraternal meal. The latter, as we shall see, already called to mind, at least in principle, the eschatological banquet at which all human beings are to find their joy in an unblemished communal existence. Meanwhile, however, we have poor folk among us and must pay urgent attention to their needs. According to the expression used by Acts, when we speak of the Eucharist we immediately speak of sharing, so that there is no longer "mine" and "yours," but rather a perfect communality. Can we fail to think here of what the Church's duty is today in face of the unjust distribution of this world's goods among its peoples?[53]

II
Meal and Celebration of the Lord

Every reader of the New Testament is surprised by the frequency with which the documents speak of food and meals in both the literal and the metaphorical senses, and even in the cultic sense. Thus, in referring to the gatherings at Corinth Paul speaks of "the Lord's Supper," a term which expresses better than the more abstract "breaking of bread" a table fellowship with Christ and the brethren. The phenomenon of which I speak raises two questions. First, why these repeated mentions of food and meals? Second, should we not go along as it were with this whole thrust and accept the suggestion of some that our own eucharistic celebration should be accompanied by an actual fraternal meal that would make clearer the meaning of the Eucharist? But even without going that far, people are inclined today to mistake the significance of food and meal in the eucharistic rite proper.

The eucharistic liturgy does of course involve bread and wine, but this food does not have as its purpose to sustain the bodily life of believers. When Paul spoke of the celebration as *"the Lord's Supper,"* he was reminding his readers that the fraternal meal associated with it was also, by the very fact of the association, prompted by the Lord himself. But he certainly did not dream of identifying the Eucharist with a meal in the ordinary sense; did he not, in fact, bid the Corinthians stay home if they wanted only to eat and drink?[1]

And yet while the bread and cup of the liturgy do in a sense supply a spiritual food, they continue to be natural realities as well; the Eucharist *is and is not* a meal.[2] For this reason, if we are to enter in any degree into the symbolism chosen by Jesus as a faithful heir to the biblical tradition, it is important that we acquire a broad, firm foundation by examining the three levels of food (I), meal (II), and religious meal (III).

I. FOOD AND LIFE

Why, then, was food chosen as a means of expressing a presence? Have not the great spiritual traditions of the race recommended rather the privation of food as a privileged means of coming into contact with the godhead?[3] Yet Jesus gives bread to eat and a cup to drink and urges his disciples to do the same in memory of him, thus giving his action a value it will keep until the end of time. A short examination of the Bible will shed some light on this contrast.

Why do human beings eat? The immediate purpose is evident: they eat in order to go on living. Thus the action of eating signifies in the Bible that the eater is very much alive. Jesus asks Jairus to "give something to eat" to the little girl he has just snatched from death: if she eats, then she is really alive! Similarly, when the risen Jesus appears in the upper room he asks his disciples: "Have you anything here to eat?"; his eating is a sign that he is alive. Consequently, the disciples in turn will take their food in gladness: the Spouse is present and alive; therefore their community too is alive.[4]

The life in question comes to human beings from the external world, thus telling them that their existence has a cosmic dimension. They see that they are in continuity with the world. According to the Bible, this experience in turn bids them recognize another and more radical dependence: their dependence on God the Creator who, after sin as before, has given and continues to give them all things, including the plants and the animals: "Every moving thing that lives shall be food for you; and as I gave you the green plants, so I give you everything" (Gen 9:3; see 1:29). The order of creation, then, is such that the life-giving relation between human beings and the universe can symbolize the no less life-giving relation between themselves and God.

The first of these two relations is a necessity for every human being who wants to go on living. The second, however, requires an entirely free acceptance. It is at this point, through non-acknowledgment of the Creator, that sin and death enter in. Human beings want to take possession of the life which the world offers them, but in the process they forget him who makes their toil fruitful and gives the seed its power to yield ripe grain. They try to free themselves from the Creator and find satisfaction in the good things the earth offers them. They are unable, however, to keep their distance from the extremes which the wise man fears and from which he prays to be preserved: poverty and riches, both of which lead human beings to forget God.[5] How, then, are they to moderate the hunger and thirst for earthly goods that can separate them from God?

God himself used the wandering in the wilderness to educate his people while he sustained their life with the manna that fell from heaven: "The Lord your God . . . let you hunger and fed you with manna, which you did not know, nor did your fathers know, that he might make you know that man does not live by bread alone, but . . . by everything that proceeds out of the mouth of the Lord" (Deut 8:3). But the people did not remember the lesson for long. Then, in order to revive their memory of the divine Giver, they had recourse, as other religions did, to the privation of food. Various measures thus helped to put the use of food in a religious perspective: rules regarding foods that might be eaten, ritual sacrifices, blessings at meals. One measure was even more radical, namely, fasting, in which temporary abstention from all nourishment opens the person to dependence on God alone.

In the course of the centuries countless individuals have tried to experience God by means of that kind of abstinence. Among them, after Elijah, was John the Baptist whose "food was locusts and wild honey."[6] Fasting creates a void that signifies in turn the utter emptiness of human beings before God.

This was not the path that Jesus followed. True enough, he began his mission with a fast of forty days; his aim, however, was not to perform an ascetical exploit but to relive, and overcome, the trials of Israel in the wilderness.[7] He lived, generally speaking, as an ordinary human being and was conscious of his difference from his precursor: "John came, neither eating nor drinking, and they say, 'He has a demon'; the Son of Man came eating and drinking, and they say, 'Behold, a glutton and a drunkard'" (Mt 11:18–19).

But he was neither a glutton nor a drunkard; he lived simply and without worry: "Therefore I tell you, do not be anxious about your life, what you shall eat and what you shall drink, nor about your body and what you shall put on. Is not life more than food, and the body more than clothing? . . . Your heavenly Father knows you need them all" (Mt 6:25, 32). In this passage he is recommending not a heedless attitude but a radical trust in him who feeds the birds. Jesus fed the hungry crowds by giving them bread in abundance, but his intention was to bring home to them the superabundance God wants to heap upon those who rely on him. Above all, as the fourth gospel explains, his intention was to urge them to seek a food that does not perish, a food that had been symbolized by the manna in the wilderness: the word of God.[8]

If, then, Jesus did not advocate the practice of fasting[9] and showed himself fully at ease in regard to the food provided by the world which God has created, this was because in the depths of his soul one thing was utterly clear: material food symbolizes another food by which God keeps human beings truly alive. John the evangelist gives clear expression to this conviction of Jesus: "The disciples besought him saying, 'Rabbi, eat.' But he said to them, 'I have food to eat of which you do not know.' So the disciples said to one another, 'Has anyone brought him food?' Jesus said to them, 'My food is to do the will of him who sent me, and to accomplish his work'" (Jn 4:31–34). It is impossible to understand the mind of Jesus fully if we do not penetrate to the secret place where the Son converses with the Father. But if we do, we will grasp the symbolic meaning of food.

What is said in the Johannine discourse after the miracle of the loaves[10] leads into the mystery of the eucharistic food; the latter accomplishes in the spiritual order what earthly food does in the material order: it communicates life. To put it more accurately: Jesus uses his gift of material bread to direct the attention of human beings to one who will give *himself* in a symbolic way as food: "All who eat my flesh and drink my blood have eternal life, and I will raise them up on the last day. For my flesh is truly a food and my blood truly a drink. All who eat my flesh and drink my blood remain in me and I in them" (Jn 6:54–56). Christians see in the bread they break both ordinary food and heavenly food; they recognize in it the bread which is itself alive and gives life to them.

II. MEAL AND ASSEMBLY

The taking of food in company adds a specifically human note to the act of eating, for the latter then becomes part of our shared life. When we eat with others and join them in drawing from the same source of life, we express our common origin and common condition;[11] it is then possible to speak of ourselves as truly "assembled." Furthermore, in Jewish practice the social act of eating together gives those present a share in the same stream of grace, thanks to the blessing that accompanies the breaking of bread.[12]

To share a meal is not simply to eat the same food together and to derive the same life from it; it is also to have an opportunity of exchanging ideas and cultivating a deeper unity of outlook. This kind of exchange already finds expression at an elementary level in the toast "Your health!" which a drinker addresses to another: the bond uniting those at table is such that the profit which one derives from drinking also brings health to another.[13] This "communion" reaches a higher level in the exchanges and discussions which table fellowship promotes; this was the origin of the Hellenistic literary genre known as the "symposium." Plato's *Symposium* remains the most polished example of the genre, but various Lukan groupings of parables which Jesus told at meals can be regarded as also belonging to it.[14] I am not stretching or twisting the historical evidence when I emphasize the importance of "speech" during meals; I shall dwell on it especially in connection with the religious meals which I shall discuss in the next section.

Sharing food and exchanging words are what give table fellowship its high social and spiritual value. The primary function of a community meal is to bring brethren together. Thus covenants between clans were most often concluded during a banquet: Isaac and Abimelech, Jacob and Laban.[15] God himself provided a "covenant meal" for Moses and the elders of Israel.[16]

In view of the unity thus intended and effected (whatever the ambiguities attendant on it because of the human condition), the presence of a treacherous guest is felt to be intolerable. The psalmist tells us of the pain he feels at such a contradiction: "Even my bosom friend in whom I trusted, who ate of my bread, has lifted his heel against me" (Ps 41:9).

It is noteworthy that the four passion narratives echo this complaint in connection with Jesus' final meal, as a way of bringing home the seriousness of what Judas is about to do: "He who has dipped his hand in the dish with me will betray me!" (Mt 26:23 par.). John adds: "Then, after the morsel, Satan entered into him" (Jn 13:27). The Adversary *(Satanas)* is also the Divider *(diabolos)* and introduces a contradiction into the heart of this man who has determined to break his relation with the Master, and do so by an act of treachery. According to John, then, Jesus owes it to himself to exclude this non-friend par excellence from table fellowship.

A meal, then, truly signifies the unity of those at table only if their hearts are already in unison. It can, however, also signify reconciliation and thereby restore broken covenants and bear witness to pardon granted. The king of Babylon invites King Jehoiachin to his table after releasing him from prison; King Agrippa issues the same invitation to Silas who had fallen into disfavor;[17] the father of the prodigal son organizes a banquet as soon as his son returns home;[18] and a jailer offers a meal to Paul and Silas who have opened the way of salvation to him.[19] Finally, the risen Jesus eats with his disciples, thus signifying their restoration to favor.[20]

At the same time, however, the union between those at table is necessarily religious as well as social and therefore implies a certain setting apart, a certain separation from others. Thus a Jew could not eat at the same table with a pagan. Peter finds himself being blamed by his circumcised brethren, even though they have become Christians, because "you have been visiting those known to be uncircumcised and eating with them."[21] This disagreement was doubtless due in part to the fact that certain foods eaten by non-Jews were unclean; but the objection sprang above all from another conviction: that those at table form a union which is intolerable between Israelites and the uncircumcised.

The freedom to which Peter has attained and which Paul claims for himself in his Letter to the Galatians (2:2) has its basis in the behavior of Jesus. Jesus is not content simply to eat with his friends, for example, at Cana or in the home of Lazarus and his sisters,[22] or even to supply the crowd with bread in abundance; he also openly shares the table of those whom the law of his people declares outcast: tax collectors and "sinners." Thus Luke tells us: "And Levi made him a great feast in his house; and there was a large company of tax collectors and others sitting at table with them. And the Pharisees and their scribes murmured against his disciples, saying, 'Why do you eat and drink with tax collectors and sinners?'"(Lk 5:29–30). When Jesus acts in this way he does so in order to signify by actions the reconciliation which he had announced at the beginning of his ministry: "The kingdom of heaven is at hand."[23] God makes no distinction between persons; if he has any preference, it is for the poor and "the sick who are in need of a physician," since all are the children of Abraham.[24]

If our own meals are ambiguous and imperfect, the reason is that they cannot bring together at one table the human beings of all times and all nations. Nonetheless the life which the food symbolizes is offered to all. For this reason the Jews held unwearyingly to the hope that the Lord would one day gather all of his own at the final "eschatological" banquet which symbolizes life given in its fullness.

When Jesus welcomes sinners to his table, he is prefiguring

not only the universal forgiveness proper to the kingdom but also
the gathering which the prophets had foretold precisely in the
form of a great banquet: "On this mountain the Lord of hosts will
make for all peoples a feast of fat things, a feast of wine on the
lees, of fat things full of marrow, of wine on the lees well refined"
(Is 25:6; see Am 9:13). In like manner, when Jesus speaks of
heaven he does not describe a sublime state of prayer but uses
instead the image of the banquet on the last day: "Many will come
from east and west and sit at table with Abraham, Isaac, and Jacob
in the kingdom of heaven" (Mt 8:11; see Lk 13:29).

This banquet, far from being reserved to Jews, is open to all
peoples. And it is not only those chosen in the first hour who are
invited, but "the poor and maimed and blind and lame," and even
"both bad and good."[25] The prophet Isaiah had already proclaimed
that all the hungry, even those without money, would take part in
this feast. So too Jesus promises the disciples who have persevered
with him in his trials: "You will eat and drink at my table in my
kingdom,"[26] at a meal which he himself will "serve."[27]

Jesus undoubtedly heard the echoes of all this at the Supper
when he gave the bread and cup as symbols of the gift he was making of himself for the sake of the multitude[28] and therefore of each
individual: "Behold, I stand at the door and knock; if anyone hears
my voice and opens the door, I will come in to him and eat with
him, and he with me" (Rev 3:20).

Is it the final banquet or the eucharistic meal to which the Son
of Man invites each individual? The commentators feel obliged to
choose the one or the other, whereas the wording should be left
ambiguous. The reason is that, far from being opposed to the
eschatological meal, the cultic meal announces and prefigures it,
as we shall now see.

III. RELIGIOUS MEAL AND PRAISE OF GOD

The eucharistic liturgy consists of a meal which cannot be
called "ordinary," since its purpose is not to satisfy the hunger of
the participants, but to communicate to them a good of a different
order. On the other hand, the "meal" involves real food and therefore cannot be described as metaphorical or even as purely spiritual. In addition, because it brings together guests of every possible origin who share the same faith, it announces and prefigures
the final banquet at which all human beings will be gathered. I
describe the eucharistic meal as "religious" in the etymological

sense of the word.[29] By way of the food it binds us to the universe; in the assembly it binds us to other human beings; by its own special nature it binds us in Jesus Christ to God himself and to his plan.

How, then, did the first Christians happen to use a meal as the way of celebrating their common link with the Lord? In answer I must first set aside certain interpretations and thereby make it possible to ask a second question: Which meals of a cultic kind would best explain the nature of the eucharistic liturgy?

Motivations for religious meals

We might spontaneously think that the reason why the first Christians gathered as they did was because Jesus had told them: "Do this in memory of me!" In fidelity to their Master who had come back from death, believers would have obeyed his command by repeating the rite he had established. This would explain an action that is quite surprising in the environment in which it occurred, for how could Jewish ears have tolerated a command to drink the cup, suggesting as it did the drinking of blood? Could such a practice have arisen except on the authority of Jesus, the Master?

Simple though this answer is, it is unsatisfactory for several reasons. If the practice of the first Christians was inspired directly by a command of remembrance that was recalled at the moment, why do Mark and Matthew not cite this command? If the words of institution came verbatim from Jesus, why were they not transmitted in identical form in the several recensions? There cannot have been a sacrosanct oral tradition, especially for the cup, which is identified now with the blood (Mk/Mt), now with the covenant (Lk/Paul).[30] The eucharistic practice of the first Christians did not owe its origin simply to the action of Jesus at the Supper, but supposed the intervention of other factors.

Some critics therefore believe that the communal meals of the very early Christians were a continuation of the meals which the risen Jesus had eaten with his disciples.[31] This thesis contains an element of truth, namely, that there was a close connection between eucharistic practice and the appearance stories. But the connection is the reverse of what is claimed! First of all, when mention is made of meals shared with the risen Jesus, the purpose is to bring home the reality of the body of Jesus who is alive again,[32] or to make the point that the risen Jesus had manifested himself during a meal at which his disciples were gathered.[33] Second, the meals of the early community provided a "vital context" for the stories.[34] Table fellowship with the risen Jesus, as presented in the New Testament, presupposes rather than explains the existence in the community of fraternal meals which everything bids us call "eucharistic."

Well, then, might not the practice of the Eucharist be connected with the meals which Jesus of Nazareth had eaten with his disciples during his earthly life? The first Christians did undoubtedly remember that table fellowship; but, despite the eucharistic meaning which believers have thought it licit to project back onto those past meals, Jesus is never in fact shown at table with his disciples alone, except at the Supper; on the contrary, the meals which the gospels look back upon with complaisance are those with "sinners."[35] As far as the meals which Jesus took with the crowd at the multiplication of the loaves are concerned, the accounts of these have been formulated with an eye on the accounts of institution;[36] that is why they sound like prefigurations of the eucharistic meal. From a literary standpoint, the accounts of institution served as a model for the accounts of the multiplication. John the evangelist makes this literary dependence explicit when, immediately after having narrated the "sign," he bids his readers see behind this new manna the person of Christ. If the accounts of the earthly meals of Jesus are later than the text of the Supper, all the more does Christian liturgical practice have priority in relation to them.

The results of this inquiry into possible motives for the eucharistic meals is very meager. Let us consider, however, the new situation created by the events of Easter: very soon, beginning at Pentecost, believers gathered in order to celebrate God's victory over death by means of the joy-filled eucharistic rite. It is doubtful that they ever explicitly thought of justifying their assemblies; in all probability they quite naturally continued on with practices familiar in their environment, while at the same time profoundly changing the meaning of these. This is the point I shall now examine by considering the "cultic meals" celebrated by Jews at this period.

Jewish sacrifices and praise of God

It is not possible in a few pages to describe in detail the nature of the various sacrifices customary among first-century Jews.[37] In any case, I am interested only in "cultic meals" and can therefore omit from consideration the principal kind of sacrifice, namely, the holocaust,[38] as well as the very important sacrifices of expiation.[39] On the other hand, the sacrifices known as "peace offerings" or "communion sacrifices" (*šᵉlamîm*, from *šalom*, "peace") included a meal at which the offerer, together with his family and neighbors, consumed the part of the victim that had been given to him after the immolation.[40] I shall discuss these under two headings: communion sacrifice and sacrifice of praise.

(a) Eucharist and communion sacrifice

Among the communion sacrifices offered in the time of Christ can be numbered the *Passover meal*, which was celebrated in the home and at which the lamb immolated in the temple was eaten. According to the evangelists, the preparations for the final meal of Jesus were of the kind also made for the Passover meal. Does it follow that the Passover rite was observed at this meal? I think not.[41] Still less can the communal meals of the early Christians be regarded as following the Passover rite, since even though a Passover atmosphere permeates them, the fact that they were celebrated at least weekly is enough to make such an identification impossible.

Another communion meal, for which Pseudo-Philo and the Qumran documents provide ample evidence,[42] served for celebrating *the renewal of the covenant*, especially at Pentecost.[43] The "covenant sacrifice" celebrated by Moses and the people at Sinai had been followed by a solemn meal,[44] and that was probably the origin of this later cultic practice. It is significant here that when Jesus says "This is my blood, the blood of the covenant," he too reminds us of the passage of Exodus.

If these brief observations are correct, it follows that Christian communal meals were related to "covenant sacrifices" rather than to other types of cultic meals that were characterized to a greater extent by expiation for sin. The Supper was basically a meal celebrating the definitive covenant of God with his new people: the gift and reception of a "food" rendered symbolically present to believers the covenant that had been sealed by the fidelity of Jesus.

Such is the result reached by my rapid survey of the religious meals practiced in Jerusalem. The first Christians were doubtless very much at home in the already highly spiritualized tradition of "communion."[45]

(b) Eucharist and sacrifice of praise

On the one hand, then, the Christian rite that was celebrated in those early years can be properly defined in terms of the "unity of life" which it symbolizes. On the other, it was carried out in a manner which likewise had contemporary antecedents. The hypothesis I offer on this point follows a path less clearly marked than the preceding; others, however, have sketched it out on several occasions,[46] and I shall patiently present the arguments for it.

To begin with, I note the fact that "prayers" are mentioned along with the "breaking of bread" (Acts 2:42). These prayers (as I said earlier) must have consisted of psalms and faith-inspired acclamations.[47] Why should they not have corresponded in fact to the *tôdâ* that characterizes so many prayers both in the Old Testament and in Judaism? But what is a *tôdâ*?

The noun *tôdâ* is derived from a verb meaning "make known"[48] and refers to a prayer which "proclaims" the saving power of God. The *tôdâ* constitutes a literary genre; C. Giraudo has produced an outstanding analysis of its nature by examining the literary structure common to a series of biblical texts and Jewish blessings.[49] The form has its proper place in the world of the covenant: the one praying (the people or an individual, e.g., the psalmist) describes past or even present distress but also celebrates some wonderful divine intervention (especially the covenant) or some great divine action, thereby proclaiming the superiority and fidelity of God. This recall constitutes the climax of a prayer of praise which, to the extent that it is always also a call for help, is already a confession that God's love will win the victory now and in the future and thus transform the life of the one praying.

Now, among the communion sacrifices *(zebah š^elamîm)* listed in Leviticus mention is made of a *zebah tôdâ*, literally "a sacrifice of [or: with] praise."[50] Although it seems impossible to reconstruct the rite in detail,[51] the critics have nonetheless attempted to determine its nature. I myself accept the explanation given in the TOB: "A sacrifice of praise seems to be a peace offering made on a solemn feast (see Num 15:3). It is doubtless the most perfect form of Israelite sacrifice; the immolation of the victim (see Ps 50:14, 23; 56:13) is accompanied by *praise*, i.e., a proclamation, in the form of thanksgiving, of the works of God (see, e.g., Ps 105; 106; 107)."[52] If this description is accurate, as I think it is, prayer of the *tôdâ* type may accompany a communion sacrifice but is not limited to that context.[53] In fact, prayer of this kind is found in many passages in which there is no question of "sacrifice."[54]

In this context I would emphasize two linguistic phenomena: on the one hand, the metaphorical use of sacrificial terminology; on the other, the occurrence of the word *tôdâ* in a legislative context.

With regard to the first: the psalms of praise often contain language that is, at least in appearance, sacrificial: "Offer to God a sacrifice of praise" (Ps 50:14); "He who offers a sacrifice of praise honors me" (Ps 50:23); "I offer you sacrifices of praise" (Ps 56:13). Some critics interpret these texts as referring to the sacrificial rite mentioned in Leviticus; others, who are more conscious of the development in the Old Testament toward a "spiritualization of cult,"[55] prefer to interpret the language as metaphorical, as already suggested by the Aramaic translation: "Offer God praise as your sacrifice" (Ps 50:14). This praise that takes the place of sacrifice is "the sacrifice that pleases God, a broken heart" (Ps 51:17) or "the sacrifice of lips," an expression taken over by the Letter to the Hebrews.[56]

This movement whereby ritual sacrifice was transformed into an offering of words—and therefore a purer offering of the human heart and its inmost dispositions—can be seen in Jewish circles that no longer sacrificed in the temple, either by deliberate choice (as at Qumran[57]) or by necessity, as with Philo in Egypt.[58] In these instances, too, a sacrifice of the lips, expressing the self-giving of the heart, became the center of religious life. Along the same lines, vegetable offerings played an increasingly important part, even becoming at times the essential element in communion sacrifices.

The second linguistic phenomenon which I mentioned confirms my interpretation. Even while the process of spiritualization was going on, legislators continued to concern themselves with ritual. Their concern was translated into increasingly minute prescriptions in which the accent was almost exclusively on sacrificial practice. It is a striking fact that these legislative texts never mention the canticles which, as Pseudo-Philo tells us, accompanied sacrifices or at least communion sacrifices: "Going down with them [Joshua] offered peace sacrifices on the altar, and all sang many canticles. . . . They offered thereon [on the altar] peace sacrifices in great numbers, and the entire house of Israel sang with a mighty voice, in the form of a psalm: 'Behold, our Lord has done what he told our fathers he would do'" (LAB 21, 8f; see 26:7; 49:8). This, then, must have been the Jewish custom in the time of Jesus: sacrifices followed by meals and accompanied by canticles.

Nonetheless—and this is the other linguistic phenomenon—the legislators themselves, despite their tendency to lay stress solely on the external rite, mention the existence of a "tôdâ-sacrifice." The expression cannot refer exclusively to the meal which completed the communion sacrifice, but must designate the meal insofar as it included a celebration of praise. The *zebah tôdâ* would thus represent the fusion of two tendencies in the biblical tradition: the one that insists on ritual sacrifice and the one that is concerned more with prayer of praise.[59]

The *tôdâ*-sacrifice can therefore legitimately be called "the most perfect form of Israelite sacrifice," for it shows that the essential thing is the surrender of self to God the Savior in a proclamation of the covenant God. A rabbinical tradition that has often been cited ever since the second century gives very clear expression to Jewish thinking: "In the days to come sacrifices will all cease, but the sacrifice of *tôdâ* will never cease; canticles will all cease, but the canticles of *tôdâ* will never cease."[60]

Let me return to the liturgy of the first Christians. Many passages of the New Testament are now clearer. In the Acts of the Apostles Christian meals are distinguished not only by "prayers" but by joy.[61] Above all, as the reader has surely noticed by now, Paul uses the verb "proclaim" (1 Cor 11:26) which, in the context, corresponds exactly to the *tôdâ*. In this perspective a suggestion of H. Schürmann acquires an even greater interest: that when the verb *eucharistein* comes at the end of sequences of nouns or verbs that seem to describe the program of Christian assemblies it is a reference to the eucharistic rite.[62] Since *eucharistein* is close in meaning to "praise," even while emphasizing the element of thanksgiving, this analogy compels acceptance. Just as praise formerly accompanied solemn communion sacrifices, so, it seems, the first Christians ate their eucharistic "meal" in a spirit of praise and celebration. They were glorifying the God who had given his Son up to death and had brought into being the community of believers, the community of the "saved."

CONCLUSION

If the Eucharist nowadays seems remote from any real experience, this is due in part to our ignorance of the Jewish and human environment in which it acquired its form and which the preceding discussion has sought to explain. We need not add an ordinary meal to the eucharistic rite in order to restore vitality to the latter; we need only become aware of the symbolism that is at the basis of the liturgy itself.

The first Christians did not invent their rites; they adopted and adapted the practices of their Jewish ancestors. Thus the "blessing" or b⁰raka was the context in which the Eucharist took shape;[63] in all probability the liturgical meal, accompanied as it was by words of praise and proclamation, had its prototype in the Israelite tôdâ. But Christians soon displayed their originality and specific character. They did so, above all, by relating their practices to the Jesus whom God had raised from the dead and with whom their own lives were forevermore associated.

While the temple was initially the place of daily prayer and of preaching, it soon yielded first place to private "houses." The result was a universalization which was impossible for Judaism as long as it located its worship in a limited geographical place.

Henceforth there was no more separation of clean from unclean; the emphasis was on the requirement of faith and authentic brotherhood and sisterhood. The eucharistic meal was not a place from which some were excluded, but a place where all believers might come together, especially the "poor," whose only personal luggage was their faith.

The assembly derived its unity no longer from the Torah, still less from this or that rabbi, even though he might be the Teacher of Justice himself. The word still was, of course, and always would be that which called the brethren together, but this word was now incarnated in the crucified and risen Jesus, the living Lord. The unity of the congregation came from this risen Lord whose very absence bore witness to his presence and whose sure coming in triumph was awaited by the brethren. In the meantime there was no longer any need of fasting, because the Spouse was now alive; the community knew that God had forgiven and renewed it because he had admitted it to share the Lord's table.

It can be seen, then, that Christianity, like Judaism, has its roots in the soil of humanity. The bread and wine are food and therefore signify new life. Taken as a whole, this food that has become a meal expresses the very life of the community; in addition, due to this food believers form a single body. Finally, this living body uses the word to praise God for his mighty deeds: the resurrection of Jesus and the establishment of his new community.

These various factors are a concretization of phenomena which can be called "universal" inasmuch as all human beings need food in order to live, must gather together in order to make their brotherhood and sisterhood effective, and, finally, must open themselves to an Other in order to achieve their fulfillment by acknowledging the gifts he ceaselessly gives them.

III
The Account of the Last Supper of Jesus:
A Synchronic Reading

Four New Testament passages report substantially one and the same episode.[1] Apart from a few details the tenor of the narrative is identical: during a meal Jesus gives his disciples the bread and cup over which he has spoken a blessing and said some words. In addition, he says a kind of farewell that supposes his death to be imminent.

The four recensions are very much alike and yet do not completely overlap. Given this fact, several methods can be used in order to get at the meaning of the account and the significance of the event being related. Scholars usually follow the historical-critical method: they look for the sources of the various texts; they try even to get back to a source-text behind the recensions which we have, and by this means to approximate more fully the meaning of the original account. This is not the path I shall follow initially, if only because of the many hypotheses that make this approach so burdensome. I shall apply the historical-critical method further on.[2]

For the moment I prefer to look directly at the account as we read it today, taking an approach which I describe as "synchronic" as opposed to "diachronic" (evolution of the text in the course of time). I want to define the internal relations that organize the various components of the present text in function of the total end-result. This set of relations constitutes what may be called the "structure" of the account. The structure is not the same as the account but it engenders, from within as it were, the several presentations of the account. These "recensions," four in number, render difficult a would-be synthetic reading of the text. It is therefore necessary to proceed methodically by first defining the bound-

46

aries of the text, then by determining its constitutive elements with the aid of an interpretation of a literary kind, and, finally, by showing the symbolic weight which these elements carry. At this point I will be in a position to recognize and situate the various relations that organize the components of the account.

Such a synchronic reading evidently depends on principles that are supplied by a number of methods. Its purpose is to grasp the relations that give the text its structure; to that end I must at times engage in analyses proper to literary criticism and at every point study the dictionary of symbols upon which the language used is drawing.

I. FIRST READING

Extent of the account

The first operation in this reading is to define the boundaries or extent of the text that is to be interpreted. This calls for a fine touch when the passage belongs to a larger narrative whole, as is the case with the present account which is located by the three synoptic writers within the ongoing "private passion."[3] Paul, however, gives the text in isolation, as it were: in the course of an indictment of abuses of which the Corinthians are guilty during the Lord's Supper he reminds his readers of that which he had handed on to them some years earlier and which he regards as a very venerable tradition. His "citation" can therefore serve as a guide in circumscribing the field of investigation by indicating the beginning and end of the text.

In the *introduction* Paul calls to mind with a brief remark— "On the night he was betrayed"—what the synoptics tell us in the immediate context of the account of institution: during his final meal with the Twelve Jesus foretells Judas' betrayal and therefore his own imminent death. It is worth noting that in Mark and Matthew this prediction constitutes the only "other" incident that takes place during the meal.[4] Luke, for his part, reports other instructions of Jesus to the disciples before the group leaves the room; on the other hand, in his account the prediction of the betrayal comes as a continuation of the second part of the institution, as though it belonged with the latter from a literary standpoint.

These various recensions make one very important point clear: Jesus has not chosen to die; his death will result from the

Mt 26	*Mk 14*	*Lk 22*	*1 Cor 11*
20When it was evening he was at table with the Twelve [disciples]. 21And as they were eating. . . .	17And when it was evening he comes with the Twelve. And as they were at table and were eating. . . .	14And when the hour came he reclined at table and the apostles with him. 15And he said to them: "I have greatly desired to eat this Passover with you before I suffer. 16For I tell you	

that I shall never eat it again until it is fulfilled, in the kingdom of
God."17And, having accepted a cup, having given thanks, he said: "Take
this and share it among you.
18For I tell you that I shall not drink henceforth of the fruit of the
vine until the reign of God comes."

Mt 26	*Mk 14*	*Lk 22*	*1 Cor 11*
26Now as they were eating, Jesus, having taken bread and pronouncing the blessing, broke [it] and having given [it] to the disciples, said: "Take, eat, this is my body."	22And as they were eating, having taken bread, pronouncing the blessing, he broke [it], gave [it] to them and said: "Take, this is my body."	19And having taken bread, having given thanks, he broke [it] and said: "This is my body which [is] given for you. Do this in memory of me."	23On the night he was betrayed the Lord Jesus took bread 24and, having given thanks, broke [it] and said: "This is my body which [is] for you. Do this in memory of me."

27 And, having taken a cup,	23 And, having taken a cup,	20 And the cup likewise after the supper,	25 Likewise also the cup after the supper,
and having given thanks, he gave [it] to them,	having given thanks, he gave [it] to them; and they all drank of it. 24 And he said to them:		
saying: "Drink of it, all of you, 28 for this is my blood of the covenant	"This is my blood of the covenant	saying: "This cup [is] the new covenant in my blood which [is] shed for you."	saying: "This cup is the new covenant in my blood. Do this, each time that you drink, in memory of me."
which [is] shed for the multitude for the forgiveness of sins. 29 I tell you, henceforth I shall not drink again of this fruit of the vine until that day when I shall drink it new with you in the kingdom of my Father."	which [is] shed for the multitude. 25 Truly, I tell you, never more shall I drink of the fruit of the vine until that day when I shall drink it new in the kingdom of God."		26 For each time that you eat this bread and drink this cup, you proclaim the death of the Lord until he comes.

49

shameful action of one of his own disciples. At the same time, however, the three gospel texts immediately interpret this death as flowing from a mysterious "necessity"; thus, according to Mark, "The Son of Man goes as it is written of him."[5] In Paul, the passive verb "he was betrayed," with no mention of the agent, suggests that the harrowing fate of Jesus is due to a plan in which God himself is at work.

The converging interpretations of Paul and the synoptics show that the account of institution must include mention of Jesus' imminent death due to betrayal. John confirms this point in his own way: in his description of Jesus' final meal he emphasizes the betrayal by mentioning it twice, just before and just after the incident of the washing of feet which replaces the account of institution (Jn 13:2, 18).

The *final words* of Paul's citation—"until he comes"—suggest, again in a brief phrase, that the eschatological verse in the synoptics (before or after the actions of the institution) is an integral part of the overall text.[6] None of the recensions fails to mention an ultimate fulfillment in which, according to the synoptics, Jesus will certainly share as one who is alive in God's presence; according to Matthew, who alone makes this point explicit, he will do so in the company of his disciples.

Whatever their location in the various recensions, these two *motifs*—deadly betrayal and definitive reunion—are as it were two boundaries within which the eucharistic text proper is located. They establish a first contrast: on the one hand, separation or death in a context of betrayal; on the other, meeting or life beyond this death, in a context of communion (with God, with the disciples).

Constitutive elements of the account

The second operation brings to light the constitutive elements of the account. I refer primarily to those which are common to the four recensions, but also to those whose absence from one or other recension can be explained by an appropriate literary criticism. Here is a list of these elements:[7]

SETTING

I have already indicated two points under this heading: (a) "On the night" (Cor 23) or "when it was evening" (Mk 17 = Mt 20), "when the hour came" (Lk 14), when Judas has begun his betrayal and Jesus is about to be handed over (Cor 23; see Mk 18–

21 = Mt 21–25 = Lk 21–23); (b) in prospect, the day of God's kingdom (Mk 25 = Mt 29 = Lk 18; see Cor 26c).

There are two further important points: (a) the context is that of a MEAL (Cor 25 = Lk 20 = Mk 22 = Mt 26), with the characteristics proper to it (a Passover setting, according to the synoptics), and (b), since death is foreseen as imminent, the context is that of a FAREWELL.

CHARACTERS

JESUS and the DISCIPLES occupy the stage. Jesus is central from one end of the text to the other, but the disciples are present at every point (implicitly so in Paul); it is to them that Jesus directs his actions and words. But two other characters are also present; an UNNAMED person, suggested by the blessing (or thanksgiving) and by the word "covenant"; and, on the horizon in Mk 24 = Mt 28, the MULTITUDE.

ACTIONS

Two main actions are described, one concerned with the BREAD, the other concerned with the CUP. Each action is presented as a totality but is made up of various gestures:

First action: Jesus takes the bread and says a blessing (gives thanks), breaks the bread and gives it to the disciples (Mk 22 = Mt 26 = Lk 19 = Cor 24).[8]

Second action: Jesus takes the cup and gives thanks, and gives the cup to the disciples (Mk 23–24 = Mt 27–28; see Lk 20; Cor 25).[9]

N.B. The words of the prayer of blessing or thanksgiving are not given; as I shall show, a blessing or thanksgiving at a Jewish meal is an act in the proper sense.

WORDS

The account as a whole contains four statements, all addressed by Jesus to the disciples:

(1) in connection with the bread, during the "bread" action; this statement introduces the element of MY BODY;

(2) in connection with the cup, during the "cup" action; this one introduces the elements of MY BLOOD and COVENANT, which are always put together, even if in different ways;

(3) the command of remembrance (Lk 19; Cor 24, 25);[10]

(4) on drinking in the kingdom of God (Mk 25 = Mt 29 = Lk 18; see Cor 26c); this statement introduces the element of FRUIT OF THE VINE.

The meal setting

The account shows the participants gathered in a single place
and at a single table. There are no comings and goings, as in ordinary stories, nor even (as at other meals reported in the gospels)
such incidents as the intervention of a person from outside the
group at table (Lk 7), the healing of a sick person (Lk 14), the short-
age of wine (Jn 2), or the "wasting" of a costly ointment (Jn 12).
The gospels do, of course, speak at times simply of Jesus taking
part in communal meals, but in these instances the important
thing is the meal or table fellowship as such: Why, the Pharisees
ask, does this man eat with tax collectors and sinners?[11] Here, on
the other hand, we have the only meal reported in the gospels
which Jesus and the disciples eat by themselves. The action
described has, therefore, this peculiarity, that it is superimposed
on the action of the meal itself and takes over the specific elements
of the latter, from the social and religious value of table fellowship
to the main gestures involved, namely, the breaking of the bread
and the sharing of the cup. A "meal" is thus the backdrop for the
account, but a meal is also the event that takes place.

In the synoptics the meal, of which there had been question
earlier in connection with the preparations for it, is mentioned
again at the beginning of the account. Jesus is initially named simply by a pronoun: "he comes" (Mk 17), "he was at table" (Mt 20),
"he reclined at table" (Lk 14). The disciples are "with him" or he
is "with them." It is then said of the group as a whole that "they
were at table and were eating" (Mk 18 = Mt 21). That which takes
place in the course of this table fellowship will provide the subject
matter of the account. The meal as framework is mentioned again
in the repetition in Mk 22a = Mt 26a and, indirectly, in the various words and expressions referring to the actions of a meal.[12]

Paul, too, explicitly mentions the meal; its ongoing function
as a setting for the action is suggested by recurring words: give
thanks, bread, cup. On the other hand, the principal person is solemnly named, "the Lord Jesus," and the date is clearly given: "On
the night he was betrayed." Everyone knew that this had occurred
at the time of the Jewish Passover.

In the synoptics the Passover situation is indicated by the con-
textual narrative; Luke is the only one to mention it in the text
itself. The Passover sheds a light that turns the ordinary table fellowship of the disciples with the Master into an occasion that is

especially rich in meaning. Not only have they shared his perilous journey up to Jerusalem and are now with him in the Holy City, but the Passover turns the thoughts of those at table (and of the reader) to a twofold deliverance: that which Israel experienced when God rescued it from Egypt and made it his special people; and that which it will experience—along similar lines, it might be said—when the Messiah comes and the glory of God is revealed. According to tradition, this future deliverance was to take place during a Passover. Thus, though it is not explicitly stated, this festive meal prolongs and climaxes the frequent meals which Jesus and the Twelve have shared; much more than any previous meal it is filled with a sense of solemn expectation.

At the same time, however, the situation here is reversed. The meal brings the guests together,[13] but it does so, at first sight, in view of a separation that seems permanent. They eat food, an action which explicitly means, according to the Bible, that life is here being sustained or renewed,[14] but the purpose in this case is to announce the cessation of life: "Never more shall I drink," says Jesus. Finally, even though table fellowship implies by its nature an unbroken unity among the participants, a rupture is here brought to light which has already broken this unity: the Son of Man is being betrayed by "someone who has dipped his hand into the dish with me" (Mk 20 = Mt 23; see Lk 21).

The account as a whole

It is against the background of this ambivalent situation that the account of institution unfolds, an account which I said a moment ago is one of a "meal within a meal" and whose constitutive elements have been listed above. A quick reading of that list is enough to show that Jesus himself plays the dominant role: the actions and words which make up the event are all his.

On the other hand, if we listen carefully to the words used, we realize that the universe of biblical faith is captured in the net of the text. In the *bread* and *cup* not only is the land present which was to provide the Hebrews with wheat and vine when their journey through the wilderness was finished, but, even more radically, creation itself is present as both gift and task. The familiar rituals of table fellowship (*bless, break* . . .) express Israel's consciousness of having received everything from God and of being a people whom he calls to unity.

Moreover, this God who has gathered Israel together and gives it life is the God of the *covenant*, which, though given and sealed in the past, still awaits its fulfillment. The covenant is with a small "group" already gathered and called to fidelity despite its infidelity, but it also meant for the *multitude*, a group without temporal or spatial limits: the Lord's plan, which will be fully accomplished on the last *day*, is universal. The banquet of the *kingdom* signifies the joy which God is preparing. While Israel waits for this fulfillment, the *blood of the covenant* calls to mind a major episode in its life: the sacrifice at Sinai by which Moses had expressed the one life shared by Yahweh and his people. Thereby the phrase also recalls the cult which preserved the *memory* of God's saving interventions and thus of his love for Israel and in which the hope of reconciliation after the separation of sin was constantly renewed. On the other hand, the blood, being *shed*, also calls to mind the lot of the prophets whom God has never wearied of sending to the people, or the lot of the just: the cry of innocent blood, beginning with that of Abel, is heard by the Lord.

Throughout the text the "word" calls those at table to a reception which becomes a participation, and to a *doing*; it bids them go beyond the immediately given and enter into a relation with an Other who is superior to themselves. It is the *cup* of *tôdâ* that is to be lifted up in praise.

In harmony with the resonances of biblical faith present in the text are the facts of an extraordinary life, that of Jesus, a child of Israel in his language, his gestures, his very body. The meal he eats with his disciples on this particular evening mirrors the ministry he has been exercising: his purpose has been to bring Israelites together in an intense, active expectation of God's reign, which is henceforth at hand; by his preaching and the meals he has taken with tax collectors and sinners he has proclaimed the extent of God's forgiveness. Because he has persevered unflaggingly in this proclamation he must now face death and shed his blood in a supreme act of deliberate fidelity. That death will bring into existence the new and definitive covenant that concerns himself and all future believers. And he is certain that he will take part in the heavenly banquet.

Articulation of the account

It is clear that all the elements of the text are linked together around the person of Jesus. They can be organized along three axes.

1. A *vertical* axis, on which Jesus is united with creation (bread and cup), on the one hand, and with God (blessing) and his reign (eschatological saying), on the other.

2. A *horizontal* axis, along which Jesus is linked to the disciples who are present and, through them, to the multitude.

3. A *temporal* axis that joins in the limited present of the account the past of Jesus of Nazareth (his Jewish speech, his life of service, his disciples gathered around him) and the future, three moments of which are suggested: the imminent death, the active community of disciples, and the final banquet.

These three axes combine to form a dynamic structure, like that formed by fields of force. Does the account in which they are operative show the same sequence that is displayed by any ordinary account: situation—event(s)—conclusion, or, in other words, a beginning, a development, and an end?

I pointed out earlier that the beginning consists of only a brief notation of the time: when the group is at table (synoptics) or the night of the betrayal (Paul). The development describes two actions of Jesus, each climaxed by a statement and including in addition—once in Luke and twice in Paul—the command of remembrance. The eschatological verse is found in two different positions: after the two actions in Mark and Matthew, before them in Luke. This verse cannot, therefore, be taken as a conclusion, or even as a result or consequence of the event reported; it is part of the event itself, although it is simply juxtaposed to the principal sayings.

Paul is the only one of the writers who puts the eschatological reference into a sentence in which by a hardly perceptible transition he himself becomes once more the subject who speaks: "For each time that you eat this bread and drink this cup, you proclaim the death of the Lord until he comes" (Cor 26). In thus picking up once more the thread of his rebuke to the Corinthians (and this in a well-defined perspective) he provides something that resembles to some extent the "commentaries" which the evangelists sometimes add to a narrative but which they clearly avoid in telling the story of the Supper. For the moment, then, I shall bracket this "liberty" taken by Paul, but I shall have to return to it later.

The account, then, as given by the synoptics, has no response to the twofold action of Jesus and no ending. It is thus radically different from the miracle stories, for example, in which the actual result of the action or words of Jesus is always expressed and in which this result is often highlighted in addition by the surprise, fear, or objections of witnesses. Why is no mention made of any reaction of the disciples to the actions which Jesus has just performed in their presence and to the words he has just spoken to them? The question is especially to the point since Jesus has given specific orders: "Take!" (Mk), "Take and eat!" (Mt), "Do this in memory of me" (Lk). How can the account ignore any and every reaction to the event, despite the mysterious character of the words spoken?

A first way of answering the question might be to look at how the synoptics proceed elsewhere when Jesus orders his disciples to do something.

It is legitimate, after all, to ask what usually ensues in other passages of the gospel in which such specific commands are given. Are there other instances in which Jesus, in direct discourse, bids his disciples perform a particular action and in which nothing is said of the execution? No, there are none: in all cases in which Jesus addresses real (or, sometimes, potential) disciples and gives them a command which calls for an immediate, concrete action, his order is always followed by reference to execution or non-execution on their part.[15] Even if we look for analogous cases outside the context of "discipleship," execution is again always specified as following or not following.[16]

In order to find commands put into the mouth of Jesus and addressed to the disciples (or to the crowd) that are not followed by mention of their execution or non-execution, we must have recourse to an entirely different type of saying: that in which Jesus gives commands or instructions that oblige *permanently* and are not connected with a particular set of historical circumstances.[17]

The account of the Supper might therefore be described as mixed or ambivalent in character. On the one hand, it tells of a particular episode in the life of Jesus of Nazareth: during his final meal with his disciples he performs actions and says words that fit only into this context. On the other hand, the overall action is not distinguishable from that of any communal festive meal; it has nothing unusual about it, except that it is described in detail and is said to have been done by the Master when in the company solely of his disciples. Therefore it simply serves to reinforce a new teaching, a revelation: what Jesus does himself and orders others to do here and now (take, eat, drink) is not limited in its meaning to the particular setting of the account and is not related solely to a precise moment in the life of the Master. Rather it has a permanent meaning that is valid for every future disciple. This, I believe, is what is suggested by the omission of any "reception" after the various commands: the commands are valid not only here and now, but permanently from this time forward.

In order that we modern readers may enter into this event which can be described from a literary standpoint as a revelatory word that commits its recipients to an action, let me go back to the various motifs as organized on the three axes which I distinguished earlier: the vertical, the horizontal, and the temporal.

II. JESUS AND GOD'S CREATED WORLD

The first action of Jesus has to do with the bread. This action is comprised in turn of several gestures or actions: taking and blessing, breaking and distributing. Note that the second of these four is put in the participial form in *all* the recensions (in the synoptics it is also coordinated with the first). On this second action, therefore, everything that follows depends: "Having taken the bread and pronouncing the blessing/having given thanks" (Mk—Mt/Lk) or "he took bread and, having given thanks . . . " (1 Cor). The same holds for the cup: "Having taken, having given thanks" (Mk—Mt).

For the action he wishes to perform Jesus chooses elements provided by the meal situation. He does not take nothingness as his starting point, any more than he did at the wedding feast of Cana, where, as St. Irenaeus points out,[18] it is water, an unspoiled creature at his disposal, that is changed into wine. In addition to being creatures of God, the bread and cup imply the labor that has transformed the fruits of the earth. By way of these elements, then, Jesus is connected with the first creation, which the Creator has entrusted to human beings.

When Jesus takes the bread he does not immediately distribute or consume it. In the eyes of a faithful Jew taking bread is inseparable from blessing it, since when he takes it he is at the same time receiving it from God.

I shall leave aside for the moment the slight distinction that must be made between "pronouncing the blessing" and "giving thanks."[19] The point that is of interest here is the vertical relation uniting God and Jesus who has just taken the bread (or the cup).

Jesus does not simply recite some prayer or other; for a Jew, to pronounce a blessing is not simply to say some words, it is an action that allows the very current of divine life to come through. The living God has empowered his creatures to transmit *his* blessing.[20] To bless is to communicate the power of God.[21] By introducing the bread into this divine current Jesus is already connecting the earth and God, thereby performing a function peculiar to human beings.

Is there more that can be said? Nothing in the account suggests that the action of Jesus is being performed by one who knows himself to be Son of God and Redeemer. He is presented simply as a human being who is linked by perfect trust and submission to the God of Israel, from whom comes all life and every gift.

Nonetheless, of these gifts that are now invested with heavenly power and that have become in a fuller sense God's gift to those at table—of these gifts Jesus will speak as if he himself were freely disposing of them: he takes it upon himself to give them a symbolic value[22] which he himself determines. There is a kind of gap between the prayer with its expression of complete dependence and the following words in which Jesus himself determines the meaning of the elements. It is as though the action of giving in which God, the Creator and Lord, manifests himself to those at table were catching up into its movement the person of Jesus himself: in the blessed bread and cup a gift of another order is proclaimed and communicated in symbol: Jesus gives himself, he *is given*. Yes, Jesus knows a divine secret that involves himself: the divine plan is mediated through the faithful love whose supreme act he himself will accomplish by dying. The blessed bread and cup signify the death he has accepted and its fruit which will be overflowing life. There is no need to name the Father; he is there.

I shall dwell for a moment on these "signifiers" in order to see the connotations they have in the biblical world and to ascertain their possible appropriateness for the new meaning they are now to have.

In the biblical world *bread* is a food which no one can do without; it also stands metaphorically for food in general.[23] Since it is that which sustains daily life it comes to human beings from the mighty Creator, who gives it to those who ask him for it.[24] Especially in the context of the Passover, bread suggests the good will of Yahweh toward his special people and therefore his constant presence.[25] Bread is meant to be shared, especially with the hungry; this sharing is the fundamental characteristic of the righteous.[26]

In light of Israel's experience in the desert where manna had been given from heaven to sustain its life, bread came also to be a sign of eschatological food.[27] In order to express the happiness of sharing in the heavenly banquet, a man who sat at table with Jesus on one occasion said: "Happy they who shall eat bread in the kingdom of God!" (Lk 14:15). Consequently, in the bread which he takes in his hands Jesus sees both ordinary food and, even more, a heavenly food.[28]

With regard to the *wine*, the first point to be made is that it is wine and not water, although we tend spontaneously to pair bread and water. In this context another consideration is at work: the element of abundance which suggests no longer mere earthly subsistence but a fullness of life that produces happiness. In the Bible, wine tends to symbolize the pleasant side of life, friendship, love, joy; at banquets it is associated with music;[29] finally, it stands for heavenly joy.[30] It is therefore the drink for feasts, the drink "to cheer people's hearts."[31]

In the account of the Supper wine is called "fruit of the vine"; like bread it is a gift from the Creator and one sign of the promised land's prosperity.[32] Observe, however, that the word used in the eucharistic verses is not "wine" but "cup." The choice of word doubtless depends on Jewish usage which distinguished various "cups" in the course of a festive meal, but in the present context the word can also have harmonics of its own. Especially in the psalms "cup" is associated with sacrifices of thanksgiving; as "cup of salvation" that "brims over," it celebrates communion with the God of the covenant, with him who is himself said to be the "cup" that is Israel's lot.[33]

In taking bread and cup into his hands Jesus is in contact with foods that are at once ordinary and festive. It is under this twofold aspect that he makes use of creation as a source of life and community among human beings. When he links this creation with God through the blessing (or thanksgiving) he gives a dimension of infinity to his own action. The created world that is present in the bread and wine is now linked to the Creator and is therefore able to signify his presence. Does not the linking of creation to God introduce into the text that covenant (in the broader sense of the term) which has united the universe to God since the moment when he created it?

III. JESUS AND THE DISCIPLES

The relation between Jesus and creation, as I have just described it, is ordered to a further relation, that of Jesus and his disciples. The Jesus-disciples axis really undergirds the entire text, for whether Jesus acts or speaks he does so at every point in function of the guests to whom his gestures and words are addressed. This horizontal dimension, which cuts across the vertical dimension uniting Jesus to God, finds expression in a number of literary contrasts which can be conveniently listed under two points of view, that of Jesus and that of the disciples.

From the viewpoint of Jesus

A synchronic reading of the text makes it possible to recognize in Jesus a consciousness which the disciples do not yet have. Thus I can perceive, with Jesus, a future that is still dark to those to whom it is promised.

A dialogical situation

In the account of the meal that brings together Jesus and his disciples there are no shifts of scene, no movements of departure and return;[34] the guests are as it were locked into the Supper room. But the account is characterized by another movement that is internal and "dialogical."[35]

From the outset this meal has a relational character: it is reserved for an intimate group, and no outsider is present. It is the final meal which the group will take together on earth, as the eschatological saying makes clear. The solemnity of the moment is intensified in that the Passover setting turns the minds of the guests to deliverance past and deliverance still to come.

It is possible to speak here of "dialogue" even though the disciples do not utter any response to the words and commands of Jesus. For during this final meal Jesus does not make a statement about the elements of bread and wine to the world in general, as if his action were here and now terminating in the materials that make up the meal. If he gives a new value to the bread and the cup, he does so essentially in order to give his own person to his followers so that they may be united to him, enter into a sharing of life with him, and thereby celebrate his gift.

The action is wholly directed to the disciples, as is perfectly clear both from the verbs "give" and "say to" and from the personal pronouns used. The disciples are bidden to take (Mk/Mt), or else it is said that *my* body is given and *my* blood shed for *you* (Lk/ Paul), the "I" and "you" being inseparably linked. The "giving" and "shedding" do indeed announce an imminent death, but reference is made to the death only in function of the disciples. The actions and words of Jesus take on their meaning only within this relation to the others at table.

But the actions and words must also be understood from the viewpoint of Jesus himself. Once they are so viewed, they show Christ to be filled with a profound desire: that he may turn this group into "his" community in this world, a living community of his own that will be established by his death and his life with God. What he has directly in mind is a state of things that will follow the imminent separation. This man who is about to die is disposing of the future: death will certainly bring separation, but from it will come the covenant that unites the disciples to God in Jesus who has rejoined his Father. In the new universe thus inaugurated, in the space that is opened up yet left empty by the Master's departure, Jesus will himself be their bread and their cup as long as the present world lasts. His new presence will not force itself upon them. Rather it will depend on their remembrance-in-action of his "passage"; it will come about through his disciples' obedience to his command through their actual, communal participation in the mystery of his life. The bread eaten and the cup drunk in the name of Jesus are here made the "symbols" of that participation, symbols that will constantly be given anew by Jesus and constantly received anew by the gathered disciples.

To the elements shared out among those at table the words restore the unity which they had in the hands of Jesus: the bread that is broken and distributed has become many pieces of bread, but it is defined in the singular as "my body"; so, too, the cup that is meant to be passed around is said to be "my blood" or "the covenant." Those who receive these gifts all enter into a communion of life with the one person who gives them to them.

Within the meal, then, another action, of another order, takes shape. Onto the familiar typology "earthly meal/heavenly banquet" that is suggested by the eschatological saying there is grafted a new typology, one that might be called "intermediate," that of the sacramental meal. The ordinary action of breaking bread begins in fact a *new* meal, the meaning of which is established by the words of Jesus. This meaning, which he knows but of which the disciples are ignorant, holds not only for the present moment, but for an indefinite future, and not only for those here at table but for every future disciple. This man who is about to die but is already master of the future leaves his presence in advance as a legacy; it will be an active presence among his followers and will make them active in their turn.

Gestures/words

Two actions are described, one corresponding to the beginning of a meal, the other to its ending; in any case, they are sequential and each is already a whole. Each is the result of connecting a series of gestures with at least one set of words. The intrinsic relation between gesture and word is very close in each instance.

In human relations gestures are sometimes enough to "symbolize" something; thus the flowers a man brings to his fiancée need no interpretation. During his public life Jesus had, of course, already used gestures to focus attention on his person; but here there is something more. As a result, whereas the traditional symbolism of the social and religious bond uniting members of a table fellowship needed no interpretation, the "effect" in the present account comes only from the words. At the same time, however, the words themselves would be unintelligible apart from the gestures that lead up to them and serve as vehicle for them. The words of Jesus establish a new meaning that is indispensable for explaining the sense he gives to his action of sharing.

The words, then, interpret the whole action. While giving bread Jesus makes it clear by his words that he is "giving himself for . . . " As he sends the cup around he states that he is "shedding his blood." The two gestures of Jesus thereby receive a symbolic import: the gift of his person in behalf of the disciples, and this to the point of shedding his blood for them.

Finally, the two actions have for their purpose to establish a relation between Jesus and the disciples that will replace the one that previously existed between them. As I said earlier, there is a meal within the meal; so too a deeper mutual presence replaces the companionship of Master and disciples.

Break/give

Jesus' action of breaking the bread is directly followed by its distribution to the disciples. The symbolism of the bread broken/

distributed is clear: the same food, when shared, gives a share in the same life. The same holds for the cup: it is one and becomes a drink for all. According to Jewish custom, the act of distributing both bread and cup was reserved for the head of the household who had first pronounced the prayer which reminded those at table of the presence of the invisible Giver.

Jesus, the central figure, follows the ritual for a meal. By mentioning each successive gesture the text lends them solemnity in a crescendo that climaxes in the distribution. The preeminence of Jesus in relation to the others at table is thereby emphasized; he does not simply, like every host, transmit the blessings of the Creator but is clearly one who, while united to God, also gives in his own name. The series of gestures keeps its usual meaning but also leads up to a statement which gives a new and surprising interpretation.

My body/my blood

By reason of the correspondence which we spontaneously see between my body/my blood and bread/wine, it would seem that this new pair is to be understood as parts of a total entity. That is, the main ritual elements making up the meal would seem to correspond to the elements of the human composite (flesh/blood) or, as some authors would have it, the elements of the Jewish cultic sacrifice (flesh and blood of the victims). In fact, the data in the text do not justify such a reading. It must be recognized, moreover, that there is no direct correspondence between "wine" and "blood"; it is only in connection with the *cup* (filled, of course, with wine) that there is any equivalence, and the equivalence is between "cup" and a reality described as "blood of the covenant" or "covenant in my blood." Consequently the pair in question here is no longer "my body/my blood" in the sense which seems so obvious to us, but "my person/covenant (of God) in my blood (that is shed)."

This lack of symmetry bids us look for a double perspective which must be defined if we are to understand the function of the new pair in the structure of the account. Not everything is already said in the words over the bread, as though the words over the cup then simply transposed it into a different register. We must pay attention to each of the two formulas in succession.

In the recensions of *Luke* and *Paul* the body is described as "given *for*" or "(being) *for*," and the covenant is sealed "in my blood (shed for you)." What is the relation that unites and distinguishes these two statements? "Body" designates the person himself who is completely dedicated (even unto death) to his mission in behalf of the disciples. The covenant in the blood (shed) states two points: a death that is violent and premature, and the universal fruit resulting from it.

In Mark and Matthew the words over the bread do not specify that the body is "given for you." But is this not implied if care is taken to understand the words in their textual framework? They are part of the overall action performed upon the bread, an action in which the verb "give" has the dominant place (in the indicative mood in Mark and in the participial in Matthew, which connects it even more closely with "saying"). "My blood" is predicated of that which is "given" to the disciples. Is it permissible to move from the obvious meaning *(give to)* to the meaning which Luke and Paul specify *(given in behalf of)*? In any event, the two ideas can be said to be so close that the more concise version of the words over the bread can, in my opinion, be read as having the same fullness of meaning (all the more so since they follow upon the invitation to "take").

Another reading of the words over the bread can be made if we take into account that in a Hellenistic environment the body can be regarded as that which unifies the varied members that compose it (see 1 Cor 12). In this perspective, the meaning might be said to be that when the disciples take in this body given to them in the form of bread, they are unified, even while remaining many, in this body and that in a sense they even become this body. Jesus would then be saying: "Until now I have been present to you, alongside you in space, and you have formed a community around me. Now, through you who are united to me, the Giver of this bread to you, I will henceforth have a relationship with all human beings and will express myself in the world."

The perspective in the words over the cup is different. The disciples may be able to become the "body" of Jesus in this world, but they cannot become his "blood of the covenant." The function of the words over the cup is rather to explain the condition required for establishing the new community that will be the "body" of Christ on earth.

In Mark/Matthew the "shedding" of the blood indicates, as it does in the other recensions, that the death of Jesus is a violent one. The formula "my blood of the covenant," which is taken from the Book of Exodus,[36] brings out the fact that the covenant in question is the one God had always been offering to Israel; now that covenant is really concluded.

Disciples/multitude

Jesus is thinking not only of the disciples and the little group here present, but of the "multitude," a term which according to the underlying Hebrew expression means all human beings. Jesus has the whole human race in view and not just the group gathered in the Supper room.

From the viewpoint of the disciples

The disciples are implied at every point throughout the scene that unfolds here; they are inseparable from Jesus whose actions and words are addressed to them alone. Without their presence there would be no account.

But here they conduct themselves quite differently than in many other episodes, for they display hardly any reaction. The texts do, of course, allow us to suppose that they eat the bread and drink the cup which Jesus offers them, but the group seems at first sight to be an addressee and nothing more. How is the important part played in the story by these others at table to be reconciled with their seeming self-effacement?

I tried to answer a similar question when I asked, from a different standpoint, why the text contains no reaction to the action of Jesus and no ending. Here I must hark back to the same point in connection with the disciples' role. Why the evangelists' seeming lack of interest in the reaction of those at table to the gifts and commandment of Jesus?

Several explanations are possible. From a literary standpoint, the device of having the others remain silent undoubtedly emphasizes their entire dependence on the action of Jesus and, as it were, their complete orientation to him. In this way the spotlight is on the giver: the only one who counts here is this man who is authorized both by the blessing asked from God and by his role in the divine plan to "give" in his own name. And indeed there can be no doubt of Jesus' preeminent role. Just as long ago when he invited the disciples to follow him, the initiative can only come from him. This is especially true now that there is question of giving them a participation in his death and his new life.

It might also be thought that the disciples remain silent because they cannot understand the mystery being entrusted to them until Jesus has actually died and risen. Only after Easter will this understanding be theirs. But are there not cases in the synoptics in which Jesus gives a glimpse of something which only the light of Easter will render intelligible and in which the disciples nonetheless react, even if only in the form of astonishment or mis-understanding? Thus after being transfigured in their presence Jesus tells them of the resurrection of the Son of Man, and Mark emphasizes the point that they did not understand his meaning and asked him about the "return" of Elijah (Mk 9:10–11).

The real or at least the principal reason emerges more clearly if we take into account another, contrasting and correlative aspect of the story insofar as the latter involves the disciples. Gathered here around the Master, they are commanded to *do* something *later on*. It is their future activity that Jesus has in view and that interests the narrators, not their present cooperation or their present sentiments. In this present hour of table fellowship they are not only invited to take the bread and receive the cup; they are urged to an action which Jesus, while himself performing it before them now, bids them perform in the future. They cannot as yet perform an action which will be theirs after his actual departure. Jesus alone is Lord of time: he anticipates symbolically both his death and the increased life it will bring to his disciples, but the disciples themselves cannot yet fully match what he does. Conse-quently, their actions now at this table must not be allowed to cap-ture our attention; these actions certainly have their value but for the reader they belong to a past that is over and done with. The important thing, as far as their own action is concerned, is the "memorial" they are to celebrate in the course of time, their future fidelity to his command, the welcome they give to the living Jesus when they gather in the certainty that he is coming to them.[37]

Finally, it was doubtless not suitable that one or other of those at table should speak in the context of the eucharistic institution. The meal which Jesus is establishing is not meant primarily for individuals, whatever the function they will subsequently exercise in the assembly, but for the community as such. This being the case, it would have been necessary for the entire group to express itself. Perhaps Mark felt this when he noted not simply that "they drank (of the cup), but that "they *all* drank of it."

A new relationship

To put it briefly, Jesus wishes to establish a new and lasting relationship with his disciples, and this relationship presupposes a twofold transformation: of himself and of the group of disciples.

Jesus the Lord

By acting with sovereign authority Jesus shows himself to be one who is master of his own destiny and who secures life for his disciples. It is in his own name that, while performing the gestures of a host, he bestows an unparalleled meaning on the blessed elements which he distributes. By his words he assigns to his person and to the death in which his ministry will culminate the power to change the situation of human beings before God. Even though his mission comes to an end in the darkness of deadly betrayal, it leads into the world of the covenant a people whom a long history of infidelity had hitherto kept in a state of indefinite waiting.

Yahweh alone could bring such a plan to its fulfillment. Yet here we see this man Jesus taking responsibility for it all: he dares to identify the effective salvation of humankind with the fulfillment of his own destiny. God's fidelity is henceforth mediated by the fidelity of Jesus and specifically by his death. But Jesus says that the disciples must "do this," not "in memory of my death" but "in memory of me." The "me" sums up the two expressions "my body" and "my blood" which are central in the respective words of institution.[38] Observe, however, that the "I" of which the command of remembrance speaks is not one who proudly contrasts himself with his disciples. This "I" is a man who is gentle and humble of heart and who literally exists only through his relationship with God.

In place, then, of an event that is recognized as being a divine intervention the account of the Supper has an "I" who speaks. His life that is given and his death are, of course, events; nonetheless the disciples are told that when they celebrate their commemoration their attention is to be on the presence of a person.[39]

Jesus is thus brought before us here as one who possesses from the outset, or has acquired by the gift of himself, a supratemporal existence. He is a mortal man and about to die, yet the vantage point from which he speaks is already on the other side of death, since he is telling those at table with him that it is he himself, *alive*, whom they will meet when they celebrate this meal.

The words which Jesus speaks over the bread and cup take but a moment to say, but into this moment they compress a future that is marked by contrast: they anticipate his absence by declaring his death and they make real here and now his new presence beyond this absence.

Death, the source of life

These statements about the person of the Lord Jesus must not be taken in isolation from the men to whom they are addressed and who by that very fact are themselves profoundly changed. In speaking of himself Jesus declares himself a servant of those at table ("for you") and of the divine plan ("covenant"). But he is not departing like any other servant of God who has completed his or her task. After his departure he will continue to be the one who gathers the disciples and, even more, gives them an existence before the Father. He will accomplish this by means of a mutual interiority of himself and his disciples which the bread and cup, given and received, will express in symbolic form throughout an indeterminate future. But this requires that the disciples recognize their deliverance to have been won by him and that they join in celebrating "his" Supper.

Jesus has indeed just announced his death and symbolized it for those at table as already under way. His gestures and words express a total stripping of self: "body given" and "blood shed" say clearly that he is departing, freely but in suffering, thus recapitulating a life spent entirely in the service of God and human beings. But by means of these same gestures and words Jesus also makes it known that he gives life. It is *for* the disciples that he strips himself of his earthly existence; it is *for* them and *for* the multitude that he concludes the covenant by shedding his blood. He thus gives the bread and cup a new meaning that extends their natural meaning as sources of increased life. They now symbolize the gift Jesus makes of himself, so that by receiving them the disciples acquire the fruit of that giving: through Jesus they are reconciled to God, and this in a definitive way.

Paul gives a splendid summation of all this when he says to the Corinthians: "Each time that you eat this bread and drink this cup, you *proclaim* the death of the Lord." What does this mean? At the future gatherings for which Jesus is now calling, the relation between himself and his disciples will be modified. I shall try to explain this before turning my attention to the temporal axis that orients the narration.

Future situation

When Jesus tells the disciples to "do this in memory of me," he looks forward to a changed situation. His death *will have taken place* and, even though its fruit remains, it will be a past historical event that cannot be repeated. The only *event* on each occasion will be Christ's coming under the veil of symbols, but that event will be as real as the celebration that brings the community together over and over again. All this means that in the account the new life Jesus will have takes definitive precedence over his death. Even though the death is at first glance the center of attention, it is in fact "overridden," as it were, in the text: on the one hand, by the meal setting, present or future, since "meal" indicates the actual existence of a community that thereby sustains its life; on the other hand, by the level at which the communion between the disciples and Jesus takes place, namely, in a sphere beyond his death.

The community's future meals will therefore not have the limited function of enabling the faithful to be present to Christ's saving death; rather they will celebrate his new life with God insofar as this is communicated to the disciples. The latter, too, must "pass" unceasingly from death to life. The past event and the present existence of Jesus are of course not separable, since the one is the condition of the other (when Jesus speaks of them, the two are superimposed in one and the same statement). Nonetheless it is the new relationship between Jesus and the disciples that takes priority.

Since the disciples will still be here on earth, this mutual relation will continue to be mediated through sensible signifiers: in the past, through the visible, concrete human being named Jesus whose native town and family were known to all; at present, through the bread and cup that are the fruit of the soil and of human labor and that can be seen and touched. The relation, however, will no longer belong to the external world, but will be of the interior order. The choice of food and drink as symbols suggests this interiority: not only will Jesus be the one who keeps his community alive, but the disciples and Jesus himself will become mysteriously one, despite an absence that must last as long as the present world lasts. Because they are associated with the bread and the cup, neither "body" nor "blood" suggests lifeless things which death will have stripped of their function; as understood in the Bible "body" and "blood" signify rather a communion of living beings.

IV. A TEMPORAL AXIS

The two preceding axes—Jesus/God and Jesus/disciples—hold the account of the Supper together. But the account itself also bids the reader situate the episode in the flow of time. This is not surprising, since every event comes at the end of a past that has prepared the way for it, while at the same time it heralds a future. The text of the Supper shows an explicit concern to locate the event within history and to bring out the sense in which the present of the narrative is an outcome and at the same time the beginning of something new.

It is worth nothing that a contrast between night and day imposes a certain perspective on the account. Jesus is betrayed at night (1 Cor); the Supper takes place "when it was evening" (Mk-Mt). But in the course of it reference is made to the "day" when Jesus will drink new wine (Mk-Mt, see Lk) and to the day of his final coming, which tradition identifies with the day of the Lord (Paul). The painful present that derives its tone from the prophecy of betrayal and death is contrasted with the future of the heavenly banquet in which Jesus will take part with his disciples and with the future of his glorious return. This contrast is comparable to another that is familiar to us: the night of the Easter Vigil and the light that flashes out in the midst of it.

Moreover, although the account is part of the larger passion narrative and is therefore immediately colored by the thought of the betrayal and the blood to be shed, the synoptics also situate it in the Passover season. The preparation for the ritual meal (Mt-Mk-Lk), the Hallel sung at the end (Mt 30 = Mk 26), the covenant concluded at this meal: these are themes that focus attention on the climax of the passion narrative as whole, namely, the appearances of the risen Jesus to the disciples. In Paul the covenant points to the parousia.

Readers may prefer to consider the text of Paul separately, since there is no question of Passover in 1 Cor 11. They can, however, find in Paul another contrast that frames the text: at the beginning, Jesus (the Lord) is said to have "been betrayed"; at the end it is said that "he will come (from heaven)." The "passivity" of a condemned man is contrasted with the sovereignly free activity of the exalted Lord. To appreciate the tension between passion and Easter we need only call to mind the thoughts and feelings of the Jews when they celebrated their deliverance from Egyptian slavery.[40]

As a matter of fact, the two relations night/day and passion/Easter overlap, since it is the night of the passion that is thus being situated in relation to the day of Easter and of the end-time, between which for the moment no clear distinction is made.

In addition to these literary contrasts which suggest a particular perspective, the account contains allusions to the past and foreshadowings of the future that establish a temporal axis. The extremities of this axis are as far distant as the eyes of those at table can see.

At the Supper Jesus sums up his past. He has reached the end of his life. The disciples he has chosen are gathered around him, representatives at this final meal of the community he has striven to assemble. Except for one of them, they are men who have followed him loyally down to the present hour, through the extremes and the ups and downs of a ministry that is now coming to a tragic end. According to Luke, Jesus at this moment emphasizes their fidelity: "You are the ones who have stayed with me constantly in my trials" (Lk 22:28). It is "with them" that he has greatly desired to eat this Passover before he suffers (Lk 22:15).

The entire ministry of Jesus provides the implicit background of this scene, since if it were not for the course his life had taken, death would not be hanging over him nor would these men be here with him. It is the mission he has received from the Father and carried on thus far without ever weakening that requires the actions he will now perform in order to prepare for the future of his community. That past shows through in the actions and words of Jesus. In addition, the gift of his person that he makes here is only the climactic expression of the attitude that has constantly been his in his dealings with human beings.

Finally, the past experience of Israel is also to be seen as present in the text. The Passover setting and the mention of the covenant call to mind the first period of Hebrew history and, even prior to that, the initiative of God, since the Hebrews were given existence as a people only for the sake of the divine plan. It is thus the entire past of Israel, with its divine interventions and all the failures and testings of a stiff-necked people, that ends in the present moment of the account. The promise that accompanies the whole temporal duration of the people is summed up in the words of Jesus and fulfilled in his death.

Openness to the future is even more explicit in the account. The immediate future is there in the coming death. The time of the Church is brought to mind since it is the time of the meal which Jesus here orders the disciples to celebrate, the meal at which he himself, though absent, will continue to be present.[41]

The journey that had its beginning long ago in the divine initiative will not get bogged down in the sands of a history that continues on endlessly. The eschatological verse says that the journey will reach its goal in the kingdom. Jesus states his own certainty of sharing in the heavenly banquet at which a "new" wine will flow. Remarkably enough, this adjective, which occurs in this context only in Mark and Matthew, is the same adjective that Luke and Paul apply to the covenant. In both cases the Greek word is *kainos*,[42] which indicates not recent origin but something that is radically, marvelously different from all that has gone before, something that in the final analysis comes from God alone.

Three successive periods may therefore be distinguished within the course of time: before the conclusion of the covenant in Jesus; between this and the reunion of Jesus and his disciples; and, last, the heavenly "time" of God's reign. In this perspective, the heart of the account is the anamnesis or remembrance that dominates the intermediate period, the period of the sacramental meal. The anamnesis, which is explicitly mentioned in Mark and Matthew, has an equivalent in Luke and Paul. The texts of the latter do not contain the command of repetition, but they do make explicit the universal scope of Jesus' action by referring to the "multitude." The multitude, which will continue to expand indefinitely, will not be able to make salvation their own unless they in their turn receive the fruit of the life-giving cross. Does this not suggest that the meal which makes this salvation symbolically present must continue to be celebrated in every time and place?

What Jesus does here, then, he does in anticipation: not only his "dying" (which he anticipates in order to bring out its meaning and to express his free consent to it), but also the giving of his presence in symbols. Through the commemoration which the disciples will make of him, this "real" presence of Jesus will light up, from within, the night of the passion that lasts through the centuries in the countless sufferings of human beings and their real "dying." The liturgical action will enable believers to express ever anew their confidence that love has conquered death.

CONCLUSION: STRUCTURE AND MEANING

The various relationships which I have been pointing out in the account of the Supper do not constitute a lifeless skeleton. It must be said, rather, that because they are structured around a single agent, Jesus, they bring into the scene the totality of what is real: God, creation, the human beings of all times.

It will be helpful to summarize briefly the route thus far traveled. During his final meal Jesus engages in a few actions that are apparently quite ordinary ones for a Jew. He takes bread and he takes a cup of wine: gestures which show his relationship with the earth and with the toil and longings of human beings. As a good Jew he pronounces a blessing that extends the action of God: in Jesus the divinely given covenant with the created universe is fully renewed, and this universe can now mediate a presence.

The attention of Jesus is directed to those at table. According to the tradition of his people, he takes the bread and the cup not only for his own nourishment but in order to share them: the food that has been provided becomes a fraternal meal. It is at this point that he intervenes in an original way: when he breaks the bread and passes the cup, he symbolizes the gift he is making of himself to the disciples and the multitude, thereby uniting them all in him. The new significance which he gives to these ritual actions is expressed in his words.

The gaze and the words of Jesus encompass the whole of time. The new community that he has just established and that will be inseparable from him is to repeat the same gestures and words he has just used. Thus the experiential present of this meal is pregnant with the future, because the Eternal One is making it co-extensive with human history.

How, then, is the present that is the Supper to be defined? The structure I have brought to light helps us grasp the meaning of the text more clearly: a change takes place, as in every narrative, but it does so here in a special way I shall try to describe. It affects the poles of the various axes, especially the person who stands at the intersection of the axes, but also the disciples and their world.

Jesus becomes one who is absent-and-present. His humanity is radically transformed by the death which he accepts and which by the divine will becomes definitive life. His "body" is no longer that which others used to see; henceforth he will express himself differently in this world, through the gift of bread and cup and through the disciples whom bread and cup unite to him.

The covenant is concluded in Jesus; it becomes new and thereby a present reality. It is no longer simply a promise, even though its effects will be manifested only in the course of time and at time's end. The disciples will give the covenant its on-going effectiveness by commemorating Jesus, because he, the crucified and risen One, will continue to be the point of reference. In him God is present, and this presence is now expressed by the eucharistic bread.

The *disciples*, too, are transformed: they "pass" from a pre-paschal to a paschal condition by being associated with the transformation that affects Jesus himself. They enjoy God's forgiveness and enter into the covenant. Consequently, they are no longer simply a band of companions gathered around Jesus of Nazareth but constitute a community united, in an interior communion, to the Christ who lives forever. By eating the one bread and drinking from the one cup they become one body, living by one life which is Jesus himself. Finally, they cease to be men who are simply instructed, men who are pretty much passive, and become responsible agents whose work is to commemorate Jesus. Their group can no longer be self-enclosed but must open itself to admit the multitude of human beings; as a result, their very cohesion supposes an openness to the entire world.

The *created world* now finds its full meaning. As we saw, the · food received from God has become a fraternal meal, a source of unity among those at table and an expression of covenant. Now, in the eucharistic rite, the bread and wine, which sum up in a way the created world, "symbolize" the body and blood of Jesus. This change affects the bread and wine at a higher level which I shall try to define in chapters on the bread and wine where I explain the meaning the verb "symbolize" has in this book. Far from casting doubt on the reality of the change in the bread and wine, the verb "symbolize" points in a profound way to the real presence of Jesus Christ in what would subsequently be called the "species" ("appearances") of bread and wine. "Change" is another word for what was intended in the term "transubstantiation."[43] The biblical text does not go quite as far in definition; it does tell us not to separate the "elements" from their ordination to the disciples, for this ordination is implicit in the "dialogical" aspect of the account.

Who is the author of this *change* that affects Jesus, the disciples, and the created world itself, and what is specific to it?

The change that occurs is not due to the gathering for a meal nor to the eating, but to *the word of Jesus.* This word, which is of a prophetic kind, is not meant as a commentary on a new rite; rather it effects the change by the very act of being spoken. According to a biblical tradition the word of God is not a simple announcement but an action, which in the present instance takes concrete form in the gesture of distributing the bread and the cup.

There are doubtless analogies between this change and those with which we are familiar in our world. Change is a manifestation of life: a child becomes an adult, wheat becomes bread, water becomes fruit, nature becomes culture.

In the case of the Eucharist, however, the change seems to be a different kind, because it is not the end-result of an immanent "development"; from this point of view it resembles the change that takes place in a miracle, which is also produced by a transcendent cause.[44] But two characteristics of the eucharistic change prevent its being put in the category of miracle.

(a) The end result of the eucharistic change is *not visible.* The new community is indeed united to Jesus Christ, but the presence of the Savior is in the mode of absence. From an empirical standpoint the bread and wine continue to exist as sensible bread and wine and continue to be earthly food. The reason is that the change is effected only in virtue of a relation to a new source of existence, which, moreover, places them in a state of continual "passage" to a different order of mediation.

The effects of the change are obviously felt in the sensible order of things: a life of charity and service reaching even to the point of self-sacrifice. But while these effects alone put the stamp of authenticity on the worship that is offered to God, they do not serve to describe the specifically eucharistic change; they belong rather to the existential order of practical everyday life.

(b) *Universality* is a second characteristic of the eucharistic change. Unlike miracles which are concerned with particular cases, the eucharistic words of Jesus embrace all the believers of every age. In this respect, there is a similarity with life itself, which is ceaselessly changing; the difference is that in the case of the Eucharist faith is required of all: "That which is born of the flesh is flesh, and that which is born of the Spirit is spirit."

A synchronic reading cannot claim to bring to light all the implications in the account of the Supper. It might indeed lead directly into the presentations which the various writers—the synoptics and Paul—give of the account, as well into a hermeneutic. We would then be able to see how the structure which I have been describing could engender different kinds of accounts. It seems preferable, however, to proceed first to a diachronic reading of the traditions and see how the text developed. I shall attempt this diachronic reading in Part II and then turn to the different presentations of the account in Part III and to a hermeneutic in Part IV.

As a conclusion to my leisurely synchronic reading I would like to reduce it to what I regard as its essentials.

The meal celebrated by Jesus is an act uniting those at table at three levels: at the earthly level, at the heavenly level which the meal symbolizes, and at the intermediate level of the liturgical action which the meal inaugurates. Everything is directed to complete communion among those at table.

This communion is brought about through a radical change which affects the agents in the scene—Jesus and the disciples—so that they reach a new mode of presence and encounter. The change is indicated in the verb *give* which describes the action of Jesus on the different levels just listed. The gift undoubtedly finds expression in the death of Jesus (gift of his body and blood); but it probably originates in the mysterious gift which God makes *to* his Son and *of* his Son. Would it not be appropriate to call this transformative action "gift par excellence" rather than "death"?

Communion through gift ends in covenant. We should observe that in the account this particular term does not connote any literary "opposite" or contrasting term: it has its meaning in itself, since it already says relation between God and human beings, between Jesus and his disciples, between the disciples and the multitude.

Finally, the account of the Supper is indispensable for explaining the account of the passion and resurrection. The reason is that it brings out the further significance of the passion and resurrection, whereas the remainder of the gospel account looks at these solely in terms of the person of Jesus himself. The account suggests that through the change which takes place in Jesus in the course of the Supper the group of disciples is likewise changed. The Eucharist "makes" the Church. The disciples, who from now on draw their life from Jesus, will in return make known the permanent source of their new existence; that is why it can also be said that the Church "makes" the Eucharist.[45]

PART II

The Traditions Concerning the Final Meal of Jesus

The "breaking of bread" and the "Lord's Supper" send us back to the gospel account of the last meal of Jesus and his disciples. It is tempting to read this account as a faithful description of that final evening, but in fact such an undertaking can be carried through only at the cost of a concordist reading, or forced harmonization, of the texts.

A first fact that is too obvious to be shunted aside is that the fourth gospel describes (Chapter 13) a final meal which Jesus of Nazareth takes with his disciples just before his arrest, but makes no mention of any institution of the Eucharist, even though all three synoptic gospels highlight this. Does this mean that there were two last suppers of Jesus? The mere asking of the question shows that it leads to a dead end: it is not possible to harmonize the two types of account at the factual level; instead, the perspectives proper to each type of gospel must be taken into account.

This being the case, why not simply examine the three synoptics in succession and then John? But the problem is even more complicated than I have just indicated, for it recurs even within the synoptics themselves. All three, of course, and 1 Corinthians as well, do report substantially the same episode: during his final meal Jesus says some words over the bread and over the cup, both of which he gives to the disciples who are present. The content is almost identical in all three accounts; and yet, if we look more closely, the differences are such as to render illusory any claim to have established a source-text. Even the two leading specialists on the subject have given up on the attempt, the one despite his desire to reach the *ipsissima verba* of Jesus, the other after having published a monumental work that is filled to the brim with the lit-

Mt 26	Mk 14	Lk 22	1 Cor 11
20When it was evening he was at table with the Twelve [disciples]. 21And as they were eating....	17And when it was evening he comes with the Twelve. And as they were at table and were eating....	14And when the hour came he reclined at table and the apostles with him. 15And he said to them: "I have greatly desired to eat this Passover with you before I suffer. 16For I tell you that I shall never eat it again until it is fulfilled in the kingdom of God."	23On the night he was betrayed the Lord Jesus took bread 24and, having given thanks, broke [it] and said:
	(18b–21)	17And, having accepted a cup, having given thanks, he said: "Take this and share it among you.	
29"I tell you, henceforth I shall not drink again of this fruit of the vine until the day when I shall drink it new with you in the kingdom of my Father."	23And, having taken a cup and having given thanks, he gave [it] to them; and they all drank of it. 24And he said to them:[24b] 25"Truly, I tell you, never more shall I drink of the fruit of the vine until that day when I shall drink it new in the kingdom of God."	18For I tell you that I shall not drink henceforth of the fruit of the vine until the reign of God comes."	

Mt 26	Mk 14	Lk 22	
26Now as they were eating Jesus, having taken bread and pronouncing the blessing, broke [it] and having given [it] to the disciples, said:	22And as they were eating, having taken bread, pronouncing the blessing, he broke [it] gave [it] to them and said:	19And having taken bread, having given thanks, he broke [it] and gave [it] to them, saying:	

Matthew	Mark	Luke	1 Corinthians
"Take, eat, this is my body."	"Take, this is my body."	"This is my body which [is] given for you. Do this in memory of me."	"This is my body which [is] for you. Do this in memory of me."
27And, having taken a cup,	23And, having taken a cup,	20And the cup likewise after the supper,	25Likewise also the cup after the supper,
and having given thanks, he gave [it] to them,	having given thanks, he gave [it] to them, and they all drank of it. 24And he said to them:	saying:	saying:
saying: "Drink of it, all of you, 28for this is my blood of the covenant	"This is my blood of the covenant	"This cup [is] the new covenant in my blood which [is] shed for you."	"This cup is the new covenant in my blood. Do this, each time that you drink, in memory of me." 26For each time that you eat this bread and drink this cup, you proclaim the death of the Lord until he comes.
which [is] shed for the multitude for the forgiveness of sins."29	which [is] shed for the multitude." 25		

1 Cor 10:16: The cup of blessing over which we pronounce the blessing, is it not a participation in the blood of Christ? The bread which we break, is it not a participation in the body of Christ?

erary criticism.[1] Consequently, if we are not satisfied with simply describing one after the other the presentations given by the synoptics and Paul but want to find out what gives these their singleness of meaning, we must try to get back to the milieus to which the four accounts owe their orientation.

Furthermore—and I do not bring this up for the pleasure of making things even more complicated!—it must be noted that the three synoptic texts report words that are lacking in Paul. The latter transmits only the verses on the bread and the cup (lines 22–50 of the synopsis on pp. 78–79—that is, Mt 26–28 = Mk 22–24 = Lk19–20). He does not know of the saying of Jesus about the wine that will be drunk "new" in the future kingdom (lines 15–21), even though an echo of it may be audible in his final words, "until he comes" (line 51). In addition, the "eschatological saying" is placed differently in the synoptics themselves, before or after the words of institution. This variation may signify that the saying does not belong to the basic substance of this tradition; may it not belong rather to the kind of tradition followed in the gospel of John?

My intention is not to succumb to the temptations either of forced harmonization or of skepticism, but to find a way that will help me to discern a certain unity of meaning amid the diversity of perspectives. How am I to proceed?

In the preceding chapter I used the synchronic method in an effort to bring to light the structure common to the various recensions and to get at the meaning of the passage more effectively. In taking that approach I was not concerned with the traditions used by the accounts as we have them. Once attention is focused on those traditions a different method proves more effective, that of tradition history.

The method I shall be applying in Part II will make it possible, first of all, to see that recollections of the last meal of Jesus found expression in two clearly distinct literary forms: the "testamentary form" and the "cultic form." Lest I confuse the reader, however, I shall give the term "tradition" a somewhat broader meaning and speak rather of "testamentary tradition" and "cultic tradition."[2] I think this first result of the method is of value not only in uncovering the genesis of our present texts but also in grasping the overall meaning of the account (Chapter IV).

I shall then apply the same method to the cultic tradition and be able to show that there are two different tendencies at work within it; these I shall call the Antiochene tradition and the Markan tradition (Chapter V).

Finally, with the results obtained from the synchronic and diachronic approaches, I shall be in a position to study the specifically eucharistic elements of the account: the words about remembrance (Chapter VI), the words over the bread (Chapter VII), and the words over the cup (Chapter VIII). I hope then to be ready to tackle the difficult question of the event itself: What exactly happened in the supper room on Holy Thursday evening? I shall then try to determine as far as possible how the traditions took form (Chapter IX). After that it will be possible to sketch out the various presentations of the account of eucharistic institution (Part III, Chapters X–XII).

I urge readers not to grow discouraged as they follow the literary analyses, since these give indispensable support to the subsequent study of the various elements in the account of the Supper. If anything must be scanted, it would be preferable that readers not exhaust themselves over Chapters IV and V on the tendencies within the cultic form proper.

IV
Cultic Tradition and
Testamentary Tradition

As I pointed out a moment ago, the New Testament adopts different perspectives in describing what happened on Jesus' last evening with his disciples. I shall try first to explain the two main directions taken: by the synoptics and Paul, on the one hand, and by the gospel of John, on the other. The first of these two traditions is in the genre of "liturgical account," the second in the genre of "farewell meal."

I. A LITURGICAL ACCOUNT

In all the recensions, the account of eucharistic institution has the appearance of being a bit of "biography," inasmuch as it reports one of the final episodes in the life of Jesus of Nazareth, just before that life comes to an end. But this narrative aspect does not provide a complete explanation for the composition of the text; a number of elements in it suggest that we see it as also influenced by the liturgy that was celebrated in the various ecclesial communities.

The liturgical factor

The account of the Supper as given by Paul shows clearly that a liturgical factor is at work. The apostle's purpose in writing to the Corinthians is to correct the abuses they commit in their eucharistic gatherings; he therefore appeals to the cultic practice that has been followed since the beginning of Christianity: "This is what I received from the Lord and have handed on to you" (1 Cor 11:23). Like the formula of faith in the resurrection of Christ, later on in this same letter, the account of institution is introduced by technical terms[1] that announce the citation of something in the tradition.[2] What Paul has passed on is probably the catechesis he himself had received at Antioch, where he was instructed in the faith as early as 35–40.

Most of the critics[3] agree that the actual worship of the Christian community had played a part in the formulation of 1 Cor 11:23b–25. Does this mean that the text can be properly called a "etiological cultic"[4] story? The purpose of such stories is to lend authority to a rite in habitual use by providing it with a foundation. In these stories the rite in its essentials is usually traced back to a mythical period of origins. This is not what we find in Paul: his account connects the Church's celebration with an historical individual, Jesus, and even with a precise date, the night of his betrayal.[5] The passage in Paul is therefore not a cultic text of a "legendary" kind. But with this reservation it is legitimate to assign the Pauline account to the literary genre known as the etiology.[6]

The same holds for the text of institution in the gospels. It is undoubtedly part of the introduction to the passion[7] and, to this extent, of a biographical narrative. Mark, however, betrays its interpolative character when in v. 22 he repeats the formula "and as they were eating" which he had already used in v. 18 in an evidently historical context.[8] He betrays the interpolative character of the text again at the end of the account where v. 25 clashes with v. 24: What is the point of the simple phrase "fruit of the vine" after the solemn words about "blood of the covenant"? Finally, the "Hallel" that is sung in v. 26 harks back to the Passover meal for which preparations had been made earlier, in 14:16–18, although no reference is made to this meal in the account of the Supper itself.

To these remarks about the awkward way in which the eucharistic text is introduced into Mark's gospel I may add some observations of a different kind. The hieratic style of the account shows that it is not intended primarily as a description of events. Thus nothing is said of the reaction of the disciples; the only words reporting their behavior are "and they all drank of it" (only in Mark, line 40), and then, oddly enough, they drink while still not knowing that in giving them the cup Jesus is giving them his "blood of the covenant." The symmetry of the invitations "take and eat," "take and drink" clearly suggests a liturgical practice. Moreover, Luke and Paul both speak of *the* cup, as though it were well known, whereas "bread" does not have an article with it. The tendency to liturgical stylization becomes even clearer if the various recensions of the words of Jesus are compared: the ill-assorted pair "body/covenant" (Lk/Paul) has been systematized into "body/blood" (Mk/Mt). The command, "Do this in memory of me," seems intended to make explicit in Luke and Paul what was already doubtless regarded as self-evident in the tradition of Mark and Matthew.[9]

The conclusion is inescapable: the purpose of the account is not directly to relate an episode in the life of Jesus but rather to proclaim a foundational action. In their worship, the Christians of every age hark back to the Supper and the action of Jesus, the theological significance of which they attempt to bring out. Does this mean that the account arose out of the eucharistic practice of the Church and has no strict historical value? Such a conclusion would go too far, as I shall now show.

The historical factor

In this text that is so evidently liturgical, elements are detectable which can hardly be attributed to the influence of public worship but can legitimately be regarded as echoes of an historical event.[10]

Despite the tendency of the liturgy to have the actions over the bread and the cup follow immediately upon one another, two of the recensions mention that a meal separated them. And, contrary to the current practice of having individual cups for the guests, Jesus, according to all four texts, passes a single cup; such a departure could not have been specified without an historical basis.[11] Furthermore, although the term "breaking of bread" very soon became a technical term for the entire eucharistic rite, the account gives equal and even greater weight to the words (though not to the gestures) over the cup.[12] All the recensions confirm this historical basis by using semitisms that point to a Palestinian origin of the account. Thus the words "blessing" and "break bread" sound strange to Greek ears.[13] Moreover, the words used by Jesus do not conform to any used at every Jewish Passover meal; they are meant to explain not the ancestral rites repeated at Passover but the present gestures of Jesus who interprets his own behavior after the manner of the prophets;[14] the resemblance to the prophets is all the clearer inasmuch as he interprets it as concerned with the future and not with remembrance of the past.

These various points certainly do not justify taking the account of institution as a detailed description of the event; they do, however, provide a solid basis for the account.

The first of the two main traditions regarding the last meal of Jesus is thus to be seen as liturgical account with an historical basis. It can therefore be described as "cultic." Its theological significance is very great.

II. A FAREWELL MEAL

The last meal of Jesus is also reported in the framework of another tradition of which the gospel of John is the best representative. It is highly probable, of course, that the Eucharist was celebrated in Johannine circles (see Jn 6). There can be no escaping the fact, however, that in place of the actions and words of institution John has the washing of feet and a long farewell discourse of Jesus. Later on I shall examine the Johannine perspective in its entirety; for the moment it is enough to call attention to the obvious existence of this testamentary form in the New Testament. Is the form to be found exclusively in the fourth gospel? A few verses in the synoptic accounts seem not to come from the cultic tradition; critics have therefore suggested various hypotheses to explain them. For the time being, let me speak of them simply as coming from a different, "non-cultic" tradition.

The synoptic echo of a non-cultic tradition

The synoptic account of institution is accompanied by a saying of Jesus that must inevitably surprise a careful reader. Here is the text:

Mt 26:29	Mk 14:25	Lk 22:18
I tell you, henceforth I shall not drink again	Truly, I tell you, never more shall I drink	For I tell you that I shall not drink henceforth
of this fruit of the vine until the day when I shall drink it with you new	of the fruit of the vine until that day when I shall drink it new	of the fruit of the vine until
in the kingdom of my Father.	in the kingdom of God.	the reign of God comes.

In Matthew and Mark this saying follows directly upon the supreme revelation about the "blood of the covenant which [is] shed for the multitude." Is it not surprising that immediately after these words the reader should hear the text speaking of the wine as simply "the fruit of the vine," a name that describes the wine of every festive meal and has none of the special character of the "shed blood" of Christ? The two juxtaposed verses (Mk 24 and 25; Mt 28 and 29) belong to two different linguistic registers, one liturgical, the other prophetic. This difference of origin is confirmed by the way in which the saying shifts its place in the gospel tradition: Luke puts it before and not after the cultic account. In Luke it is quite at home in v. 18 where it follows smoothly upon the preceding text (which is peculiar to Luke), especially since v. 17, on the cup and the sharing of it, prepares nicely for it.

The sequence of verses in Luke helps explain how Mark could have come up with his odd text in which the cultic words of Jesus over the cup (Mk 24b) come only after the disciples have already drunk from it. If we excise the words of institution over the cup we see that the sequence Mk 23, 24a, 25 fits neatly beside Lk 17–18:[15]

23 And, having taken a cup,
      having given thanks,
      he gave [it] to them;
      and they all drank of it.
	17 And, having accepted a cup,
	      having given thanks, he said:
	      "Take this
	      and share it among you.

24a And he said to them: [24b]	

25 "Truly, I tell you,
      never more shall I drink
      of the fruit of the vine
      until that day when I shall drink it
      new
      in the kingdom of God."
	18 For I tell you that
	      I shall not drink henceforth
	      of the fruit of the vine
	      until
	
	      the reign of God comes."

Everything suggests that in Mark the words about the blood of the covenant were introduced later on into an account in which v. 25 commented in its own way on the distribution of the cup and the action of drinking from it (v. 23)

I note further that the verb "give thanks" *(eucharistein)* in v. 23 may suggest a Hellenistic setting, as does v. 17 in Luke; on the other hand, in speaking of the action with the bread (v. 22) Mark uses the verb "bless" *(eulogein)*, which is typical of a Palestinian setting. My hypothesis, then, is that Luke has preserved a special tradition which Mark has broken up; by joining the words over the cup (24b) to the words over the bread Mark has further shifted the emphasis to the institution of the Eucharist.

In any event, the eschatological saying in Mk 25 = Mt 29 and in Lk 18 remains very important; it helps us enter into the very thinking of Jesus, since it is a gospel saying which the critics almost unanimously regard as having come from Jesus of Nazareth without being altered by the early Church.[16] Understandably, then, since exegetes like to have their feet solidly on the rock of history, they tend to take this "authentic" saying as the starting point and generative nucleus of the tradition about the last meal of Jesus.[17] Their mistake is to go on thinking of it as properly cultic, no matter what explanation they give of its origin. But there is nothing to justify this assumption, and I shall place the words provisionally among the non-cultic sayings of the tradition.

The tradition in Luke 22:15–18

In the gospel of Luke the eschatological saying, far from being simply juxtaposed to the cultic account, as it is in Mark, is introduced by vv. 15–17 which mention another cup, not identical with the one in v. 20. Here is the eschatological saying in its Lukan context:

> [14]And when the hour came he reclined at table and the apostles with him. [15]And he said to them: "I have greatly desired to eat this Passover with you before I suffer. [16]For I tell you that I shall never eat it again until it is fulfilled in the kingdom of God." [17]And, having accepted a cup, having given thanks, he said: "Take this and share it among you. [18]For I tell you that I shall not drink henceforth of the fruit of the vine until the reign of God comes."

Widely varying explanations have been given of this passage that comes before the account of institution. Consequently, before offering my own hypothesis, it will be appropriate to mention a few of them.

In the most recent technical analysis of the Last Supper texts H. Patsch thinks it possible to maintain the unity of vv. 15–20 by reading it as a *history-based catechesis* in which the last meal of Jesus is seen as following the Jewish Passover ritual.[18] According to Patsch, the cup mentioned in v. 17 corresponds to the *Qiddush* cup,[19] which is the first of the Passover meal. The words over the bread then follow quite naturally (v. 19), and the words over the cup of the covenant refer to the third cup of the Passover rite (v. 20). The words in Lk 15–18, which is original and certainly from Jesus himself, are those in which he states both his desire to celebrate the Passover with his disciples (v. 15) and his intention to abstain from eating it and from drinking of the cup until the coming of God's reign (v. 18). The absence of the principal foods found in the Passover meal is to be explained in the light of early Christian celebrations. Thus, if the Passover lamb is not mentioned, this is because it had no theological significance that could be compared with that of the words of Jesus and, above all, because the custom of eating a lamb had necessarily been dropped when the celebration became a daily or weekly one, especially in the case of communities distant from the temple. On the other hand, the first cup had to be mentioned because Jesus in his role as father of the "family" would have had to drink this, thereby making his subsequent abstinence all the more meaningful.

Such a reconstruction, which unifies the entire sequence of verses in Lk 22:15–20, is not impossible, but it suffers from a congenital weakness: it is not possible to prove that at his final meal Jesus followed the Passover ritual.[20] Instead, then, of making the entire explanation rest on a weak hypothesis, it seems preferable to acknowledge that vv. 19–20 must in fact have existed in separation from vv. 15–18 and that Luke has combined two independent units. In addition, this is the view of most critics.

Whence, then, comes the first of these two units, Lk 22:15–18? Two hypotheses have been proposed which again invoke a Passover ritual, Jewish in the one case, Christian in the other.

H. Schürmann reads these verses as a reflection of a primitive account, historical in kind, which located the institution of the Eucharist in the course of a Jewish Passover meal. Luke took vv. 19–20 from another, etiological tradition with the intention of making the content of the earlier presentation more explicit.[21]

This hypothesis, however, runs up against two major difficulties. As the author himself readily acknowledges, it results in a quite complicated reconstruction of 15–18 + 19–20 as a unit.[22] In the original historical account (15–18) the cup which Luke mentions in v. 17 was the cup of institution; it would therefore have corresponded to the third cup of the Passover meal; but in the reconstructed unit, vv. 15–20, the cup in v. 17 can no longer be the cup of institution, since this is now expressly named in v. 20, and must therefore represent the first cup of a Passover meal. This kind of complication is hardly an argument in favor of the hypothesis. The second difficulty: if the account from which vv. 15–18 were taken intended to describe a Jewish Passover meal, how could it reduce the ceremonial to a single cup? If the rites involving the lamb and the bitter herbs were omitted in that account, why not the cup as well? Or did the cup have a special theological significance which cannot now be recaptured?[23]

In short, according to Schürmann Luke tried to make a single account out of two traditions about the Supper, one historical, the other cultic and etiological, but both relating to one and the same Passover meal of Jesus. I agree that the text of Luke shows the existence of two traditions with different origins; but I challenge the claim that both traditions refer to a "meal which follows the Passover ritual."

J. Jeremias, for his part, thinks that an early Christian liturgical custom provided the model for Luke's text.[24] For the early Christian custom he relies on the work of B. Lohse, who thought it possible, on the basis of *Epistola apostolorum* 15, to reconstruct a Passover feast celebrated by the "Quartodecimans" on the evening of 14 Nisan, that is, on the same date as the Jewish feast.[25] According to Lohse, this Christian feast (which would date from the seventies of the first century) was a kind of "anti-Passover"; that is, in protest against the joy that marked the Jewish feast with its commemoration of deliverance from Egypt, Christians obliged themselves to fast during it for the conversion of their fellow Jews who did not believe in Christ. Only at three in the morning, when the Jewish feast would have been over, did Christians celebrate their own cult in the form of an agape (using unleavened bread) that was combined with the Eucharist. In Lk 22:15–18 Luke (or his source) would have given the basis for this Christian practice of fasting: Did not Jesus himself, at his final Passover, renounce further eating and drinking until the reign of God should have come?

It would be difficult to deny a connection between the Quartodeciman custom of a Passover fast for the conversion of the Jews and Jesus' announcement of his intended abstinence (if indeed that was the meaning of the text). But this leaves a number of problems still unresolved. Where in Luke's account is there anything about the Quartodeciman reading of Exodus 12? What role did the cup play? Above all, where does the New Testament make any mention of a liturgy using unleavened bread?[26] Here again, an historical and literary reconstruction is being erected on the head of a pin; it is not possible to assert a dependence of the Lukan text on the reconstructed Quartodeciman liturgy.

In view of the difficulties raised by these various hypotheses we may ask whether it is absolutely necessary to make the two traditions on the final meal of Jesus in Lk 15–20 dependent on a Jewish or an already Christianized Passover ritual.

Many years ago now, H. Lietzmann[27] hypothesized that in the beginning Christians followed a Palestinian custom and celebrated a meal in joyous expectation of the proximate return of the Son of man, a meal, therefore, in which the perspective was eschatological. Gradually, as a result of contact with Hellenism, a different tradition arose that put the emphasis on remembrance of the sacrificial death of Jesus. The earlier tradition led to the celebration of a non-eucharistic agape, the second to the celebration of the eucharistic cult. This hypothesis (two types of meal in the early Church) could not, however, explain the data in the texts.[28]

K. G. Kuhn gave Lietzmann's hypothesis a new twist and came up with an explanation that merits careful consideration.[29] In his view Luke 22:15–18 describes a Christian meal eaten in joy, while vv. 19–20 contain a prophecy of the death of Jesus. The first of the two traditions is distinguished by its central theme "the service performed by Jesus" (Lk 22:27–30; see Jn 13) and by an eschatological point of view (Lk 22:15–18; Jn 14–16; Acts 2:46); the second reports the words of eucharistic institution, which interpret the death of Jesus in the framework of a theology of covenant and of what Kuhn calls "vicarious expiation" (22:19–20).

This is the general direction which I myself shall take. I shall not, however, rely in any way on the quite shaky hypothesis that Luke's account refers to a Passover meal, Jewish or Christian. I too think that two traditions regarding the final meal of Jesus developed at a very early date. Unlike K. G. Kuhn, however, I shall argue not from the content (eschatological or not, sacrificial or not) of the text but from the literary form in which the two traditions (one cultic, to be studied in the next chapter, and the other non-cultic) are expressed. As for the non-cultic tradition, the literary form of the "testament" seems to me to do most justice to the data of the text. Let me discuss it now.

The "testament" as a literary form

Inasmuch as the explanations offered for Luke 22:15–20 lead to impasses or rest on weak foundations, I have long wondered[30] whether it would not be appropriate to assign the passage to the literary genre of the "testament." Most of the critics acknowledge the existence of such a genre, but its study and interpretation are still in an early stage.[31]

The *texts* which make it possible to analyze the "farewell discourse" as a literary form are fairly numerous; they occur in the Old Testament,[32] in Jewish apocryphal literature,[33] and in the New Testament.[34] The passages have one thing in common: shortly before his death a man offers advice to his relatives. Almost all of the passages use such formulas as: call together *(kaleō)*, rejoin one's ancestors, ordain by way of last will and testament *(entellomai)*, and "my children." Certain themes recur frequently: gathering, prophetic vision, testament, false leaders, imitation, intercession, and finally death.

The circles in which this form arose could hardly have been the clan or the community. We should look rather to sapiential literature which bears the mark both of apocalyptic and of a measure of concern for history. In it we find the revelation of secrets, consolation, hope, and pseudonymity, but also the haggadic genre, that is, the reinterpretation and actualization of biblical texts.

The *literary form* of the farewell discourse can be determined on the basis of all the passages in the dossier (some forty texts), by listing the principal themes or motifs and by tentatively suggesting a structural model.

The only motifs I shall retain are those that appear at least four times in the various testaments that have been studied. Relying on the detailed analysis of H. J. Michel,[35] I shall list them in order of decreasing frequency.

In almost all of the texts a man recognizes that his death is near (no. 1). He addresses a well-defined audience: his sons, his relatives, the leaders of the people, or even the entire people (no. 2). In an exhortatory discourse he gives an historical survey of the way in which God has acted toward them and in which human beings have behaved for good or for ill. The hearers are thereby encouraged to live uprightly, like their patriarch (no. 3). Finally, there is an account of the death and burial of the one who pronounced the farewell discourse (no. 4).

Into this common framework various other motifs may be introduced. An *apologia pro vita sua* by the patriarch whose life has been exemplary or whose failings have been instructive (no. 5) sometimes crowns the retrospect in no. 3, or else leads into a prophetic vision of the future, whether proximate or truly apocalyptic (no. 6). The setting for the discourse may be a meal with a blessing

(no. 7) and with kisses, embraces, and tears (no. 8). Advice is sometimes given regarding burial (no. 9).

Here, finally, are three less frequent motifs: appointment of a
successor (no. 10), invitation to prayer (no. 11), last counsels (no.
12).

With this list of themes in mind I shall attempt to elucidate
the structure of the farewell discourse. Certain characteristics are
especially interesting from the viewpoint of this book.

(a) A man about to die takes leave of his own by gathering
them around him for a "farewell"; it is he himself who calls them
together to hear his last words (nos. 1 and 2). The gathering sometimes takes place at a meal (no. 7), a motif which occurs seven
times.[36] On three occasions the meal has a cultic context,[37] and
twice it leads up to a blessing,[38] so that the communication of
divine favor turns the meal into a sign of divinely guaranteed communion between testator and heirs. In at least three instances the
meal is one of reconciliation between estranged brothers, in the
presence of their father or mother: the reconciliation of Esau with
Jacob,[39] of Joseph with his brothers,[40] and perhaps of Isaac with
Ishmael.[41]

From the viewpoint of the testator the meal, when it occurs,
does not simply serve as a framework for his farewells; it is this
farewell in action; sometimes it has a cultic context. From the
viewpoint of the heirs, the meal is a sign of communication with
the testator (who communicates God's favor) and among the heirs
themselves (because of their communion with the testator).

(b) The dying man addresses a lengthy exhortation to his children, predicting rewards or punishments, advising them to do
works of mercy and charity, and, above all, urging them to live in
fraternal amity. To lend weight to his exhortation, the speaker
recalls the great and wonderful acts of God as well as the past
behavior of human beings (no. 3). Sometimes the dying man even
offers his own life as a model (no. 5). Finally, he ventures to predict
the future of the community and even the end of time (no. 6).

I cannot pass in review here all the testaments mentioned in
the Bible and in the apocrypha. For the sake, however, of a better
understanding of the non-cultic verses in the eucharistic account
it will be helpful to look at what the New Testament offers by way
of such testaments.

The relevant New Testament passages are related not to those
of the Old Testament, where the patriarch's exhortation takes the

divine blessing as its point of departure, but to the *Testaments of the Twelve Patriarchs*. Like the latter, the New Testament texts take human uprightness as their point of departure. The outline does not vary: uprightness brings blessing while wickedness brings a curse; the emphasis may be on the past,[42] the present, [43] or the future.[44]

Here are some examples from the New Testament. Paul's farewell address at Miletus (Acts 20:17–38) is in the testamentary form. He calls the elders together and predicts his death (nos. 1 and 2); he enlarges on his exemplary life (no. 5) and says he is without fault in regard to his hearers. In his exhortation he prophesies the coming of false teachers and divisions (no. 6) and expresses his concern about apostolic succession (no. 10). He prays for a blessing on them (no. 7); the actual farewell finds expression in tears and embraces (no. 8).[45]

The second letter to Timothy clearly looks forward to Paul's proximate death (no. 1); the teacher and model (no. 5)[46] offers several exhortations that are intended to put his readers on guard against false teachers (no. 6).[47]

The genre is perfectly clear in John 13–17. This farewell discourse even has the typical expression "my little children" as well as such recurrent themes as prophetic foresight, intercession, imitation, and so on. I shall return to all this in the chapter on the fourth gospel.[48]

What, then, is the significance and importance of the testamentary form? It makes it possible to bring out what is happening in a change as important as death, a change of generations. One period is ending, another beginning. If I believe that eternity is present in time, does this not mean that the eternity which dwells in me wants to continue creating time? The making of a last will and testament reflects our instinct for survival: at the moment when human beings are on the point of ceasing to live, they hope to triumph over the cessation of time by making a testament. The point of a will and testament is not simply to bequeath the things we possess but to pass on the moral and spiritual wealth that we have acquired in our lifetime, that is, to pass on our very being and, in a way, to outlive our own death. The making of a testament manifests the omnipotence of the eternal God. For this reason, whether there is question of Abraham or Jacob, or Paul, or even Jesus, the problem arises of the mode of survival, which here takes the form of "successors." Human beings cannot by their own power conquer time; therefore they must hand things on to others. In this way they seemingly fulfill for themselves the proverb "I shall not wholly die." This pagan desire is now transfigured by divine intervention.

The testamentary tradition regarding the final meal of Jesus

After this short explanation of the testamentary form it is easy enough to show the significance of the verses that seemed out of place in the liturgical account of the final meal of Jesus. It is vain to imagine with Lietzmann that there were two successive customs in the early Church: one, the "breaking of bread," which was supposedly celebrated in a spirit of eschatological joy; the other which, under Paul's influence, emphasized the sacrificial death of Jesus. Nor is it enough to modify Lietzmann's thesis and say, with K. G. Kuhn, that one tradition emphasized eschatology and fraternal service, while another stressed the theme of the redemptive death. The need is rather to specify in a more exact way the two ways of reporting the final meal of Jesus: one is properly cultic and the other is existential; one is liturgical, the other testamentary.

The only tradition which John passes on is the tradition of the farewell discourse. Luke, on the other hand (as I shall show in Chapter XI), incorporates the cultic tradition within the testamentary tradition by making the account of institution part of a kind of farewell discourse that runs from v. 7 to v. 38. Mark and Matthew are content simply to add an echo of a farewell discourse at the end of the liturgical text.

CONCLUSION

Since two traditions are intertwined in the gospel account that has come down to us, is it possible to specify the function of each? In particular, what is the function of the "farewell discourse" that is still present in the text of the Supper, though this is eminently liturgical in character?

By locating the cultic account in the framework of the passion the evangelists show how Jesus, foreseeing his departure from this world, meant to maintain a personal link with those he would be leaving behind. How was he to remain present in his absence? The Eucharist was a first response, but it was not the only one.

Another, non-cultic, tradition gives another answer to the question. This man who is about to die leaves a testament for his disciples during the time that must pass before he can be reunited to them. In its own way this tradition tells the disciples how they can continue in union with him who is now risen from the dead and forever alive: namely, by an existential attitude of service and love that reflects the way Jesus himself had lived in this world.

Both traditions are in fact indispensable. A first examination shows that they correspond to the two dimensions of the Eucharist which later theologians distinguished as *sacramentum* and *res sacramenti*, that is, the rite and the life which the rite signifies. The "sacrament" has value only because of the "thing," that is, that which it signifies, namely, Jesus Christ and the love in the Church. As we might put it today, authentic cult or worship is inseparable from life.

Deeper insight, however, bids us not to interpret the two traditions as referring to two realities of which one is simply the effect of the other. Cult and fraternal service are not on the same level nor of the same order. What is the relation betweeen them? People usually think of service as the result of cult: the Eucharist produces "love" as its effect. In a sense this is quite true, but does it follow that service can exist only because of cult? Evidently not, and this is why I think it preferable to see the two as signifier and signified rather than as cause and effect.[49]

The presence of the testamentary tradition in the eucharistic texts and especially the fact that John can simply pass over the cultic tradition help make it clear that existential love is the only "reality" by which the church truly draws its life from Christ, but they also make it clear that the Eucharist is the source of this life. It follows that the cultic way, while continuing to be at the center of Christian life, *is not the only* way by which Christ continues his presence in the midst of his disciples; love and service are likewise a privileged way. Cult is not dismissed; it is simply given its proper place in relation to the life of love that characterizes Christians.

V

The Two Tendencies in
the Cultic Tradition

The cultic tradition behind the four recensions of the account of the Supper finds expression in the verses that tell of the institution of the Eucharist, excluding the "eschatological" saying, as I showed in the foregoing chapter. The synoptic presentation of the texts (on pp. 78–79) will help us see how they are alike and how they differ.

A comparison of the recensions shows that they come from two clearly different formative milieus; the same cultic tradition takes two forms showing two different tendencies.

I. THE TWO TENDENCIES

Paul and Luke alone mention the command of remembrance (line 33); they alone separate the actions with the bread and the cup by the words "after the supper" (line 37). In their presentations of the tradition the statements of Jesus are asymmetrical: for "body/blood" they have "body/covenant." Finally, their vocabulary has fewer semitisms and seems to reflect a Hellenistic environment. Because of Paul's connections with Antioch I shall henceforth refer to this tendency as the *Antiochene tradition.*

Mark and Matthew have in common a strict parallelism between the words "This is my body" and "This is my blood." Semitisms abound: in addition to the word "blessing" (*eulogēsas:* lines 25–26), which I mentioned earlier, there is the expression "for the multitude" (*hyper [peri] pollōn*, lit. "for [the] many"), which would have been unintelligible to a Greek. The tendency which both of these recensions share is clearer in Mark and can

96

therefore be called the *Markan tradition*; it originated in Jerusalem or Caesarea. Matthew, as I said, shares this tradition, but with some slight variations.[1]

The *two traditions*[2] thus briefly described report one and the same episode. Without claiming to have gotten back to a single source, two eminent specialists on the subject have tried to determine which of these two forms of the tradition is the oldest. Jeremias concludes in favor of the Markan version,[3] Schürmann in favor of the Antiochene.[4] Such contradictory results might incline a reader to be skeptical, if not about the possibility of a successful outcome, at least about the value of the methods used; but in fact the contradiction simply warns against hasty generalizations. Let me look briefly at the factors taken into account in both arguments: vocabulary, style, theological motifs.

Whenever the *vocabulary* of a text is clearly semitic, the text comes from a Palestinian or Syriac setting and is likely to be quite old. But even if it be supposed that the words in question are all authentic semitisms,[5] it does not follow that the tradition containing them is older; the reason is that a fully Greek word may in fact be a successful translation of a semitism belonging to a very ancient tradition. Even if a Greek word or turn of phrase (in Paul, for example) cannot be "back-translated" into Aramaic, this is no proof that it does not correspond in any way to an underlying Aramaic word or formula.

Nor is *style* a decisive criterion. Take, for example, the words over the cup in Luke and in Paul: in Luke, unlike Paul, they are continued by a participle that is in the nominative case: "which is shed for you" *(to hyper hymōn ekchynnomenon)* but is in apposition to a dative ("in my blood": *en tō haimati mou*), thus yielding a quite un-Greek construction. But from the principle that Luke, being a good writer, cannot be the author of such an addition, two conclusions are possible: (a) he is passing on a pre-Lukan tradition; or (b) he has taken these words from the Markan tradition ("which is shed for many": *to ekchynnomenon hyper pollōn*), while substituting *hymeis* (you) for *pollōn* and thus identifying the multitude of Mark with the Christian community.

Finally, the theological *motifs* (or themes) operative in the redaction of the account must be carefully checked. This is essential for the motifs of "expiation" (by one for all) and "covenant." According to some critics,[6] these motifs could not have been used in combination during one and the same period in the formation of the text. A decision on this point depends on the historical evidence at our disposal regarding their presence or non-presence in the contemporary Jewish world.

The preceding observations are intended to moderate the rashness with which critics sometimes try to show the priority of the one or the other tradition and to establish that the one is the source of the other. As a matter of fact, most of the critics recognize that old and new are combined in each tradition and even in each text. Consequently, even when scholars favor one tradition over the other, they are not thereby justified in dismissing the other, for it can help to bring out nuances in the preferred tradition.

In my own opinion, there is one strong argument for some priority of the Antiochene tradition: its much less hieratic character. The reference to the meal (line 37) separating the two sayings of Jesus could hardly have been introduced into a text as unified as Mark's. Conversely, the polishing effect of continued liturgical use would explain quite nicely the strict parallelism evident in the Markan tradition.

For this reason, even though I am not saying that the Antiochene tradition is closer than the Markan to the origin of the text, I think that a careful analysis of the recensions should begin with the Antiochene tradition. It is in that order that I shall examine them in an attempt to get back to the text behind each of the two traditions.

II. IN SEARCH OF THE TEXTS BEHIND THE TWO TRADITIONS

The *Antiochene tradition* finds expression in Luke and Paul. A first variant between their two recensions appears in the words over the bread (line 32): "This is my body which [is] for you" (Paul); "This is my body which [is] *given* for you" (Luke). H. Schürmann thinks Luke's formulation is to be preferred because it contains the participle *didomenon* and a back-translation into Aramaic would require the equivalent. He then tries to show how and why Paul came to drop this verb. P. Neuenzeit, who takes the contrary view, criticizes this explanation as over-subtle.[7] Which view is to be accepted? Since it is easier to add to a traditional text than to remove something from it, I opt for Paul's more restrained version; in adding the verb Luke was doubtless trying to render explicit and also bring out more strongly the aspect of gift that was implied in the words of Jesus.

The second important variant is in the words over the cup

(lines 47–48): "This cup is the new covenant in my blood" (Paul); "This cup [is] the new covenant in my blood which [is] shed for you" (Luke). Here the same two critics agree that Paul represents the original text. Since the resultant Greek is so poor, the addition in Luke, making his text parallel to Mark's, is doubtless not his work. It is enough to choose one of the two possibilities which I indicated above when discussing *style* as a criterion of priority, and to assign the addition to an earlier stage in the transmission.[8]

There is a third point. It will be observed that both Paul and Luke use the verb *eucharistēsas* (line 25) in the words over the bread. Given that it is appropriate to get back whenever possible to a Palestinian setting, it may be thought that the two redactors used this Greek verb to translate the Aramaic verb which presumably lies behind Mark's *eulogēsas*, "pronouncing the blessing" (lines 25–26).[9] In regard to the expression "for you," which Paul and Luke have in the words over the bread and Luke also in the words over the cup, instead of "for the multitude" which Mark has in the words over the cup, the critics usually maintain that Mark's formula could easily have been replaced in the liturgy by a personalized expression.[10] But despite the agreement of the majority of critics I am not sure that *hyper pollōn* is older than *hyper hymōn*, since the developing tradition could more easily have passed from the "you" of an intensely experienced liturgy to the "many" of a liturgy intent on greater universality.[11]

Allowance being made for the limitations of this initial inquiry, here is a text that might reflect the Antiochene tradition known to Paul and Luke:

> And having taken bread, having pronounced the blessing, he broke [it] and gave [it] to them and he said: THIS IS MY BODY WHICH [IS] FOR YOU. DO THIS IN MEMORY OF ME. Likewise, after the meal, the cup, saying: THIS CUP [IS] THE NEW COVENANT IN MY BLOOD.

The *Markan tradition*, which is found in Mark and Matthew, must be set beside the Antiochene tradition. The parallelism of "This is my body," "This is my blood," which so clearly distinguishes the Markan tradition, seems to be late, for if it had existed from the beginning, it could have been changed only with difficulty. On the other hand, the reader is surprised to find Paul himself using a formulation in which body and blood are already strictly paralleled: "The cup of blessing over which we pronounce the blessing, is it not a communion in the blood of Christ? The bread which we break, is it not a communion in the body of Christ?" (1 Cor 10:16). Since this symmetrical formulation occurs in the same letter in which, shortly after, the Antiochene tradition is cited, it must necessarily belong to a concomitant and therefore contemporary tradition.[12]

In addition, Markan "stylization" is not carried through as consistently as scholars claim. A perfect parallelism would require that the two sayings be constructed on the same pattern and therefore that the words over the bread have a complement comparable to that in the words over the cup. H. Schürmann even goes so far as to say that "considered in isolation, the words over the bread, lacking as they do any explanatory complement, are an insoluble riddle."[13] This is especially the case since the words over the bread are followed by those over the cup with no mention of an intervening meal.

As for the supposed impossibility of back-translating the formula into Aramaic, Jeremias has shown that the objection is unfounded. In the words over the cup the two successive genitives in apposition to the word "blood" ("of me" [for "my"] and "of the covenant") seem to pose a problem, but specialists have shown that semitic languages require a different distribution of words than Greek does.[14]

Let me now venture to offer a formulation of the text known to Mark and Matthew:

> And as they were eating, having taken bread, having pronounced the blessing, he broke [it] and gave [it] to them and he said: THIS IS MY BODY. And, taking the cup, having given thanks, he gave [it] to them and he said to them: THIS IS MY BLOOD OF THE COVENANT WHICH IS SHED FOR THE MULTITUDE.

On page 101, in synoptic form are the reconstructed two branches of the cultic tradition; words common to both are in italics.

Some critics have risked succumbing to reductionism as they try to get behind these two traditions to a single primitive form. In order to achieve their goal they have had to take into account the theological motifs operative in the redaction of the texts; such a procedure involves a method other than the simple literary criticism I have been applying up to this point.[15] When I state my own

	Antiochene	Markan
1	↓ 7	As they were eating,
2	*having taken bread, having pronounced the blessing,*	
3	*he broke [it] and gave [it] to them and he said:*	
4	THIS IS MY BODY	*THIS IS MY BODY*
5	WHICH [is] FOR you	↓ 13
6	Do this in memory of me.	
7	Likewise, after the meal,	↑ 1
8	the cup	And taking the cup,
9		having given thanks,
10	*saying:*	he gave [it] to them, *saying:*
11	THIS CUP [IS]	THIS IS
12	THE NEW *COVENANT* IN *MY BLOOD*	*MY BLOOD* OF *THE COVENANT*
		WHICH IS SHED *FOR* THE
13	↑ 5	MULTITUDE

view that the Antiochene tradition is the older of the two, I do so only to explain why I turn to it first in each comparative analysis.

This first probe of the cultic tradition has shown that the four recensions go back to two differently oriented types. There was, of course, an interaction of these two traditions in the development of the texts as we now have them. It is nonetheless possible to describe the different orientations of the circles in which the two traditions arose. The Antiochene tradition seems to emphasize more the "personal gift" given by Jesus and to mirror a theology of covenant that is not cultic in character, as I shall explain in the proper place. The Markan tradition proves to be more directly liturgical; but, while regarding the gift of Jesus as the fulfillment of Jewish sacrificial rites, it too emphasizes the personal nature of this gift. All these points will emerge clearly from a study of the Old Testament motifs at work in the recensions of the two statements of Jesus.

VI
The Words on Remembrance

"Do this in memory of me," says Jesus after the words over the bread, at least in the tradition known to Luke and Paul. To the relationships already uniting the personages of the account this command adds a new one, no longer between speaker and addressees but between this man, now present but soon to become absent, and those who will survive him. The new relationship unites future believers with the living Christ, and the Church with the period of the Supper.

In my synchronic reading of the account of the Supper I was satisfied to point out the structural function of this relationship;[1] it is time now to examine its content. This requires that I enter into the biblical world of memory (I) and time, in order then to discover the function of remembrance in Jewish worship (II) and thereby to understand better the formula which Jesus used (III).[2]

I. MEMORY AND ENCOUNTER WITH GOD

For the Bible, unlike ourselves, "to remember this or that person" is not simply to call the person to mind by a purely interior act. It is also to act in a certain way: memory and action are intrinsically connected.[3] For example, when God "remembers" Noah, Abraham, and Rachel, he immediately confers a blessing upon them.[4] This link between memory and action is characteristic of the root *zkr* (and its derivatives, e.g., *zikkarôn*), the Hebrew verb for "remembering," which is always an action with an effect.

Remembering the God of the covenant

When memory plays a part in the relations of human beings with the biblical God it has surprisingly extensive implications.

Above all, it presupposes that there already exists between these two unequal partners a solid bond in which God has taken the initiative by his past promises and interventions and to the permanence of which he has pledged himself. But while God is forever faithful to his covenant, the people or individuals in it prove unfaithful with the passage of time. Their "forgetfulness" amounts to a real separation.

Consequently, the Bible echoes with calls to "remember," addressed by human beings to God or by God himself to human beings. Israel pleads with Yahweh to intervene in its favor: it feels the need to renew ties with a God whom it experiences as absent, since it has suffered a misfortune it deems undeserved, or because of its sins.[5] These calls for God's remembrance of his people indicate not only that separation from him is insupportable, but also that God can do away with it. Through reciprocal remembrance the original relationship will be, and in fact already is, restored: Israel (or the praying individual) is confident that God will remember and, in the name of his covenant, exert once again his life-giving power.

Still more numerous are appeals from God that Israel remember its divine election, "enter into its heart," and mend its ways. The prophets in particular urge the people never to forget God's saving interventions, which he is always ready to repeat in order to win their renewed fidelity.[6] Deuteronomy gives this type of exhortation a universal extension, since it is the lack of such remembrance that has caused the disasters which afflict the people, and it is by "remembering" that they will escape death.[7]

The first act of "remembering" on the part of human beings in the Bible is to become conscious again of the covenant—that objective reality that is always alive in the depths of the people's hearts despite their constant forgetfulness of it. Philosophers tell us, with good reason, that the past creates the very being of persons and directs them toward their future: a human being is, first and foremost, a history. Biblical revelation teaches us that this history is a history of love, a history of the covenant between God and his people.

The next step in remembering is for Israel to realize that some past intervention of God at a particular time and in a particular place (e.g., at Mamre or on Horeb) is still meaningful for it today, even though that event does not cease to be past. A particular historical event is called to mind, and its special meaning for the people becomes relevant once again. This being so, it would be a mistake to interpret these texts as simply legendary illustrations of God's goodness to Israel.[8]

But it is characteristic of contact between human beings and God that there can be no question of a static encounter, a simple gazing upon him in wondering or grateful contemplation. As soon as the people stand before God they find themselves in the presence of a plan in which God takes the initiative. The covenant does not link two equal partners; when human beings encounter God they find that a bond with him already exists; they can therefore count on forgiveness and reconciliation; and, finally, they are projected into a future which God himself opens up to them and which they have the responsibility of realizing in the flow of time and in their individual "histories," transient creatures though they are.

Remembering God the Creator

As a result of their reflection, the Jewish people realized that the various covenants God had struck with Israel were but explications in the course of time of a fundamental covenant: the covenant established by creation itself. Thus the Jewish memory looked back beyond the God of the Sinai covenant to the God who had been at work from the very beginning.

> I look up at your heavens, shaped by your fingers,
> at the moon and the stars you set firm—
> what are human beings that you spare a thought for them,
> or the child of Adam that you care for him? (Ps. 8:3–4 JB).

In the view of the psalmist as he looks with astonishment at the wonderful work of creation,[9] when God "remembers," he "cares." Is the covenant with Israel anything but a renewal of creation as the latter is brought to light again from under the rubbish of sin? To descend to the inmost depths of memory is to (re)enter the presence of the Creator.

It might be said with some simplification that human memory is the sediment left by time; the "sediment" is more or less consciously known, but in any case it is always real. Is memory not also an attempt to control time and imitate eternity? Or it might rather be said, for other reasons, that memory is a path linking human beings with the Eternal One. When I bring the past to mind I am, in the final analysis, once again renewing contact with him who establishes me in existence, if indeed it be true that human beings draw breath from the breath of God. When I reach this point of my origin and am in communion with God, I realize simultaneously that there is a future, a "still-to-come," which is his secret. Through memory, then, the present that is mine finds itself caught up in a creative movement that is divine.

If this contact with God through memory spurs me to act in accordance with my creaturely conditions and with the covenant, the reason is that God himself is always acting. He did not stop working after creating the world: his unceasing creative activity sustains and fructifies human action, even while leaving it its own proper mode of acting.[10]

Memory and action are thus the two sides—the internal and the external—of the relationship between God and human beings. God saves human beings—which is certainly a "memorable" action; when they remember this action, they renew their fidelity to the covenant.

II. MEMORY AND CULT

Memory as understood in the Bible is co-extensive with the entire existence of human beings because by its very nature it involves a relationship with God. But memory is exercised in a privileged way in cult, a very complex institution that retains its true and valid meaning precisely because of its connection with memory.

Cult and story

The element that is characteristic of Israelite cult is not sacrifices or feasts, for in this regard Israelite cult has analogies with the practices of neighboring peoples. The characteristic element (in addition to its progressive "spiritualization"[11]) is the role which memory plays in it. What is celebrated is the great deeds of Yahweh that have marked the history of the chosen people. God was not satisfied to enter into a solemn covenant with Israel; both before and after that moment he intervened in its history, and it is these interventions that the people regularly celebrate, thereby keeping the memory of them alive.[12] Reminders of the prophetic or Deuteronomic type are thus supplemented by more existential reminders: the feasts of the calendar, commemorating the main divine interventions in which God shows his fidelity to his covenant.

As a way of showing that this or that encounter between the God of the covenant and the people has a permanent importance, God himself has turned the event into a feast by prescribing that the event be commemorated. This process is very clear in the case of Passover: "This day shall be as a memorial *(lᵉ zikkarôn)* for you. You shall make this pilgrimage in order to celebrate a feast for the Lord. From age to age shall you celebrate it; this decree is immutable" (Ex 12:14 JB). The same holds for other feasts (for example, Shelters[13]), for the sabbath,[14] and even for the altar of sacrifice: "You yourselves have seen how I spoke to you from heaven. . . . You shall make me an earthen altar. . . . In every place where I shall commemorate *(ʾazkîr)* my Name, I will come to you and bless you" (Ex 20:22, 24 JB).

The commemoration of the Name means the presence during cult of God himself and his power to bless. In fact, it is really God who "remembers" in a special way on certain days and in certain places. The people, for their part, "remember" by following the prescribed rites and calling to mind this or that great deed of Yahweh. What happens at such moments? The subjective remembering of believers has no power to give life to a past event;[15] rather, God's past action as such has an enduring power which believers are urged to acknowledge and draw upon. The past event did not concern only the people to whom it was directed at that time; in them Yahweh saw all of their descendants.[16] That is why the Mishnah can comment: "In celebrating the feast, we must act as though we ourselves had come up from Egypt" (*Pesahim* X, 5). A like invitation to the faithful to think of themselves as present when God performed his great acts was already implicit in Deuteronomy's identification of the present generation of Israelites with the generation in the wilderness: "The Lord our God made a covenant with us in Horeb. Not with our fathers did the Lord make this covenant, but with us, who are all of us here alive this day" (Deut 5:2–3).

A feast therefore means that one of God's great deeds is present to the celebrating assembly. This actualization, or operative presence, is accomplished through the proclamation of a *story* or account of a divine action that continues to have consequences even now. Believers, far from being able simply to make use of that action, are urged to be united to it by making themselves present to it.

The account thus has as its function to transmit the experience of Yahweh's intervention to coming generations. All have an obligation to hear and remember. Fulfillment of the obligation can be seen in the questions which the children ask on the eve of Pass-over and which the adults are to answer.[17] The word increasingly becomes the essential part of the rite, because it is the primary means of reviving memory of the past. What past? Not the nation's own past glories, though these are recalled, but the past salvation which God bestowed on the people in their distress. The past thus continues to be a revelation of God.[18]

The encounter of the people with God in the liturgy so clearly entails a "presence" here and now to God's great acts that the word "see" can be used in speaking of the cultic action: "Come, you *shall see* the acts of God who terrifies human beings by his feats. He turned the sea into dry land, they crossed the river dry-shod; now we rejoice in him" (Ps 66:5-6 JB; see 46:9). After the people have "heard the story which our ancestors have passed on to us,"[19] the verb "see" indicates that they are in the presence of God as he acts now in their own history. The cultic assembly does not imagine that the historical event is repeated in its historical factness, for that is impossible; rather by jointly commemorating it the assembly makes the meaning of that event its own and moves forward into its own future.

Cult and everyday life

As I pointed out earlier, remembering is not simply an inter-nal act; it has a potential for outward expression in action, and the potentiality must be fulfilled. Otherwise, as the prophets say in their indictments, cult becomes unauthentic: Of what value are ritual practices if there is no respect for justice?[20] Cult in isolation is an illusion.

Is there any difference between memory exercised by individ-uals and memory that plays a part in cult? When offered by a peo-ple to whom the covenant has been entrusted, cult is a response to the express will of God, who has commanded the commemora-tion; the divine presence at this cult is therefore ensured and this as the result of a freely given gift and not of human action, still less of magic. The encounter with God that is expressed in ges-tures is, I might say, of a "sacramental" kind.[21] Furthermore, since cult is offered specifically by the assembled community, by means of rites that express unanimity and obedience, it is the community as such that is disposed to make its own the spirit of the Lord. The community is renewed by "remembering" him and is rendered capable of living upright everyday lives.

To become conscious of a past that is filled with God's action is at the same time to become conscious that this action extends to the entire universe. Cult therefore contains an element of unlimited proclamation; it not only involves the participants,[22] the psalmist's brothers and sisters,[23] and the poor and lowly of Israel,[24] but it issues a call as well to the peoples at the ends of the earth:[25] "Praise him, all you peoples," and proclaim the Name of him who is Lord of heaven and earth.[26]

Present and past

How is it possible to maintain that the present of cult is distinct from the past act which it commemorates, and yet continues to be identical with it? If we are to be convinced that this is not a fantasy on Israel's part, we must keep in mind the principal tenet of biblical anthropology: human beings are not first and foremost individuals, but members of a people in and through which they exist; they in turn contain in their loins all their descendants. This is what is meant by the expression "corporate personality."[27]

We must also, and above all, grasp the biblical conception of time in its relation to eternity. What is time? Not an empty framework in which the actions of human beings take place and then are swallowed up, nor a mere sequence of juxtaposed moments. Time is the turbulent reality of successive human generations that hand on the torch of life which is the Creator's gift, that are present to one another, and that thus constitute a people which God for his part embraces in a single, comprehensive gaze.[28] Time, it might be said, is the projection outside God of life that in the final analysis is God himself and that he shares with human beings.

Time is thus the unfolding of eternity, so that the moment, far from being simply a point between two other moments or a point of departure for movement into a still unclear future, is a "present" belonging to God and inseparable from the divine project as a whole. Time as conceived in the Bible must not be confused with cyclical time, for by its nature it is also time that moves toward a fulfillment and completion. This is because time includes the action of God himself, or else it does not exist at all.

Turn the telescope around and look through the other end. Eternity is not an endless temporal duration; it does not come "after" time but is "within" it, giving it its dimension of full reality, which is God present to becoming. Human beings must therefore discover for themselves the presence of the eternal in time; they must bring to light this depth dimension of time. All this supposes that human beings have an essential relation to God, without whom they can have no life. So, too, time does not exist apart from eternity.

The God of Israel thus performs certain acts which of themselves, and not by reason of human imagining, control the flow of time; they have a dimension of eternity that makes them always present to those who remember them. Memory is time seen as a single whole; this applies to God as well as to human beings.

III. DO THIS IN MEMORY OF ME

An improved understanding of biblical memory and its relation to cult enables us also to understand better the words of Jesus: "Do this in memory of me."

According to the experts, the Greek verb *poiein*, "do," when used in such context, signifies directly a cultic action.[29] The verb is evidently to be translated as an imperative, not an indicative, since Jesus is telling his disciples to act as he has acted. He is not explaining the change in the bread and wine, but urging them to an action, namely, to eat and drink, or, in other words, to receive what are meant as gifts, as the words "for you" or "for the multitude" indicate.

What is the "this" that the disciples are to do? At first glance, or as a hurried reader might think, it refers to the meal which Jesus has taken with his disciples; but such an interpretation proves inaccurate. A careful reading of the text shows that according to Luke and Paul the command refers to the total action Jesus has just performed over the bread. When Paul adds the same command after the saying over the cup, he is careful to state his meaning exactly: "Each time that you eat this bread and drink this cup . . ." and, further on, "Whoever eats the bread or drinks the cup of the Lord unworthily. . . ."[30] The "this" refers not to the entire meal taken at the Supper, but specifically to the actions and words over the bread and the cup.

The phrase "in memory of me" translates the Greek *eis tēn emēn anamnēsin*, which is equivalent, it seems, to *eis tēn mou anamnēsin*.[31] The noun is not *mneia* (mention, anniversary) or *mnēma* or *mnēmeion* (emblem, commemorative monument, tomb) or *mnēmē* (faculty of memory, remembrance as a psychological act), but *anamnēsis*: the act of calling to mind, an action which causes remembrance.[32] Consequently, it is better to avoid the term "memorial" when speaking of the Eurcharist, since "memorial" does not signify an action taking place but an action already completed (a written account of recollections, or a monument of some kind). Furthermore, since the preposition *eis* (lit. "into") in the anamnetic formula suggests movement, it would be better to translate: "Do this in order to make remembrance of me."[33]

Origin of the formula "in memory of"

What is the source of the formula "in memory of"? I may mention, for the reader's information, an explanation that was current at one time: the Christian eucharistic meal was supposedly a variation on the "funerary banquets" in which the Greeks commemorated their dead.[34] In this explanation, the Lord's Supper, like the Hellenistic "memorial meals," was celebrated in memory of the death of Jesus. But this hypothesis is unacceptable for three reasons. The Palestinian formula *eis anamnēsin* is not found in the supposedly parallel documents. Funerary banquets took place on the anniversary not of the death but of the birth of the person comemorated. Finally, these banquets very soon became secular events.[35]

There is no point in looking outside of the Bible for the source of the formula; the parallelism between it and the commandment of Passover remembrance shows clearly where it came from:

This day shall serve you for a remembrance (*l*ᵉ*zikkarôn*).
You shall celebrate it (Ex 12:14).

Do this for a remembrance (*eis anamnēsin*) of me (Luke/ Paul).

Eis anamnēsin clearly corresponds, at least in its form, to the *l*ᵉ*zikkarôn* of the ancient Passover.

As a matter of fact, the resemblance of the Supper text to the Passover text is not limited to the sentence "Do this in memory . . . " but extends to the entire organization of the two accounts.[36] In both, a saving event of vast significance is in the offing: the departure from Egypt and the cross. Each account tells how the event is prefigured in a sign (*l*ᵉ*'ôt:* Ex 12:13) which, be it noted, is taken from the realm of food and nourishment: the Passover meal of the Hebrews during the night of the exodus and, at the Supper, the distribution of bread and a cup by Jesus. The sign refers there-

fore to the *near future*. But the command of repetition also connects it with the *distant future:* down the centuries it will proclaim the same event, but as an event now past; it will be a
"remembrance" (*l^ezikkarón*: Ex 12:14).

It is by a figure or image, the Passover meal, that the "exodus"
from Egypt is set before the ancestors as something still to come,
and it is by the same prophetic figure that their descendants will
be reminded of it as something which has already taken place. In
like manner, Jesus prefigures the immediate future—his death for
the sake of his followers—by means of a gift of bread and wine
which he identifies with the gift of his person. In the command of
repetition the same sign is addressed to a distant future in which
it will make known the same event, but as an event now past. By
means of this anticipatory sign believers will appropriate the grace
which is the fruit of a death that for them is now in the past.

Let me summarize the relevant points. On the eve of its occurrence, the imminent saving event is prefigured in a sign. This sign
is to be repeated in cult, thereby becoming for the community that
celebrates it the means of remembering the event now past. The
sign refers to one and the same divine action but is ordered to two
different futures: one proximate and momentary, the other distant
and ongoing. It has a double function: as prophetic it looks forward; as cultic it creates a link with the past.

It is noteworthy that the account repeated in cult is not of the
saving event which is to be commemorated, but of its prefigura-
tion. Is this because the sign, being originally prophetic, continues
to be pregnant with the future? As a matter of fact, the deliverance
of the ancestors, which is commemorated over and over again by
the Passover meal, ensures the eschatological deliverance of the
children of Israel. In the case of Christians, Jesus' gift of himself,
which is signified by the eucharistic sharing, ensures their own
future "passover" and the final banquet.

This makes it clear that the event being celebrated, though
now in the historical past, is also a pledge of a definitive future
fulfillment. From this point of view, the sign, considered in its initial prophetic significance, not only refers to the key event which
it proclaims, but in addition is already pregnant with everything
that will take place in the history of the people, up to and including the fulfillment of heaven.

But while the accounts of the Supper and the exodus display
the same structure, they also differ profoundly by reason of the
"me" whom Christians remember.

The "me" that is Jesus

The event being commemorated is no longer the departure from Egypt. There is indeed still question of a salvation that has been bestowed, and the two dimensions of the sign, the prophetic and the cultic, are retained. But there is also something entirely new: what is being remembered is now *identified with a person.* The event being celebrated is still God's action, but it is God's action in the person of Jesus.

In order that the reader may see more clearly the shift that has taken place, let me compare the formula used at the Supper with the lasting "remembrance" of the action of the woman who anointed Jesus at Bethany: "Wherever the gospel is proclaimed throughout the world, what she has done will also be told in remembrance of her *(eis mnēmosynen autēs)*" (Mk 14:9 JB).

The remembrance in this case is of a particular action: that of the woman who anointed the body of Jesus beforehand for its burial. This gesture will not be forgotten, for it will be included in the proclamation of the gospel. At the Supper there is again question of an action, not however of one that is purely momentary but of one that recapitulates the entire life of Christ. By "his" body and "his" blood Jesus signifies the mystery of his death; by foretelling the salvation of the multitude he indicates that the fruit of this death is universal. In addition, since the reference is to the person in the full sense of the word, the act includes by implication all that led Jesus to acceptance of the cross, namely, the mission which he continues to the end in fidelity to God and human beings. Finally, the invitation to eat and drink signifies that Jesus intends to involve the disciples in his own destiny by assimilating them to himself and even transforming them into himself.[37]

Although the "me" that is Jesus becomes the focus of the reader's attention, it takes the place not of Yahweh himself but of the great deeds of God, of which it is the crown. The event that was the deliverance from Egypt is "fulfilled" in it, as are all of the Lord's interventions in history. This "me" is astonishingly comprehensive.

It is now possible to understand better the meaning of the liturgical action for which Jesus calls. It renders me present, not, strictly speaking, to the final meal of Jesus but to what that meal signified: the life which Jesus gives to his disciples by dying on the cross. In his body and his blood Jesus sums up the gift of his entire life and his constant fidelity. The liturgical action renders me, and each of us, present to the announcement of the death of Jesus, which it signifies, and gives me a share in the new life of the risen Lord. Here we have once again the three dimensions of memory: (1) by means of the present cultic action (2) we go back to the Jesus who at a point in history manifested and made real the definitive presence of God the deliverer, and (3) who gives an everlasting salvation.

The eucharistic liturgy places us collectively in the presence of Jesus who gives his life for me and who asks me to act as he acted, or, more accurately, who gives himself to me as food and thereby asks me to act by means of his own power to act, which is now present within me. He is here, and I did not realize it! He is here, and so I open myself to the multitude of human beings. When I descend into the depths of my memory, I encounter Jesus my Savior whom God raised from the dead and who is henceforth more me than I am myself.

The new situation

Let me get back to the main thread of my exposition by focusing attention on the new situation created by the command of remembrance.

Jesus here establishes a nexus between two actions. One is that which he himself performs in offering himself for the multitude during a meal shared with his brethren as he is about to suffer. The other is the action of his disciples in their future assemblies. The former will soon belong to a past which like other things human tends to fade into oblivion. The latter is of the future but is modeled on the one that preceded it.

From one point of view these two actions do not overlap except in an imagination that turns away from reality; the action of the disciples is not identifiable with the action of Jesus. And yet from another point of view and in virtue of the connection which Jesus established between the two, the action of the disciples has meaning only in function of his own; at a deeper level it must even be identical with his. How is it possible, despite the erosion of time and despite the distance between them, for the past to go on really acting in the present?

The possibility is created by the fact that the Easter event of Jesus is not swallowed up by time but rather stands over it. The people whom that event has brought into being render themselves present to the action that is the foundation of their existence,

namely, the acceptance by God of the "sacrifice" of Jesus on the
cross. The Lord's Supper is in reality a feast at which the Church
renews its adherence to the risen Jesus and, in him, to God the
Savior.

Seen in this perspective, the eucharistic anamnesis applies to
Jesus what had been said of the Jewish Passover, and requires the
disciples to act as the Israelites did at their Passover feast. It is not
God who is urged to remember, but human beings, for these must
struggle against their tendency to forget the action that grounds
their existence. When they renew their remembrance of Jesus they
are invited to become like him and thus to let his action and presence find expression in and through them. It is clear, then, that we
are far removed here from any subjective conception of memory,
such as is found in, for example, a "commemoration" of the dead.
The eucharistic action is not a monument to be erected before
God; it is an actualization of the event that was Jesus. The "day"
is a day that is still, even today, a day for me: unceasing thanksgiving, a laying hold of the eternal in time, an opening to my true
destiny.

Is the formula "Do this in memory of me?" all that is needed?
I think not. It would be naive to think that the command is enough
to produce what it says. Memory easily degenerates into reified
habit.

The Jews were careful to remain in contact with the word of
God by means of a rite—a feast—which expressed the presence of
that word (e.g., Ex 13:9). But, like other peoples, they also
invented equivalents for this commemorative action; these equivalents were simply lesser forms of a feast. Thus the incense placed
on the loaves of permanent offering turned them into a memorial.[38] The Bible did not advocate the use of tattoos or amulets, but
just as the Israelites set up stones as an "eternal reminder" of a
pact (for example, at the crossing of the Jordan[39]), so too they were
to put a tassel containing a violet thread on the hem of their robe.[40]
They also made phylacteries for themselves, but these ended up as
excuses for not acting in accordance with the law. These little
receptacles contained the most important words of the law and
were attached to forehead or arm. Moses had said: "You shall bind
them [my words] as a sign upon your hand, and they shall be as
frontlets between your eyes"; the Jews took his metaphor literally
and gave the Shema a material form by placing it in a leather recep-
tacle which they wore on their persons; some Jews even used phylacteries as a means of attracting attention.[41] Let none of us cast a

stone at them, for the same kind of corruption threatens all "practicing" religious people.

In the final analysis, all the measures taken to keep memory alive are ineffectual as long as God does not take a hand in the business. Of old it was realized that the law would ultimately have to be written in the human heart. Today the Spirit must remind us of the actions of Christ. That is precisely what Jesus promised that the Paraclete would do: "He will bring to your remembrance all that I said to you" (Jn 14:26). The Holy Spirit is the living memory of the Church. Consequently it is not, strictly speaking, a human action that makes believers present to Jesus during the eucharistic liturgy, but rather God himself acting through his Spirit. And what is then produced is not an encounter but a complete "synergy."[42]

At the concrete level, however, memory is exercised by means of the "account" of what Jesus said and did. The function of the account is to put me in the presence of the event that is the saving cross. Let me immediately call the reader's attention to a deterioration that took place at a rather early date. The account called attention to the letter of what Jesus had said and done. Attention gradually shifted from the meaning, which is inseparable from the sayings and actions, to the literal wording of the sayings, thus leading readers and hearers to concentrate on the problems involved in the "transubstantiation" of the bread and wine and the remaining "species." It is true, of course, that in saying what he did over the bread and the cup Jesus expressed the meaning of his self-giving unto death: he enables those who share his meal to receive the act by which he saves the world and to share in his sacrifice. Only the celebration in its entirety, with its implied acceptance of the gift of bread and wine, reveals the full significance of the eucharistic banquet and of the presence of him who announces and symbolizes his saving death.

CONCLUSION

The command to remember Jesus Christ is an exhortation to the Church to renew its contact with its source: that is the purpose of memory, although this case is special since in Jesus the Church comes in contact with God at work. The Church finds in Jesus the meaning of its very existence and is thereby disposed to let God and Jesus act through it.

In this remembering the Church is asked not only to say the

words of "consecration" but to celebrate a "meal": not a meal that directly satisfies bodily hunger, but the eucharistic meal that includes preparation, consecration, and communion. Only then is the wish of Jesus fulfilled.

Remembrance of Jesus is dynamic: it gives a forward thrust to the Church that has in this way renewed its contact with its Lord and that must express in its everyday life what Jesus himself experienced and lived on earth: the love of God that grounds love among human beings.

Let me suggest, finally, a symbolic analogy that will help us to accept the mystery of a past action that exerts an efficacy down the centuries.

Day after day we repeat: "The sun has risen," even though we know perfectly well that the sun does not "rise," and that on the contrary the earth each morning enters the presence of the sun, the center of the system in which it exists. The same holds for the action of Jesus in sacrificing himself for all human beings. He is henceforth the center of the "Christian system" inasmuch as he is the one on whom all depend and from whom all receive life. Day after day I say that I am actualizing that action, rendering it present; I know perfectly well, however, that the contrary alone is true. Each morning *I* become present to the sacrifice of Jesus which, though an action within past time, has a supratemporal dimension and allows me to be present to it despite the distance created by time, which from my point of view flows on unceasingly and inexorably. As a result, time itself acquires not only a footing in eternity but a dynamism that is solidly rooted in the saving act of God and opens me to an all-embracing reconciliation.

VII
The Words Over the Bread

The words of Jesus over the bread need to be read in their immediate context, since they serve there to interpret the action he has just performed.

Markan Tradition (M)		Antiochene Tradition (A)	
Matthew	*Mark*	*Luke*	*Paul*
Having taken bread and pronouncing the blessing,	Having taken bread, pronouncing the blessing,	And having taken bread, having given thanks,	took bread and, having given thanks,
[Jesus] broke [it] and having given [it] to the disciples, said:	he broke [it], gave [it] to them and said:	he broke [it] and gave [it] to them, saying:	broke [it] and said:
"Take, eat, this is my body."	*"Take, this is my body."*	*"This is my body which [is] given for you. Do this in memory of me."*	*"This is my body which [is] for you. Do this in memory of me."*

Context of the words

The words over the bread are difficult from the viewpoint of literary criticism. As I pointed out earlier, it is hardly possible to determine their original tenor, since there are no cogent reasons for assuming the original presence or absence of the phrase "for you," which modifies the word "body," and for assuming, in consequence, that one of the recensions must derive from the other.[1] In addition, account must be taken of two traditions, the Markan and the Antiochene. Since it is not possible to decide which tradition is original, we must look to the context for light on the text.

This context plays a part at three levels. First of all, in all the recensions the words over the bread are paired with those over the cup. Consequently, the complete meaning will not be had until the latter have been studied. Meanwhile, however, the words over the bread must be studied in their own right, even if the scope of the analysis is limited.

117

Secondly, the words are closely connected with the gestures that precede them: blessing, breaking of bread, distribution. These gestures, too, determine the interpretation.

Finally, and most important, the words "This is my body," which are the essential ones spoken by Jesus at this point, do not occur in isolation in any of the recensions. The Markan tradition introduces them with an imperative, "Take," and thereby directly involves the disciples in what is said. The Antiochene tradition likewise implies the involvement of the disciples by adding "for you" to "body" and by introducing the command of remembrance. As a result, the relational aspect of the entire scene, which I pointed out earlier,[2] intrinsically modifies the words over the bread. For this reason, at every step in the analysis I must keep in mind the reference of the words, "This is my body," to the others at table.

Before interpreting Jesus' statement let me examine the words that make it up.

This (touto)

This demonstrative pronoun does not refer simply to the material object which Jesus takes in his hands. It is true, of course, that *touto*, even though in the neuter gender, can stand for the masculine *houtos ho artos* ("this bread").[3] But since Jesus' statement comes after the ritual described in the preceding active verbs, the word "this" now has a richer meaning which it is important to understand.

To begin with, in keeping with Jewish tradition, a blessing has been spoken over the bread, which has thus become liturgically, and not only naturally, a gift of God. Therefore it now has a "symbolic" value over and above its inherent value as earthly food.

Furthermore, the bread that has been broken is not intended simply to nourish each guest individually. As a single loaf that is shared among many at a communal meal, it establishes a union among those who eat it, since all share in a single source of life.

Finally, this bread is "given" to the disciples, explicitly in the three evangelists, implicitly in Paul. The giving expresses the relationship which Jesus, the host, is establishing with them, his guests. This bread comes to them from his hands; it is deliberately shared with them. Even before the statement in its entirety can determine the meaning, the pronoun "this" points not simply to the material bread as such but to a food that has already been removed from its ordinary profane condition and been turned into a means of establishing a relation: in secret with the invisible Unnamed One who is present, openly with Jesus, the host who shares it with them.

My body (to sōma mou)

Before determining the sense which these words have in their present context, let me recall the various meanings that the word *sōma* can have in the world of the Bible.[4]

When Semites use the word "body," they are not referring to the organism that is at the human being's disposal, but rather to the person insofar as it is able to express and manifest itself, or to the person insofar as it enters into relations with the universe and with other human beings. In biblical anthropology, human beings do not merely have bodies, they *are* bodies. Therefore, since Jesus, like every other human being, expresses himself through his body, the expression "my body" refers to his person insofar as it is related in a concrete way to other human beings and to the whole of creation.

The word *sōma*, when thus understood, is almost equivalent to the Hebrew word *bāsār;* the latter, however, adds to the preceding description overtones of creaturely weakness and is usually to be translated as "flesh" (thus Isaiah says: "All flesh is like grass"). Many authors suppose that *sōma* in the present context represents the Hebrew *bāsār* (or Aramaic *bisrā*).[5] Other critics are reluctant to accept this hypothesis: Why (they ask) did the synoptics and Paul not choose the Greek word *sarx* (= "flesh"), as John the evangelist was to do in the discourse on the bread of life? Furthermore, post-biblical Hebrew prefers the word *gūph* when speaking of the person or self in its relation to other human beings.[6] Finally, the Septuagint uses *sōma* to translate many other words beside *bāsār,* especially words that refer to the person when looked upon solely from outside and treated as an object: a slave, something abandoned, even a corpse.[7] For these reasons many critics today are of the opinion that *sōma* too can refer to the human being insofar as it is destined for corruption and death. This being the case, the word's range of meanings suggests two alternative lines of interpretation: the person in relation to the universe, or the person as destined to die.

The context in which the words occur points in the second of these two directions. Jesus has just said that he will be betrayed.

He will speak in a moment of the blood that he is to shed for the multitude. Finally, the verb "give," used to describe his action in distributing the bread, suggests a comparison with the Isaian prophecy of the Servant.[8]

Is Jesus therefore saying that he is giving himself as the victim of a cultic sacrifice which will expiate for the sins of the world? In support of such an interpretation scholars sometimes appeal to an ancient text that is cited in the first letter of Peter where the behavior of Jesus is being offered as a model for Christians: "he who in his body *(en to sōmati autou)* carried *(anenegken)* our sins upon the wood" (1 Pet 2:24). The phrase "in his body" evidently means "upon himself": Jesus took our sins upon himself, just as the Servant of God (Is 53:12 LXX) "carried" *(anenegken)* the sins of "the multitude." If the comparison be accepted as a valid one, it must be noted that Jesus performs his action as a martyr who accepts death in behalf of sinners; for while the verb used can at times have the meaning of "offer in ritual sacrifice," it cannot have this meaning in 1 Peter, since if it did, sins would be the material of the offering, which is impossible.[9] Furthermore, body and blood as paired terms do not belong to the cultic language of the Bible. Therefore, when Jesus speaks of "my body," he is referring to his life that is given even to the point of accepting death, but in a sacrifice that is personal and not cultic.

In summary: the words "my body" can have two meanings; they signify either the person of Jesus insofar as it expresses itself (but this meaning requires that the words be separated from their context) or the person of Jesus as destined for death. If the second meaning is chosen, is it to be concluded that Jesus is therefore prophetically announcing his death? I think that this connotation is secondary, and this for two reasons: first, in the Markan tradition (and in Paul) the reader already knows that Jesus will be delivered up to death; second, and more importantly, the main emphasis is on the symbolism of the bread which, as food, gives life. But death is certainly present in the background, and it was important to recall this fact. The life which the bread, that is, the body, gives, comes through the death of the body.

My body which [is] for you (hyper hymōn)

In the Antiochene tradition the body is immediately described as being "for you." The critics are almost unanimous in understanding the words "for you" in light of the cultic model of expiation. That is: in speaking as he does, Jesus is presenting himself as the one who in dying offers God the true expiatory sacrifice by which human beings are really reconciled with God.

Is this reading well-founded? Admittedly, the words over the cup, with their reference to blood that is shed, suggest this line of thought. On the other hand, only Matthew's recension adds the final phrase "for the forgiveness of sins" and thus explicitly introduces the theme of expiatory death. In the older recensions there is no question of sin.

In face of this difficulty most of the critics argue that the preposition *hyper* is enough by itself to compel an interpretation along the lines of expiatory sacrifice. The author of the article on *hyper* in Kittel's *Theological Dictionary of the New Testament* has this to say: "No matter how one may assess the direct influence of Is. 53:11f. on the self-awareness of Jesus and primitive Christian christology, the beneficial quality *(hyper)* of the death of someone . . . can be understood only against the background of the sacrificial concepts of the OT."[10] According to this passage, the preposition *hyper* is intrinsically connected with the Old Testament sacrificial mentality. I venture to challenge this view and shall therefore look at the evidence once again.

The basic meaning of *hyper* is "above" or "over," whence its connotation of "covering, protecting, defending" and its use to express the idea of "in favor of" someone or something. *Hyper* has a wide range of applications. Let me note at the outset that the substitutional sense, "in place of," is very rare in the New Testament.[11] Here are some examples of the regular uses of this preposition. One can take a stand for another,[12] be concerned about another,[13] spend oneself for another.[14] Paul is ready to risk being accursed for the sake of his Jewish brethren,[15] and he rejoices in the sufferings which, he says, he endures "for you."[16] In all these usages, *hyper* indicates that an action will profit someone.

Christological texts follow the same pattern. Christ "died for us,"[17] "for us sinners."[18] He even "died for our sins,"[19] according to a bold expression that comes at the end of a strange development of the meaning and explains why the critics have generally taken the approach they have to this preposition. For when sin is given as one of the reasons for Christ's acceptance of death, the reader spontaneously understands the text as saying that his death redeemed us from sin, and spontaneously deduces that this death is to be interpreted in accordance with the biblical idea of sacrifice for sin.[20] I may add that in the time of Christ "expiatory sacrifice" was very popular.[21] All this explains why the critics have detected cultic overtones in the words of Jesus over the bread.

The generalization that *hyper* has an expiatory meaning supposes, however, that two points have already been clearly established. The first is that, as Kittel's *Dictionary* puts it, the statement "Christ died for us" derives from the words over the cup at the institution of the Eucharist and, more specifically, from Mark 14:24, which is said to be the earliest recension and to have a sacrificial meaning.[22] But this argument is circular, since there is no proof that Mark supplies the earliest text of the Supper story or that in his text the words have a cultic meaning. The reasoning behind such a statement is not based on literary evidence but is an answer to a theological question: How could the death of Jesus effect the justification of all human beings? As I have shown elsewhere,[23] the cultic-sacrificial interpretation which Paul gives of the death of Jesus is only one among others to be found in his letters; it is also the least frequently offered, being found only in rare texts that are not easy to understand.

The second point that is falsely supposed as established is that *hyper* always has reference to sin when it is connected with the mention of the death of Jesus. Such a reference does exist in some cases,[24] but Paul also uses *hyper* in situations not concerned with sin. Here is but one example: Paul has just said that "Christ died for the wicked," and he continues: "A person will hardly be ready to die for someone upright, though perhaps one might accept death for someone truly good."[25] In this context, *hyper* ("for") does not require the reader to think of an "expiatory sacrifice." This connotation might possibly be present in the statement that "Christ died for the wicked," but it is surely absent from the two parts of the next sentence, dealing as they do with the "upright" and the "truly good" for whom there is no question of making expiation. Yet the preposition *hyper* is used throughout.

As confirmation that *hyper* is not necessarily connected with expiatory sacrifice, I must point out that the death of Christ is often explained not by the need to save human beings from sin, but by love, even if "salvation" is implied. "The Son of God . . . loved me and gave himself up for me"; "God shows his love for us in that . . . Christ died for us."[26] Love includes far more than ransom from sin. John makes this clear when, for example, he says: "There is no greater love than to give one's life for those one loves."[27] And when John says that Christ "consecrates himself for us," the meaning is not that Christ looks upon himself as victim of an expiatory sacrifice but that he is making it possible for his disciples to join him in his role as the Son who belongs to us in virtue of his creaturely condition.[28] At this profound level, "expiation" would carry its original meaning of "reconciliation," that is, the restoration of human beings to a condition in which they can dialogue with God.

When, then, Jesus says "my body . . . for you," he is not directly saying that his body will be offered in a sacrifice of expiation as the "one" victim given for "all." This meaning can certainly be read into the formula in light of the context of death in which it is found. But the symbolism of food suggests that another interpretation is the primary one. The direct meaning of the words is: "I give myself as food so that you may live"; such is the sense, in context, of *hyper* ("for," "in favor of") since human beings eat in order to have life.[29]

A corollary needs to be stated explicitly. In the words over the bread Jesus is not announcing that he accepts death as a "means" of salvation; he is announcing rather that as a result of his fidelity unto death to God and human beings he will be present to his followers by becoming their food and giving them life through himself.

The words are doubtless spoken with death on the horizon, but the death is a saving death. It is life, therefore, that provides the controlling perspective. Jesus is saying that beyond the death which he is accepting as part of God's plan and out of love for us, he has power to remain our life-giving food in the new world of the covenant.

This is (touto estin)

I have thus far been clarifying the meaning of the words that make up the statement over the bread, as well as the proclamation of life which the statement contains. But a delicate question remains: What is the nature of the identity being asserted between the bread and the body of Jesus? To say that in Aramaic no copula is used in this type of sentence is simply to avoid the issue. The Greek text, after all, regards the inclusion of a copula as necessary. Furthermore, the juxtaposition of "bread" and "body" compels us to see a close connection of some kind between them. Are the bread and the body simply compared? Or are they really said to be identical, and, if so, what kind of identity is being asserted?

The answer to these questions is conditioned by one's philosophical or religious position, to such an extent that the same words—e.g., "real," "substantial," and "figurative"—may be used with quite different meanings by the various parties to the discussion.[30] I shall therefore try, first, to situate the words of Jesus in the context of the biblical world in which they were uttered; then to look at them from the viewpoint of semantics; and finally to interpret them in light of a particular understanding of the idea of "symbol."

(a) The exegetes agree that, taken as a whole, what Jesus said and did over the bread and the cup is a form of *behavior peculiar to the prophets* of the Bible.[31] The latter often mime their message in gestures that are at once figurative and efficacious.

Thus when the prophet Agabus wishes to warn Paul of his (Paul's) coming imprisonment, he takes Paul's girdle and binds his own feet and hands with it (Acts 21:11). In order to announce the impending deportation of the inhabitants of Jerusalem, whom God intends to punish for their infidelity, Ezekiel is obliged to shave his head and scatter his hairs to the wind. Then he is told: "Thus says the Lord God: This is Jerusalem" (Ez 5:5). The prophet asserts an identity between his gesture and the destiny of the city; his hearers understand that their fate will resemble that of the prophet's hair. The prophetic action mimes a coming event, which is then stated more explicitly in words.

There is a second element in the biblical understanding of such actions: they are efficacious. That is, the prophet does not simply look forward to the event; rather, his action anticipates it and in a sense brings it to pass. Thus when Jeremiah puts a yoke on his own shoulders as a way of saying that Jerusalem will fall under foreign domination, the false prophets quickly break the yoke in order to keep the prophecy from being fulfilled (Jer 17—28). Some biblical stories are even clearer. Elisha bids King Joash strike the ground; he immediately does so, but only three times. The prophet then says: "You should have struck five or six times; then you would have struck down Syria until you had made an end of it, but now you will strike down Syria only three times" (2 Kgs 13:19). There is a real connection between the king's action and the battle that is foretold; the connection is between signifier and signified, the latter being a consequence of the former by reason of the efficacy attributed to it: If the king had struck five times instead of three, he would have routed the enemy.

The reader will have noticed that in the passage from Ezekiel there is a turn of phrase—"This is Jerusalem"—that is analogous to the words of Jesus over the bread. When interpreted against this prophetic background, the verb "to be" in the words over the bread does not establish a direct *material* correspondence between the bread and the body. Interpreters are usually quite clear on this point. Thus J. Dupont writes: "When interpreted in the context of Semitic and biblical modes of thought, the most natural meaning of the words over the bread would be: 'This signifies my body,' 'This represents my body.'"[32]

The question then arises: Is it still possible to speak of a "real presence"? In order therefore to "provide a basis for the doctrine," Dupont has recourse to Paul, for whom this bread is "a communion in the body of Christ" (1 Cor 10:16), and to John who has the statement: "My flesh is truly food" (Jn 6:55). This is all very well, but does this extrinsic addition to the words of institution help to determine in what the "conversion" of bread into the body consists?

(b) In asking this question I do not imply that what was said under (a) is erroneous; it is simply incomplete. The words and action of Jesus can indeed be located in the category of prophetic mimesis, and they possess the efficacy which is characteristic of that kind of activity: by eating the bread the disciples are united to the "body" of Jesus. The sign of bread produces a communion with Jesus. But what precisely is to be understand by the signifier "bread"? In order to answer this question I must recall the *dialogical situation* in which Jesus spoke, as I pointed out at the beginning of this chapter. An explanation of that situation requires in turn a digression into some ideas from linguistics and semantics.[33]

All words are addressed by a "speaker" to an "interlocutor."[34] To the extent that they say something and are addressed to someone, they have two poles: one determinative, the other significative. When I say: "This is my bread," I am making an informative or "constative" utterance;[35] that is, I am reporting that this thing is bread and not a stone. But my statement is also "performative," inasmuch as I am telling my interlocutor to recognize that the bread belongs to me and not to someone else. On the one hand, then, I "determine" the nature of the object called "bread"; on the other, I "signify" to the interlocutor that it belongs to me. Depending on the disposition of the speaker and the interlocutor the words carry a greater or lesser degree of meaning.

The degree depends on the "performative" authority of the speaker and the "competence" of the interlocutor.[36] First and foremost, the interlocutor must understand the language being spoken (if the language is English, he must realize, for example, that I am not speaking of something having been "bred") and must recognize the authority of the speaker (I have the right to say that the bread is "mine"). These conditions were fulfilled in the case of Ezekiel and his hearers: they knew the prophet's reputation and recognized that the prophecy would really be fulfilled.

In the account of the Supper, the dialogue is explicit: the words "Take" and "for you" refer to those to whom the statement of Jesus is addressed. His words do not simply define some new state of the bread; they immediately order the disciples to do something: to take, to receive. They are not a self-contained proclamation but a call to receive the bread and thereby become an agent in the accomplishment of the sign itself. There is much more involved here than in the usual prophetic signs of the Bible. The mimetic action of Jesus requires for its completion a corresponding action of those at table with him.

The nature of the signifier confirms that last observation. In the case of the Last Supper there is question not of the scattered hairs of a prophet or of blows struck upon the ground by a king, but of "bread," which is a food to be eaten. True, it is not said that the disciples actually ate, but the text does say that they were told to eat. In Luke and Paul, the words that follow immediately ("Do this in remembrance of me") show that the eating was to be repeated later on after the death of Jesus. The fact that there is question here of bread is enough by itself to prove that the "performative" utterance of Jesus finds its completion only in the implicit response of the disciples as they eat the bread he gives them. The dialogical situation in which the words are uttered shows that Jesus is inviting the disciples to eat a special food, his body. What does this mean?

At this point the linguistic element of signification or meaning becomes primary. One and the same word, "bread," can in fact convey a variety of meanings. If I say: "This is the bread of life," I give the signifier ("bread") a sense that is different from its natural meaning (bodily food) and is perceptible only to interlocutors who are familiar with a certain way of thinking proper to the world of faith or the world of the Bible.

The meaning here is no longer single and univocal as it was in the example given a moment ago: "This is my bread" (I must acknowledge that the bread belongs to the speaker). In this new context, the word "bread" is open to several interpretations. The interlocutor may interpret the expression "bread of life" as meaning a living wage or a wisdom that confers contentment or the heavenly manna of the Apocalypse. It is thus the mind of the interlocutor that understands the expression "bread of life" to have a particular meaning. He "recognizes" this meaning; that is, with the aid of his own culture and its familiar archetypes he establishes a communion of thought with the speaker. The latter has engaged in a "performance" in which he gives the signifier "bread" a meaning different from its natural meaning and calls upon the interlocutor to recognize this meaning.

I have now taken a further step beyond the first, which located the action of Jesus in the genre of prophetic action. In that first step his action was seen to be real and not fictitious, to the extent precisely that he possessed authority. In the second step I have shown the "performative" nature of Jesus' utterance: his words do what they say to the hearer. But a third step is still required for a full understanding of what the transformation of bread into the body of Jesus involves.

(c) In this third step I shall locate the signifier "bread" of our text in the category of *symbol*. If readers are properly to understand this new step they must realize, above all else, that "symbolic" is in no way opposed to "real," contrary to what is supposed by minds accustomed to an ontological approach to the world. Such minds must undergo a true intellectual conversion if they are to grasp the difference between symbol and sign.[37]

What, then, is the nature of "sign"? Let me begin with a lower form of sign, the "signal." At this level, the signifier "smoke" (for example) leads those present to perceive a signified, which is "fire." Smoke is a sign of fire; smoke and fire are two entities of the same order, existing independently of the mind that perceives them. That is why smoke cannot be said to "symbolize" fire.

In other instances of "signs" the signifier immediately calls to mind something else, but this time a reality that belongs to a different order and can be grasped only by the mind. What was said a moment ago about the plurality of possible meanings which a word or statement may have also applies here; in this new context, however, attention must be focused more closely on the signifier.

Depending on the "performance" of the speaker and/or on the "competence" of the interlocutor a signifier such as "water" can symbolize freshness, fruitfulness, destruction, and so on. In and of itself, "water" is not a symbol any more than bread or light or any other object in this world is; rather the human mind, on the basis of its cultural background or the activity of the unconscious, establishes an understanding of this or that aspect of a signifier that is already freighted with what the mind puts into it or discovers in it. Thus it is the mind that determines or perceives the symbolic value of a material reality such as water.

When I consider "bread" as a signifier I can see in it not only everyday food but realities which belong to a different and hidden order of things and which I decide to "manifest" or make visible through it: the bread of life, the bread that is wisdom, and so on. The signifying term brings together, unites, and establishes a "symbolic" relationship between two realities that are on different levels.

A "sign," then, is separable from that which it signifies, since it exists independently of the mind as a reality capable of having a variety of meanings. A symbol, on the other hand, participates in that which it represents, and it becomes a symbol only through the activity of the mind that unites these two realities of different orders. The dialogical situation has thus led into the *language of symbols.*

Let me now apply these various considerations to the words spoken over the bread. In uttering them Jesus gives the natural function of bread a further role. The bread continues to be earthly food that is given by God, but now it is also a food of a different order, since it is said to be the body of Jesus. The bread thus acquires a new value which it derives both from the words of Jesus and from the acceptance of these words. The mind of Jesus gives meaning to the words; the mind of the disciples, by accepting what he says, acknowledges its efficacy. The bread retains its function as bread, and in this sense it is not the body of Jesus; but the bread also becomes the body of Jesus, and in this sense it is no longer ordinary bread. Paradoxically, for Jesus as for the believer, the eucharistic bread *is and is not* bread, it *is and is not* the body of Jesus.

The statement that "the bread *is and is not* the body of Jesus" sums up the twofold value of the one bread. It shows that there is question here not of the ordinary material thing called bread, but of a reality that has been transformed not only by the blessing but specifically by the words of Jesus: "This is my body." In the strictest sense, that is, the sense which Jesus gives to the words and which the disciples perceive, "the bread *is* his body." At the same time, however, and from a different point of view (that of the senses and of a mind not enlightened by faith), the bread *is not* the body of Jesus.

The end result of this lengthy digression is a nuanced understanding of the verb "to be." People often understand it as the verb which identifies visible things that are *on the same level.* But in the light of what has just been said it must be acknowledged that the human mind can use the same verb to express an identification of a visible reality with a reality of another order: in this instance, an identification of bread with the "body" of Jesus. It is obvious that Jesus does not mean to give his physical body to be eaten; the "body" in question can only be the spiritual, heavenly reality of the risen Lord. At the Last Supper he bids his disciples eat this bread, knowing that by doing so they will enter into communion with his person, with him who exists solely "for you," is faithful unto death, and trusts in the God who is to raise him up.

Before undertaking a second reading of the words of Jesus, let me stress the limits of the preceding inquiry. It led to a description of the words of Jesus as a symbolic statement within a dialogue that is meant to establish a community which will survive the death now threatening the speaker. Am I saying, then, that there is no difference between the eucharistic statement and other symbolic statements? No! Two basic factors give the eucharistic words a place apart. The first is that since they are "performative" the quality or status of the speaker determines their value. In this case, the speaker at the Last Supper possesses a unique authority, so that the mystery of the eucharistic symbolism is simply one aspect of the overall mystery of the person of Jesus Christ. The eucharistic bread is thus not merely one symbol among others but expresses an aspect of the mystery of God's Word who has taken a human countenance for himself.

The second factor which differentiates the symbolic relation in the Eucharist from other symbolic relations is to be seen in the action which the addressees are required to perform. The man who gives a bouquet of flowers to his fiancée symbolizes his love by means of the gift. In giving us bread to eat Jesus symbolizes his love not by a gift external to himself but by giving his very self in the form of food. This is encounter at its deepest possible level, for in giving this bread he gives *himself.* It may be said, then, that in one sense the eucharistic mystery is the supreme symbol, the supersymbol, because the relation between speaker and addressees is one of reciprocal assimilation. More accurately, the eucharistic bread has an effect that is the opposite of the effect of bread at the natural level: the believer eats this bread, but it is the body of Jesus that assimilates the believer, and not vice versa. To accept the eucharistic bread is to acknowledge the mystery of Jesus Christ.

Second reading of the words over the bread

When set in their dialogical context the words of Jesus reveal the meaning they have in both the Markan and the Antiochene traditions. The "for you" which in the Antiochene tradition makes explicit the purpose of Jesus' statement has an equivalent in the Markan tradition in the invitation: "Take!" I shall therefore take as my starting point the seemingly more enigmatic formula in the Markan tradition.

Is it possible to say that as they stand the words "are meaningless," as is claimed by some critics who think it necessary to rely also, and even exclusively, on the Antiochene tradition? Their judgment is in fact a superficial one. Is it really believable that the Markan tradition suppressed the Antiochene qualifier "for you," even for the sake of establishing a closer parallel between the body and the blood? More importantly, these critics fail to grasp the dialogical situation in which Jesus utters his invitation to "take" his body.

The words were taken literally and given an erroneous interpretation by believers who understood "body" as referring to the physical constitution of Jesus and unhesitatingly identified the material bread with his physical body. This approach led at one time to what was called the "stercoran" interpretation; in this view there is a real "impanation" of Jesus in the host, with the result that the communicant physically digests the bodily organism of Jesus. It is worth noting how Paul, while emphasizing the reality of the Lord's body that is received at this Supper, avoids suggesting any material eating of the physical body.

It must be said that this kind of excess finds no justification in Paul. In 1 Cor 11:26, the verse that completes his eucharistic account, the words "eat" and "drink" do occur: "For each time that you eat this bread and drink this cup, you proclaim the death of the Lord until he comes." But instead of "eat this body" and "drink the new covenant," he says "eat this bread" and "drink the cup." It is true, indeed, that the bread and cup are a bread and cup that have become part of the Eucharist; nonetheless the eating and drinking refer to human actions that have for their object the natural foods involved. Furthermore, in the concluding verse just cited Paul does not say "You become one with the Lord," but rather "You proclaim the Lord's death." He is not expressing here the idea of communion with a person, still less the idea of assimilation, through eating, of a being which is materially present. He says only that to share the Lord's supper (bread and cup) is to share in the salvation Christ won for us by his death.

In the other passage in which Paul speaks of the Eucharist (1 Cor 10:16), the situation is reversed from the linguistic point of view: "The cup of blessing which we bless, is it not a communion in the blood of Christ? The bread which we break, is it not a communion in the body of Christ?" While the reference here is still to the bread and the cup, the envisaged effect is no longer a proclamation of the salvation that has been received, but rather a communion in the "body" and the "blood." The words "body" and "blood" do not occur in 1 Cor 11:26. Conversely, the words "eat" and "drink" do not occur here. Instead, there is question here of "the cup which we bless" and the "bread which we break"; the verbs now refer to gestures which are, properly speaking, part of a ritual.

Paul thus avoids any formulation that might promote a materialistic identification of the species with the body and blood of Christ. But if he thus excludes possible excesses of this kind, neither does he allow the reader to diminish the realism of his statements, in the manner, for example, of that devout and lamented scholar, Joachim Jeremias. Because Jeremias rigidly interprets "is" as meaning "signifies, represents," he sees in the words of Jesus

> a double simile . . . which has its formal analogy in the manner in which the prophets of the Old Testament announce future events parabolically. . . . Jesus made the broken bread a simile of the fate of his body. . . . "I go to death as the true passover sacrifice" is the meaning of Jesus' last parable.[38]

On this view it is no longer possible to speak of a real identity between the body and the bread; one must limit oneself instead to the idea of a comparison or parable. But in taking this position Jeremias overlooks the nature of language as I have tried to explain it.

The language of Jesus is "performative." He addresses his disciples, not in order to give them a definition of the bread which he has just broken and distributed, but to urge them to recognize his very self in the bread they share and thereby to form the community that will be called "the Church." He thus begins a new mode of presence to his disciples, not through any prolongation of the incarnation but as the risen Lord who sustains the life of the Church. It is as though he were saying: "Until now my body has been here among you, and I have encountered you through this body which is familiar to you. But now I am departing, and henceforth you will encounter me in a different way, namely, in this bread which I have distributed to you. From now on, I am present to you through this bread which you share in my name."

By his act of sharing the bread and by the interpretative words that accompany it Jesus establishes an identity between the eucharistic bread and his body that will make this body present, despite its absence, to his disciples and the world. This communion, be it noted, has a twofold effect: not only is each individual invited to union with Jesus Christ, but this union in turn leads to authentic community with the others who are invited.

The words "Take; this is my body" do not say everything. They undoubtedly do indicate the way in which Jesus makes himself present after his death, but, despite the meaning of the word "body," they say nothing *explicitly* about the condition required for this new kind of presence, namely, his death. The context suggests this necessary condition, and the Antiochene tradition makes it explicit by saying "body which is for you": it is because of the personal sacrifice of Jesus that the new presence becomes a reality. The other statement of Jesus over the cup brings this out with full clarity: the shedding of his blood establishes the new and definitive covenant between God and human beings.

Despite this reservation, the words over the bread, even when taken in isolation, open the way for the disciples to a full communion with Jesus and with other human beings. The bread retains its ordinary function as food, but the words of Jesus also give it a new function as a heavenly food that sustains the Church. The biblical narrative does not immediately entitle us to consider the bread apart from its intended role in the relationship which Jesus establishes with his disciples or apart from the liturgical context of the saying. As I pointed out in Chapter III, the saying must be located within the structure of the narrative; it is from that structure that it derives its true meaning.

SUPPLEMENTARY NOTES

1. Transubstantiation

The reader may have observed that in my exposition I have avoided speaking of "transubstantiation," since this word does not appear in the scriptures. On the other hand, it is part of our usual theological language, and the reader therefore has a right to some brief explanation of it. I prefer, however, to let Bernard Sesboüé, a theologian who is an expert on the subject, do the explaining:[39]

> *The idea of substance* causes hopeless confusion nowadays because its meaning for the modern scientific mind is completely different from that which it had in ancient philosophy (and which it still has in modern philosophy, although the terminology used is different).
>
> *Meaning of the term in the contemporary mind* (what I might call its popular meaning): substance is the empirical reality that is regarded as the material or substratum of any given thing; it shows a certain homogeneity of structure and belongs to the phenomenal order. *Examples:* the substance of my coat is wool; the substance of bread is wheat or barley or rye.
>
> *"Philosophical" meaning of the term.* I offer two definitions: "It is being . . . as possessing a unity and cohesion and seen at the level at which the intellect grasps it and affirms its reality."[40] Or: it is the active principle that organizes a certain number of components into a whole; it is the totalizing and concrete unity of a set of phenomena, and that which turns them into a being that has meaning.[41]
>
> *Examples:* the substance of my coat is that it is a certain kind of garment intended to protect me from the winter cold and to look good on me (insofar as clothing is an adornment). The substance of bread is that it is a food. Bread is no longer wheat; it has been negated as wheat and as a product of nature and has undergone a series of changes wrought by human labor (it has been milled into flour, kneaded into dough, and cooked in the oven)—changes which have unity and meaning in that the pur-

pose of all of them is to turn wheat into human food. There has been no "transmutation" of the wheat in the "alchemical" sense of the word. In a real sense, though one only analogous with the case of the Eucharist, there has been a "transubstantiation" of wheat into bread. The "substance" of bread is the immanent unity of a set of causalities and finalities. This case differs from that of the bottom of a bottle which I use as an ashtray (example suggested by J. de Baciocchi): in the latter case I have changed the finality but the object has remained the same and can once again become the bottom of a bottle. Bread cannot become wheat again. . . .

In view of what has been said, the judgment of identity ("This *is* my body") at the level of being is fundamental. I am not evading the issue or playing on words. For at the level of being a choice must be made: "The bread remains bread or it becomes the body of Christ."[42] That is why the words *transfinalization* and *transignification*, though accurate as far as they go, are inadequate to the extent that they could suggest a merely extrinsic change. "Substance" supposes a unity of both causality and finality: Christ acts on this bread and wine in a manner which we cannot represent to ourselves but which has its basis and counterpart in the action which he exercised on his own body during his passion.

The situation being what it is in our cultural world, it is understandable that, without surrendering anything of what has just been said, the documents on eucharistic agreement should avoid the "boobytrapped" word *transubstantiation*. The Les Dombes document, for example, clearly emphasizes the action of Christ "who binds himself in his words and in the Spirit to the sacramental act, the sign of his presence given."[43] It avoids the word "substance" and speaks instead of the "reality given in the signs of the bread and wine" and of "ultimate truth." The judgment of identity is unequivocal: "They [the bread and wine] are henceforth, in their ultimate truth, beneath the outward sign, the given reality," that is, his body and blood.[44] A helpful notes adds: "This does not mean that Christ is localized in the bread and wine or that these latter undergo any physico-chemical change."

Sesboüe also notes that the Council of Trent took up three subjects which are on quite different levels and that its procedure in dealing with them differed in important ways: on the first two subjects (real presence and change in the eucharistic elements) it reached its decisions without hesitation, while on the third (the word "transubstantiation") there were numerous discussions.[45] He concludes:

> The term "transubstantiation," taken in isolation, is not the subject of a dogma. The dogma defines the real presence given by Christ in the Eucharist. What the Church has always maintained is that the word "transubstantiation" is very apt for expressing this presence. It has never said that it is impossible to give authentic expression to the presence in another vocabulary. This is why it has never cast doubt on the correctness of the eucharistic faith of the Orthodox Churches, even though they have always refused to use the word "transubstantiation."[46]

2. The Duration of the "Real Presence"

The word "transubstantiation" is an attempt to define how the Lord makes himself really present during the liturgical action. It leaves open, however, the question of how long the presence lasts. Is it limited to the time of the celebration or does it continue beyond this? I shall try to answer this question as an exegete by approaching it from two points of view.

(a) If Christ has a lasting presence in the bread and wine, it is not because of any physico-chemical change in these foods,[47] but solely in virtue of his word. Since, therefore, his word has supra-temporal validity, *the consecrated bread and wine cannot return to the profane world as long as they remain assimilable food.*[48] This explains why the Dombes Agreement, in keeping with an already ancient tradition, urges "respect" for the reserved eucharistic sacrament.[49] The Orthodox have always placed the reserved sacrament behind the iconostasis, and Catholics have always put it in a privileged place in the material building which symbolizes the Church made up of living stones. Does not the Eucharist "make the Church"?

(b) The preceding answer needs to be completed by a proper understanding of the words of consecration, which do not say simply "This is my body," but "Take! This is my body for you." Jesus is not satisfied to say, through the words of the officiating priest and by the power of the Spirit, that he is here in this new mode of presence. He says more specifically that this presence seeks encounter. Far from being static, it is an invitation, an urgent call, to receive this eucharistic bread. The presence of the Lord in the eucharistic gifts cannot, therefore, be reduced to a simply "being here." Moreover, the word "gift" can be misleading; in the Eucharist there is in fact rather a "Giver"; by his action, and through his Spirit, the risen Lord seeks to give his very person to the Church and thereby awaken in it an active remembrance of the divine covenant.

VIII
The Words Over the Cup

Markan Tradition (M)		Antiochene Tradition (A)	
Matthew	Mark	Luke	Paul
And, having taken a cup	And, having taken a cup	And the cup likewise after the supper,	Likewise also the cup after the supper,
and having given thanks, he gave [it] to them,	having given thanks, he gave [it] to them; and they all drank of it.		
saying: "Drink of it, all of you,	And he said to them:	saying:	saying:
for *this is*	*"This is*	*"This cup* [*is*]	*"This cup is*
my blood	*my blood*		
of the covenant	*of the covenant*	*the new covenant in my blood*	*the new covenant in my blood."*
which [*is*] *shed* for the multitude for the forgiveness of sins."	*which* [*is*] *shed* for the multitude."	*which* [*is*] *shed* for you."	

The words over the cup are unusually rich in content, since they sum up in a very brief form the meaning and significance of the life of Jesus of Nazareth.

Jesus has unwearyingly preached the reign of God and as a result he is now faced with imminent death. He has gathered a group of faithful disciples around him. In these final hours he must tell these followers the meaning of the present and the future in God's plan. Two terms sum up this message. First, he no longer preaches simply the "reign" of God, but announces the *covenant*, a term that calls to mind the long historical journey of Israel and speaks of God's presence to his people. Jesus tells his disciples that the covenant with God is now definitely renewed, that is, that eternal life is given to him and that he shares it with his disciples by giving them the cup to drink.

This life comes to him, however, through death; that has always been the ultimate lesson he has taught his disciples. Here it provides the second key term in the words over the cup: the *blood shed.* It is useless for them to preserve their life; if they do, they will lose it. On the contrary, they must lose their life, for then they will gain it for good.[1] Life is given to those who accept the risk of death in fidelity to the covenant. At this point the reader must not reverse the elements of the problem. The revelation Jesus is giving here is concerned not with death as something supposedly to be sought but with the life that comes through death. The order of precedence is radically important, for if the elements are reversed one ends up connecting the death of Jesus solely with redemption from sin or with what is called "reparation," whereas in fact the goal in view is the fullness of life.

The words over the cup require a revision of the very idea of sacrifice. As I shall show, the Eucharist is essentially a "sacrifice of praise" in which the disciples glorify God for having made life victorious over death in Jesus.

I. SETTING OF THE WORDS

The words over the cup, which bring the account of institution to an end, have come down in two traditions, the Markan (M) and the Antiochene (A), each of which inseparably links "covenant" and "my blood that is shed." The covenant with God is proclaimed; that through which this covenant comes to human beings is the blood of Christ. The two traditions differ in the way in which the two terms are correlated. The cup is identified with "the covenant in my blood" (A) or with "my blood of the covenant" (M). In both cases, to drink of the cup offered by Jesus is to become a beneficiary of God's covenant. But for A, to drink is to enter into the covenant established by the blood of Jesus, whereas for M it is to receive the blood of Jesus insofar as it is covenant blood. The difference in emphasis must be taken into account in interpreting the words. As for the nuances peculiar to each tradition—"for you" (Lk) or "for the multitude" (M), "for the forgiveness of sins" (Mt)—these will be explained after I have examined the elements common to the two traditions.

In addition to having an almost identical form, the words over the cup resemble the words over the bread in three important ways. First, they too occur in a *dialogical context.* They follow upon the giving of the cup to the guests and are intended to explain the meaning of this action. They explain why the disciples have already drunk (Mk) or why they are invited to do so either explicitly (Mt) or implicitly (A). Luke expressly says that the blood of Jesus is shed "for you" who are present, "you" to whom he is speaking. The words must therefore be read not apart from this context, but precisely as an invitation to the guests to share individually in the action of Jesus and to receive the benefits that flow from it.

Second, like the words over the bread, those spoken over the cup belong to the *prophetic genre,* that is, they comment on a meaningful action and are meant to be "efficacious." Thus the bread and the cup have similar meanings: both have to do with nourishment taken by eating or by drinking, which together form one complete action. This is important because it shows that there is question not of purification but of an increase of life. The prophetic action of Jesus is effective in increasing life through communion with him.

The third resemblance is that both sets of words use *symbolic language.* Consequently, the verb "is" does not directly assert a material identity between "wine" and "covenant" or "my blood." This claim is confirmed by the fact that Jesus speaks of "cup" and not of "wine." The verb "is" paradoxically unites the signifier "cup" with a signified that is defined differently in each tradition. As in the case of the bread, the cup *is and is not* the cup and the reality which it proclaims.

These resemblances are accompanied by two differences which make it possible to pinpoint the special character of the words over the cup.

The first difference comes from the context. According to M, Jesus said a "blessing" over the bread, but here he "gives thanks."[2] What is the point of this? There is doubtless an echo of the historical fact that the second set of words was said "after the supper" (A). But there is more to the expression as can be seen from the content of the verb. In ending his eucharistic action Jesus does indeed offer thanks for the meal that has been eaten, but his words make it clear that the meal is not an ordinary one but one in which the plan of God—the establishment of the covenant through the blood of Jesus—is brought to fulfillment. As in the *tôdâ* of the old covenant,[3] Jesus completes his journey by relating himself to the plan of God to whom the glory belongs. The Church of the second century will likewise sum up its "Eucharist" precisely as an act of thanksgiving to God.

The other difference is in the fruit acquired by the action of Jesus. The final "unity" between God and human beings which Jesus celebrates is symbolized by the cup itself, which is one and, unlike the bread, cannot be broken up. The bread shared was one in the hands of Jesus but it then became many small pieces; by receiving it the many disciples were to become one and even, according to the words over the bread, the one body of Christ. The cup remains one even while the disciples drink from it, just as does the covenant, that inclusive reality that comes from the one God and has become personal in the one Jesus Christ.

The likenesses and differences of the two sets of words already give an idea of the advance made in moving from the one to the other. Like the bread that is shared, the cup is, of course, distributed; moreover, the two sets of words have the same structure and announce a new union of Jesus and his disciples. But the words over the cup complete those over the bread. In what way? Not because the blood and the body are supposedly the two components of the human being,[4] but because the second statement makes some further points. The words over the bread undoubtedly express the unreserved gift of Jesus and his desire for communion with the disciples; but they leave unsaid the relation of this final gift to the plan of salvation that is known as the covenant. The words over the cup make known to the disciples the full meaning of Christ's activity, which was wholly in the service of communion of life between God and human beings and which now climaxes in a violent death that is freely accepted out of fidelity.

II. QUESTIONS OF TERMINOLOGY

If I am to comment in an orderly manner on the two traditions of the statement over the cup, I must first determine the meaning of the principal words which are common to both but whose full meaning may escape the reader.

Cup

The word "cup" has a number of metaphorical meanings in the Bible,[5] two of which seem to be used in the text. Drinking together during a meal usually symbolizes the fact that the guests form a community; from this point of view the cup is a "cup of communion" with Jesus and among the disciples themselves, especially since, contrary to the custom of the day,[6] only one cup is used. In the description given by Paul, who emphasizes the divine origin of the unity symbolized, this cup is a "cup of blessing" (1 Cor 10:16).

Should reference be made, in virtue of the context, to the "sprinkling cups" in which, in Old Testament sacrifices, the blood of immolated animals was collected for sprinkling?[7] The parallel is at a quite superficial level. Nor should we imagine, even though there is question of the shed blood of Jesus, that the cup here is the cup of God's anger, as though God were taking vengeance on his Son for the sins of human beings.[8] On the contrary, the cup taken by Jesus is drunk just before the Hallel and is, in the psalmist's phrase, a "cup of salvation" (Ps 116:13).

In the eyes of Jesus this cup probably had a second meaning which was likewise a classic one in the Bible. "Cup" often means the fate in store for someone; thus Jesus asks the sons of Zebedee, "Can you drink the cup that I shall drink?" (Mk 10:38f). He is referring to the cup which in Gethsemane he will ask the Father to remove from his path (Mk 14:36) and which he now accepts because it symbolizes the covenant won by his fidelity unto death. He knows that God will bring him safe and sound through the decisive hour (Jn 12:27).

Covenant

Though I shall not attempt to outline here the very complex theology of "covenant," I must describe in broad lines what the Bible understands by this term."[9]

In his love-inspired plan God made a pact between himself and his people whereby he guaranteed them not only life but all blessings: land, fertility, descendants, and so on, provided they on their side observed the prescriptions set down by the Lord himself. This covenant was not conceived as a "contract" between two equal partners,[10] but as a treaty between a sovereign and his vassal. The former promises certain advantages, and the latter binds himself by an oath of fidelity. The covenant, in which the sovereign always has the initiative, has thus two constitutive elements: a real agreement between the parties, and the observance of set conditions.

The first element, the agreement, affects both parties, God and the chosen people, but there is an immediately evident difference between them. God is Lord of heaven and earth, while Israel is only a particular people. From the beginning God declares his openness to all the nations for whom Israel is called to act as a priestly mediator (Ex 19:5f). This projected expansion of the covenant will become a reality only at the end of a movement of concentration. The covenant is first made with Israel and its ancestors, but it then settles upon David and finally on the Servant of God as depicted by Isaiah.[11] The movement of concentration comes to its term with the death of the Servant, but it is followed by a movement of expansion in which the "multitudes" receive justification. Such is the universal scope of the covenant as planned by God and concentrated at this point in Jesus.

The second element, the obedience of the people, likewise undergoes a development. God is looking for a faithful servant who does not betray the agreement made with him. But how is he to win the required obedience from this stiff-necked people? For if the aim of the covenant is a communion of life, it supposes an agreement of wills. God's will cannot change, since he is faithful by his very nature, and therefore it is the will of the people that must gradually alter for the better. The transformation takes place in a movement from the external to the internal. In the beginning, the law, which expresses God's will, takes the form of a code of precepts, though it is not limited to this. In its source the law is basically God himself expressing his desire and love and seeking to establish a communion with his people. He will therefore interiorize the law in them until it becomes his very Spirit acting in their hearts and eliciting the proper response from them. In this sense the covenant becomes a "new covenant," to use the phrase that is repeated in the Antiochene tradition.

This first transformation leads to a second which prepares the way for New Testament revelation. In the beginning, two types of condition were required of Israel: the practice of a cult determined by precise rules and the practice of justice in everyday life. But the concern for ritual observance often got the upper hand over a concern for a life according to the commandments and even became dissociated from it. Thanks to the preaching of the prophets this deviation was gradually unmasked, and it was realized that cult has value only if conduct is upright; more than that, fidelity in everyday life, inspired by the clinging of the heart to God, is the authentic "sacrifice." These two conditions are combined and expressed in what the New Testament calls "spiritual worship," that is, a life that is truly guided by the Holy Spirit and that offers true worship to the Father.

In my blood which [is] shed

Whatever the biblical background of each of the two traditions,[12] the blood in question here is literally the blood of Jesus.

The "my" which controls the phrase shows beyond a doubt whose blood it is that is shed.

In general, blood is regarded in the Bible as "the soul of the life" and belongs to God alone.[13] This belief has two corollaries. The first is existential: no one has the right to "shed the blood" of human beings, that is, to kill them.[14] The second is ritual: blood has a sacral character and therefore may not be consumed along with the flesh in cultic meals following an immolation but is set aside in order to be poured out on the altar, which represents God. The blood is thus "given back" to God.[15]

In reading the words of Jesus over the cup must the interpreter opt for an existential meaning or for the Old Testament cultic meaning? The answer is not easy but the existential meaning seems required by two evident literary data. First, the verb "shed" (Greek *ek-chinnō*) is used exclusively, at least in the New Testament, to describe the violent death of a human being. It is taken from the commandment in Genesis and is used above all of the death of martyrs and, more particularly, of persecuted prophets or the suffering just man.[16] The same word is used in describing the deaths of Jesus and Paul.[17] In saying that his blood will be shed Jesus thus shows that he is going wittingly to his death.

On the other hand, the verb "shed" is not the one currently used in cultic literature, which instead uses "sprinkle."[18] To this may be added the fact that there is a basic difference between the action of sprinkling and the action of "drinking." The disciples are not being invited to use the cup in order to sprinkle themselves with the blood of Jesus;[19] they are being invited simply to drink it. Consequently, there is question not of the purification gained from expiatory sacrifices through the sprinkling of the sacrificial blood,[20] but of a drink and therefore of increased life. This remark is enough by itself to guide the symbolic interpretation of Jesus' action.

Why is the blood of Jesus shed? The answer sometimes given is that this was "God's plan," as can be seen from the many occurrences of "it is necessary" or "it was necessary" in the gospel tradition. The phrases were the fruit of Christian reflection on the event, as the disciples of Jesus sought to situate the scandalous happening in a plan foreseen from all eternity. But this scriptural understanding, taken for granted by the first Christians, requires some clarification. If Jesus "must" pursue his mission to the end, this is because he is motivated by love. If the "must" is turned into an arbitrary divine decree, God becomes a kind of tyrant who "takes vengeance" on his own Son for the sins of humankind. Since I have discussed this subject at length in my previous book,[21] I shall simply remind the reader here that the death of Jesus was caused directly by malicious human beings who responded in this way to the unyielding fidelity of God's envoy; it was the climax of the long history of persecution inflicted by human beings on the prophets and the upright. Christian faith sees in the fidelity and love of Jesus the beginning of a new human race that is reunited to God in its depths of its being.

The preposition "for" (hyper)

Jesus says that his blood is shed *for* the disciples and for all human beings. The preposition has commonly been understood as taken from the cultic language of the Old Testament and as therefore requiring a sacrificial interpretation of the cross. I have already gone into this matter in connection with the words over the bread and shown, I trust, that *hyper* need not have this cultic sense but can be understood as meaning "in our favor."[22]

III. THIS IS MY BLOOD OF THE COVENANT
WHICH IS SHED FOR THE MULTITUDE

The formulation of the statement over the cup in the Markan tradition is taken word for word from what Moses says at the covenant sacrifice on Sinai.

The Sinai account

After receiving the tablets of the law ("the Book of the Covenant"), that is, the decalogue[23] or covenant code,[24] Moses comes down from the mountain and joins the entire people in a "communion sacrifice." It is at this point, when the people pledge themselves, that the covenant is effectively made. Here is the text:

> [6]Moses took half of the blood [of the immolated animals] and placed it in cups; with the remainder of the blood he sprinkled the altar. [7]He took the Book of the Covenant and read it to the people. The people said: "Everything that Yahweh has said we shall put into practice, we shall obey it." [8]Moses took the blood, sprinkled the people with it, and said: "Here is the blood of the covenant

which Yahweh has made with you on the basis of all these prescriptions" (Ex 24:6-8).

The sacrifice described here is par excellence the "communion sacrifice" that unites God and the people. The account of it has no parallel in the Old Testament,[25] since this is the only instance in which the blood is sprinkled not only on the altar but on the people as well.[26] The characteristic traits of a covenant are to be found here: God, who has taken the initiative by calling Moses to the mountain, has stipulated the conditions of the "contract," and the people now bind themselves to observe them.[27]

What, then, is meant by the phrase "blood of the covenant," which occurs in Moses' explanation of the rite he has just performed? After the immolation, which does not signify "human suffering" but is necessary in order to procure the blood, two ritual actions (sprinkling of the altar, which stands for God himself, and sprinkling of the people) frame a dialogue that brings about a contract (Book of the Covenant on God's part and promise of fidelity on the people's part). The rite supposes the contract for which it provides a framework, and is not the same as the contract; it makes it possible to *symbolize* the communion effected between God and the people.

Communion sacrifice and "expiatory" sacrifice

Since the Markan formulation refers to a communion sacrifice, I must briefly explain the place of such sacrifices within the sacrificial cult of the Old Testament and Judaism.[28] In addition to communion sacrifices[29] there were sacrifices of "expiation," which gradually became the predominant type in Israelite sacrificial cult (sacrifices of reparation, sacrifices for sin). In these, blood had "expiatory" value; that is, thanks to it, the sin of the people was wiped away, although in fact it was firmly believed that Yahweh alone did the forgiving.

"Expiation" became so large a part of Jewish thinking that a first century targum turns the account of the covenant in Exodus into a expiatory ritual: "Then Moses took *the half of* the blood [from the immolation] *that was in the bowls for sprinkling,* sprinkled *the altar with it to make expiation for* the people, and said: 'Here, *this is* the blood of the covenant which Yahweh has made with you on the basis of all these prescriptions'" (Targum on Exod

24:8).[30] No longer does Moses sprinkle the people; instead the author makes the action of Moses conform to the sacrifices of expiation of his own time, as the italicized words show.

The letter to the Hebrews proceeds in a similar manner, while combining texts from various sources:

> [19]When Moses had proclaimed each commandment of the law to all the people, he took the blood of calves and goats, and then some water, scarlet wool, and hyssop, and he sprinkled the book itself and all the people, [20]saying: "This is the blood of the covenant which God has commanded for you" (Heb 9:19–20).

In the context of the "new" covenant the author of the letter to the Hebrews alters the original meaning of the Mosaic sacrifice by changing blood from a symbol of communion into a means of purification.

This is not the place to reflect on what "sacrifice" is,[31] but it is important at least to realize how much human beings are inclined to concentrate on their own "sin" and to seek deliverance from it by all sorts of means. Fortunately, Jews continued to offer sacrifices of praise, thus making it possible to go back to the authentic tradition of covenant sacrifice as found in Moses' sacrifice at the foot of Sinai. When Moses spoke of the "blood of the covenant," he was explaining the sense in which blood expressed a communion of life between the people and their God, since he could presuppose the practice of the law that was written down in the "Book of the Covenant."

My blood of the covenant which [is] shed for the multitude

Jesus says: "This is my blood of the covenant." The word "my" indicates as it were a monopolization of the Mosaic formula, for when Jesus takes over this ancient way of expressing the making of a covenant, he radically transforms it.

Just as blood joined altar and people, so Jesus is both on God's side by reason of his mission and obedience and on the side of human beings by reason of his death. He links God and humankind: his blood joins the two. There are thus differences between the action of Jesus and the sacrifice of Moses or later Jewish sacrifices. First, the blood in question is not the blood of animals but the shed blood of Jesus himself. In the past God had granted forgiveness on the occasion of blood being shed that was exterior to the offerer; now he grants it on account of the blood which Jesus himself sheds because of his utter fidelity to the covenant; in Jesus the covenant with God is henceforth established.[32]

Another difference is that the blood is not sprinkled on persons who receive it passively; rather the cup must be "drunk" in accordance with the command of Jesus. This means that the blood requires some cooperation from the disciples. It is not possible, then, to interpret the effectiveness of this blood of Christ in the categories of "magic." The dialogue which Jesus has instituted with his disciples continues in their action of "drinking the cup" which is offered to them.

Using a different vocabulary I might say that in the action of Jesus Jewish sacrifice passes from the realm of figures to the realm of reality, from ritual sacrifice to personal sacrifice. The same passage marks the whole of Christian life. The prophets had strongly emphasized interior dispositions and the practice of justice. Paul, their authentic heir, makes clear the sense in which Christian worship must become a "spiritual worship":[33] obedience and love alone define the scope both of the personal sacrifice of Jesus and of Christian cult.

The letter to the Hebrews, for its part, reinterprets the sacrifice of Sinai in the categories of purification: the death of Jesus is the final sacrifice that liberates human beings forever from the sacrifices of the old covenant.[34] The author shows an "almost incredible boldness"[35] in daring to make the death of Jesus a prolongation of cultic sacrifices, even if a prolongation that is also a fulfillment and completion. It may be said with many modern authors that the sacrifice of Jesus is, in a sense, an "anti-sacrifice,"[36] for the "my," which is the controlling word in the statement, shows that there has been a passage to an order other than the ritual and that from now on the covenant is made real through "spiritual worship."

The Markan tradition draws upon Isaiah when it specifies that the blood is shed "for the multitude,"[37] that is, for all human beings. The perspective peculiar to Isaiah will be discussed in the next section, for it had a long history. But even the simple statement ("for the multitude") already creates a major problem which I sketched earlier in my short study of the preposition *hyper*. In order to grasp the meaning of *hyper*, it is necessary to appeal to Jewish belief regarding expiatory sacrifices; the fact remains, however, that the Jewish mind of the New Testament period was convinced that a given set of rites (those of Kippur, for example) could of itself bring God to grant his forgiveness to the entire people. How could this have been?

In my book *Face à la mort: Jésus et Paul* I tried to show that Paul is able to use several different vocabularies. Among these one that draws upon the symbolism of the courts helps to understand or, more accurately, to express the anomaly I have just described. This judicial language supposes a semitic anthropology according to which the human race is not a crowd of individuals but, first and foremost, a *single* reality that is created by God. Thus Paul believes he can solve the problem by appealing to the first Adam: just as the sin of Adam had universal consequences, so the action of the opposite prototype, Jesus, affects all human beings.[38]

For the forgiveness of sins (Mt)

Only Matthew extends the interpretation of the words over the cup by adding that it brings the forgiveness of sins. In so doing he makes explicit a biblical idea, namely, that the covenant pre-supposes the forgiveness of sins. Matthew follows Isaiah more closely than Mark does;[39] as a result, for him the death of Jesus has as one of its functions to expiate for sins.

Matthew thus reminds us of what is indeed an important aspect of the death of Christ. If I have insisted on showing that the essential thing in the Markan and the Antiochene traditions alike is the gift of the covenant, this does not mean I have forgotten the very condition of an authentic covenant, namely, the forgiveness of sins. It is good, therefore, that Matthew should recall this dimension of the mystery of Christ's death.

Conclusion

The symbolism of "drinking the cup" is ample confirmation that the words of Jesus over the cup are centered and based not on expiation and on the sin from which he sets human beings free but on the life-giving covenant. As I pointed out earlier, Jesus does not ask his disciples to "sprinkle" themselves with his blood; he tells them to drink of the cup. People drink, however, not to purify themselves but to nourish themselves and live more fully. In con-nection with baptism pastors insist on the necessity of immersion in the water that purifies human beings of sin, and the condition should evidently be fulfilled. But a constant recall of this kind of purification can cause the very intention of the text on the Supper to be obscured and narrowed. The emphasis in Jesus' words over the cup is on the invitation to share in the covenant which gives life in abundance.

IV. THE NEW COVENANT IN MY BLOOD
WHICH IS SHED FOR YOU

The Antiochene formulation focuses attention directly on the covenant, since the cup is identified with the covenant, which is called "new" in accordance with Jeremiah. On the other hand, the formula also speaks, with Isaiah 53, of blood that is shed, and it thus transforms the tradition of the communion sacrifice reported in Exodus. A brief survey will situate these various dependences.

The new covenant

The history of the Israelite people was made up of violations of the covenant and subsequent efforts to renew the pact with Yahweh. After many fruitless attempts at renewal,[40] the "Book of the Covenant" was rediscovered in 622 under King Josiah.[41] The discovery gave rise to the "Deuteronomic Reform," which restored Israelite cult to its proper form and of which Jeremiah was a strong proponent.[42] The reform effort, however, did not achieve lasting success. Why the new setback? At this point the prophets had to ask themselves a fearful question: Shall we continue in the same direction, or must we look for something new?

One thing is certain: many prophets remained convinced that since the covenant was from God it must, despite everything, endure through the generations. Yes, they said, in the end God will win out because of his own fidelity, his *hesed*.[43] It is at this point that Jeremiah's originality appears. Until he came on the scene, it had been human beings, led by the kings, who had taken the initiative in efforts to renew the pact; for Jeremiah it is God himself who will act. This prophet no longer speaks of "renewing the covenant," but rather of a "new covenant" (Hebrew: *berît hadassa* = Greek: *diathēkē kainē*):

[31]Days are coming, says the Lord, when I shall make a *new covenant* with the community of Israel. [32]Not like the covenant which I made with their fathers when I took them by the hand to lead them out of the land of Egypt. They broke my covenant; but I remain master among them, says the Lord. [33]This is the covenant I will make

with the community of Israel after these days, says the Lord: I will put the law in the depths of their being and write it on their hearts; then I will be their God and they will be a people for me. [34]No longer will they have to instruct one another, telling one another: "Know the Lord!" For they will all know me, from the least to the greatest, says the Lord, because I will forgive their wrong-doing and no longer remember their sin (Jer 31:31–34).

This prophecy of Jeremiah, even though radically new, is fully in line with the tradition; it explicitly[44] repeats God's plan as described at Sinai: Yahweh is the God of Israel, and Israel is his people. The dynamic movement inherent in the covenant will reach its term on the last day, thanks to a renewal that does not originate in human beings but will nonetheless penetrate their very hearts.

Jeremiah's only concern is the newness of this covenant; he sees only its fulfillment and says nothing of any rite, for the law of God will be wholly interior. Ezekiel says the same thing some twenty years later:

I will give you a new heart,
I will put a new spirit in the depths of your being. . . .
I will put my spirit in the depths of your being,
and I will make you walk according to my laws. . . .
You shall be my people, and I will be your God (Ez 36:26–
    28).

The law is thus none other than the very Spirit of the Lord. The code given at Sinai had remained external to human beings, merely telling them what they had to do in order to please God. By the gift of the code God had indeed already revealed his will to them and had come to meet them, but now Jeremiah and Ezekiel proclaim that God will no longer simply issue his commandments, his law: he will give *himself* in his Spirit. No longer will it be up to men and women to accept the precepts and then do the best they can (offerings and sacrifices, acting justly, etc.) to live in communion with God; now God himself will come and produce fruits of holiness within their hearts.

The prophecy of the new covenant did not, however, have any profound effect on Jewish life. The tendency already manifested in the time of Josiah was greatly strengthened in the period of the return from exile under Ezra and Nehemiah,[45] as the latter erected the hedge of the law around Israel. The history of Judaism continued to be marked by an increasing concentration on the observance of the law (and sacrificial practice).

This was the case, for example, in the monastery of Qumran, near the Dead Sea, which by the time of Jesus had for two centuries been sheltering the members of the "community of the new covenant"[46] or "of the eternal covenant."[47] These individuals looked upon themselves as the chosen remnant of Israel, to whom the Teacher of Justice had been given.[48] In their belief in divine forgiveness and in their practices they displayed indeed some resemblances to the Christian faith.[49] Their sacred meals, moreover, had nothing in common with the sacrifices in the temple, but simply expressed a deep longing for the coming of God's reign. On the other hand, nothing suggests the kind of interior renewal that Jeremiah had predicted. The determination of the Qumranites to be completely faithful to the law did not point to the existence of a truly new community but rather to efforts at renewing a community still living under the old system. Not in this way was the prophecy of Jeremiah to be fulfilled, but thanks rather to those who prepared the way from afar for the other element in the Antiochene formula: the shed blood.

The covenant in my blood which [is] shed for you

Here, as in the Markan formulation, covenant and blood are again paired, a phenomenon found elsewhere only in the text in Exodus 24. This shows that the account of the sacrifice at Sinai continues to exert an influence on the tradition; the picture drawn there still serves to express the communion between God and people.

But how did Christians come to speak of a "covenant in blood which is *shed*"? The answer requires that I turn to another line of thought and behavior. The prophets had not been satisfied simply to proclaim in words the coming of the Spirit who would transform the people from within; they also remained personally faithful to the divine covenant to the point of shedding their blood for it. But they did not themselves draw conclusions from their own experience, except in the enigmatic figure of the Servant of God in Second Isaiah.

The prophecy of the Servant of Yahweh contains elements lacking in the prophecy of Jeremiah and unknown to the com-

munity at Qumran. In his concern to emphasize the newness of
the covenant Jeremiah focused his attention entirely on the ideal
he had in view. He passed over in silence the active presence of
someone who would act as intermediary between God and Israel,
as Moses, for example, had in the covenant at Sinai. Nor did he
mention the ritual of the sprinkled blood that would seal the covenant when the moment came. Finally, he did not explicitly adopt
a universalist perspective, even though this was already present in
the covenant of Sinai.[50] The poems of the Servant, however, do
include all these elements which were constitutive in the covenant
of Israel with its Lord.

Let me recall, then, the salient traits of this person who will
be the covenant in his own person,[51] since here the entire divine
plan is concentrated in a being who becomes mediator between
God and the people. What the prophet has directly before his eyes
is no longer the blood of animal victims that represented in ritual
form the commitment of the people; his focus is on the *experiential* commitment of a human being: the Servant who is faithful
unto death. This Servant, who in his person is a covenant of the
people, brings about, by the gift of his "soul," the communion
with God which the blood rite had signified.

The poems of the Servant effect a kind of linguistic shift. It is
true, of course, that existential language has the upper hand in the
texts: the Servant has exhausted himself and been despised;[52] he is
a man of sorrows[53] who "handed over *(paredothē)* his soul to
death"[54] and who because of our sins was delivered up for the good
of the multitude.[55] But this "personal sacrifice"[56] with its universal
consequences is also described in cultic terms: the Servant is the
new Moses who "sprinkles the nations"[57] and again offers the
"sacrifice of expiation."[58] The reader must not, however, be mis-
led by this cultic language, for it has become metaphorical, using
familiar categories to state an inexpressible reality: just as the sacrifice of expiation was regarded as having value for all of Israel, so
the personal sacrifice of the Servant has universal value.[59]

The prophecy about the Servant thus provides new light for
understanding how the blood shed can have universal value. On
the other hand, the prophecy seems to lack one element by comparison with Jeremiah's prophecy of the new covenant: Isaiah does
not describe the covenant as "new." But the absence of the adjective becomes understandable if we reread Jeremiah carefully, for
he describes the covenant as "new" in contrast to the "old." This
contrast, however, had no place in Isaiah because he was con-

cerned not with replacing the old covenant with a new one but with showing how the covenant was to be brought into existence, namely, by the personal work of the suffering Servant, who is a figure of an Israel that has become faithful.

Furthermore, Jeremiah explains a little further on that this covenant which he has described as "new" (only in that passage!) is the "everlasting" covenant of God with his people.[60] Well, a few years later, Third Isaiah likewise describes the Servant's covenant as "an everlasting covenant."[61] The prophecy of Isaiah is thus in clear continuity with that of Jeremiah: it shows the path which the perfect Servant must take in order that the everlasting covenant may be established.

The covenant is always on the horizon; but the means foreseen—the death of the Servant—becomes real only in a limited degree in the life of any given prophet. The development leads therefore to a call for the perfect Servant to make his appearance. There is nothing surprising in this. The historical development which I have recounted could not have been recounted if I did not know of the appearance of the perfect Servant in the person of Jesus. This fact does not involve me in a vicious circle, but simply shows the movement proper to all real understanding.

Jesus says, then, that "this cup is the new covenant in my blood which [is] shed for you." The new covenant will be established by the event of his death on the cross. According to Paul, the prophecy of Jeremiah has been fulfilled: there exists a new covenant that is made real in the Holy Spirit who fulfills the ancient law.[62] As a man of faith, Paul knows that Jesus by his voluntary death has given the Spirit and that the Spirit makes the covenant a personal reality in each believer. He supposes therefore that an act has been placed which was very different from even the most careful practice of the law and which consisted rather in a personal fidelity to the covenant, a fidelity leading even to the shedding of blood.

The words of Jesus over the cup derive their existential tonality from the "my" that accompanies "blood" and from the "for you" that establishes the dialogue between Jesus and his disciples. I may add that, unlike what is to be seen in the poems about the Servant, there is no third party here speaking of the man who will shed his blood; Jesus speaks for and about himself. The fact that blood is shed makes it possible, therefore, to recover the values not only in the tradition of the persecuted prophets and the suffering just man but also in Isaiah's prophecy of the Servant of God which had gradually been banished from the mainstream of tradition.[63] The fulfillment had to come before the prophecy could be understood.

Let me sum up. The monks of Qumran thought that they could effect a renewal of the covenant not by offering blood sacrifices but by practicing an ever more strict fidelity to the law of the Mosaic covenant, while postponing divine forgiveness to the end of time. The Antiochene tradition, however, shows that the prophecy of Jeremiah is fulfilled rather by way of Isaiah's prophecy about the Servant of God. This personage has become a reality in Jesus of Nazareth, who in fact has shed his blood for the human race. The word "blood" replaces the "soul" or "person" of Isaiah's poems. In using it, the Antiochene tradition shows that Jesus is *also* fulfilling the Mosaic covenant. But the most important thing in the words of Jesus is their "personal" perspective.[64]

CONCLUSION

The words over the cup complement the words over the bread in certain ways. In the words over the bread Jesus is asking his disciples to form a community around him whose presence will be expressed in the bread that they receive together. The words over the cup tell the disciples that through Jesus, present among them, they will enter the covenant established by the blood which he sheds for the sake of the human community.

The words over the cup make definitive use of certain Old Testament phenomena. They repeat to some extent the cultic vocabulary of the Old Testament but also transfigure it by applying it to the personal action of Jesus. Old vocabulary, new reality: this is what I would like to bring out, at the end of this brief study, on the basis of the two traditions in which the words of Jesus have been handed down. In describing these two traditions, I have no intention of giving preference to the one or the other, either on grounds of a supposed greater antiquity or on grounds of content. In keeping with the method I have been applying, I want to use both traditions in getting at the meaning of the words.

Two major contributions are in fact to be found in both traditions. The first is the revelation of the establishment of the covenant, a point emphasized in the Antiochene tradition. By drinking of the cup the disciples enter into the covenant instituted by Jesus; they thereby make real the oneness symbolized by the single cup: oneness with Jesus, oneness among themselves, and therefore oneness with God himself. The prophecy of Jeremiah regarding the "new covenant" so long awaited by Israel is now fulfilled.

The second contribution of the words over the cup is their revelation regarding the blood of Jesus. It has two aspects. First, there is a revelation of the fidelity of Jesus to the covenant, a fidelity maintained to the very end as he sheds his blood. Second, in consequence of the language used in making this revelation, there is a definitive passage from the ritual order to the personal. It is no longer the blood of animals that symbolizes the covenant, but the blood of Jesus himself; this blood, moreover, symbolizes the covenant not in a figurative way, as at Sinai, but in a real way on Golgotha and therefore in a real way also at the Supper when Jesus passes the cup. When the disciples drink the cup, they show themselves no longer satisfied to be merely "sprinkled," as passive recipients, with the redemptive blood; they are active, and they actively unite themselves to the fidelity of Jesus in order that it may be a source of new life for them.

Because the words over the cup make use of a cultic vocabulary to express an action—the acceptance of death—that belongs to the existential order, they are accompanied by certain dangers which later interpreters have not always avoided. The focus of both traditions is on the symbolic action with the cup by which Jesus expresses the fruit—namely, the covenant—of the gift he is making of himself. The action certainly implies attention to the wine in the cup, but the wine is not, any more than the bread, the direct object of interest, despite what critics sometimes suggest in discussing Mark.[65] In both traditions, the Markan no less than the Antiochene, the eucharistic action as a whole is the focus of attention; the bread and the wine are never isolated from the total action by which Jesus establishes his community.[66] Yet in later centuries the elements as such have often been overemphasized and to some extent separated from the action which gives them their meaning.

The other danger attaches to the language used. People have been quick to move back from the existential to the cultic, despite the meaning of the words themselves.[67] I am not denying, of course, that the eucharistic action is cultic in kind or that it requires rites for its performance. The point is rather that this cultic action has no coherence apart from the existential behavior whose value and meaning it symbolizes.

The words over the cup do not say everything. They must be

completed by the other data of the gospels. In particular, the words do not say in what the "new covenant" consists. The answer to this question is given by the testamentary traditions (Chapters IV and XI) and especially by the fourth gospel (Chapter XII). Instead of the account of institution, and at the point where the latter would come, John tells of the washing of feet and the "new" commandment: "Love one another!" This commandment is the new law that is written in hearts, the new covenant that is established by the blood of Jesus who gave his life for those he loves, and by the Holy Spirit who makes Jesus Christ present and enables believers to act in accordance with the covenant.

IX

The Traditions and the Event

Readers of this book will have asked themselves, perhaps impatiently: "But what actually happened?" Our Christian faith does indeed embrace Christ the Lord as confessed in the Spirit by the first Christian communities, but in the final analysis it is also based on a foundational historical datum: on a certain Jesus of Nazareth who lives in Palestine at a certain time and who carried on a ministry of word and work among his fellow human beings. It is therefore natural to want to get back to the past event—in this case, the Last Supper—to which the texts and our liturgy bear witness.

The historical quest

The question is a legitimate one, provided that it be understood correctly and that the answer be sought in the proper way. If I have deferred the answer until this point, I have done so chiefly for two reasons.

The first is *methodological.*[1] What is given to us Christians of a later time is not directly an event but a text that reports the event and interprets it in the process. In any and every quest of historical knowledge students of the past have access to the "facts" only through accounts in which these facts are presented not simply and purely as they happened but as they were reported by contemporaries. Except for the people who directly experienced the event, there is no such thing as a "brute fact" existing independently of the words used in reporting it or, consequently, of the perspective of the reporter. And even those who directly experienced it perceived it according to their subjective disposition and then transmitted it as seen from a given point of view.

157

Historians therefore have a twofold task: to expound what the texts say, and to define that of which they speak. My first and primary task, therefore, was to present the various interpretations of the event; that is what I was doing in the preceding chapters as I studied the "traditions" about the Supper. The time has now come to tackle the second task, that of explaining as far as possible the event that took place in the upper room, or of defining that which gave rise to the various traditions.

I have a second, *dogmatic* reason for deferring until now this investigation of the event itself. Christian faith does indeed presuppose a historical event which by and large can be ascertained as such. But in the final analysis faith is not based simply on this authentification of the event; if it were, we would reduce it to an act of unaided reason and would end up calling in question the intellectual honesty of those who do not accept Christianity. No, Christian faith is based on the text that has been transmitted by a community of witnesses who speak in it of Jesus Christ in whom they believe, and not simply of the Galilean whom any of his contemporaries might have met. These witnesses are the indispensable mediators of the event of Jesus who was exalted as Lord.

The essential question in this area, then, is not: "Did the event take place exactly as reported by so-and-so?" nor: "Which details are historically certain?" but rather: "How did the witnesses perceive it, and how have they transmitted knowledge of it to me?"

In looking for the answer it is not enough for me to drop my line, as it were, into the interpretations and fish out what I find more pleasing or what I regard as "earlier" from a literary viewpoint and therefore "more credible." I must accept the New Testament in its entirety, because it is the relation between the traditions that will yield the meaning. This is why in the preceding chapters I have taken into account both the testamentary tradition and the fourth gospel, even though these are only indirectly relevant to the mystery of the Eucharist.

Principles

The principles that will guide my study are of two kinds.[2] The first is *theological*. In order to proceed correctly in the inquiry I must avoid two contrary positions, both of which I regard as extreme. One is the position of R. Bultmann, who claims to have no interest in the pre-Easter Jesus; the other is that of J. Jeremias, who bases biblical theology entirely on an historical reconstruction of the words and actions of the pre-Easter Jesus. The former, in my opinion, ends up in gnosticism, and the latter gets mired in an illusory positivism; both sacrifice everything else to a fantastic search for an "origin" and differ only in locating this origin in a distant or less distant past: the primitive Church or the pre-Easter Jesus.

Unlike these two authors and many others who share their views I think that the New Testament message does not emerge from knowledge of the one or the other of the terms of the relation (which then becomes an alternative: the pre-Easter Jesus *or* the interpreting Church). It emerges rather from the very relation that connects the interpretations of the Church to that without which there would have been no interpretations, namely, Jesus of Nazareth.[3] Therefore, while I agree with Jeremias that the search for the pre-Easter Jesus is necessary, I cannot identify the truth of the message solely with an "historical residue," not even if this be supplemented by a psychological application intended to stimulate devotion or by an existential application in the Bultmannian manner. The truth of the message is to be found in the interdependence of interpretations and event. This is what determines the value and, at the same time, the limits of historical inquiry. Historical inquiry is necessary, but it becomes meaningful only as part of a complete hermeneutical effort.

The second principle is *methodological* and has to do with the criteria that make it possible to get a more accurate picture of the pre-Easter Jesus. There are two such criteria and they interact with one another.

The first may be called the *criterion of difference.* When I compare what the gospels say about Jesus with what I know of the contemporary Jewish world and early Christianity, I find both similarities and differences. I can regard as authentic that which cannot have come either from the Jewish environment or from early Christianity. The application of this criterion brings out the radical originality of Jesus, that which distinguishes him from his age.[4]

This criterion is, however, one-sided and brings with it the danger of removing the person from his environment. Jesus of Nazareth could, after all, have spoken and acted as a good Jew, as for example when he believed he would rise on the third day. Moreover, when any given expression proves to be strictly from the post-Easter period, there is the danger that on this point Christianity may be cut off from its founder. In such instances, the problem has to be put in another way: Are there equivalent ways of speaking to be seen in Jesus and the early Christians? An example will explain what I mean: Must Jesus have spoken expressly of "vicarious expiation," as some modern authors demand, or is it enough that he showed himself to be "pro-existence," a "man for others"?[5]

The second criterion is the *criterion of consistency*. It presupposes that the expressions of a personality or a teaching all come from a single center which binds the various elements into a whole. If therefore I am persuaded, by appropriate means, that this or that saying of Jesus is authentic or that this or that New Testament datum is certain, I can bring the resultant global knowledge to bear on texts which are still uncertain after analysis of them. The consistency gained, of course, might have been imposed from outside by the early Christians or by the exegetes themselves, but it alone offers a valid approach to the personality of Jesus. For example, while the eschatological perspective adopted by Jesus may justify historians in accepting this or that saying as his, it must not be forgotten that Jesus deliberately adopted a theological perspective as well.[6] The application of the criterion of consistency depends in practice on the idea that the New Testament is a single body: knowledge of the whole plays a role in knowledge of the parts.

Each of these two criteria is necessary for any more than a fragmentary grasp of the reality. The first criterion has the value of being analytical and of showing what belongs exclusively to Jesus, but even if all of its results are added together it is not an adequate tool for "reconstructing" the personality of Jesus. The second criterion has the value of creating a synthesis and making it possible to view the person of Jesus as a single whole, but it depends more than the first on the subjective outlook of the exegete. Yet the second criterion is no less necessary, and the first serves as a control over the provisional synthesis that is obtained.

For the sake of orderly procedure I shall try first to view the event through the accounts as a literary genre and through the component parts of the accounts, that is, the words and actions that are reported. Then I shall look at the event from the various angles made possible by the light of Easter.

Readers should not let themselves be too quickly disillusioned by the limited results a historian can obtain. As a general rule, what is historically certain is somewhat vague, and what is sharply defined is usually not historically certain. They should not grow impatient at having to traverse the labyrinths through which students of the event must pass, and should realize that the historian has not finished his task until he has shown what the first interpretations of the event were (interpretations that bring the sacred books to a close).

I. THE ACCOUNTS

The account of the institution of the Eucharist at the final meal of Jesus is but an episode in a more extensive narrative ("biographical" in the broad sense of the word) to which the name "gospel" has been given. On the other hand, I have shown, especially with the help of St. Paul, that the eucharistic text belongs to a literary genre other than history: it is an "etiology."[7] An account of this type, as I noted, has for its purpose to provide a basis for a cultic action regularly celebrated by a religious community; the foundational account depicts the action itself. But while the critics agree in placing the eucharistic account in this literary category,[8] the categorization gives no answer as yet to the question of the real origin of the Christian celebration: Does the account convey simply a cultic legend which the post-Easter community produced in order to validate its current practice, or does it report a remembered action of Jesus himself? To call the account an etiology is to leave this question still unanswered.

In the not too distant past some scholars claimed that eucharistic practice originated in the early community, which supposedly took its cue from the contemporary custom of sacred meals, whether Jewish or pagan. Although comparative religion is no longer so widely accepted as a tool for interpreting the information given in the New Testament, it is nonetheless important to evaluate the validity of these comparisons.[9]

As a matter of fact, even if it be allowed that the Christian community was influenced by contemporary customs, a number of questions still remain unanswered. I pointed these out in an earlier chapter when I was describing the literary genre of the account: the single cup, the words of Jesus that are of a prophetic kind and not in keeping with the customs of the Passover meal.[10]

Meanwhile there are several facts that argue for a connection between the text of the Supper and an action of Jesus of Nazareth. These facts vary in kind and importance.

In his first letter to the Corinthians Paul refers to his earlier stay in the city, in about the year 51. At that time he had passed on to the faithful the eucharistic tradition he himself had received.[11] He was therefore familiar with the content of this tradition before going to Corinth for the first time. If the formula in 1 Cor 11, that is, the Pauline account of the Supper, was of Hellenistic origin, he must have received it during his stay in Antioch in about 40–42. If it was of Palestinian origin, it must have come from an even earlier period and been in use at the time of Paul's conversion in about 35. The time that elapsed between the death of Jesus[12] and either of these dates seems utterly insufficient for the development of a cultic legend.[13] It is therefore reasonable to think that the tradition must have been inspired by, or have originated in, an action of Jesus which the community had remembered.

Another fact that argues for an attribution of eucharistic institution to Jesus is that when the gospels report other meals taken by Jesus during his ministry or by the risen Lord during the appearances, they never date these events. In the case of the Supper, however, Paul specifically says that that the action attributed to Jesus took place "on the night he was betrayed," and all the synoptic accounts say the same thing in their own way.

Finally, the testamentary tradition, which is later than the cultic tradition and independent of it, immediately focuses the reader's attention on a meal which Jesus took with his disciples on the eve of his death. This tradition embodies the memories of those who were present at that farewell meal.

These arguments for a pre-Easter historical basis of eucharistic practice lead, it seems, to only a limited certainty; that is, they provide a solid basis, but no confirmation of details. A study of the actions and words of the account will yield more specific results.

II. THE ACTIONS

Two factors seem to have been at work in the redaction of the "etiological" accounts of the Supper: the cultic practice of the Church, and historical reminiscences. Both factors influenced the traditions, each having a preponderant role in turn. At the level of the redaction of the present gospels, as I showed in Chapter IV, biographical reminiscences frame the cultic tradition (that is, the words of institution), which the seams in the text make it possible to set apart as an independent whole. Conversely, at a deeper level the cultic tradition thus preserved tended to blur the historical memories which it itself might well have been conveying, and the perspective proper to it as cultic ended by gaining the upper hand. There are three indications that this process was at work.

Although Luke is a witness to the testamentary tradition, he preserves the information about the cultic tradition by integrating it into his text—a sign that this information is regarded as indispensable.

An examination of the two branches of the cultic tradition itself shows that Mark and Matthew directly link the two actions over the bread and the cup, and are unaware of the meal that separates the two in Luke and Paul. The mention of the meal in the latter two authors is a reminiscence of an historical fact. Its omission in Mark and Matthew shows that with the passage of time celebrating Christians no longer felt any need of this reminder.

Finally, although the testamentary tradition as preserved in Luke seems to refer to a meal eaten in a Passover atmosphere, the cultic tradition has removed any explicit mention of the Jewish feast.

Let me list now the historical elements that can be detected in the present account as a whole.

(a) Contrary to the hypothesis proposed by W. Marxsen,[14] the tradition of a *meal* taken by Jesus with his disciples on the night before his passion does have historical value. First of all, this meal is a typically Jewish meal, since there is question of a "breaking of bread" and a "blessing" (or thanksgiving). Second, and most importantly, the Lukan and Pauline recensions retain a reference to this meal between the two liturgical actions; such a reference is unusual in a stylized cultic tradition. Finally, the singing of psalms that marked the end of a Jewish meal is mentioned in Mark 14:26 after the cultic action. It is doubtful that the remark is a redactional addition meant to lend the meal a Passover character, for it raises more difficulties than it resolves.[15] It represents rather a pre-Markan relic of a tradition that regarded the final meal of Jesus as a Passover meal; the preparation described in Mk 14:12–16 would belong to the same tradition.[16] This earlier tradition, however, cannot claim historical certainty, as I shall explain shortly. It is indeed certain, on the other hand, that the final meal of Jesus was celebrated in the festive manner and in a Passover atmosphere; various points in the description place this beyond doubt.

(b) I have already mentioned, as a typically Jewish aspect of this meal, the rite of the *breaking of bread*, which marked the

beginning of ordinary Jewish meals.[17] Here indeed it is said to have
occurred "as they were eating." It does not follow from this that
the meal was a Passover meal,[18] because in the time of Jesus the
Passover meal followed the same pattern as every other solemn
Jewish meal; it is practically impossible to distinguish the two.[19]

(c) The accounts tell of two *unprecedented* actions of Jesus
during the meal. His first innovation was to pass a single cup
around among his disciples. Usually the guests had individual
cups. The only text that mentions a common cup for all the guests
dates from the second century.[20] The single cup is another historical reminiscence, since it can hardly have sprung from the creative imagination of the primitive community.[21]

Another departure from Jewish custom is the words that
explain the act of giving. It is true, of course, that at the Passover
meal the children ask for explanations of various ancient rites that
are characteristic of this meal; the analogy, however, is purely formal and does not account for the words of Jesus. He acts here as a
prophet explaining *his own* symbolic gesture.[22] In addition, as I
pointed out earlier, his interpretation looks to the future and not
to the past.

These various points, then, are historically certain. The same
cannot be said of some further points that are often emphasized.
In particular, Jeremias vigorously maintains that Jesus celebrated
his final meal according to the ritual for Passover. He endeavors to
refute the many objections raised to this position,[23] and even
builds his entire interpretation of the text on this hypothesis,
which he is convinced reflects the reality. It cannot be said, however, that his arguments have convinced the critics generally.[24]

Critics ought also avoid speculating about the Jewish Passover
rites—the Passover lamb and the bitter herbs—that are not mentioned in the eucharistic texts. Jesus may, of course, have eaten the
lamb and the herbs, but if he did, no conclusion can be drawn from
the fact. Nor is there any basis for typological considerations
based on the red color of the wine that was drunk.[25] The only question calling for a response is whether or not Jesus himself ate the
bread and drank the wine; I shall offer an answer when I discuss
his words. Finally, I, like many others, am cautious about the supposed "declaration of abstinence" which Jeremias attributes to
Jesus. It can be deduced only from an interpretation of Jesus'
words which, as will be seen, does not command acceptance.

III. THE WORDS

Literary criticism makes it possible to discern behind the present recensions the following words:

This is my body which [is] given for you.

This cup is the new covenant in my blood which is shed for you.

I tell you, never more shall I drink of the fruit of the vine until I drink it new in the kingdom of God.

It is the last of these statements that provides the historian with a starting point, since it has all the signs of complete authenticity. I shall examine it first in itself and then in its context in Luke.

Mark 14:25 and Luke 22:18

According to these words, when read independently of the context in which Luke has placed them, Jesus fully realizes that his death is at hand; he also makes it clear that his own death will not halt the reign of God which he has proclaimed throughout his ministry.

An application of the criteria of difference and consistency shows that the words are authentic.[26] Jesus speaks not as a Christian would speak after Easter but as a good Jewish believer whose eyes are fixed on the end of time; nor does he show any concern about the eventual fulfillment of his words (as Christians will be concerned later on). On the other hand, he expresses himself here in a manner consistent with what we know of him from the best attested historical tradition: he uses no apocalyptic imagery but only the image of a banquet; in both the teaching of Jesus and in the Bible generally a banquet is a favorite symbol of the joy of the elect.[27] In addition, the perspective in these words remains vague; there is no Christian specification of what Jesus will accomplish; there is no thought of his resurrection or his return for a forty-day period; the end of time is not fulfilled now in his person; and, finally, the future is not made more explicit than it is in the classical predictions of the Old Testament prophets. There is only one difference, but it is an important one: Jesus is sure of sharing in the banquet on "that day."

Did Jesus utter these words at his final meal? Is there any reason to deny that he did? Not only do the three synoptic evangelists report them as said on that occasion, but their content is fully suitable to a farewell. It can be said, then, that these words give the historian access to the mind of Jesus of Nazareth in this final hour.

From a first point of view, then—that of his vertical relation to God—Jesus faces his imminent death with utter confidence that God will be victorious. He tells his disciples that he will take no more earthly meals, but only in order that he may share one day in the heavenly banquet, when the reign of God comes. The text provides a very valuable historical certainty.

Luke reports this saying at the end of a short discourse of Jesus which suggests further implications, although these are not without their difficulties:

> [15]"I have greatly desired to eat this Passover with you before I suffer. [16]For I tell you that I shall never eat it again until it is fulfilled in the kingdom of God." [17]He then accepted a cup and, having given thanks, said: "Take this and share it among you. [18]For I tell you that I shall not drink henceforth of the fruit of the vine until the reign of God comes" (Lk 22:15–18).

H. Schürmann believes that these verses are a fragment of the oldest narrative tradition regarding the final Passover meal of Jesus.[28] In my opinion, however, as I explained earlier,[29] they have a different origin: they belong to a tradition of a testamentary kind. In accordance with that tradition, Jesus, when about to suffer, says farewell to his disciples, and does so in a Passover atmosphere; he tells them that their table fellowship with him will cease until the promises of God are fulfilled.

According to a straightforward reading of this text, Jesus says that he greatly desires to eat the Passover with his disciples, but, since he is about to die, he will not be able to do so until the end of time. In like manner, by sharing a cup with his disciples for the last time, he wants to associate them with the thanksgiving he has just offered to God. This is his last evening of earthly fellowship with them. V. 18 thus says substantially the same thing as v. 16; the two verses are fully parallel and an example of a very venerable semitic tradition, thus placing us on solid historical ground. In v. 16 Jesus completes what he has said in v. 15; in v. 18 he comments on his action in v. 17, which Luke has remembered. The words of Jesus thus tell his disciples of his entire confidence in God as he faces imminent death.[30]

It would be strange if in this context of a farewell Jesus were interested solely in his own destiny. Matthew is indeed the only writer to make explicit the communal dimension ("with you") of the eschatological banquet. It is to be observed, however, that Jesus speaks of the presence of the disciples at the actual earthly meal: "I have desired to eat this Passover *with you*" (Lk 22:15) and that John brings out the purpose of Jesus in washing the feet of his disciples: to enable them "to have part with" him (Jn 13:8). At this Passover of his passion he lives out his own destiny and wants his disciples to be associated with him. By means of this final meal he symbolizes at the same time the banquet of eschatological communion. The actions of eucharistic institution thereby acquire the value of a communion that anticipates the final banquet.

Moreover, given the thinking of Jesus, can we imagine him conceiving the eschatological banquet as simply a tête-à-tête with God? In any case, his words imply a reunion. In addition, the reference to the kingdom locates the scene in the context of community. But, then, why is this aspect not explicitly stated in all the texts? The answer is doubtless that the tradition was interested primarily in preserving what had to do with Jesus and his Father, in order to emphasize the unique role of the former: he, after all, is the reason for the community's existence.

Perhaps, too, there was a desire to recall the problem caused by cessation of his earthly presence and the void left by his departure: how could there be a communion with him beyond his death? The answer is given fully in John's "discourse after the supper."[31] There, however, Jesus speaks in such Johannine tones that historians find it difficult to base their findings on these words in their present form. The same is not true of the short discourse which Luke places after the words of institution; these sayings as a whole go back to Jesus of Nazareth. In them Jesus asks the community members to live as "servants" of one another.[32] These texts undoubtedly show traces of adaptation to the situation of the Church to which Luke belonged, but they surely also express what Jesus of Nazareth might have said.

It seems, then, that Jesus foretold something regarding the community he has established around him. Anachronism must be avoided, of course: we must not ask what Jesus was thinking about the "Church" in the modern sense of this word.[33] Yet it is a fact that Jesus addresses the gathered twelve, the twelve whom he looks upon not as a group apart but as the remnant of Israel.[34] He gives instructions to these disciples who will find themselves alone after his departure, but in their persons, as the gospel constantly makes clear, he also speaks to the multitude of future believers.

The historian can therefore claim that Jesus acted as if the group of disciples was to continue in existence during the period of separation, thanks to the bond which would still unite them to his person. This is the import of the final instructions Jesus gives his disciples before leaving them.

This general but very important answer given by the testamentary tradition is supplemented in the cultic tradition by some important clarifications regarding the nature of the union Jesus will maintain with his disciples after his departure. As a matter of fact, the explicit answer to the question of the community's continued existence is given only by the words of eucharistic institution.

The words of eucharistic institution

The historian recognizes that these words are required by the foregoing behavior of Jesus; that is, the actions so solemnly described call for words to interpret them. The influence of the Christian cultic tradition has been such, however, that the historian does not dare to involve himself with them as he does with the eschatological saying (Mk 14:25). Yet he must compare them with Mk 14:25 in order to determine what Jesus was in fact saying.

(a) *The words over the bread*—"This is my body which [is] for you"—are transmitted in the context of an action that enjoys a high degree of historical probability. As I have pointed out several times, the rite of the breaking of bread, which included a blessing, was a part of every Jewish meal. On the other hand, this meal is the last which Jesus will eat with his disciples because he will soon be dead, and therefore he sets the tone by speaking mysterious words that give the classical gesture an unparalleled significance. What precisely do the words mean on his lips?

As my literary study of the words over the bread has shown,[35] the various recensions express the same thought: Jesus says that as he gives the bread to his friends, so he gives his life for them. The dialogical context and the nearness of death make the words highly probable on the lips of Jesus. Moreover, the words are in harmony with the eschatological saying: the latter speaks of a reunion at the final banquet, while here Jesus clarifies the new mode of his presence ("my body") and the meaning of his entire existence, namely, that it is a life of service ("for you").

The two criteria which I explained earlier corroborate the historical value of the words over the bread. The criterion of difference makes it clear that Jesus is not here providing any of the explanations to be found later on: there is no basis for seeing in them a prediction of his resurrection or a clarification of the precise meaning of his death. The words are not "Christian" in the post-Easter sense of the term.

The other criterion, that of consistency, likewise argues for placing the words in the mouth of Jesus. They use the "symbolic" language of which he is fond. In addition, he does not explain his action, but is satisfied to take a familiar Jewish gesture and turn it into a symbolic expression of the gift of himself which he is constantly making to others and which here includes the acceptance of death for them.

Some authors think it possible to elicit a further meaning from the words over the bread. According to them, the preposition *hyper* ("for you") shows that Jesus is here presenting his death as expiation for the salvation of the disciples or even, according to some, of the "multitude."[36] I cannot accept this interpretation. There was indeed a widespread view in Jesus' time which interpreted the cultic sacrifice of expiation as meaning that the death of the victim could expiate for the sins of the people as a whole. It is not impossible that Jesus knew of this view, although no trace of such an awareness shows in his words. In order to show that, on the contrary, Jesus is aware of this view and accepts it, the authors in question adduce the preposition *hyper*, claiming that it evidently refers to an expiatory action. But as I showed earlier in analyzing the words over the bread,[37] there is nothing to make this interpretation inevitable. The claim that this is what Jesus means really introduces into the argument a particular theological conception of his death. In my view, the words have another meaning.

As I tried to show earlier,[38] Jesus saw his death coming and did not seek to escape it but rather gave it a place in the divine plan. He situated it in the series of murders of the prophets and just men, although on a higher level than the others. For he knew that by reason of his unique relation to his Father and to all human beings, his existence had a significance extending to the entire race, just as his wonder-working activity "symbolized" the salvation that was to come upon the world.[39] In this sense, Jesus can be said to have seen his death as having a universal salvific significance. But is his language therefore the language of cult? The question calls for a nuanced answer.

First of all, I know that Jesus showed no interest in ritual sacrifices except to criticize abuses of them. The criterion of consistency forces me to ask: Why then should he, at the last moment, have altered his ways of speaking and looking at reality by adopting a terminology based on practices in which he had no interest? It is we moderns who tend to attribute to him a terminology traditional among us. Nonetheless, to the extent that by his words he establishes a rite meant to signify his sacrifice, his action has a cultic tinge to it.

Furthermore, this regrettable interpretation is based on an erroneous conception of what expiation is. In the Jewish notion of sacrifice the victim does not obtain forgiveness, God grants it on his own; the blood only symbolizes the attitude of the human being who asks God for reconciliation. Jesus does not attribute "redemption" to himself; he is satisfied to be faithful to the covenant to the end. He does know, however, that God will give his fidelity a vast and even universal significance. It is God who blesses this man who has lived and now dies so that God's reign may be established, and it is God who makes the action of Jesus salutary for the race. The idea of redemption underwent the same development as the idea of resurrection; that is, the primitive community evolved in its view of the agent at work. According to the early formulas, God himself raises Jesus; in the next stage, Jesus "is raised" by God; finally, in John, the Son raises himself. The same is true of redemption: only implicitly could Jesus have thought of himself or, at least, have spoken of himself as Redeemer.

The historian will think, then, that in announcing the gift of himself through service (Lk 22:27) Jesus opens up, without yet making it fully clear, the authentic perspective for interpreting his own death: it is a sacrifice of communion. It will be up to God to do the rest, that is, to raise him from the dead and to bestow the fruits of his life on the disciples and perhaps on the multitude of human beings.

(b) *The words over the cup*, while fundamental, cause the historian more difficulties than do the words over the bread. Let me remind the reader of the tenor of these words as established, at the end of my earlier literary study, for each of the two forms of the cultic tradition:

> This is my blood of the covenant which is shed for the multitude.
> This cup is the new covenant in my blood which is shed for you.

In giving the cup to drink Jesus symbolizes the meaning of his mission, which is to transmit the life of God through the covenant that is bound up with his voluntary death.

In the view of some authors, there is an obvious proof that these words are from Jesus himself: the call which is implicit in Mark and Matthew to "drink the blood" of Jesus the martyr was so shocking to Jewish religious sensibilities[40] that it could not have been invented by the first Christians; only on the authority of their Master could the disciples have been invited to perform an act so revolting to them.

I find the argument puzzling, even if the invitation to drink be historical. This is because the argument presupposes a strictly physical identification of the wine with the blood of Jesus that is missing from the Antiochene formulation, in which the cup is connected with the covenant. On the other hand, the texts suggest much more: the complete—personal and substantial—reality of the blood shed in the course of a violent death.

It is advisable, therefore, to take a different approach by comparing the words over the cup with the eschatological saying, which all three synoptics have (Mk 14:25 par.) and which is certainly authentic. A couple of correspondences leap to the eye: the context of imminent death in which Jesus now finds himself, and in Paul/Luke the adjective "new," which is equivalent to the "new" applied to the act of drinking at the heavenly banquet.

But there are also major differences between the two statements. In the one, the reign of God is still to come, and no information is given on how long the delay will last; in the other, the covenant, as understood in the light of Easter faith, is already present. This present actualization has no equivalent in the words over the bread, and there is question of its historical authenticity.

By his miracles Jesus certainly prefigured the reign of God and therefore the salvation of the race, and he even proclaimed that the reign was already there "among you." Nonetheless, there are two respects in which the words over the cup seem not to be in accord with Jesus' usual way of speaking. First, in the gospel sayings and discourses that are attributed to him the word "covenant" never occurs. Is it not surprising then that it should suddenly make its appearance at the Supper?

The same question must be asked regarding the overall content of the words over the cup. The words over the bread do no more than say symbolically how Jesus conceived his entire existence, namely, as an unstinting service of his fellow human beings. In the words over the cup, however, he does not simply say that this gift of himself includes a violent death for our sake; he goes on explicitly to proclaim what the awesome fruit of his "shed blood" will be. The only equivalent in the synoptic gospels to such a statement is the saying in Mk 10:45: "The Son of Man has come to give his life *as a ransom for the multitude.*" The presence of the word "multitude" makes the two statements even more akin; for even if this term was not necessarily included in the original formulation of the words over the cup, the content of these words would still be analogous since the "covenant" concerns at least the whole of Israel and is usually co-extensive with the plan of God in all its ramifications. But I have elsewhere shown at length that Jesus did not utter the Markan saying in its present form and that the words are a Christian explicitation of an authentic saying preserved by Luke: "I am among you as one who serves."[41]

In summary, the criterion of coherence, as applied both to vocabulary and to content, induces me to ask whether an explicit revelation of the significance of his shed blood and therefore of his death can be attributed to the historical Jesus.

An observation of a literary kind adds weight to the foregoing pieces of evidence. Mark's brief statement: "And they all drank of it," comes in prematurely in the account of institution, and I have inferred from this that it must have belonged to a tradition other than the cultic, namely, the "testamentary" tradition[42] which Luke uses in 22:15–18. One deduction seems obvious: Mark has combined two cultic traditions, one containing only the words over the bread, the other containing the words over the cup. This hypothesis would explain the existence of the Lukan "short text" which did not have the words of institution over the cup.[43]

Historians ask, finally, for an explanation of the juxtaposition in Mark/Matthew of *two* sets of words over the cup, one cultic, the other eschatological. Since they must regard the latter as exhibiting the better claim to authenticity, they will be inclined to think that the cultic words over the cup do not surely go back to Jesus himself, at least in their present form.

According to the Synoptic writers, Jesus conducted himself as the last of the prophets. On the one hand, he proclaimed the coming and even the presence of God's reign, and criticized the entrenched narrowness of his contemporaries with their legal subtleties and cultic formalities. Above all, he performed actions and spoke words, the implications of which his disciples would bring to light as they penetrated their meaning and applied the truth in them to various situations. In view of this process, some historians

have been led to suppose that the words over the cup do not nece-
sarily go back to Jesus himself but are the result of explicitation
by the Church. I add, however, that the cultic tradition has never
lacked these words. Moreover, although they may not be among
the *ipsissima verba* of Jesus, they are indispensable as the finished
expression, in Jewish categories, of what Jesus did for us in accordance with his Father's plan. Christian faith, enlightened by the
Holy Spirit and by experience of the paschal mystery, made these
words an expression of the mystery of salvation in its fullness.[44]

This hypothesis runs into numerous difficulties, however,
which it is useless to gloss over. These are a warning not to accept
the hypothesis without careful reflection. To begin with, in this
final hour of his life on earth Jesus could very well have used the
word "covenant" to sum up the meaning of his mission, even
though the word does not occur in any of the sayings attributed to
him elsewhere in the gospel. Furthermore, was it not natural that
at the end of this last festive meal he should have pronounced
words over the cup, and should even have done so twice? Finally,
and above all, does not the hypothesis overestimate the interpretative powers of the primitive Church? It need not be thought
impossible, then, that Jesus himself should have uttered the words
over the cup.

But do these difficulties invalidate the arguments proposed by
those who maintain the hypothesis? Readers of the present book
will recall my earlier conclusion that we cannot know with certitude the precise historical form of the words of Jesus, since the
two traditions transmitting them, the Markan and the Antiochene, are not in agreement. Readers are now being asked to take a
further step and decide whether Jesus really spoke the words over
the cup. It is quite understandable that they should hesitate; the
simplest course is to accept the historical attribution.

If, however, some decide to accept the hypothesis, others
should not criticize them on the grounds that they take from Jesus
a saying which is very important for his consciousness of his destiny. True enough, Christian faith obviously needs a historical
ground; it does not, however, require that all the words attributed
to Jesus be historical, since this faith is in Jesus the Christ, that is,
Jesus as interpreted by the primitive community in the light of
Easter. If, then, for reasons regarded as valid and sound, this or
that saying of Jesus is judged to be an explicitation by the Church
of what Jesus himself thought, Christian faith is no less authentic,
as I have tried to show in detail in my book on methodology, *The*

Gospels and the Jesus of History. In the present instance, the
words over the bread bear historical witness to the consciousness
of Jesus as he accepted death "for us" and to his will to give himself to his disciples.

In any reading of the evidence, Jesus himself provided the
basis for the symbolic or "sacramental" interpretation of his
death, since his saying is "ritual" in the sense of being symbolic.
Did Jesus therefore "institute" a rite? It seems that the answer
should be "yes," since on the one hand the strict parallelism
between bread and cup justifies us in speaking of the Markan tradition as liturgical,[45] and, on the other, the Antiochene tradition
clearly says the same when it shows Jesus saying: "Do this in
memory of me." But are these last words really from Jesus
himself?

(c) *The command of remembrance.* I said earlier[46] that the
structure of the Supper account calls for something to be said
about the future, since to the extent that the account is cultic, it
implicitly legitimizes the relation between the liturgy celebrated
by the community and the foundational event. The legitimation
would be facilitated by the connection between the eucharistic
command of remembrance and the command that is part of the
Jewish Passover feast: "This day shall be for you a memorial day"
(Ex 12:14). All this would be quite obvious if Mark's account
included the command of remembrance, since the content of this
account is eminently cultic. Yet it is precisely the Markan tradition that lacks the command. Nonetheless I have found it possible
to maintain that the command of remembrance is part of the very
structure of the account.[47]

The question remains, however: Did Jesus himself formulate
the command? The criterion of consistency requires great pru-
dence in answering. Beyond a doubt, Jesus was utterly convinced
that the group of twelve would continue after his death and be
faithful to him. On the other hand, as I have pointed out several
times, nowhere else does he ever emphasize a ritual precept.

There is a literary argument that might serve to intensify
doubts about the historicity of the command. If the precept came
from Jesus, why did it disappear from the Markan tradition? But
in my view this argument carries little weight since, as I repeated
a moment ago, the pre-Markan tradition is so "liturgical" that it
needs no command of repetition. "A rubric is obeyed and not put
into the text."[48]

There is another and better argument: Paul's duplication of

the command (he has it after the bread as well as after the cup) and the hortatory turn he gives it indicate that the eucharistic tradition has a tendency to add rather than to omit.

For these combined reasons many historians do not attribute the command to Jesus himself.[49] But then it remains necessary to show in what sense the command only makes explicit the thinking of Jesus. I shall raise this question in Section V of the present chapter, where I attempt a description of the genesis of our texts. For the moment, however, I ought at least to say how Jesus expresses his certainty (which the command presupposes) that he will continue to be present among his disciples, not simply because he will have risen from the dead but also because (he is convinced) the table fellowship which he began with his disciples while on earth will continue. The answer is that he chooses the symbol of bread, that is, of life-sustaining food, to express his lasting presence among his followers. His followers in turn regarded this symbol as necessary if they were to express his real presence among them. The disciples were not content simply to pray: "Maranatha!" They also experienced his presence during their gatherings, and to such an extent that Paul would call upon believers to "recognize" the body (1 Cor 11:29). The command "Take! Eat!" likewise makes explicit the certainty Jesus has that he is dispensing life by means of the food thus given.

IV. THE EVENT

Am I now in a position to gauge what must have occurred in the upper room in Jerusalem? My reconstruction is in any case hypothetical, and I shall be careful to point out the two possibilities that historians can see from their reading of the text. Further reflection may add new elements and enrich the following reconstruction. In the suggested text that follows I put in parentheses those elements that are challenged on historical grounds by a reasonable number of critics:[50]

In the season of Passover, when evening had come,
Jesus ate a final meal with his disciples.
At the beginning of the main course (= after the preliminary
    dishes)
Jesus takes bread and says the blessing;
he breaks it and gives it to his disciples, saying:
"This is my body for you."

At the end of meal, having taken the cup and given thanks
(and having said: "This cup is the new covenant in my
blood which is shed for you"),
he says to them:
"Never more shall I drink of the fruit of the vine until that
day when I shall drink it new in the kingdom of God."

The text as a whole is quite satisfying at first glance, despite
the difficulties which I have raised and tried to face. Furthermore,
if the words in parentheses be set aside, the remaining text con-
forms in surprising fashion to assured historical data: "Breaking
of bread," the early name for the Eucharist, is given a solid basis.
The various textual or stylistic variants in the text of the words
over the cup become more understandable, since these words do
not have behind them the solid tradition of the words over the
bread. Finally, there are two facts which confirm the reconstruction: first, Luke has the command of remembrance only once, and
this after the words over the bread; second, there is evidence that
until the third century the Syrian Churches knew of a Eucharist
using only bread.[51]

As the reader can see, the reconstruction leaves many points
unsettled. One thing is clear: by his words and actions Jesus instituted a symbolic order which Christians now call "sacramental."
But while he himself celebrated a rite that expressed the meaning
of his death in symbolic form and in ways which were in continuity with his habitual behavior, he also left his words open to
deeper understanding by his disciples. That, and not the sure
determination of an historical residue, is the essential thing. It is
therefore important to take the entire New Testament tradition
into account.

V. TRADITION AT WORK

The sole purpose of the reconstructed test just proposed is to
ensure a solid basis in past history. But the basis is not the last
word; it is rather a point of departure and allows for the further
impact of a unique experience: the experience that "Jesus who was
dead is alive!" Easter colors the interpretation of all past events.
Everything is now seen in a new light, for believers are certain that
they have entered the eschatological phase of history, not only
because they are sure of the banquet to come but also because it is
evident to them that in Jesus Christ the covenant has been sealed.

On the other hand, it is also certain that the first Christians began to gather without delay in joyful assemblies and that these meetings brought a flood of reminiscences: of the final events of Jesus' life during his passion but also of the teachings of the incomparable Master. It was in this vital atmosphere that the eucharistic tradition took shape. The reconstruction which I shall give of the development claims to be nothing more than an attempt to describe the successive changes which our present texts underwent. The "stages" which I shall distinguish should be regarded not as separate phases but rather as reflections of dominant themes in the evolution of the thinking of the Christian community.

In the beginning was the tôdâ

In their meetings the first Christians reacted as good Jews by joyously celebrating the God who had delivered his Son Jesus from death and was bringing them too into the eschatological kingdom. There was no reason now for going to the temple for the immolation of a sacrificial animal; it was enough to gather for the "meal" which followed upon the sacrifice and in the course of which they glorified God for having thus delivered Jesus from the bonds of death. They were simply celebrating the traditional tôdâ.[52]

More than anything else, and prior to any "reflection," the "breaking of bread" is marked by expressions of eschatological joy. The Lord will come; of this these Christians are convinced, as their earliest acclamations, the maranathas, show.[53] The reign of God has become a reality in Jesus, and Jesus will return. Christians thus experience now, under the veil of figures, the eschatological banquet which Jesus had proclaimed.

On the other hand, as the first Christians remember the recent past and especially the final meal eaten with the Master, they think of his death as salutary; the very fact of the resurrection which the Father has worked for him brings this aspect of his death home to them. For the moment, however, they think only of the past from which Jesus has been delivered.

The covenant concluded and the summons to remembrance

Very quickly, as the early documents show, Christians made use of the Bible to express their joy and to explain the events that had taken place. The result was two interpretations of the new situation. The prophecy of Jeremiah made it clear that the new covenant was now in existence; this line of thought gave rise to the "Antiochene" eucharistic tradition. A second line of thought went back further to the covenant sacrifice offered by Moses at Sinai; thinking of this kind was stimulated by the Passover atmosphere in which the decisive events had taken place.In both of these interpretations the controlling idea was the covenant which had finally become a reality in Jesus and in the community that gathered to celebrate.

Did the participants in these gatherings gradually become conscious of their liturgical character? This is highly probable, since we are told that "they devoted themselves to the breaking of bread and the prayers." We may therefore think that the command of remembrance, in which Jesus said that this was to be done in his memory, made its appearance very quickly. The element of remembrance would have been taken for granted by those who thought of the Eucharist as a kind of fulfillment of the covenant sacrifice of Moses. Those, on the other hand, who thought in terms of the new covenant would have had to urge themselves to the repetition of an act that would now be liturgical. This would explain the presence of the command of remembrance after the words over the bread.

The saving death

Finally, the first Christians were soon recalling the Isaian prophecy of the Servant of God; they saw Jesus fulfilling the destiny of the Servant in his own life and death. At this point the sacrifice of Jesus was seen as an expiation for the "multitude." "Expiation" served chiefly to define the meaning of the death of Jesus; it said that this death had a universal significance which turned the community outward to embrace the entire race. The preposition *hyper* then took on a more specific meaning: Jesus sacrificed himself in order to redeem from sin.

At what point did the words over the cup take shape? The answer is difficult, but it was probably when Christians began to concentrate their attention on the covenant and on the fact of the cross. The words over the cup then received a twofold formulation in keeping with the two lines of thought already mentioned: that which focused on Jeremiah's prophecy and that which focused on Moses' sacrifice.

Jesus present in a liturgy

Once the words over the cup were added a new liturgy came into being. The *tôdâ* became a sacrifice of praise commemorating the new covenant as not only obtained by the shed blood but also lived in the presence of Jesus himself.

In the Antiochene tradition continuity between the two sets of words is obtained by placing the second set "after the meal" but without venturing to specify further what Jesus did over the cup. As an ending Paul adds the command of remembrance as well as the reference to the return at the end of time.

In the Markan tradition the continuity is worked out much more carefully, to the point of making the bread and cup completely parallel.

In both, the primacy of the relational aspect of the liturgy is maintained. That is, the aim is not to teach that the elements are changed (this is presupposed) but to celebrate the covenant that has been wrought by the saving death of Jesus and that anticipates the eschatological reunion.[54]

PART III

The Presentations

Readers who have courageously followed me this far through the maze of the investigation are ready to reap the fruits of the inquiry. And in fact the time has come to present the several texts themselves. But these readers must not foster false expectations. They perhaps want to be given obvious facts and unqualified certainties, whereas in fact the results I have reached are based in good part on hypotheses. But is this not so in every undertaking in the human sciences? "Historical certitude is never more than a probability which it would seem perhaps unreasonable to question—or at least there would be insufficient reason for doing so."[1] This assessment holds for the last meal of Jesus and for the traditions which transmit recollections of it.

The inquiry has nonetheless led to the ascertainment of traditions behind the present texts. I first showed that recollections of the final meal of Jesus take two forms, the testamentary and the cultic. The cultic in turn shows two major variations: the Antiochene tradition (Lk/Paul) and the Markan tradition (Mk/Mt). Against this background I have explained the diverse meanings found in the three main statements of the cultic tradition: the words on remembrance, those over the bread, and those over the cup. Equipped with this somewhat more detailed knowledge of the elements making up the cultic tradition, as well as with the results of a first assay of the testamentary tradition, I have been able to attempt some understanding of the historical event itself. At this point, a new task presents itself: to show how the several authors composed their texts on the basis of the traditions available to them. This is the end result sought by the method known as tradition history.

What route am I to follow in studying the various presentations of the text? The critics usually proceed by examining the alterations made in the original texts. In dealing with the account of the Supper they are admittedly less confident than when dealing with the synoptic texts of the threefold tradition, and most of them allow that they cannot prove the direct dependence of Luke or Paul on Mark. They also prefer to speak of an *Ursprungsform* rather than an *Urform*.[2] Have they, in doing so, correctly applied the method of tradition history? I fear not, as I have tried to show elsewhere.[3] In my opinion, the inquiry must start with the structure of the account rather than with some form of the text that is assumed to be original except perhaps for a few nuances.

It is precisely here that the synchronic method which I applied in Chapter III, at the end of Part I, is once more appropriate. Back in Chapter III I showed that the account of the Supper manifests a *structure:* three axes—Jesus/God, Jesus/disciples, and present/future—serve as points of reference for the communication of a message, the message of a profound transformation that affects Jesus (a new manner of bodily presence), the group of disciples (who become the community of the risen Lord in this world), and their earthly meal (which becomes a communion of a new kind). In these three areas a threshold is crossed; there is a passage from one state to another. Such, in my view, is the structure of the Supper account.

The evangelists and Paul each make use of this dynamic structure according to the needs of their various ecclesial communities; this explains the variants in the content of the texts. These communities could not be asked to repeat a single text in which every word was irreplaceable; each had to speak the living word and then "translate" the message for its own use. This is still the task of interpretation even today.

In this third part of my book I treat the several recensions in different ways. I place Mark first as an example of a tradition being reused in the service of a "gospel" (X). In order not to make the discussion excessively long, I have thought it advisable to speak of Matthew only when he shows major differences from Mark. I then show how Paul actualizes the tradition by specifying its nature and significance (XI). Next to be discussed is the testamentary form which, in Luke, serves to enclose the cultic form so that the whole becomes a short "farewell discourse" (XII). Finally, in what is the climax of New Testament revelation, John the evangelist transposes the entire gospel tradition (XIII).

X
The Message of Mark

Even though Paul quotes the account of eucharistic institution some twenty years before Mark, it seems advisable to start with Mark's presentation of the last meal of Jesus. My reason is that, writing as he does as early as the 70s, he is the first to place the account of the Supper in a biographical context.

It is an interesting fact—and a source of weariness to other scholars—that no year passes without one or two articles appearing on the Markan interpretation of the Supper. On the other hand, it is disconcerting to see the variety of titles given to the passage. Here are several from the most recent publications: "The Institution of the Eucharist,"[1] "The Promises of the Last Supper,"[2] "The Interpretation of Jesus' Death and the Establishment of the Church."[3] What, then, is the meaning of the text? This is the question that must be answered at the term of my inquiry—although, when I read one quite recent study,[4] I ask myself whether any answer is possible.

My purpose is to see how Mark organized an account on the basis of the traditions familiar to him. The problem to be resolved is not an historical one but one of theological perspective. To determine what this perspective is I shall read the text in light of the different contexts in which it is placed. I shall begin with the broadest, which is that of the gospel as a whole (I); then I shall move in closer and examine the setting of the account in the story of the passion (II) and in relation to Passover, which creates the atmosphere of the chapter in which the account occurs (III); finally, I shall turn to the text itself, inclusive of the words about the heavenly banquet (IV).

183

I. SUPPER AND GOSPEL

The gospel as a whole illumines the cultic account to such an extent that the latter appears as a kind of summary of the gospel. By its very nature the gospel shows how the Supper text is to be understood; through the stories it tells about meals and about the behavior of the disciples it helps the reader to enter more deeply into the meaning of the Supper.

The cultic account must be read in the same perspective as the gospel in its entirety. What does this mean? Mark's intention is not simply to tell the life story of a man who can be ranked among the heroes of this world and whose memory he wants to keep alive. As seen by Mark the believer, Jesus is not only a figure of the past whose marvelous life is to be recounted; he is still alive now as the one who reconciled humankind to God at the cost of his death on the cross. The events related are relevant to the Christians of every age, who can see their own history reflected in them. In other words, the gospel is a "good news" which proclaims that the reign of God announced by Jesus of Nazareth (Mk 1:15) has begun for us in the life, ministry, death, and resurrection of this same Jesus. This message must be received by faith, and it is to faith that the risen Lord still addresses himself today through the Jesus who spoke the words of the Last Supper.

The eucharistic meal is the last in a series that punctuates the ministry of Jesus; at the same time, however, its special character makes it profoundly different from the meals that preceded it.

This is not the first time that the disciples have shared bread with Jesus. Have they not worked alongside him, to such an extent that they "did not even have a chance to eat" and at times had to worry about finding food for the crowds that followed Jesus or for their own small group?[5] It is quite natural, then, that at this Passover they should busy themselves preparing for their rabbi's "Passover meal" and that, once again, the action of eating together should symbolize for them the life they share with their Master.

The many meals they had shared up to this time had not left the disciples with simply the memory of table fellowship with their Master. These meals had also taught them his most important lesson, for in preferring to eat in the company of tax collectors and sinners Jesus had manifested the supreme freedom with which he overturned the barriers set up by the religious authorities in order to exclude from table fellowship, and therefore from life itself, those who did not observe the law. Those surprising meals had symbolized in a transparent way the universality of his message: the reign of God that is at hand is available to every human being. The disciples were already prepared, in principle, to hear this cardinal aspect of the message being expressed once more in the words of Jesus at the Last Supper. Here, in direct continuity with his earlier behavior, Jesus tells them that his blood is shed "for the multitude" and therefore not only for the faithful in Israel. Besides, had Jesus not explicitly said, a short time before, that the good news would be "preached to all the nations" (13:10)?

These last words are part of Jesus' announcement of the eschatological persecution the disciples will have to endure: they will be delivered up and hated even by their relatives, but those who persevere to the end will be saved (13:13). But before this prophecy of the spread of the gospel through the fidelity of its witnesses even to death is fulfilled in the course of history, Jesus himself first fulfills it perfectly and shows its full meaning at the Last Supper, where his body and blood are given "for the multitude."

The disciples could have understood all this, at least if the Supper story be understood in the light of the gospel as a whole. But did they in fact understand? The text does not say. By its silence it continues another line of development in Mark's gospel, according to which the disciples usually do not understand the situation in which they find themselves. The gospel depicts them as failing to penetrate the mysterious depths of the reality they are experiencing.[6] After the second prediction of the passion they are still arguing about who among them is the greatest (9:34); during the very last days of Jesus' life they complain about the woman who has just wasted a fortune in perfume (14:5). They do indeed assert their good will (see 14:19, 31) and are ready to act as Jesus asks them (14:23b), but they are silent in face of his sovereign action as he proclaims the gift of his life. Why is this? It is because until the centurion's proclamation of faith before the dead Jesus on the cross (15:39) no one enters into the secret of the Son of Man.

One reason for the disciples's failure to understand is that this final meal differs from earlier ones; the mysterious words over the bread and the cup presuppose faith in the mystery of the passion and death of Jesus. How could the disciples, who still had an earthly vision of God's reign, have understood that by these words Jesus was transforming the manner of his presence and thus the nature of their community?

Thanks to the setting provided by the gospel as a whole, the account of the Supper ceases to hang in the air and acquires instead the teeming richness of an extraordinary episode in an already long and extraordinary history. Its uniqueness will emerge even more fully from an examination of the passion story of which it is a part.

II. SUPPER AND PASSION

The cultic account is located in the last part of the gospel, that is, in the lengthy unit that is the story of the passion and resurrection. This narrative sequence does not simply tell of how Jesus died on the cross; it opens onto the endless horizon provided by the meeting to which the risen Lord summons his disciples in Galilee (14:28; 16:7). The two aspects of life and death are also found in the cultic account: Jesus says that he is going to die, but he also proclaims that in his shed blood a covenant is concluded in behalf of the multitude of human beings. In addition, is not the silence of the disciples in the face of Jesus' announcement and interpretation of his destiny an omen of their absence during his supreme trial? The account of the passion (in the strict sense of the term) and the resurrection unfolds in a series of events which the account of the Supper already includes in, as it were, digest form.

More specifically, the account of the Supper is located in the first part of this lengthy whole, that is, in the "private passion" (14:1–22). The first Christians regarded the sequence of events making up the "private passion" as an indispensable prelude to the "public passion" (14:43–15:47). They could not simply leave the reader in the presence of a Jesus who is almost mute, one who not only is the victim of human wickedness but also seemingly has no choice but to endure his sufferings. It was therefore necessary to show that this man who was to rise from the dead had gone knowingly and deliberately to his death. The "private passion" has its climax in the story of Gethsemane,[7] which shows Jesus first rejecting death and then accepting the fact that God his Father does not will to save him from it. The reader now knows that this man who does not open his mouth to complain when he is mistreated (see 1 Pet 2:23) has painfully but deliberately accepted the death that comes upon him. He is able, therefore, to face it, and to do so alone—a point emphasized by the pericopes surrounding the episode in the Garden of Olives: the prediction of the scattering of the disciples (14:26–31) and their actual flight (14:50).

The story of the private passion thus contains two major and overlapping themes: the inevitability of the death that already has Jesus in its grasp, and Jesus' consciousness of being free in the face of this death. Death is about to crush him, and yet, when seen from within and interpreted, its meaning changes: it is in a sense already conquered because this man who is about to die gives himself with sovereign freedom.

On the one side is the baseness that marks the conduct of the priests and scribes, then finds concentrated form in the person of Judas, one of the twelve, and finally spreads outward again to the entire group of disciples, who will abandon Jesus. On the other side is the gentle strength of this man who knows his fate to be inescapable and consents to it out of fidelity to the mission he has received and made his own.

This sharp contrast is reminiscent of the paintings of Georges de La Tour who juxtaposes light and darkness as if they were impenetrable to one another. The same juxtaposition that runs through the private passion is to be seen even in the literary organization: pericopes in which darkness prevails alternate with others in which light dominates. A quick survey of the story will make this clear.

The introduction, which places the whole account in the context of Passover, tells the reader of a secret plot: certain authorities are looking for a way to arrest Jesus and have him executed (14:1–2). Against this dark backdrop there is immediately played the scene of kingly anointing at Bethany. Not only does Jesus defend the woman's extravagant gesture: "She has perfumed my body in advance for its burial." He also predicts, in the context of what has just been done, that the gospel will be proclaimed "throughout the world." He will die, but death has no ascendancy over the good news of which he is the messenger (14:3–9). Then darkness descends again: Judas betrays Jesus (14:10–11), but it is immediately succeeded by light, as Jesus organizes his own Passover with complete freedom to dispose of everything around him: a feast is in the making (14:12–16). Once the meal begins, the horror of the betrayal returns, this time predicted once again by Jesus (14:17–21). This is followed by the account of institution, in which the death that brings cruel separation paves the way for a life of communion, the highest form of life. In addition, Jesus relates this last meal with his disciples to the eschatological banquet that he knows awaits him in the kingdom, for he is certain that God will reign victoriously (14:22–25). In a final contrast, he somberly prophesies that the disciples will scatter and Peter will deny him, but he also tells them that after he has risen he will go before them all into Galilee (14:26–31).

But the text does not simply juxtapose darkness and light and show them alternating; it also suggests that light will win out. The scenes in fact are not merely contrasted; there is also progress from each to the next. The progress is easy to detect, especially in the three episodes that culminate in the cultic account. When preparing for the Passover meal Jesus displays a real gift of clairvoyance such as is appropriate for one who is fully aware of all that is going on. He then shows himself master of the situation by revealing the presence of a traitor, even though the man has acted secretly and with guile: Jesus is an authentic prophet. Finally, he shows himself to be more than a prophet when in a symbolic gesture he gives his body and sheds his blood, thereby sealing the covenant of God with the multitude.

The reader must avoid interpreting the eucharistic words and gestures of Jesus as simply a liturgical action that introduces a rite to be observed in the future. To begin with, Mark says nothing about any repetition of what Jesus does here. Furthermore, the words over the cup do not say that Jesus "is going to shed" his blood, as though he were simply delivering a prophecy, more important indeed than those that have preceded, but of the same order nonetheless. No, the text says that he "is shedding" his blood, here and now.[8] Symbolic words or gestures are not simple announcements of what is to come; in them a reality is being enacted before our eyes, a reality that *is* and *is not* the thing said or done. In the actions and words of the Supper Jesus is "expressing" his death, he is "experiencing" it. A climax is reached here that cannot be surpassed: not only is Jesus aware of his coming death and consenting to it; his words freely make it already a fact.

By introducing the account of Gethsemane a few verses later Mark revives the contrast, but in a form which his preceding text hardly leads the reader to expect: on the one hand, at the Supper, a man who goes voluntarily to death; on the other, in the Garden, a man who wants not to die. This "conflict" in the presentation is acceptable only to a reader who approaches with respect the mystery of the personality of Jesus, a perfect human being who adheres to God without reservation but also remains fully human.

If the scenes in the Markan story are not only contrasted with one another but suggest a progress, then the comparison made a moment ago with the paintings of Georges de la Tour is inadequate. The impression which his pictures convey needs to be complemented by that derived from the works of another painter. At the end of a long artistic life Georges Roualt found a way of letting the glory of the risen Lord shine through the bruised face of the Son of Man. The light of Easter does not remain external to the darkness of the passion but penetrates it and shines through it.

III. SUPPER AND PASSOVER

The account of the passion and resurrection begins with the words: "It was now two days before the Passover and the feast of Unleavened Bread" (14:1). This chronological notation, which recurs frequently throughout the text[9] as a way of locating the events in time, is an invitation to speak briefly of the significance of this Jewish feast for Jesus and his disciples, as well as of its significance in the eyes of Mark.

The Jewish feast of Passover

Israelites were expected to make the trip to Jerusalem each year in order to celebrate the "great feast" with the family or in some other group. Lambs were slaughtered in the temple on the afternoon of Nisan 14, which ordinarily fell in April. At the same time, as a symbol of the purity of the home in which the action of him who had delivered his people from Egyptian slavery was to be commemorated, every trace of yeast was removed and the eating of leavened bread was forbidden for seven days.[10]

On the evening of this same day the Israelites were asked to celebrate the deliverance of their people. They were to recall how during this night they had been liberated from Egyptian slavery and how later on God had again rescued them from the exiles into which their constant sinning had led them.[11]

The feast was not only commemorative, it also roused in the hearts of the celebrants the eschatological hope that on some future day the Lord would deliver Israel permanently from every evil, and this through the mediation of a Messiah.[12] Is it surprising that among an oppressed people this hope should at times have been reduced to the hope of an immediate political liberation? This would explain the caution of the high priests and scribes who did not want to arrest Jesus "during the feast," since some persons looked upon him as a political Messiah and there might therefore be "a tumult among the people" (14:2).

On the other hand, the feast of Passover had in the course of the centuries acquired a very deep religious meaning, becoming as it were the epitome of God's great deeds in the history of Israel. Among the documents that might be cited to show the wealth of meaning concentrated in Passover I choose for examination the targum on Exodus 12:42, a theological text that dates from the end of the first century at the latest. I am surely not being venturesome in thinking that for Jesus and his disciples, as for other fervent Jews, the feast with its many echoes and overtones was an intense experience.

> [The night of Passover] is a night of watching and is set aside for redemption to the name of the Lord at the time the children of Israel came out redeemed from the land of Egypt. Truly, four nights are those that are written in the *Book of Memorials.*
>
> The *first night:* when the Lord was revealed over the world to create it. The world was without form and void and darkness was spread over the face of the abyss (Gen 1:2) and the Word of the Lord was the Light, and it shone; and he called it the First Night.
>
> The *second night:* when the Lord was revealed to Abram, a man of a hundred years, and Sarah his wife, who was a woman of ninety years (Gen 17:17), to fulfill what the Scripture says: Will Abram, a man of a hundred years, beget, and will his wife Sarah, a woman of ninety years, bear? And Isaac was thirty-seven years when he was offered upon the altar. The heavens were bowed down and descended and Isaac saw their perfections and his eyes were dimmed because of their perfections, and he called it the Second Night.
>
> The *third night:* when the Lord was revealed against the Egyptians at midnight (Ex 12:29; Wis 18): his hand slew the first-born of the Egyptians and his right hand protected the first-born of Israel to fulfill what the Scripture

says: Israel is my first-born son (Ex 4:22). And he called it the Third Night.

The *fourth night:* When the world reaches its end to be dissolved: the yokes of iron shall be broken and the generations of wickedness shall be blotted out; and Moses will go up from the desert (and the king Messiah from on high). One will lead at the head of the flock and the other will lead at the head of the flock and his Word will lead between the two of them, and I and they will proceed together.

This is the night of the Passover to the name of the Lord: it is a night reserved and set aside for the redemption of all the generations of Israel.

Targum on Exod 12:42[13]

This Poem of the Four Nights sums up the whole range of God's action in behalf of his people. The celebration of Passover recalls not only the foundational memory of the departure from Egypt, but also the creation of the world (first night) and the end of time (fourth night). And at the center of the text is the birth and "sacrifice" of Isaac, which recall the marvelous way in which God intervened in order to found his people; as Jewish legend has it, God triumphs over death by "raising" the son of Abraham so that the latter's posterity may continue.[14]

Each night is witness to a transformation, as can be seen from the contrasts that punctuate the text: between dark chaos and light, deadly barrenness and birth/resurrection, the death of the Egyptians and the survival of the Israelites, the chains of evil and a walking in freedom. In each instance God rescues his people from a deadly crisis in order that they may maintain and intensify their life.

The reason for this is that life belongs to God. That is what is to be understood by the expression "Book of Memorials." These "memorials" are not of a vanished past but of a Living One who is always at work. Israel does indeed "make remembrance" of its Savior God, but in doing so it celebrates, first and foremost, him who takes the initiative in "remembering" his people and intervenes in behalf of his indestructible covenant.[15]

The feast of Passover is a joyous celebration because it turns minds and hearts to the final, permanent deliverance from evil. Provided the expression be properly understood, this feast might be called the "feast of challenge." God intervenes and challenges the guilty order established by human beings that leads to subjection, slavery, and impotence, whether because work has been turned into an idol or the law has been misunderstood or religion has been abused. In this order everything becomes an instrument of oppression, oppression which God cannot tolerate and from which he wants to deliver his people. Yes, even though Passover at times becomes a tool of revolutionary political movements, it remains the feast of liberation, the feast of a God who makes it possible for life that has been crushed to rebound when set free.

Such must have been the atmosphere in which the twelve assembled. How much more deeply must the meaning of the Passover festival have entered into the mind of Jesus who knew himself destined to be delivered up to death but also to the living God who sets human beings free! But if the events reported took place in the atmosphere of Passover, does it follow that Mark was satisfied simply to call the Jewish Passover to mind in this way? Did he not wish also and above all to situate the Jewish Passover in relation to its prolongation, the Christian Passover?

Jewish Passover and Passover of Jesus

This chronological setting for the events which Jesus experienced before his passion seems to be confirmed by the emphasis placed on the account of the preparations for the Passover meal.

> [12]On the first day of Unleavened Bread, when they sacrificed the Passover lamb, his disciples said to him: "Where will you have us go and prepare for you to eat the passover?"[13] And he sent two of his disciples and said to them: "Go into the city, and a man carrying a jar of water will meet you; follow him, [14]and wherever he enters, say to the householder, 'The Teacher says, Where is my guest room, where I am to eat the passover with my disciples?' [15]And he will show you a large upper room furnished and ready; there prepare for us." [16]And the disciples set out and went to the city, and found it as he had told them; and they prepared the passover (Mk 14:12–16).

The reference is seemingly to the Jewish feast, the feast of "Unleavened Bread." A careful examination shows, however, that

while the Jewish feast provides the temporal setting, the feast celebrated is in fact that of Jesus: *his* Passover or Passage.

In its literary genre the narrative just cited is not a report of
an event or even an eye-witness testimony.[16] The elements of legend that mark the recognition of the place for the feast are reminiscent of the story of Samuel and the finding of Saul's asses (1
Sam 10:3–5). In addition, the close parallelism with the description of the entrance into the Jerusalem (11:1–6) suggests that the
later story is modeled on the earlier; since Jesus has come up to the
holy city to celebrate his Passover there, someone must have prepared a room for him, despite the fact that the city was filled to
overflowing with pilgrims from all over Palestine. Finally, the nar-
rator takes pains to show how Jesus not only acts as a
"clairvoyant"[17] but also exercises a "control from a distance" over
persons and places. Under these conditions it would be a mistake
to use the few descriptive elements in the text in order to visualize
the scene, and it would be an error to read the passage as referring
solely to the "Jewish" Passover.

In my hypothesis Mark is describing the Passover *of Jesus*.
Verses 12–16 lay surprising stress on the connection of the feast
with his person. The question which the disciples ask already
points in this direction: "prepare for *you* to eat the passover," and
Jesus accepts the emphasis, for he speaks of "*my* guest room,
where *I* am to eat the passover"; when he adds "with *my* disciples," he shows that it is *his* community that is to assemble there.
The conclusion is inescapable: as Mark sees it, the disciples prepare for the Passover which Jesus will experience. But there is
more, as I shall explain: according to Mark the Passover of Israel
is fulfilled in Jesus; and if it is fulfilled in him, then there is a transition from rites to person, from the ritual order to the personal
order.

Confirmation of my hypothesis is to be seen in the fact that
the description of the Supper contains no reference to the Passover
lamb or to the bitter herbs or to any other detail of the Jewish Passover meal.[18]

From the Passover of Jesus to the Christian Eucharist

Mark's emphasis on the Passover of Jesus reflects profound
understanding on the part of the primitive Church, which saw the

Israelite Passover as authentically fulfilled in the event of the death and resurrection of Jesus.

As heirs to the Jewish tradition, the first Christians did not invent another feast in order to celebrate the salvation which God had wrought in the exodus and exaltation of Christ. They simply understood the traditional feast of their people in a new way and celebrated the Jewish Passover as something Christian or "Christic."[19] The Jewish Passover feast included, and still includes, in addition to the meal, a basic liturgical element: a free rendition of the account of the deliverance from Egypt that opened the way to the promised land. When Christians celebrated their own Passover, they told, instead, the story of the passion and resurrection of Jesus. In this way the texts took shape that constitute the oldest stratum of the gospels. In place of the story of the exodus, Christians during their feast told of the Passover meal of Jesus with his disciples, the meal proper to his Passover, in which he celebrated his death in advance and gave expression to his trust in the God who sets human beings free.

This is the effect of the telescoping process that brought into a single focus the Jewish Passover and the Passover of Jesus, which is the prototype of the Christian Passover celebrating the resurrection. In a remarkable way the Christian feast thus completed the Jewish Passover and inherited its spirit: God delivered in the past, God delivers now, God will deliver in the future. In the eyes of the first believers Jesus had become the true Passover lamb, so that they had no need of a ritual lamb.[20]

It is understandable that a number of elements characteristic of the Jewish feast should have been retained in the account of the Supper: the dating, the solemnly prepared room, the community gathered for an evening meal. On the other hand, the various rites have not been kept because they referred to the departure from Egypt, and remembrance of the latter has been replaced by remembrance of the event of the cross.

In addition, the first Christians, like all Jews, longed for the definitive coming of the Lord and for final and universal deliverance. Though Passover was an actualization of a past event, it was also clearly future-oriented. The celebration of Passover was indeed a celebration of the birth of the people: the exodus in the case of Jews or the saving death of Jesus in the case of Christians. But at the same time it also included expectation of a saving intervention by the Lord who is coming and of the last day of God's earthly reign.[21]

IV. SUPPER AND HEAVENLY BANQUET

It is time to turn attention once again to the text of eucharistic institution. It contains some noteworthy details; in particular it is immediately followed by a saying that locates the present event in relation to the end of time. An examination of these slight modifications and of the added saying makes it possible to enter more fully and accurately into Mark's perspective.

"Dialogical" situation[22]

Those who approach the account of the Supper will naturally focus their attention immediately on the words of institution: What do they mean? What is their real significance? But readers risk going astray if they isolate the words of institution as though these did not have their place in a relationship between Jesus and his disciples, which the former initiates in the course of a table fellowship. And in fact interpreters have often concentrated on what are called "the species," which have therefore ended up being to some extent absolutized. The parallelism of the two sets of words, which is more pronounced in Mark than in the Antiochene tradition, has even been taken by some[23] to be the sign of an already "sacramentalist" tendency.

But, as I pointed out earlier, this scene differs from many others in which Jesus seems to be uttering timeless truths: here he addresses himself explicitly to the twelve. His actions and words over the bread and cup do not terminate there as though they had reached their goal; rather they imply, on the part of the group of addressees, a genuine receptivity without which they would not exist.

As I made clear earlier, the structure of the cultic account established in advance some relation between Jesus and the disciples. Mark the evangelist lays special emphasis on this point: he repeats the statement that "he gave [it] to them" (14:22, 23) in both cases says something which indicates an activity on the part of the guests. In v. 22 there is the imperative *Labete*, usually translated as "Take!"[24] and in v. 23 there is the phrase: "And they all drank of it." The direct response to the "giving" of Jesus is the silent, but implicit, acceptance of the disciples. The imperative "Take!" is noteworthy inasmuch as in Jewish practice of that time the distribution of bread was usually not accompanied by any invitation to the guests.[25] As for the words "And they all drank of it," they occur, oddly enough, *before* the words which explain that the

cup contains the blood of the covenant. As I indicated, this is probably a vestige of a testamentary tradition.[26] I think, nonetheless,
that in the eyes of Mark the writer the words have a specific function in the account, namely, to show the role of the disciples, their
readiness to receive the gift offered to them by Jesus.

The significance of the scene is thus to be found first and foremost not in the transformation of the bread and cup or even in the
meaning assigned to the bread and cup, but rather in the establishment of a community that is united to Jesus in a special way. The
action over the elements is subordinate to this purpose. Through
the gift which the Master symbolically makes of himself the group
of twelve enters now (and will remain after the departure of Jesus)
into a close contact with their host: they will be inseparable from
him who is leaving them. The community thus established is a
new community which nothing can destroy, even if, while time
lasts, its members must experience the presence of Jesus in the
mode of absence.[27]

The words of institution

The dialogical situation helps to a more correct understanding
of the eucharistic words, because it keeps readers from abstracting
the words from their setting and purpose, namely, the new community which Jesus establishes and which draws its life from his
gift.

This is clear in the case of the words over the cup, since the
blood which Jesus "sheds" is covenant blood. The blood shed, that
is, the violent death, signifies the perfect fidelity of Jesus; by being
faithful to the point of shedding his blood Jesus the Just One seals
the definitive covenant with God. He does so first of all for himself, but because he thereby fulfills the prophecy of the Servant,
the covenant is also directly intended "for the multitude."[28] By his
saving death Jesus makes available, not only to the twelve but to
all human beings, the communion with God which he himself has
lived fully, to the point of making the supreme gift of himself.[29]
Finally, everything is placed in the perspective of the coming
kingdom.

In the words over the bread, on the other hand, the Markan
tradition does not say that the body is "given for you." In the
absence of any explanatory description, how is the reader to
understand "body" here?

Some critics interpret the term with the help of the words over the cup; they make "body and blood" two components of the human individual or two components of a Jewish cultic sacrifice. As I explained earlier,[30] this approach to the problem is invalid.

There is in fact a basic principle that must guide the student: in the semitic mind the word "body" refers directly not to the physical organism but to the person insofar as it is capable of expressing itself to other persons and to the world. With this supposed, two readings of the compact sentence "This is my body" are possible.

Some interpreters take their cue from the fact that in the Greek sentence, "Touto estin to sōma mou," the subject of the statement is not "touto" but "to sōma mou," so that it should be translated as "My body, behold it!"[31] It is as if Jesus were saying: "Until now I have expressed myself to you through my bodily presence: I have spoken to you, I have gathered you together; henceforth I will express myself among you through the action of this meal, through this blessed bread which I give you to share among you." He will be present no longer through his "fleshly body" but to the extent that his disciples gather in his name and receive the bread which he will continue to give them from God. In this type of interpretation Jesus is saying that he will henceforth express himself in this world in a different way than he did during his earthly life; it is through the eucharistic meal that he will maintain contact with his disciples and be present to them down the centuries.

Does it follow from this that because the group of disciples or the celebrating community shares such a meal they become in the strict sense the expression of Jesus, his manifestation in this world? Is Jesus saying: "Behold my body, namely, you who eat the bread which I give you"?

Such an inference would lead to a view that is Pauline in character, namely, that the community is, in the final analysis, the "body of Christ," the body of the risen Lord. But the text gives no hint leading in this direction. Jesus is speaking here of his own body and of his own way of maintaining contact with his followers in the future.

This first interpretation does have some validity, but it runs into difficulty insofar as it ignores, or at least bypasses, the main theme of the death of Jesus as imminent and even already present symbolically. This theme, which is given greater intensity by Jesus' consciousness of it, is certainly dominant in the "private passion," as I indicated in the preceding section. In fact, it is pre-

cisely at the Supper that Jesus explicitly states the meaning of his
death. Furthermore, this first interpretation does not seem to do
justice to what Mark suggests, literarily speaking, in the immediate context.

As a result a second interpretation may prove more satisfying.
It is based on the fact that the expression *to sōma mou* occurs only
twice in Mark: here and in the account of the anointing at
Bethany, when Jesus responds to his disciples, who are indignant
at the woman's "wastefulness," by saying: "What she could do she
has done: she has perfumed my body in advance for my burial"
(Mk 14:8). Only one other time, in 15:43, does "body" refer to
Jesus, but without the personal pronoun; on this occasion it means
his corpse. Given the linguistic context, should not "my body" be
connected with the death of Jesus in 14:22 as well? I am not saying
that "body" here means "corpse." I mean rather that while keeping the underlying idea of "body" = "person," we should understand Jesus as saying that he is going freely, deliberately to his
death. The action of giving the bread represents the action of giving himself; the fact that he gives it to the twelve shows that he is
dying for human beings. *Sōma* would therefore designate the person of Jesus of Nazareth as advancing toward the violent end of
his earthly mission. Why is "body" used, rather than some other
term such as "I"? Doubtless in order to avoid any suggestion that
the person of Jesus is wholly a prey to death.

This second interpretation provides a more satisfactory link
than the first between the words over the bread and the words over
the cup; the two statements do not refer to the two components
of the human person or of a sacrifice, but represent a progression.
When Jesus says "This is my body," he is declaring his acceptance
of his death. When he gives himself, with the bread, as food,
he shows that his life is communicated to others. Finally, in
the words over the cup he makes it clear that this gift of himself
bears fruit in a universal salvation: the "covenant for the multitude."

Let me say a few words, finally, on the relation of this reading
to the structure of the cultic account as elucidated back in Chapter
III. The message, here again, is the change in the mode of his presence which Jesus is announcing: despite his death he remains with
the disciples in a new way. The group of disciples is also transformed: it becomes a community with its center of gravity in Jesus
who has "died for the covenant" and is mysteriously present. As

regards the "elements," that is, the bread and wine, Mark makes no clear statement about a change in them.[32] I shall come back to this point further on; for the moment it must be said that they too are affected by the changes in Jesus and the group of disciples, but the extent of the change in them will have to be determined more closely.

What of the other factor intrinsic to the structure of the cultic text, namely, the present/future axis which ensures the continuity of the eucharistic celebration? When I speak of "future" in this context, I am not referring to the eschatological time of God's reign to which allusion is made in v. 25; I shall turn to this aspect shortly. Here I am referring to the period of time during which believers will be gathering at the "table of the Lord." Since the command of remembrance is lacking in the Markan text, is there any basis in the latter for a repetition of the eucharistic action?

Two considerations point to such a repetition. First, and in general, the fact that the Supper is celebrated in the context of Passover suggests that the Supper is to be repeated in virtue of its connection with the Jewish feast. The reference to "blood of the covenant" (see Ex 24) likewise links this episode with the annual celebration of the Jewish practice. Finally, the parallelism between the two statements of institution, as well as their juxtaposition (without any separation by reference to a "Supper"), surely reflects a liturgical practice already current among Christians; this being so, was there any need to mention a command of repetition?

There is a second consideration that suggests repetition. It is the reference to the "multitude" alongside the reference to the twelve. According to the scriptures, the ancestors of Israel who had experienced the foundational event had passed on the memory of it to their descendants; from generation to generation these descendants had recounted and actualized this "memory" on the basis of their tradition. It is not impossible that in Mark's eyes the twelve who witness the event of the last meal of Jesus are the "ancestors" of the multitude of believers yet to come.[33] That multitude will be the new Israel that continues to experience and celebrate the salvation made known by Jesus at his final meal. The few considerations offered on the receptivity of the disciples at the Supper may serve as confirmation of this interpretation.

In this way the gap is bridged between an action of Jesus that is addressed solely to the twelve, to the exclusion of any other guest, and the same action as nonetheless envisaging all the believers who will profit from the covenant which Jesus proclaims here.

The eschatological perspective

Finally, the change that takes place looks to the future, as is required by the idea of a covenant with God that extends through all future time. This implication in the idea of covenant is made explicit in the "eschatological" saying which Mark (or his source) places immediately after the words of institution. No transitional statement connects the two sets of words, not even the formula, "And he said to them," although this is used to introduce the words over the cup (14:24a). Mark therefore regards v. 25 as an intrinsic part of the eucharistic text even though in and of itself it belongs to a different type of tradition.[34] "Truly, I tell you, never more shall I drink of the fruit of the vine until that day when I shall drink it new in the kingdom of God" (Mk 14:25).

The perspective inherent in the covenant for the multitude had already shown what the fruit is of the gift which Jesus makes of his life; it pointed to a future whose extent is not defined. In the words over the cup, however, the perspective of Jesus' death took precedence over that of the future and of coming glory; the emphasis was on the fact that his shed blood is the means of establishing the covenant.

In the eschatological saying the emphasis is reversed. The death of Jesus continues to be implied in the statement "Never more shall I drink," but it is as it were absorbed by the certainty of participation in the final banquet. Jesus has indeed just said that he is shedding his blood, and he certainly says here that he will no longer celebrate Passover in this world, but he also says very clearly that he is filled with an unbounded confidence: he is certain that he will share in the banquet on the last day. He gives his body and blood, therefore, with the prospect of an assured final joy. Far from dwelling on his proximate death, and still less on the sufferings and injustice this death entails, he focuses his gaze wholly on the success to be achieved by God.

There is a word in the eschatological saying that describes the divine success. The wine of the heavenly banquet is said to be "new" (kainon), that is, not "recent" as opposed to "old,"[35] but radically different, newly created, unexpected, just like the new earth and the new heavens. Here is something to set the heart dreaming! It is noteworthy that the word "new," which in the Antiochene tradition describes the covenant, occurs here in the context of the "last day."

A detail which Matthew is careful to add seems to be lacking in Mark. In describing the heavenly banquet, Jesus does not say that he will drink the new wine "with you." But in fact this detail is not required, since a banquet is immediately thought of as shared with others; this is especially true among the Semites. Furthermore, after having carried on his ministry in the company of his disciples and having now forged them into a community with him after his death, how could Jesus find delight in a solitary face to face relationship with God? Mark's omission of the words "with you" can be explained: in his view the incomparably important role of Jesus in the "private passion" and especially at the Supper required that the emphasis be on his person: everything is focused on him.

But this concentration does not have the last word in the account. Everything is indeed focused on the passage of Jesus and on the final banquet which Jesus already glimpses on the horizon, but the essentially important thing is nonetheless the work accomplished by Jesus, namely, the establishment of a new community that draws its life from him. The "eucharistic" meal is thus related to the eschatological banquet. The cultic action is intended only for the intervening period; the presence of the "body" of Jesus, which is manifested through the meal eaten in the name of Jesus, has its full meaning only in function of the eschatological banquet to which it leads. The Eucharist is therefore celebrated only during the period that precedes the final coming of God's reign; it does not have an absolute value and must always be seen in relation to the "heaven" which it prefigures but is not.

CONCLUSION

As seen in relation to the cultic tradition which I tried to define in preceding chapters, Mark shows a considerable expansion that enables the reader to avoid the pitfalls set by a merely liturgical practice. The Markan account gives condensed expression to the paschal mystery of the covenant that is established by Jesus. This man whom we know to be living today, this man who has proclaimed the reign of God and tomorrow will make it a reality by being faithful even to the point of shedding his blood: this man tells us very succinctly, in word and action, the purpose of his life and his death. That purpose is to restore the communion of all human beings with the Father and in accordance with the Father's plan. Since this covenant has not yet reached its full fruition, it must be experienced symbolically through a new mode of presence and union. When the disciples eat the bread and drink the cup which Jesus has blessed in the name of God, they express the fact that Jesus is alive. In an obvious sense he is already present, but it is a presence despite absence, a presence wholly directed to the coming banquet at which all will reach their fulfillment in God.

When seen as part of the gospel story, the account of the Supper proves to have profound roots in two ways. The action performed here by Jesus crowns his earthly life; in it he takes hold of his destiny, as it were. He does not go to his death as to a fate that is simply forced upon him by his enemies, as though he did not grasp its deeper meaning, namely, that this death crowns his mission and renews the covenant of God between God and humankind. No, in this final hour Jesus makes it splendidly clear that he gives himself freely in order to be completely faithful to God and his fellow human beings.

More accurately—and in this we see how really deep the roots of Jesus' action go—he is faithful to his people. He is heir to what we now call the "Old" Testament; he recapitulates in himself the lengthy history of the covenant which God has ceaselessly renewed with his people. Jesus in his person is the true Israel. That is why in the Eucharist there is question not simply of a gift of himself but also of the covenant which flows from that self-giving and by which he renews the history of the human race. He thereby brings to fruition the deepest longing of the people, God's firstborn, from which he comes forth and to which he belongs for ever.

How shall I characterize the Markan account of institution in light of this twofold background? The act of Jesus that crowns and completes the Jewish Passover is not only ritual but existential. In time past God had delivered his people when he intervened in their behalf at the exodus; his action had challenged the unjust order to which the people had fallen victim. By his action on this night Jesus challenges the Jewish order in which the powerful of his time had imprisoned the children of Abraham: he gives his life not only in obedience to God but also in fidelity to the authentic tradition of his people. By so doing, he inaugurates a new order of things, the order of love that prevails over the order of ritual and law. Believers who repeat his action and from it receive life according to the Spirit must in their turn challenge the order in which they are always in danger of rigidifying the inexhaustible dynamism of the love of God who makes all things new.

XI
Paul and the Lord's Supper

It is a surprising fact that Paul the theologian does not develop a systematic view of the Eucharist as he does of baptism. In the letter to the Romans he shows how the sacrament of initiation unites believers closely to the death and resurrection of Christ; the theme is one to which he readily refers elsewhere as well.[1] Yet nowhere in the Pauline corpus would there have been any discussion of the Eucharist if the Corinthians had not disturbed the founder of their Church by the manner of their eucharistic gatherings. Did Paul speak of the Eucharist in his oral preaching? Did he, like so many theologians after him, make it a major theme of his teaching? We cannot be sure that he did, because the needed evidence is lacking. It can be said, however, that the two passages which we do have, both of them in the first letter to the Corinthians,[2] are extremely important and revealing.

In his effort to heal the divisions at work in the recently established Corinthian community Paul spends the first four chapters of his letter on a vigorous assertion of the "folly of the cross,"[3] a theme that must be kept in mind if the letter as a whole is to be understood. He then gives answers to questions asked by his correspondents on a wide variety of subjects.[4] The first eucharistic text occurs in a passage on pagan cultic meals (10:14–22), while the second conveys Paul's reaction to the conflicts that arise in the community during the celebration of "the Lord's Supper" (11:17–34). In both instances, Paul reminds his readers of eucharistic traditions and gives his personal interpretation of them.

There is a third passage that may possibly have a eucharistic meaning: 1 Cor 10:1–6, which speaks of the "spiritual" food and drink that the ancestors of Israel received in the wilderness. The content of these verses was in the back of Paul's mind when he wrote the two eucharistic texts. I shall refer to it in passing.

When Paul responded to the questions asked by the Christians of Corinth, he was addressing people familiar with the customs of the day; he was not concerned to fill in this background for twentieth-century readers. A modern historical reconstruction is therefore based on information that is fragmentary and subject to constant revision. I must nonetheless attempt a comprehensive presentation, even while realizing that another synthesis is possible.[5]

I could pick up here where the preceding chapter left off and begin my reading of the Pauline texts with the passage in 1 Cor 11 in which Paul gives the text of eucharistic institution. This would enable me to attend, first of all, to that which Paul emphasizes, namely, the coming together that constitutes the assembly, and, secondly, to his special point of view in regard to the essential meaning of the celebration, namely, that it proclaims the death of the Lord. Only then would I turn to the theme of the communion with Christ which the sacramental meal produces (1 Cor 10). But, instead of this seemingly more systematic approach to the texts, I prefer to follow the order of the letter itself and therefore to begin with the passage (1 Cor 10) which cites a peripheral eucharistic tradition and gives Paul's commentary on it.

I. CULTIC MEALS AND EUCHARISTIC COMMUNION

I shall be following here the twists and turns of Paul's letter, which are such that he requires three chapters (8–10) for a nuanced reply to the questions the Corinthians have asked him. Initially, there is as yet no question of the Eucharist but only of food offered to idols: Can this be eaten without danger of idolatry? Paul then goes on to a closer look at the problem inherent in cultic meals: they establish a real communion with the divinity they are meant to honor. At this point he is forced to make a comparison between, on the one side, cultic meals and their effect, and, on the other, eucharistic practice and the resultant constitution of the "body of Christ," which elsewhere he calls the "Church."

Christians and idols

The Christians of Corinth lived in a world that was filled with idols. In the many temples of the city sacrifices were offered to various gods on all kinds of occasions; they might be inspired by personal devotion,[6] or be performed during civic ceremonies, or

be part of the meetings of guilds or clubs. After a part of the immolated animals had been burned, the remaining portions were
returned to the priest and to the offerer of the sacrifice. These portions would then be eaten either at public banquets held in a building attached to the temple or at meals in the home; in the second
case, they had either been brought there from the temple or had
been bought in the marketplace where surplus sacrificial meat was
sold.[7]

Christians obviously did not offer sacrifices to idols, but were
they allowed to eat food that derived from idolatrous worship?

At the level of principle the answer is simple enough. Since
idols have no real existence, the flesh of animals sacrificed to them
has not in any way been changed but remains "neutral." Besides,
Paul says, "food will not commend us to God. We are no worse
off if we do not eat, and no better off if we do" (8:8). Therefore
"eat whatever is sold in the meat market without raising any question on the ground of conscience" (10:25). At the same time, however, distinctions must be made in regard to actual behavior,
depending on whether the food is eaten at an ordinary meal or at
a cultic meal. This is the point that Paul will explain in a series of
discussions running through chapters 8–10 of his letter.

If there is question only of an ordinary meal, believers who
understand the unreality of idols are free to eat any food whatsoever. They must however have consideration for their "weaker"
brethren who are not sufficiently enlightened and are still afraid
that the eating of such food will put them in contact with idols; if
they follow the example of their better instructed brethren they
may do what their conscience forbids them to do. As far as Paul is
concerned, even though there is no "incarnation" of a god in the
flesh of the sacrificed animal (especially since idols have no real
existence), believers must do everything to avoid scandalizing others: "If food is the cause of my brother's falling, I will never eat
meat."[8] In order to encourage others to make such a renunciation
Paul tells them of his own behavior: far from holding on jealously
to his rights as an apostle, he has preferred to abandon these rights
so as to "become all things to all" his brothers and sisters.[9] In this
way he qualifies his initial pronouncement of radical freedom; he
says now that it is proper to abstain from such foods if other people still imagine that these are something more than simple foods.
Yes, "'all things are lawful,' but not all things are helpful."[10]

If, on the other hand, there is question of a cultic table fellowship, is it enough to be considerate of the consciences of the breth-

ren? No: the danger here is that Christians will not only scandalize the weak but will compromise their own faith. The danger, once again, is not due to some power supposedly present in the immolated food. It is rather that Christians who feel sure of their complete freedom, since they have only contempt for false gods, and who therefore sit "at table in an idol's temple" (8:10), may fall back into their past errors. Are they not persons upon whom "a quite recent association with idols" has left its impress?[11] The apostle thinks it necessary, therefore, to put recent converts on their guard against imprudence in this matter.

He begins his exhortation by giving his own behavior as an example: instead of allowing himself every right, he practices a strict asceticism and deals harshly with himself.[12] But his reaction is determined above all by a key conviction which he wishes to keep alive in the Corinthians and which he has set down at the beginning of this entire section of the letter: "Although there may be so-called gods in heaven or on earth . . . yet for us there is one God, the Father, from whom are all things and for whom we exist, and one Lord, Jesus Christ, through whom are all things and through whom we exist" (1 Cor 8:5–6). Paul's intense and even triumphal certainty of this "oneness" explains both the radical lack of importance that he attaches to "food offered to idols" and his disapproval of participation in pagan cultic meals. Any turning back and any divergence, even if only potential, from the faith are unacceptable. The apostle is fearful for the faithful of Corinth because they are immersed in a polytheistic atmosphere. Let them be mindful of the history of Israel, for even the chosen people did not manage to avoid abandoning the living God. All of them had crossed the Red Sea and all had been fed with manna from heaven, and yet many of them succumbed to the attraction of false gods. Therefore "let those who think that they stand take heed lest they fall."[13] Past events prefigure what can happen to the Corinthians even today: they in their turn risk abandoning their consistent adherence to the faith and falling into idolatry.

Having reached this point in his discussion, and wishing to strike a decisive blow against the idolatry that threatens, Paul shows his readers that cultic meals taken with pagans are radically incompatible with the meal that unites Christians to the one and only Lord:

[14]Beloved, flee idolatry. [15]I address you as intelligent people; judge for yourselves what I say. [16]The cup of bless-

ing which we bless, is it not a communion in the *(koinōnia tou)* blood of Christ? The bread which we break, is it not a communion in the *(koinōnia tou)* body of Christ? [17]Since there is but a single loaf, we, the multitude *(hoi polloi)*, are a single body because we all share in *(ek tou . . . metechomen)* this single loaf. [18]Look at the fleshly Israel: are not those who eat the sacrificed victims in a communion with the *(koinōnoi tou)* altar? [19]Am I saying, then, that food sacrificed to idols is really anything? Or that an idol is really anything? [20]Not at all! But since what they sacrifice they sacrifice to demons and not to God, I do not want you to be in communion with *(koinōnoi)* demons. [21]You cannot drink both the cup of the Lord *(potērion Kyriou)* and the cup of demons *(potērion daimoniōn)*; you cannot share the table of the Lord *(trapezēs Kyriou metechein)* and the table of demons. [22]Or do we want to rouse the Lord's jealousy? Are we stronger than he is? (1 Cor 10:14–22).

Two points in this passage make it clear that Paul's primary concern is that the Christian's adherence to the God of Jesus Christ should be complete and unalloyed. First, Paul, authentic Jew that he is, is evidently inspired here (as earlier in 10:7) by the Canticle of Moses,[14] a text that gives passionate expression to the contrast between the one God who has heaped his gifts upon Israel, and the idolatrous behavior of the chosen people:

> They have dishonored their Rock, their salvation. . . . They sacrifice to demons who are not God. . . . They have made me jealous by their empty idols. . . . They ate the fat of their [the pagans'] sacrifices, they drank the wine of their libations   (Deut 32: 15, 17, 21, 38).

The second point: the chiastic arrangement of Paul's text shows that the theme which gives the passage its structure is the theme of idolatry and not the more obvious one of the two meals:

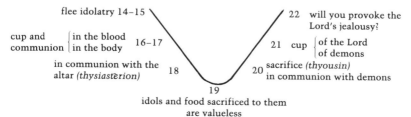

Within the chiasmus the text emphasizes a competition between pagan meals and the eucharistic meal; therefore, as Paul sees these, they resemble each other. In order to show in what the similarity resides, I must first clear away a question regarding the elements of the two meals: if the victims sacrificed, like the idols to which they are sacrificed, are nothing, must the same be said of the bread and the cup of blessing? Certainly not! The context clearly requires a negative answer, and further confirmation comes from Chapter 11 in which Paul condemns the behavior of those who "do not recognize the body" and care little about respect for the religious act which they perform. Since the answer to the question is in the negative, it may seem that the argument lacks a solid basis. But this is only because the verses are not concerned with the elements as such, but with the effect which participation in a cultic meal produces in the participant.

Paul reads into any and every table fellowship, whether pagan or Christian, a belief he has inherited from early Israel: "Those who eat the sacrificed victims are in communion with the altar."[15] In the thinking of Paul, as of his contemporaries, the act of sharing in a cultic meal signifies a close connection between the guests and the power to which the victims have been offered.

But is there not a contradiction here between the emptiness or non-existence of idols, on the one hand, and the real result that is nonetheless produced by a cultic table fellowship, on the other? An unexpected shift in focus, however, removes this difficulty: behind the victims and behind the nothingness of the idols stand the demons, who are real. In the final analysis, pagan cultic meals establish a link with demonic powers.[16] The eucharistic meal, on the other hand, links the participant with the living Christ. The incompatibility between the two types of meal is thus to be found in the divergent terms of the relationship into which the human participants enter. They cannot be table fellows both of those who honor demons and of the one Lord. In summary: at the formal level of "entrance into a relationship" there is a similarity, but at the concrete level there is an immense difference, since the act of drinking from the Lord's cup and being at his table has the effect of uniting the participant to him who alone merits an unreserved adherence. Paul continues to think in terms of his principal theme, which is the exclusiveness of the Christian's belonging to Christ.

In fact, the main terms that keep recurring in the passage all express the same idea, namely, participation or sharing, but in differing degrees of intensity. The verb habitually used is "share" (met-echō). The other word used, koinōnia (or koinōnoi), is in principle synonymous with met-echō, but here it seems to have a narrower meaning. A short semantic study will show this to be the case.[17]

In its habitual use, the Greek word koinōnia signifies that a relation exists between persons in regard to some object; there exists among them, for example, a communion in thought or a community of interests, such as can be the basis of some kind of "society."[18] When used by itself the word can even signify the "community of faith and material goods" that unites the first Christians (Acts 2:42). Ordinarily, however, the object of the participation or sharing is given in the dative case or in a prepositional phrase. Thus people are associated in a common work such as the collection;[19] they may also share the same faith[20] or, conversely, the "unfruitful works of darkness";[21] they can participate in the spreading of the gospel,[22] in the sufferings of others,[23] or in distressful situations that must be alleviated.[24] A community of spirit is thereby established among persons;[25] it shows itself, or is deepened in varying degrees, according to circumstances.

Contrary to current Greek practice,[26] Paul sometimes uses the word with a dependent genitive. He can express the idea of "communion with Christ," for example, by saying "koinōnia of the Son"[27] or, as in the eucharistic text, "koinōnia of the body, of the blood of Christ." In this usage the word koinōnia seems to mean more than participation or sharing; it seems to denote a very close union, a truly personal communion between the faithful and Christ, whether directly or through the bread and the cup.

Is it possible to specify further the nature of this communion in the body and blood of Christ? Any response must, above all else, avoid treating the body and blood as substances in which the recipients would participate. Such an approach would project a Hellenistic perspective on a passage which is evidently semitic in its outlook,[28] with "body" and "blood" referring to the aspects under which the believer enters into communion with the person of Christ. Furthermore, Paul's statement looks directly to the action of blessing the cup and the bread, and the result it has in view is not an alteration of the elements but a communion of persons. Consequently, one must not look to the idea of "eating Christ" for a principle that will shed light on the new communion established by the eucharistic liturgy.

Some scholars have followed another approach that is suggested by the similarity which Paul presupposes between the eucharistic meal and pagan cultic meals. Is it not possible to speak here of a "belonging" that becomes a kind of identification of believers with their god? Before doing so, it would be necessary first of all to study more closely the Greek texts that seem to suggest an experience of mystical identification with a divinity. But in any case, the religious universes of the Greeks and the Bible are profoundly different.[29] Therefore, even if it be possible to speak of such an identification for pagans, the same will not necessarily be true for Israel and Christians, both of whom had far too great a respect for the divine transcendence and otherness to dare imagine such a "fusion" between believers and God.

Paul himself in fact shows a way that leads to an authentic understanding of this "communion" with Christ. He says repeatedly that believers have "died with Christ,"[30] have been "crucified with him,"[31] and will be "raised up with him";[32] we "shall live with him,"[33] so that our life, which at present is "hid with Christ in God," will be "life for ever with him."[34] Thus, while asserting a communion of the most intense kind possible, Pauline "mysticism" always respects the distinction of persons.

The best expression of this new state is given by Paul himself when he speaks in the name of all believers and says: "I live, but it is no longer I who live; Christ lives in me. As for my present life in the flesh, I live it in faith in the Son of God who loved me and gave himself up for me" (Gal 2:20). In this well-known passage he is not contrasting present life and future life but, within the present life, life prior to faith and life after it. The new life does not eliminate the self and replace it with the godhead; rather the new life is a continual breakthrough of the life of Christ into a self which, far from disappearing, is ceaselessly made new. Christ is henceforth the only source of the believer's life and being.

The Eucharist, then, involves neither magic nor theophagy, as is shown by what Paul says about Israel in the wilderness. The corroboration is all the greater since in both cases there is question of an "eating" and even, though at different levels, of "sacraments":

> Our fathers were all under the cloud, and all passed through the sea, and all were baptized into Moses in the cloud and in the sea, and all ate the same spiritual food and all drank the same spiritual drink. For they drank from the spiritual Rock which followed them, and the Rock was Christ (1 Cor 10:1–4).

The eating to which Paul refers is evidently a "spiritual" eating that has nothing to do with any absorption of the divinity, as understood in the Hellenistic mysteries; rather it is the risen Christ who by his real presence takes believers into himself. The cult practiced by Christians is therefore "spiritual" not in the sense that it has no place for the body, but in the sense that the body is that of the risen Lord. If we were "all . . . made to drink of one Spirit" (1 Cor 12:13), it is because the risen Christ gives the Spirit to all who take part in the eucharistic act.

The body of Christ

I am now in a position to study the verses which contain a eucharistic formula and, more important, to study Paul's commentary on it. Paul's intention in setting this ancient tradition in the context of cultic meals is to highlight the closeness of the bond which the Eucharist creates between believers and their Lord. It is a bond that excludes any relation with demonic powers; it also establishes an intimacy with Christ which down the centuries has been the source of extraordinary religious experiences.

Attentive readers will be surprised by the idea that binds the verses together. Here is the passage once again:

> [16]The cup of blessing which we bless, is it not a communion in the blood of Christ? The bread which we break, is it not a communion in the body of Christ? [17]Since there is but a single loaf, we, the multitude, are a single body because we all share in this single loaf (1 Cor 10:16–17).

Verse 16 cites pre-Pauline eucharistic phraseology, as can be seen from the terms used: "cup of blessing" is not a Greek expression, and "bread which we break" is typically semitic. Furthermore, Paul is here recalling something already known and accepted by the Corinthians. The inverted order cup/bread might, according to some authors, reflect a peripheral tradition on the sacrament; others—rightly, in my opinion—attribute it to Paul, who adopts this way of leading into the sentence on the one loaf, which is the main focus of his interest here.

Many interpretations have been given of these two verses. The reader would be bored if I were to review them in detail; I shall therefore simply point out two possible directions the interpreter may take.

According to one reading, v. 17 introduces a teaching, which is out of context here, on the unity of the Church that is the fruit of the one eucharistic loaf. The antithesis one/many certainly does suggest that the single loaf creates unity among the many who share it. Moreover, the community is based not on the fact that all sit at the same table but on the special character of the bread which all eat; for in this gift it is Christ himself who is given. So far, the interpretation raises no problems. But those who propose this first interpretation go on to read the passage as if the union produced did not directly have to do here with the relation of the gathering as a whole to Jesus Christ, but only with the relations of the members among themselves. In the final analysis, the passage would be an appeal for continued union among believers.

It is true indeed that the Eucharist is a source of cohesion in the Church, but is this what the text is talking about here? Such a reading requires making the two verses a parenthesis within a passage in which the controlling idea is the unqualified adherence of Christians to Jesus Christ alone.[35] Furthermore, if Paul's intention here again were to urge his addressees to respect their brothers and sisters, would he not emphasize more the point that since they are a *single* body they should avoid destroying this union under pretext of freedom?

Another approach must therefore be taken to the meaning of verses 16 and 17. Their place in the overall chiasmus (vv. 14–19) requires the interpreter to compare them with their counterpart, v. 21: "You cannot drink both the cup of the Lord and the cup of demons; you cannot share the table of the Lord and the table of demons." The emphasis in verses 17 and 21 is on the exclusive character of the eucharistic meal. If the loaf given is one, the intimacy with Christ which the entire congregation gains from it will tolerate no additional bond of union.

The surprising thing about this short passage is the shift that occurs in the use of the word "body." In v. 16 the body is evidently the individual body of Jesus himself,[36] the body which died and is now alive. In v. 17, however, it is "we, the multitude" who "are a single body," and it is difficult to argue that the "body" here is still the individual body of Jesus. We do not become Jesus himself. How, then, is it possible to speak of "body of Christ" and "a single body"?

Some critics feel obliged to fall back on the gnostic idea of the "Primal Man."[37] But why should they seek help in a phenomenon attested only later when they have at hand two other possible keys to understanding?

The first is the one Paul himself develops two chapters later when, in the light of an ancient fable of Aesop, he considers the body to be that which gives unity to the multiplicity of members (12:12–26). But I am reluctant to accept this idea as operative in 10:17, because in the context here Paul is not using Hellenistic language as he is in 1 Cor 12.

I prefer therefore to see at work here another, clearly semitic idea, that of "corporate personality,"[38] with which Paul is no less familiar, as can be seen in, for example, Chapter 5 of his letter to the Romans. In the perspective given by this idea Paul is saying that we are incorporated into the individual body of the risen Jesus so that a constitutive and permanent bond unites us to it and makes us dependent on it. The thought which Paul is conveying is the same as that conveyed by *koinōnia* when used in the intensified sense it has in 1 Cor 10; the only difference is that attention here is on the effect of the *koinōnia* for the entire community of believers. The ecclesial body of Christ, which has been established by baptism, continues to be shaped and to receive life through the eucharistic meal and this in a privileged way.

*

This first passage, written in response to a particular situation, provides a deeper understanding of the sacramental meal. While baptism has already given form to the "body of Christ," the Eucharist is this body's food; when believers express themselves in the eucharistic action they maintain and strengthen their personal union with Christ and become, together, the community that belongs to him forevermore. This is the communal fruit of the Eucharist.

In a further passage Paul will explain the sense in which the Lord's death—the source of salvation and of the Church—is celebrated in the sacrament.

II. EUCHARIST AND GATHERING

Paul has shown how the eucharistic meal completes the covenant of God with humankind because it creates a close communion with Christ who makes all believers one body with himself.

A little further on in the letter Paul compares the liturgical gatherings of the Corinthians with the tradition about the last meal of Jesus. In so doing, he provides the first liturgical witness to the continuity between the Supper and the Church's celebration of the sacrament.

This continuity is one of the major problems faced by historians and theologians: How did the Church pass from Supper to Mass? Paul will open up some lines of study that may lead to a valid hermeneutic of the biblical data.

Once again, the Pauline text I shall be examining is not a theoretical exposition of its subject, but is occasioned by very concrete difficulties which the Corinthians have been experiencing at their eucharistic gatherings. Paul exhorts the faithful to celebrate the Eucharist in an authentic way. His pastoral intention here, as always, is supported by a theological vision. In this passage the vision concerns two points: first, the requirement that there be no rift in the union of believers as they gather at the table of the risen Lord; second (as we shall see further on), the profound significance of the sacramental action.

At the beginning of Chapter 11 Paul has congratulated his flock: "You maintain the traditions as I have passed them on to you" (11:2). But then, after having settled a question regarding the attitude to be adopted by women in the assemblies (11:3–16), he shows his dissatisfaction with the way in which "the Lord's Supper" is being celebrated.

The passage can be divided into three parts. First, Paul condemns the behavior of the Corinthians (17–22); then he reminds them of the tradition received "from the Lord" and shows the implications of this tradition for the meaning of the cultic action, on the one hand, and for unworthy participants, on the other (23–32); finally, he gives instructions on the behavior to be observed during the celebration (33–34).

[17]And, since I must now give instructions, I cannot congratulate you, because you come together *(synerchesthe)* not to your advantage but to your detriment. [18]First of all, when you come together in assembly *(synerchomenōn hymōn en ekklēsiai)*, there are divisions *(schismata)* among you, I am told, and I partly believe it, [19]for there must be factions *(haireseis)* among you in order that those who are tried and true *(dokimoi)* among you may be recognized. [20]Then, when you gather in com-

mon *(synerchomenōn . . . epi to auto)*, it is not the Lord's
Supper *(kyriakon deipnon)* that you eat *(phagein)*. [21]For
when the eating begins *(en tōi phagein)* each person goes
ahead *(prolambanei)* with his own meal *(to deipnon
idion)*, and one person is hungry while another gets
drunk. [22]Do you not, then, have houses in which to eat
(esthiein) and drink? Or do you scorn the Church of God
and intend to shame those who have nothing? What am I
to say to you? Am I to congratulate you? No, on this point
I do not congratulate you. [23]For I received from the Lord
(parelabon apo tou Kyriou) what I then passed on *(pare-
dōka)* to you:

On the night he was betrayed *(paredideto)* the Lord
Jesus took bread [24]and, having given thanks, broke [it]
and said: "This is my body which [is] for you. Do this
in memory of me." Likewise also [he took] the cup after
the supper, saying: "This cup is the new covenant in my
blood. Do this, each time that you drink, in memory of
me."

[26]For each time that you eat this bread and drink this cup,
you proclaim the death of the Lord until he comes.
[27]Therefore whoever eats the bread or drinks the cup of
the Lord unworthily will be guilty in regard to the body
and blood of the Lord. [28]Let each person *(anthrōpos)* test
himself and then eat of this bread and drink of this cup,
[29]for those who eat and drink without recognizing *(mē
diakrinōn)* the body, eat and drink their own condemnation *(krima)*. [30]This is why many among you are sick and
weak, and a good number have died. [31]If we examine
(diekrinomen) ourselves, we will not be judged *(ekrino-
metha)*. [32]But in judging us *(krinomenoi hypo Kyriou)*, the
Lord corrects (educates: *paideuometha*) us, in order that
we may not be condemned *(katakrithōmen)* along with
the world.
[33]Therefore, my brothers, when you gather to eat
(synerchomenoi eis to phagein), wait *(ekdechesthe)* for
one another. [34]If anyone is hungry, let him eat at home *(en
oikōi esthietō)*, lest you gather *(synerchēsthe)* for your
condemnation *(krima)*. I will settle the other points when
I come.

Contrasts in terminology

The passage has a polemical tone. To the behavior of the Corinthians Paul opposes his own conception of the Lord's Supper,
one that is based on the tradition he has received. This basic oppo-
sition finds expression in two contrasts that are reflected in his
vocabulary. First, many expressions for "gathering together" are
contrasted with terms pointing in the opposite direction. Five
times, thrice in succession at the beginning, Paul speaks of "coming together" (vv. 17, 18, 20 and 33, 34) "in common" (20), "in
assembly" (18), so that the title "Church of God" in 22 could be
paraphrased as "the believing community that comes together."
On the other hand, there are "divisions" (18), "factions" (19), and
actions done by individuals for themselves in isolation, as when,
for example, each person sits down to eat in advance or feasts
without heeding the hunger of others.

This contrast is subordinated to another that controls the
entire passage. On the one side, there is the "Lord's Supper" *(kyriakon deipnon)* which the community "eats" *(phagein)*[39] and
which is the reason for its coming together. On the other, there is
"his own meal" *(idion deipnon)*[40]. These two meals clash because
it is the Lord himself who calls his community to a single
gathering.

The Lord's Supper

Historians uses these contrasts in order to determine what
went on at "the Lord's Supper" in Corinth. One fact is certain: the
faithful gathered (how often?) for a meal that included the celebration of the Eucharist. The presence of the Eucharist is shown by
the usual expressions for it: "eat the bread" and "drink the cup,"
as well as by what Paul expressly says, namely, that "the body and
blood of the Lord" are involved. On the other hand, it is not said
that the Corinthians explicitly invoke the words of Jesus at his
final meal. Nor is any information given about the organization of
the ceremony: Does the Eucharist proper take place at the beginning of the meal, or at its end, or even during it? Or do the two
actions over bread and cup serve to frame the meal? No sure
answer seems possible,[41] but certainty on this point is not indispensable for understanding Paul's reaction.

"The Lord's Supper" can therefore be described as a whole
consisting of a Eucharist that is celebrated in conjunction with a
fraternal meal and that is the raison d'être of this meal. The meal

is not to be identified with the "agape,"[42] a custom which dates from the second century at the earliest and presupposes that a complete separation of meal from sacrament has already taken place.

As I said back in Chapter I,[43] the "Lord's Supper" took place in the home of one or other of the faithful. The food doubtless included more than bread or wine, but it is difficult to be any more precise. There is nothing surprising about the fact of such meals: they resembled others of the same period,[44] although they were also distinguished from these not only by their specific religious character but also by the mingling of guests from different social strata. The meals cannot be regarded as mere preliminaries or "appetizers" for the Eucharist, since they surely also had for their function to give the experience of "living together," which is a basic form of human behavior[45] and, indeed, the foundation on which the Church is built. In addition, these meals made it possible to feed the hungry,[46] not only for humanitarian reasons but also, and above all, in order to give expression to the concrete Church, which must reject distinctions between rich and poor.

All this is the good side of what the Corinthians did at their "Lord's Supper." But the coin had its reverse side as well.

Paul's reaction

What did the Corinthians do that was blameworthy? Some did not wait for all the guests to arrive before beginning to eat; they even went so far as to get drunk while others present went hungry. The result was the clashes of which Paul had been told: clashes, in all probability, between believers who were better off and others of modest means, who perhaps arrived late because their work had delayed them or who perhaps were kept away from the better stocked tables. There may have been sociological reasons for the tensions among Corinthian Christians and for Paul's response.[47] Thus the desire for equality and unity among the members of the assembly may have been inspired by a movement for the integration of the poorer classes into more affluent society. Or, again, it is possible that Paul was so insistent because he was trying to provide a powerful antidote for other divisions within the community. All these considerations are helpful in showing the sociological impact of the "Lord's Supper." It is important, however, to assert unequivocally that Paul's reaction originates primarily, even if not exclusively, in his faith, as I shall show.

How does Paul react to the scandalous individualism and inequality in the Corinthian eucharistic assembly? He has no thought of believers sharing their goods beforehand so that all the guests will be on the same level from the start. Nor do we find him exhorting them to pool all their possessions, as is suggested by some of the summaries in the Acts of the Apostles.[48] Still less does he think of having the faithful eat in socially homogeneous groups, though this would have been in keeping with contemporary custom.[49]

His goal is quite different: the actual unity of the assembly as such in the course of the "Lord's Supper." Whatever the social status of the participants (free or slave, rich or poor, etc.) or their respective "merits" (as givers or receivers), unity is required because this is the *community* of believers whom the risen Lord has called together. The identity of the Host who receives them and who has given himself up for all who belong to him makes any separation intolerable. The guests should therefore wait for one another in order that all may share together in the one meal. Moreover, it is only by so acting that they will truly respect the impoverished members and avoid showing contempt for the "Church of God," for it is one and the same faith that brings them all together at the eucharistic table.

Through baptism believers have become one, as Paul had written to the Galatians: "As many of you as were baptized into Christ have put on Christ. There is neither Jew nor Greek, there is neither slave nor free, there is neither male nor female; for you are all one in Christ Jesus" (Gal 3:27–28). It *is* possible, then, to celebrate the Eucharist while paying no heed to the presence of the brethren or with each person acting only for himself or herself? The conclusion is obvious: The Lord's Supper presupposes that the assembly "is together" as "one body." Otherwise there can be no Eucharist.

Paul is therefore asking not so much that the food be equitably shared (though he is doubtless suggesting this) as that the properly communal aspect of the Eucharist, and thus its religious significance, be respected. He is so permeated by the holy presence of Christ that in order to bring out the seriousness of the liturgical action he unhesitatingly invokes the judgment[50] which strikes those who do not recognize what they are doing when they unduly confuse their "own" meal with that of the Lord. If they are concerned only to eat because they are hungry, then, says Paul, let them do it at home! As he writes, the thought of judgment brings with it the threat of concrete sanctions: sickness and death may ensue.[51]

This last assertion surprises us because it seems to reflect a quasi-magical view of sacramental abuses and therefore of the rite itself. In trying to understand its meaning, it is worth noting what Paul doubtless had in mind when he recalled the example of the Israelites in former days: although all had received "the same spiritual food and drink," all were not therefore pleasing to God; many of them fell into idolatry and were struck dead in the wilderness (10:1–6). So too a sharing in the gifts of Christ does not automatically guarantee salvation, contrary to what "enlightened" Corinthians, people at home with the Hellenistic mystery cults, seem to have thought.

Paul therefore insists that each person examine his or her own attitude, for the behavior of believers toward the brethren and toward the sacrament must be in harmony with what is being celebrated; otherwise the eucharistic action will be not only fruitless but a source of condemnation. The meal puts believers in contact with the risen Lord and therefore in an "eschatological" situation, which is a situation of judgment, for he who calls the community together and is mysteriously present is one who is already exalted in glory. This is why Paul urges his addressees to understand what it is they are doing when they gather for the Lord's Supper.[52]

In order that the Corinthians may be better able to recognize the body of the Lord, Paul reminds them of the tradition which he has previously passed on to them. But he proceeds in a rather surprising way, for why should he reproduce the account of institution in its entirety when his correspondents are already quite familiar with it and especially when it has not been the object of doctrinal objections? Paul himself does not provide an answer to this question, and commentators are therefore obliged to fall back on hypotheses.[53]

It cannot be said that Paul wanted to remind his correspondents of the sequence of actions at the Supper so that they might follow it exactly in their own liturgy. His tone is far too solemn for this to be his main concern. The tone is in fact similar to that of a later passage that deals with the resurrection of Jesus Christ (1 Cor 15:1–5).

The context suggests a better explanation. Paul feels obliged to correct the way in which the Corinthians eat the bread and drink the cup of the Lord, because their present disorder is such that their gatherings result in disunity, or the very opposite of what the Lord's Supper is intended to produce. Above all, the participants are so lacking in earnestness that their activity contains hardly any *reference to Jesus Christ*. This is all the more true since certain "enlightened" folk so abandon themselves to excesses of eschatological joy that they end up ignoring the event in which their faith originates: the cross of Jesus.

Let me explain this answer to the question. Paul probably thinks it important to cite the account of institution because it contains the words of Jesus himself. He has two reasons for citing it. By reminding the readers of the command of remembrance, the text makes it clear that the celebration is a response to the express desire of the Lord himself. Secondly, and above all, the words of Jesus express the meaning of his actions at the Supper and the saving value of his gift of himself on the cross. They must therefore be spoken in a worthy manner over the bread and cup which are shared at the meal, so that the content of the words may leave its impress on the celebration.

As a matter of fact, when Paul speaks of the way in which the Corinthians perform the eucharistic rite, he mentions only the actions and the foods: "bless the cup," "break the bread" (10:16), "eat the bread and drink the cup" (11:26, 27), and makes no reference to any words pronounced as a means of bringing out the meaning inherent in these actions. Does the Lord's Supper not require, then, an explicit reference to the words spoken by Jesus? Does it not require even more a reference to the death of Jesus who is now Lord? The remainder of the text will supply the answer.

III. THE LORD'S SUPPER AND THE LORD'S DEATH

After reminding the Corinthians of the traditional account of the Supper Paul goes on, without any break in the rhythm, to an important commentary on the Lord's Supper of the Corinthians: "Each time that you eat this bread and drink this cup, you proclaim the death of the Lord until he comes" (1 Cor 11:26). The statement is a surprising one. On the one hand, death has been overcome in the case of the risen Lord. On the other, is not the purpose of the eucharistic meal to renew the guests' participation in the present life of Christ? Why, then, this emphasis on the celebration as a proclamation of the Lord's *death*? The answer requires, first, that I show what Paul understands by the words I have just cited; second, that I call attention to the way in which he passes on the tradition; finally, that I explain what the word "proclaim" means.

The death of the Lord

Observe, first of all, that Paul does not say "death of Jesus" but "death of the Lord." He cannot think that Jesus died for good, because the glorified Christ is forever alive and will return. His purpose, therefore, is not to emphasize the distressing aspect of the passion—and yet he does insist here, and only here, on the "death" as such of Jesus Christ! Why does he do it? It is not impossible that he is here challenging the Corinthian "enthusiasts," who are overly ready to lose sight of Calvary with its tragic element and to think of themselves as already in heaven. But he surely has something more in mind here, and it emerges when we look at his reference to the death of Christ in the light of his theology as a whole.

The letters of Paul show how deeply Saul of Tarsus was "gripped" by his experience of the Christ who had emerged from death and had come to meet him, of the Christ who had joined him on the way and had then associated him with the mystery of his own passion and resurrection. "He gave himself for me!" Paul cries. Yes, "we are now justified by his blood."[54] The starting point of Paul's thinking is always the cross of Jesus; this is especially true in 1 Corinthians where he begins by telling his correspondents that his message is "the word of the cross."[55] But Paul sees the cross as God's victory over death itself, because the Christ who gave himself out of love for us has been raised up as the first fruits of a multitude of brothers and sisters.[56] The phrase "death of the Lord" is thus a shorthand statement of the salvation which Jesus has made available to all human beings by his perfect fidelity in carrying out his mission.

The theme of Christ's death recurs in the theology which Paul elaborates in connection with baptism as the sacrament by which human beings enter the new covenant. He says that believers are baptized "*into (eis)* the death of Christ"[57] not "in" it but "into" it. This wording of the letter to the Romans finds its explanation in the phrase Paul has used here in 1 Corinthians: all the Israelites "were baptized *into* Moses *in* the cloud and *in* the sea" (10:2), cloud and sea being the element in which the Israelites were baptized, while Moses is the person *to* whom they were dedicated. In like manner, Paul says in the letter to the Romans that believers are henceforth dedicated to the person of Jesus, that is, the person of him who "died for us": "If we have become connatural with the likeness of his death, we will also be so with that of his resurrection."[58] The baptismal rite thus symbolizes both death to the world of sin and resurrection to life.

What, then, is the relationship Paul establishes between the death of the Lord and the community's eucharistic meal? In order that the reader may better understand this relationship, let me reread the cultic account which Paul has included in his answer to the Corinthians.

The tradition repeated by Paul

As I showed earlier in this book,[59] none of the recensions of the Supper text can claim to be the source of the others. It is therefore legitimate to point out where the emphases are placed in the account cited by Paul.

> [23]On the night he was betrayed the Lord Jesus took bread [24]and, having given thanks, broke [it] and said: "This is my body which [is] for you. Do this in memory of me." [25]Likewise also [he took] the cup after the supper, saying: "This cup is the new covenant in my blood. Do this, each time that you drink, in memory of me."
> [26]For, each time that you eat this bread and drink this cup, you proclaim the death of the Lord until he comes.

Since Paul is not working within the narrative context of the synoptics, he briefly describes the setting for the institution: "On the night he was betrayed."[60] In this way he preserves the existential character of the scene and its location in the saving plan of God. This succinct evocation of the passion as the setting of the Supper is enough to specify the symbolic action by which Jesus expresses the fruit of his death. Unlike Luke, Paul does not say in so many words that Jesus "gives" the bread and the cup to the twelve, because the act of "giving" is implicit in the words: "he was betrayed."

The words over the bread make it clear, as in the Antiochene tradition generally (but without the verb "give" which Luke has[61]), that the bread blessed and distributed is "the body *for you*." Paul's version of the words emphasizes the personal relation of Jesus with the community: not with the distant "multitude," but with the present assembly, which at the Last Supper was made up of the twelve disciples, and which today comprises the gathered faithful of Corinth.

The words over the cup, on the other hand, say nothing of "for you" and are formulated in a strictly "objective" way: "This cup is the new covenant in my blood." Paul seems bent on stating an irrevocable fact: the utterly unconditional covenant that is now sealed by the "death of the Lord." Not only does he emphasize the identity of the cup with the covenant rather than with the blood (as in Mark), but he also does not think it necessary (as Luke does) to specify those for whom this sovereign covenant is meant. Simply by speaking of a "new" covenant and adding, by way of commentary, a reference only to the cross of Jesus, the apostle brings into focus a central concept in his theology.

It is easy to see in all this the man whose experience of sudden encounter with the risen Lord showed him that his Jewish faith was open to a fulfillment which transcended all of Israel's hopes and radically transformed the human situation. Mark did not think it necessary to speak of anything more than a "covenant" in the line of the one concluded on Sinai. Paul, however, speaks of a covenant that is *"new,"* using an adjective that occurs in a variety of contexts in his writings: "God . . . has qualified us to be ministers of a new covenant, not in a written code but in the Spirit," so that "if any one is in Christ, he is a new creature" and, by reason of his baptism, must walk in newness of life "in the new life of the Spirit."[62]

It is immediately after saying that the cup is the new covenant in the blood of Christ that Paul repeats the command of remembrance (it occurs but once in Luke): "Do this, each time that you drink, in memory of me."[63] Paul certainly intends to rectify the attitude of the Corinthians by reminding them the Lord himself presides at this meal. Above all, he is urging them to remember[64] that the relation of human beings to God has been changed by the death of Jesus and that the community meal celebrates a limitless and always present love. But the repetition of the command of institution also provides a kind of "subjective" counterpart to the objective statement: "Likewise also the cup," in which no mention is made of Jesus' gesture of giving his disciples the cup to drink. When believers remember, they recognize that they benefit from the Lord's gift of his life and covenant. The relation Jesus/believers is therefore not put in abeyance, as it were, by the unqualified character of the words over the cup. The reason is that to the sacrifice of Jesus with its unlimited fruit there must correspond, on the part of his disciples, an act of celebration by which the ever present gift is affirmed and accepted down the centuries.

Paul, then does emphasize the "death of the Lord" in connection with the Eucharist. This does not mean, however, that he fails to recognize the same basic structure which I studied back in Chapter III. The relation of Jesus with God is expressed in the reference to thanksgiving (v. 24); his relation with his disciples is highlighted by the repeated anamnesis (24, 25); the past/future axis emerges in the temporal references within which Paul frames the account: "On the night he was betrayed" (23) and "until he comes" (26), which define the time of the Church.

The act of proclamation

"You proclaim the death of the Lord," says Paul. The formula is not an imperative,[65] as if it represented a new obligation added to the liturgy. The Corinthians do not have a "duty" of proclaiming; rather they proclaim by the very fact that they gather in the Lord's name. In response to the action of Jesus who showed in his Supper both the meaning of his death and the union it would produce between himself and his disciples (present and future), the celebrating community makes itself receptive of the gift and does so by using the literary genre of the *tôdâ*.[66] It is probable that the community formulated this proclamatory aspect of its action, but in what words? Critics suggest various possibilities.[67] In any case, following the example of Jewish prayers at table which take the form of commemorations of God's great deeds, Christians gave free rein to their joy.

According to both the Antiochene and the Markan traditions the earthly Jesus at his final meal announces his death in the sense that he predicts it; he anticipates it in a symbolic way, thus showing that he accepts it, and he explains its meaning and fruit. But the celebrating community does not have to "announce" the death of Jesus in the sense of predicting it: Christ has already died, and that death in time is now past and cannot be predicted. Nor can the community anticipate his death, for the Jesus with whom it gathers does not still have to undergo his death on Calvary.

What is left, then, that can be a real echo of what the twelve experienced as they gathered around their Master at his final meal? What is left is the interpretation of the meaning and the acceptance of the fruit. By repeating the gestures and words of Jesus and by receiving the bread and the cup the community "commemorates" his action, that is, his death in which (according to Paul) the stake was our salvation and the new covenant was inaugurated. This is why Paul can go on to say, without any break: "Each time that you eat this bread and drink this cup, you proclaim the death of the Lord until he comes."

The translation of Paul's Greek verb as "proclaim" rather than "announce"[68] points the way by which we can enter into the thinking of Paul here. To proclaim is to announce authoritatively that a salutary event has taken place.[69] The event reaches the hearers through the act of speaking that is normally part of a cultic act.[70] In this particular cultic act, however, the action itself is an official "word": eucharistic worship is different in kind from the silent magic that can express itself only in nonsensical formulas.[71]

Who does the proclaiming at the Lord's Supper? Not the individuals who make up the community, still less some one person among them, but the assembly as such, or, more accurately, the Lord who is present in the assembly. It is the host who stands pledge for the proclaimers, those who speak in his name.

By the very fact that the community exists and celebrates its Supper it proclaims the life-giving power of the death of Jesus. As Paul sees it, the assembly does not "recall" a distant past event but proclaims a present salvation that is given because the past event has permanent value. The Lord's death alone gives birth to his community through baptism; through the Eucharist that same death keeps the new body in existence. At his final meal Jesus did much more than establish a means by which he might remain present to us after his death. He also expressed by this meal the union that would henceforth exist between himself and his disciples because he was going to his death in fidelity to his Father. For his death draws believers into a sharing of the life which the Father gives him in return. In the eucharistic assembly the covenant established with God is celebrated by celebrating its source: the death of the Lord. In a profound sense, the liturgical meal symbolizes the death of the Lord and its abiding efficacy.

To whom is the proclamation addressed? Those authors who, unlike me, read the text as meaning "Proclaim the Lord's death," that is, as a command, a statement of a duty to be carried out,[72] think that the eucharistic celebration is a "means" of preaching Christian salvation to others or bestowing salvation on those participating. I have difficulty accepting this reading. For one thing, salvation is acquired through faith and baptism. For another, Paul's purpose is to make the Corinthians aware of what they are doing when they gather for the eucharistic meal: How seriously they must take this meal if in it they are proclaiming the Lord's death!

The baptized, who accept the cross and love of Christ as the source of their existence as believers, find in the Lord's Supper a way of giving constant expression to their new life and of strengthening it through union with the mystery of him who died and rose for us. To celebrate the Eucharist is thus to renew participation in the death of Jesus; it is to proclaim the always liberating, redeeming, reconciling significance of that death.[73]

To celebrate the Eucharist is also, finally, to proclaim together—but, says Paul, only "until he comes." In other words, the Lord's Supper will find its fulfillment and its termination at the parousia, when—to use an image from the gospels—the Lord will provide the heavenly banquet in the company of God himself. "Until he comes" shows the "relative" nature of the Lord's Supper; the latter is not to be confused with the heavenly banquet. Paul says here what the synoptics say in their own manner: "I shall not drink henceforth of the fruit of the vine until the reign of God comes." Remarkably, then, while the eschatological perspective in Paul's treatment has moved outside the cultic account to v. 26 and is not included in the words attributed to Jesus, it has nonetheless been retained. It is evident that no account of institution in the New Testament authorizes its omission.

The time of the Eucharist stretches between the night of the betrayal and the day of the final coming. The Eucharist has value only by reference to future realities. In this sense, it is already and, at the same time, is not yet the very reality of life with God. But in the sacrament which the assembled community celebrates the presence of the Lord Jesus is continually manifested despite his absence, while the faith of the ecclesial community is continually proclaimed and its life continually renewed.

There is a secondary question that may be raised: When Paul speaks of "death," is he also thinking, as he does in baptism, of an effect produced in each believer by the actual dying of the Lord? Is the eucharistic celebration simply a matter of declaring our faith by receiving the gift offered to us by him who gave himself up for us? Or does the term "death" including a "death-dealing" element that actually touches the lives of those gathered for the celebration? I have explained elsewhere[74] that when Paul talks to the Corinthians about his sufferings as an apostle he replaces the Greek word *thanatos*, "death" (used here in 1 Cor 11:26), with *nekrōsis*, which means a dying, a death in process, an ongoing death, as it were. Here is the passage: "We ceaselessly carry in our bodies the dying *(nekrōsis)* of Jesus, in order that the life of Jesus may also be made visible in our bodies" (2 Cor 4:10).

This statement of the apostle applies to every believer. In connection with baptism Paul speaks of a "being buried with [Christ] into his death" so as to die continually to sin. In my opinion, the Eucharist likewise "actualizes the action of Jesus in dying, his 'necrosis,' as Paul calls it."[75] Not, of course, in the sense that the sacrament of life causes death, but in the sense that, according to Paul, it reminds Christians they must die to everything that divides, so that life may flow through them and the community of Christ may be ever more closely united. Through the eucharistic meal Jesus continues to sustain and deepen in believers the fidelity to God and other human beings which he himself demonstrated when he accepted his death. To announce the Lord's death is therefore not only to proclaim the salvation that springs from his love for us; it is also to assert that the living Christ is today killing in us the seeds of division that constantly threaten his community. And in fact the Churches have always regarded the Eucharist as the sacrament of unity.

CONCLUSION

Is it possible to summarize Paul's contribution to an understanding of the Eucharist? He himself provides no synthesis, but only reactions to what his correspondents tell or ask him, and this makes any general statement difficult and liable to be tendentious. However, he does show—and in this he is unique—how even the most ancient ecclesial traditions can be inflected so as to provide norms of behavior. Unlike the evangelists, he did not feel bound to locate the memory of Jesus' final meal in a biographical context. He was dealing with Christians who thought that their eucharistic practice was authentic but who at the same time showed little consistency in harmonizing their concrete attitudes with the teaching they had received. Faced with this situation, Paul turns "serious" and focuses on what is "interior."

His seriousness shows in his emphasis on the "death of the Lord." While the Corinthians tended to rejoice quite simply in the praise of God, probably in the manner of the gatherings described in the *Didache*, they also allowed themselves to lose interest in the poorer brethren and to indulge in real excesses. Do not some of them become drunk, even while others in the assembly lack necessities?

The situation is an intolerable one. As elsewhere—for example, when he writes from Corinth and brandishes Christ crucified before the eyes of the Galatians (3:1)—so here Paul forcefully reminds the Corinthians that when they celebrate the Eucharist they proclaim the "death of the Lord." Here again the crucified Lord stands before them, as one who has indeed returned from death but also as one whose wounds are still visible. The gift of self and service of the brethren must be the marks of every Christian.

Paul is not a killjoy, but he does want the community that celebrates "the Lord's Supper" to be conscious of its dignity, that is, attentive to all the brothers and sisters; otherwise its meal will no longer deserve to be called "the Lord's Supper." This liturgical action deserves its name only if it is celebrated in an atmosphere of brotherhood and sisterhood. If unity is to be real, there must be a minimum of union among those present, as Jesus himself had pointed out: "Before placing your offering on the altar, go and be reconciled with your brother!" Only then will the Lord's Supper be a living reminder of the salutary effectiveness of the death of Jesus.

Paul is not only serious; he also calls upon believers to develop a profoundly interior attitude to the Eucharist. The unity he demands of the Corinthians is not imposed from outside, but is to be a fruit engendered by the celebration itself. Of course, everyone already knew that Jesus was now present among his followers through the gift of bread and wine; but the words of the traditional account of the Supper hardly explained the kind of union Christians had with Christ as a result of the Eucharist or the new relationship they had among themselves.

By making use of a peripheral tradition about "communion" in the body and blood of Christ Paul is able to show the essential nature of the eucharistic liturgy. For, in making the point that the bread is the body of Christ he does not use the verb "to be" here but chooses, probably from an old tradition, the word koinōnia, which means "communion" in the fullest and most comprehensive sense of this term. "Communion" implicitly includes what is said in the verb "to be," but refers immediately to the fruit received through acceptance of this bread and this wine: the bread which we break is a communion in the body of Christ. Paul's statement thus brings out the finality of the eucharistic action.

To be in communion is to participate in the definitive covenant which Jesus has made with God. This participation evidently takes place through communion in the personal body of Jesus, but this in turn signifies directly an entrance into the covenant.

This entrance into the covenant is a personal act; that is, the relation between believer and Jesus is a relation between individuals. Paul is thus equivalently saying what is said in so many words in the fourth gospel: the good shepherd knows each of his sheep.

The union between believer and Jesus is effected in the mode of an assimilation, in accordance with one of the symbolisms Paul uses to express redemption. The symbolism of reconciliation is completed and, in a sense, crowned by that of assimilation, which human beings use in an effort to bring out the way in which interpersonal relations can be established. "Assimilation" here has nothing to do with an imaginary mystical "fusion," but respects the distinctness of the two persons involved. What is meant is a dialogue of love that is pushed to the extreme, that is, a dialogue leading to the fullest identification possible without destruction of the personality. Through communion the believer becomes really one with Jesus Christ.

To have communion in the body of Christ is, finally, to live as the very body of Christ, for it is Paul who introduces into theology the idea of that "ecclesial body" which we call "the body of Christ." The closer the intimacy with Jesus, the closer the presence to other believers. At this point Paul touches on one of the deepest of all mysteries, if indeed it be true that the paradox of human existence is to be found in the fact that human beings are at once individual persons and essentially social beings. Believers in Jesus become more fully themselves and more closely associated with their brothers and sisters, the more intimately united they are to their Savior.

XII
The Testament of Jesus
According to Luke

I shall be developing here the conclusion reached in Chapter IV, namely, that Luke has located the account of eucharistic institution in the immediate context of a non-cultic tradition which proves to be a testamentary tradition about the last meal of Jesus. It can be maintained that the Lukan account of the passion, which begins with Jesus' announcement of his imminent death and ends with the burial, follows the overall pattern of a "farewell discourse," similar to those found in the *Testaments of the XII Patriarchs*. The accounts of the arrest, condemnation, crucifixion, and death of Jesus are, of course, quite developed, showing that interests peculiar to the primitive community have caused a concentration on, and expansion of, the final part of the pre-existing testamentary pattern. Despite this alteration, however, the pattern is clearly discernible in the following table which shows the parallel between the sequences in Luke and that in the *Testament of Naphtali*.[1]

The table highlights the arrangements of the farewell discourse within which Luke has placed the tradition of eucharistic institution. He introduces his account with a prologue (22:1–14) that omits the anointing at Bethany and has two parts, each beginning with a reference to the coming Passover: "The feast of Unleavened Bread, called Passover, was approaching" (22:1); "The day of Unleavened Bread came, on which the Passover lamb had to be sacrificed" (22:7). The first section (1–6) is equivalent to the announcement of the patriarch's coming death (n. 1).[2] The second section (7–14) shows Jesus, like the patriarch, summoning his followers to a gathering (no. 2).

The meal then begins (nos. 3–4), during which Jesus will say

230

TESTAMENT OF NAPHTALI — MODEL TESTAMENT — LUKE 22:1–38

MODEL TESTAMENT (based on 32 biblical and apocryphal testaments)

Naphtali ref	TESTAMENT OF NAPHTALI	MODEL TESTAMENT	LUKE 22:1–38	ref
		PROLOGUE		
1, 1–2a	His sons arrive	Proximate death	The death of Jesus is imminent	1–6
		Summons	He takes the initiative	7–12
1, 2b	He prepares a meal	Meal	regarding the Passover meal	13–14
		TESTAMENT		
1, 3–4	I shall die after this meal	I am about to die	I shall die after this meal	15–18
			Body given. Blood shed	19–20
1, 5–2	My happy past in an ordered world:	My past	The traitor is preparing my death	21–23
3, 1–5	Play your part in it	+ exhortation	As I have served, ⇅ you also are to serve	27 / 24–26
			⌐ The Kingdom is given to me / It will be given to you	28–30
4, 1–5	You will sin: captivity, conversion, return	Your future	Sin of Peter and his return	31–34
8, 4–10	Do good and God will bless you	+ exhortation	(do not fail)	32a
		My successors	strengthen your brethren	32b
9, 1	Bury me at Hebron	I bless you / I am about to die / My burial	⌐ Trials are coming + exhortation full of imagery	35–36
			All shall be fulfilled	37(–38)
		EPILOGUE		
9, 2	He ate, drank . . . died	Death	(PASSION AND DEATH)	
9, 3	Buried as he wished	Burial	(BURIAL)	

Left-column bracket (5–8, 3): Visions of future, esp. Levi, Judah — Tell your sons to be faithful to them

N.B. 1 5–8, 3   28–30   35–36: elements of the model testament that are frequently found

N.B. 2 ⇅ : elements inverted in 24–27 (where the exhortation precedes the reference to the past)

his farewell (no. 7). The farewell contains three sections referring respectively to the present, the future, and the aftermath of his death: he announces and mimes his coming death (15–23); he tells his survivors how they should act (24–30); finally, he tells the community of disciples what is in store for them in the near future (31–38).

I. ANNOUNCEMENT AND MIMESIS OF THE DEATH OF JESUS (22:15–23)

The farewell discourse proper begins in the presence of the disciples as they gather for a meal, and it contains two groups of statements (vv. 14–18 and 21–23) which frame the cultic tradition (19–20). Each group of statements shows that this man who is about to die has clear knowledge of his destiny and places his trust in God; he knows whither he is going, and he defines what it means to be his follower.

The first part of the discourse contains two groups of verses (14–16 and 17–18), which are rendered parallel by their respective final verses:

14And when the hour came he reclined at table and the apostles with him. 15And he said to them: "I have greatly desired to eat this Passover with you before I suffer. 16For I tell you that I shall never eat it again until it is fulfilled in the kingdom of God."	17And, having accepted a cup, having given thanks, he said: "Take this and share it among you; 18for I tell you that I shall not drink henceforth of the fruit of the vine until the reign of God comes."

The actions mentioned are each followed by two statements:

ACTIONS	14coming to table for the Passover	17ataking the cup and giving thanks 17ba gift to be shared
WORDS	15desire for the Passover 16before suffering; motifs this is the last time	18 this is the last time

The *situation* is clearly described: Jesus is facing death, since he is about to "suffer," that is, "die,"[3] and since he will not again celebrate the Passover and drink the cup until the end of time.

The *feeling* which Jesus experiences is a strong desire[4] to celebrate this final Passover with his disciples. Is it possible to state this feeling more exactly? He does not want to suffer or die, but, since his death is in fact imminent, he does want to celebrate the Passover once again with his little band and unite himself in spirit with all of Israel as it celebrates the memory of its deliverance from Egypt, a memory now enriched with overtones added by a long past and with all of the people's expectations.[5]

The precise *motif* is sounded in a biblical manner by calling to mind the end of time, when God himself will bring Passover to its fulfillment,[6] that is, he will provide the reality which the feast anticipates liturgically. The second statement makes the same point by alluding to the coming of God's reign.[7]

The *behavior* of Jesus on this occasion is described in semitic fashion with the aid of the paired verbs eat/drink. He tells the disciples that he is here eating and drinking for the last time on earth, and that he will then go to his death. If his words are read without any preconceived ideas, they say clearly that he shares the festive meal with his disciples and drinks from the cup.[8] This final meal on the feast of Passover crowns the meals, both everyday and festive, which he has taken with his disciples and with sinners during his earthly life.

In short, these verses are meant to show Jesus very desirous of being with his disciples to celebrate the great feast of Passover on the eve of his death.[9] This new patriarch clearly announces his imminent painful death and, at the same time, the profound joy he derives from certainty about the final banquet that God will provide at the end of time. Meanwhile, and despite his departure, he will ensure his presence in the community during the time of waiting for that definitive reunion. That is the point of the next verses.

Vv. 19–20 contain the account of eucharistic institution:

[19]And having taken bread, having given thanks, he broke [it] and gave [it] to them, saying: "This is my body which [is] given for you. Do this in memory of me."
[20]And the cup likewise after the supper, saying: "This cup [is] the new covenant in my blood which [is] shed for you."

The essential structure of the cultic tradition is preserved in this account: with three axes serving as framework—Jesus/God, Jesus/ disciples, present/future—a radical transformation takes place in

Jesus (whose bodily presence will be of a different order than in the past) and in the group of disciples (which becomes a community gathered around Jesus at a cultic meal).

The account as presented by Luke has two distinctive aspects. First, for him, as for Paul and unlike Mark, the cup is identified not with the blood of the covenant but with the "new covenant" in the blood of Jesus "which is shed for you." As a result, Luke makes the farewell discourse of Jesus culminate in the new covenant. But if it be remembered that *diathēkē*, the Greek word for "covenant," is from a root meaning "to make a will or testament by an effective disposal," then there is justification for interpreting Jesus' act of giving himself as a "testament" that establishes the new people of God.

The second distinctive aspect of Luke's cultic account is that the liturgical coloring so prominent in Matthew/Mark has yielded place to a presentation of an historical kind. The account directly recalls the past occasion when Jesus and his disciples were together at the end of his last day on earth. The historical character of the account is emphasized by the fact that Jesus speaks not of the "multitude" but only of "you," the disciples gathered around him that day. In the group thus brought together in unity (plural "you") Jesus does doubtless have in mind the community made up of the believers of all times, but he is especially concerned with the individuals who are actually present and to whom his farewell words are addressed. On the other hand, the event is not wholly of the past, for there is a command of "remembrance," an order that the disciples celebrate the memory of Jesus. The community, now established through a bond with Jesus that has become internal, is to continue in existence after his passion and to remain until the end of time.

The two verses (19–20) containing the cultic account have a function in the farewell discourse, for they symbolize by a (two-fold) action the new mode of Jesus' presence to his disciples. This theme is new in relation to earlier testamentary literature. Not only does Luke, like Mark, stress the point that Jesus "gave the bread" to the disciples; he also explains that the body "is given for you." The reader must be careful to note that in announcing what will come to pass Luke uses the present tense, not the future; he does not say that the body of Jesus *will* be given or that his blood *will* be shed.[10] By using the present tense Luke shows the highly symbolic character of Jesus' action; because the action is introduced into the farewell discourse it mimes his death.

A second group of statements (vv. 21–23) completes the frame within which the mention of the eucharistic rite is located. First, Jesus tells the disciples that one of those at table with him is ready to betray him. He sharply contrasts himself and this individual:

> 21"But behold, the hand of him who is betraying me is helping itself at this table with me. 22For the Son of Man is going as it has been decreed. But woe to that man by whom he is being betrayed!"
> 23And they began to ask one another which of them would do this.

Luke uses the word "table" here, instead of "dish" as in Matthew and Mark, probably in order to emphasize the table fellowship and therefore the terribly contradictory situation of the traitor.[11] He does not, of course, like John, go so far as to show Judas departing from the supper room and leaving Jesus alone with "his own,"[12] but the openness of the indictment justifies us in thinking that the traitor is not part of the group to which the farewell discourse is addressed. It might be said, then, that these verses correspond to the summons of his family by the patriarch who will shortly die.

Luke's intention in placing these words after the account of institution is not to make the reader think that Judas received the body and blood of Christ in "communion" (Matthew and Mark seem to have tried to avoid this scandalous implication by placing the revelation of the betrayer before the cultic meal). If Luke had wanted to depict an infamous "communion of Judas,"[13] he would have laid greater emphasis on it. In his view, Jesus proceeds as he does in order to ensure the cohesiveness of this group of sons who alone may hear what the father of the family has to say just before his death. Another probable reason for the order in Luke is to make readers ask themselves whether they too share the Lord's table and yet betray their fellows. Believers must ask themselves whether they are faithful to the call of Christ which they have heard.[14]

The situation is clear. Jesus has called his disciples together at his last meal in order to tell them that he is about to leave them until the day when he sees them again in the kingdom of God. Above all, however, he wishes to tell them that he will remain present with them liturgically through the eucharistic rite, by reason of the new covenant that he will establish by shedding his blood. He has to give some last explanations to these "believers" who, as the eucharistic symbolism reveals, have become one with him, and thereby ensure the complete cohesiveness of their community. The patriarch can now begin his exhortation that will reveal the meaning of the lives of his own.

The patriarch is Jesus, who has just asserted his complete confidence in God: he will be delivered from death and will remain present to his disciples. My reading of the verses that follow will therefore be made simultaneously at two levels. At the level of form I shall note the analogies that exist between the pericopes in Luke and the characteristic motifs of the testamentary genre. At the level of interpretation I shall be pointing out the parallel between the kind of life the disciples are exhorted to lead and the experience, past or soon to come, of Jesus himself. His death is imminent, but for that reason his gaze is already fixed on what lies beyond death; in this twofold perspective he sums up the essential traits of his own life and projects them as an ideal for the life of his disciples.

II. PRESENT SITUATION OF BELIEVERS (22:24–30)

The exhortation of Jesus comes shortly after the words of institution which foretold the close communion between disciples and master. It explains how this vital unity is to find expression in everyday life, namely, by conduct that is inspired by the conduct of Jesus of Nazareth and supported by his promise and victory.

The exhortation has two parts which correspond to the two aspects of the one mystery of Christ. Service of the brethren (22:24–27) corresponds to his death, and the prospect of coming glory which gives strength to the disciples of Jesus (22:28–30) corresponds to his resurrection.

A life of service (22:24–27)

The disciples have heard Jesus speak of a "kingdom" or "reign" (22:18) and are therefore anxious to know which of them will be the most important person in it. In response, Jesus speaks of his own behavior, which should be the model for theirs:

[24]They came down to arguing among themselves
about which of them was to be considered greatest.
[25]He said to them:
"The kings of the Gentiles

act as their lords,
and those who hold sway over them
are called benefactors.
[26]Not so among you.
Rather let the greatest among you
be as the youngest.
and let him who commands
be as one who serves.
[27]For which in fact is greater:
one who sits at table
or one who serves?
Is it not the one who sits at table?
But as for me, I am in your midst
as one who serves."

This short explanation corresponds rather closely to the section of a testament in which the dying man looks back over his devout past, and to the exhortation that flows from the assessment (no. 5). Here, indeed, the exhortation precedes the reference to the past, but this is due to the behavior of the disciples, for it is in relation to their rivalry that Jesus speaks of his own past. This flexibility in applying the testamentary form does not prevent our recognizing it here, since the relation among the component elements remains the same.

This passage is nonetheless distinguished from other testaments by its mention of the quarreling disciples. The dispute breaks the continuity of the monological discourse and thereby lends interest to those Jesus is addressing. They have hardly gathered when they fall to disagreeing among themselves and thus fragmenting their new-found unity. It was not enough for Jesus to get rid of the traitor, for here a source of discord is already visible.

This last remark calls for some clarification of the situation. We have here indeed a patriarch who recalls his own past life; above all, however, we have Jesus who is seeking to associate his disciples fully with his own destiny and who, to that end, seeks to deepen the table fellowship that unites him with them.

The quarrel among the disciples, which is not extraordinary by ancient standards, provides an excellent context for the exhortation of Jesus.[15] He has not only shown a special preference for the meal as an image of the community formed by human beings in covenant with God, but has added the further image of service at table. Thus when the master of the parable returns to find his servants keeping watch, he "will don his working garment, seat them at table, and go about serving them" (Lk 12:37). In Jesus' eyes, his own life is a service: "The Son of Man has come not to be served but to serve."[16] This saying, which is recorded by Mark and Matthew, has its Lukan equivalent here in the farewell discourse, where the emphatic "I"[17] seems to make it a more direct expression of Jesus' thinking. "But as for me, I am in your midst as one who serves." Jesus is here summing up the meaning of his entire life; John will express that meaning symbolically in the gesture of washing the disciples' feet.[18]

By contrasting service with ambition in his own behavior Jesus shows what the authentic attitude of disciples must be—not of the twelve alone but of every disciple. I say this because, prior to Easter, the twelve are not yet the leaders of the Church, inasmuch as they are not yet the privileged witnesses to the risen Christ; at this point they rather prefigure the new people of God that gathers around Jesus. They cannot as yet be described as in a position of authority over the other faithful, but represent the future Church in its entirety. Consequently the exhortation of Jesus here applies to all members of the people of God.[19]

Among these members, however, some aspire to be great and powerful, to be leaders. Jesus does not utterly reject this secret ambition of human beings, for it may express a deep sense of human solidarity. But it may also cloak a tendency to dominate, and therefore Jesus establishes a clear contrast between "the greatest, those who hold sway and give orders, those who sit at table," and "the youngest, those who serve." Who, then, can be called leaders in the people of God? Those who serve. In this context, however, Jesus is not urging humility but revealing a new order of things: in God's people the greatest is the littlest and the leader is the servant, the one who, in imitation of Jesus, acts as "one who serves."

While, then, the meal symbolizes the community of brothers and sisters, this community is held together not by the authoritative control of those whose concern it is to maintain order, but by mutual service. Jesus says to all members of the new people: "Do you want to be leaders? Then be servants!" Such is the testament describing Christian life as a life like that of Jesus who gave his blood for his disciples and for all human beings. The fruit of the eucharistic meal, therefore, is the appearance of servants who will be true "leaders" among their brothers and sisters.[20]

In trying to summarize what Jesus has been saying here it is enough to cite the answer which Jesus gives in the fourth gospel to the Greeks who want to "see" him: "If anyone serves me, let him follow me. And where I am, there my servant will also be." To this he immediately adds: "If anyone serves me, my Father will honor him." The prospect of reward and honor corresponds to the second panel, as it were, in the diptych of Jesus' exhortation.

The prospect of glory (22:28–30)

In their exhortations the patriarchs told their sons they would be rewarded for their fidelity if they obeyed the law and practiced fraternal love.[21] Jesus takes the same approach, but with what a difference! For it is "I," Jesus, who will determine the reward in store for the disciples:

> [28]You are the ones who have stood by me
> in my trials.
> [29]And I for my part confer a kingdom on you
> as *(kathōs)*[22] the Father has conferred
> a kingdom on me,
> [30]so that you may eat and drink at my table
> in my kingdom,
> and sit on thrones
> to judge the twelve tribes of Israel.

In a tremendous leap Jesus connects the present situation with the end time: the time of the kingdom of which he had spoken prior to the eucharistic instruction, the time when human beings shall be reunited at the eschatological feast.

The springboard for the promise is the disciples' faithful following of the Master all the way to this final meal when he is threatened from every side. In the trials he has had to endure, Jesus has had the faithful support of the disciples—a support that amounts to the "service" he called for a moment ago. They have joined forces with him in time of trial and they will one day be rewarded: they "will sit on thrones to judge the twelve tribes of Israel." These men who had been "servants" will then become "judges," in a complete reversal of situation.[23] Nonetheless, Luke's interest seems to be focused essentially on the prediction of the "kingdom" that is given to Jesus and that will also belong to the disciples.

Over against trials, then, stands the kingdom promised to those who have followed Christ in his humiliations. In the present context, however, Jesus does not at all emphasize the dark side of the contrast. He speaks rather as if he were already with his Father in glory and already possessed of a majesty no patriarch could have claimed. In keeping with the testamentary genre Jesus links past and future: he has sure knowledge. Unlike the patriarchs, however, he shows himself master of the future. The reason is that God his Father has given him the kingdom by testament,[24] so that he can speak of it as "his own."

In keeping with the occasion, namely, a meal, Jesus calls to mind the table fellowship with himself which the disciples will enjoy in his kingdom. When he said earlier that he would no longer drink of the fruit of the vine until the reign of God came (22:18), he had not explained that the disciples would enjoy the eschatological banquet with him (whereas Matthew adds "with you"). He does make this point now. The final banquet is already present for Jesus, and he leaves as his testament to the disciples a promise of definitive participation in it.

III. THE NEAR FUTURE (22:31–38)

I must now return to the period immediately following the supper, for the reward which Jesus announces is reserved to the end of time. At present, the disciples must look forward to trials that are about to shake them badly. The community that will some day gather in heaven is now to be scattered as a result of Jesus' death, and Jesus must strengthen it, while also heartening the man whose task it will be to bring the community together again. The disciples are unaware of the misfortune that is about to descend upon them; Jesus must therefore warn them all the more urgently.

There are two short passages, one on the scattering of the community and on the leader who must unite it once more (22:31–34), the other on the seriousness of the impending trial (22:35–38).

Peter and the community (22:31–34)

One of the problems caused by the death of the founder of a community is the problem of succession (no. 10). Luke knew the tradition about the prediction of Peter's denial; he gives his version of it,[25] but introduces it with a passage peculiar to him:

> [31]Simon, Simon, Satan has claimed you
> in order to shake you in a sieve
> as they do with wheat.

^{32}But I have prayed for you
that your faith may not fail.
As for you, when you have come back
strengthen your brethren.

Critics are not forcing the text when they see here a concern for ensuring succession in the office of shepherd. The immediate interlocutors are Jesus and Simon whom he has chosen to be the "rock" of the future community and who is here called by his original name, as though Jesus wanted to call attention to the ordinary man behind the "leader" of the community.

In fact, however, the real actors on the stage here are Jesus and Satan. This is the hidden reality which Jesus now makes known to the entire group, as is suggested by the plural personal pronoun ("Satan has claimed you [plural] in order to shake you [plural] . . . ") and by Simon's position in relation to "your [singular] brethren." Jesus has seen Satan fall from heaven, for he himself had triumphed over him.[26] Nonetheless Satan now makes his "entrance" as a combatant by prompting Judas to betray Jesus[27] and by claiming the right to scatter the disciples. Jesus is quite familiar with the mysterious activity of the Adversary.

Once again, Jesus is able to thwart this activity by his prayer. As a result, Simon's faith will not be lost in the terrible trial; God will win out in the end. Luke has his own way of showing that the confusion of the disciples will be only momentary: he omits the tradition of their actual desertion[28] and says simply that the wheat will be shaken in the sieve, thus causing the chaff to fly away (Am 9:9).

There is another sign here that Jesus is handing over the role of leader to Simon: he will not himself reunite the flock in Galilee;[29] rather it is Simon who, thanks to the prayer of Jesus, will strengthen his brethren. Simon's faith will not have been completely lost and therefore he will be able to rebuild the community once he has "come back," that is, when he shall have "put himself to rights again." The meaning of the expression will become clear only after Simon has benefited from the appearance to him of the risen Lord.[30]

Peter's own foolish claim in the very next verses (33–34) is in striking contrast with the concern of Jesus for all the disciples and with the sovereign foreknowledge of him who as Master of time links future to present. The shadow makes the light all the brighter. Perhaps Luke intends Peter to stand here for all leaders of the Church, since they too can fall.[31] The acquisition of authority should not make leaders imagine that they are henceforth unshakeable and already fully settled in heaven as it were.

The struggle begins (22:35–38)

But at present the light shines only in the heart of Christ, and the farewell discourse moves on with pitiless realism: the future is dark, the sword is inescapable:[32]

> [35]And he said to them: "When I sent you out
> without purse or bag or sandals,
> did you lack anything?"
> They answered: "Nothing."
> [36]He said to them: "But now
> let him who has a purse take it;
> the same for him who has a bag;
> and let him who has no sword sell his cloak
> and buy one.
> [37]For I tell you, this passage of scripture
> must be fulfilled in me:
> 'They counted him among the criminals.'
> And in fact what has to do with me
> is coming to its fulfillment."
> [38]"Lord," they said, "here are two swords."
> But he answered them: "It is enough."

Jesus—unlike his hearers who show a complete lack of understanding of the situation—is evidently not urging armed rebellion.[33] Rather he is warning his disciples of the hatred that will be directed at them, just as the patriarchs told their sons of the dangers that would threaten them (nos. 5 and 6).[34] The reason for Jesus' warning is obvious: it is all up with him, since the Servant of God is about to be listed among the criminals,[35] and the same fate awaits the disciples.

This man who is about to die predicts that the community is entering upon a period of its life that is quite different from the serene days when the disciples gathered around Jesus of Nazareth at the beginning of his earthly ministry. At that time brother helped brother; there was freedom and no need to worry about the morrow.[36] Now they must anticipate imminent harsh trials. At this point, Jesus plunges into the darkness in the Garden of Olives, like a wrestler who is about to sweat blood.

Thanks to the testament of Jesus the cultic tradition acquires a new meaning in Luke. The eucharistic meal must indeed continue to be celebrated, as the command of remembrance requires, but Jesus now speaks of the paradisal world of the heavenly banquet as coming only after an unrelenting struggle against evil. The idyllic period of earthly life with Jesus of Nazareth is over, but the banquet in paradise is not yet here. The time of the Church is beginning, the time of struggle with destructive powers; the Church will be able to carry on this struggle because of the new presence of him who entrusts his cause to the Father and departs to face death alone.

IV. CULT AND LIFE

The farewell discourse in Luke is clearly not as extensive and comprehensive as the one in John. Nonetheless, constructed as it is with the help of traditions which Luke chose not to revise completely, the passage does shed light on the new situation created by the departure of Jesus. The traditions at Luke's disposal, which came either from the tradition he shares with Matthew and Mark or from sources of his own, have been organized in such a way that the reader is given the entire testament of Jesus. In other words, the testament cannot be reduced to the institution of the Eucharist, even though the latter keeps its place at the heart of it.

In proceeding thus, Luke shows himself to be an evangelist par excellence. He was not free, as Paul was, to juxtapose an account of institution and an exhortation to love; he had to locate everything within a farewell discourse that includes even the words of cultic institution. According to Luke, Jesus was not satisfied to establish a new ("sacramental") mode of presence resulting from his sacrifice; at the same time he communicated the existential meaning of the sacramental action by developing the themes of fraternal service and of watchfulness amid trial in expectation of the final banquet.

Let me compare once more *the text of Luke* and *the testamentary tradition*. Most of the motifs found in this genre appear in Luke: setting of imminent death, convocation of the disciples for a meal during which the coming death is announced, exhortation to behavior like that of the dying man in his past life, encouragement with the prospect of a wonderful future, warning of the seriousness of the survivors' situation as one of ceaseless struggle.

But certain departures from the testamentary genre are also

significant. On the negative side, nothing is said of the burial, although the Markan tradition speaks of this at the anointing in Bethany.[37] Why is this? Probably because the end of the passion story will be taken up with the burial, but also because Jesus is here interested only in the community that will continue after his death.

There is, on the other hand, this further, positive difference, that Luke lays quite a bit more emphasis on certain elements in the testamentary tradition. The meal occupies the foreground and, with the insertion of vv. 19–20, even becomes a cultic meal (as it already was, perhaps, in the *Testament of Naphtali*). The disciples are not passive witnesses: thus the announcement of a traitor greatly puzzles them (23); they argue about who will be greatest among them (24); Peter reacts vehemently to the prediction of his testing (33); and when the disciples are questioned by Jesus, they show their failure to grasp the situation (35, 38). The "discourse" of Jesus thus tends to turn into an instruction in dialogue form. Is he still a "dying" man who is leaving a testament, or is he fully in control of events?

Finally, the past comes into the picture only as an argument for the fidelity of the disciples. Jesus looks primarily to the future: to the reward appointed for those who on earth will have remained his faithful companions (24–28), or to the recovery of Simon and the others (32), or, finally, to the threatening situation of the disciples (36).

The cultic tradition is colored by this entire setting. It acquires meaning from the service to be done in sustaining the community which the eucharistic meal seals and symbolizes. It is related to the eschatological banquet, as it already was in the common tradition, but with this difference, that the context of the relationship here is one of struggle to remain faithfully united to Jesus and to join him in transforming the world. The Eucharist is not simply a rite to be performed; it is an action that, like a concave mirror, both focuses light and reflects it back: it contains within itself in summary form both that past meal of Jesus and the meal that is still to come; it announces the definitive banquet; it keeps the community united and confident amid trial and death.

Finally, let me look at the text of Luke from the standpoint of the two basic perspectives proper to the testamentary form: that of the testator and that of the testatees.

The viewpoint of the testator

While his enemies and Judas are preparing death for him (vv. 1–6), Jesus bids his disciples prepare the Passover meal which he will celebrate in his own fashion (7–14). This twofold preparation serves as prologue to the final action of Jesus; it is a prologue that has his person as its unifying factor. Jesus goes to Passover and to death with full awareness of what he is doing.

Jesus establishes the meaning of the Passover he celebrates: that meaning is his own death. Does he not announce that he will not share a meal again with his disciples until the day of the heavenly banquet? He makes clear as well the consequences of his departure. Yes, his death is at hand.

It is even here at this moment. As I pointed out earlier, Luke uses the present tense of the verbs that describe what is about to happen. This is clear in the case of the words of institution, but he does the same elsewhere. Thus, unlike the Jesus of Matthew, who uses the future tense, the Jesus of Luke exposes the hand of him who *is betraying* him (*paradidontos*) and says that the Son of Man *is going* (*poreuetai*) and *is being betrayed* (*paradidotai*). Jesus is master of time and sees his death as now present, just as he confers (*diatithemai*) the kingdom now and judges that what is written of him is now being fulfilled (*telos echei*).

The viewpoint of the testatees

Testamentary literature shows the farewell meal as being an act of communion with the testator and a meaningful bond of communion among the testatees. The observations made on the text of Luke can be grouped under those two headings.

Communion with Jesus

Luke emphasizes the meal, which is mentioned in each of the pericopes analyzed, except in the one on the betrayal and in the final exhortation. It is his way of symbolizing the participation or communion of the disciples in Christ. The meal of the present moment is being taken with Jesus who "serves" at table; the meal at the end of time will be taken with Jesus who bestows the kingdom. In between these two there is the cultic meal which Jesus orders eaten in memory of him; this meal resembles the meal which they are eating now and which already symbolizes the death and new life of Jesus.

The disciples who have shared their master's trials during his
earthly life are asked to serve as he did, in union with him, and
with the prospect of a table fellowship to come in heaven.

The apostles are eating and drinking with Jesus for the last
time, until they eat and drink with him again in the kingdom. By
agreeing to share in his bread and his cup they become participants
in his passage from old life to new life. They attach themselves in
a symbolic way to his body that is being handed over; they receive
his blood that is being shed. Since the communion in his death is
real, the mimesis too deals in reality. The words of Jesus deal in
reality, for because of them and of the gift of the body given and
the blood shed the twelve implicitly "pass" and "die" with him,
so that they may be able also to rise with him. The communion is
real in historical time (the time of the Last Supper) and it will be
real in heavenly time (the time of the final banquet); it must therefore be no less real in the intervening time of seeming separation.
This parallelism and continuity is the basis of the "real presence"
of Christ (the basis, that is, of the eucharistic mystery), since communion supposes a real presence.

Communion of the apostles among themselves

By including in his account the exhortation Jesus gives when
he finds the disciples quarreling about who is the greatest among
them, Luke shows that there can be no domination, jealousy, or
rivalry among brethren who share the same Supper of the Lord. A
commitment to brotherhood must unite the sharers of Jesus' table;
each must even want to be the servant of all. It is clear that this
aspect of the Supper narrative corresponds to the theme of the reconciliation of estranged brethren in the testamentary literature.

The branding of Jesus' betrayer can also be interpreted in light
of the communion among the disciples. The incident takes place
not before the eucharistic meal but immediately after it and thus
stands in violent contrast with the communion, symbolizing as it
does the anti-communion of the traitor. Then, and only then, Jesus
can exhort the disciples to a life of fraternal service and to perse-
vering fidelity.

By locating the words of institution within a farewell discourse Luke brings out very clearly the role of the eucharistic lit-

urgy in Christian life. The cultic tradition even has a privileged place within the testamentary tradition, inasmuch as the account of institution summarizes, in a way, the entire farewell discourse, and the latter becomes an explanation of how the liturgical action assimilates the disciples to the living Lord. The liturgical action has value only if it expresses its efficacy in concrete fruits: faith and fidelity amid trials, hope of promised glory, love brought down to earth in service to the brothers and sisters.

There is therefore no question of choosing between the cultic tradition and the testamentary tradition, since both are indispensable for showing the deeper meaning of the new presence of Jesus after his death. Both give expression to the same divine mystery, namely, that the disciples are invited to become other Christs, as understood by the saints.

XIII
The Eucharist According to John

The fourth gospel offers a very original treatment of the tradition regarding the Lord's Supper and the sharing of the bread. On the one hand, it stands apart in that it has no account or words of sacramental institution and that by its exclusive emphasis on the relation of each believer with Christ it distances itself from any and every "organization" of Christian life and highlights instead the new commandment of fraternal love. On the other hand, Johannine symbolism often invites the reader to look beneath the words and behind the gestures of Jesus for a deeper meaning which some interpreters regard as sacramental.

It is not surprising, therefore, that many critics have chosen one or other of these two directions within the gospel. Some think that John adopts a clearly antisacramental outlook in which faith alone is required of the disciples of Jesus. Thus while Bultmann keeps three passages with eucharistic overtones,[1] he nonetheless believes them to have been added by an ecclesiastical redactor who was anxious to make up for the lacuna in John. Some critics—E. Schweizer and H. Strathmann,[2] for example—go even further and maintain that the entire gospel, including the three passages just mentioned, must be interpreted along lines that if not strictly antisacramental are at least antidocetic; any residual sacramental overtones are only peripheral.

At the other extreme, O. Cullmann finds sacramental teaching throughout John's gospel; his principle is that wherever such an interpretation is possible, it should be asserted and attributed to the author.[3] W. Michaelis has vehemently challenged this systematization,[4] but it has continued to find adherents, such as E. Hoskyns and A. Corell, and many Catholic writers, such as B. Vawter and E. Niewalda.[5]

In view of these two extremes, the first need is to define the terms in the debate, since to speak of Johannine sacramentalism is not to say that John shares our classical conceptions (for example, in regard to the words of institution or to bread and wine as the elements) or even the idea of sacrament that can be found in Ignatius of Antioch.[6] The second need is to define the criteria that allow a passage to be read as having sacramental significance. It is not enough here to appeal to the interpretation which second-century Christian writers give of John;[7] each text must be examined on its own merits. This is what R. Schnackenburg and R. Brown have done with great care.[8]

It is quite obvious that John was familiar with the early Church's sacramental practice of baptism and the Lord's Supper; it is therefore possible that this or that episode or statement of Jesus was deliberately chosen in order to call these sacraments to mind. This is the direction in which I shall move, with the aim of showing to what extent there may be a sacramental dimension in John. I shall take up this question in the second part of the chapter.

In the first part, which carries on the discussion in the preceding chapters, I shall inquire into the meaning which the final meal of Jesus takes on when it is located in the context of a lengthy farewell discourse.

I. THE TESTAMENT OF JESUS

The critics unanimously describe chapters 13–16 as a "farewell discourse,"[9] but they do not usually draw conclusions from this fact for their interpretation of the cultic tradition. Luke has retained the latter, while incorporating it into a farewell discourse;[10] John, however, has a farewell discourse to the exclusion of the cultic tradition. What is the significance of this state of affairs?

1. Let me first quickly recall the arrangement of the Johannine discourse. In the course of his final meal, after a very solemn introduction (13:1), Jesus founds the community of disciples by washing their feet (13:2–20) and by getting rid of the traitor (13:21–30); the community which he establishes is thus knit together by the master's service to them and by faith in his word (13:10; 15:2–3). His action must continue to be the prototype and living source of the disciples' way of life:[11] "I have given you an example (hypodeigma) so that as I (kathōs) have done for you, you may also do" (13:15).

The word "example" can be misleading, since it may be understood as an invitation to "imitate" the behavior of Jesus, whereas in fact the word "as" *(kathōs)* conveys the idea of origination rather than exemplarity.[12] It certainly does set up a comparison: the relation of love among the disciples should be like the relation of love that unites Jesus to the disciples. But there is more than that. It is as if Jesus were saying: "By acting in this way, *I give you the power* to act in the same way." There is an evident similarity here to the commandment of remembrance: "Do this in memory of me," inasmuch as both formulas express a will to exercise a control over future time. Their objects differ, however: the commandment of remembrance has to do with liturgical action, the farewell discourse with service to the brethren. According to John, the community is founded upon and kept in existence by mutual service as much as by eucharistic worship; "have part with" (13:8) corresponds to "communion" (1 Cor 10:16).

This entire introduction to the farewell discourse ends in a cry of victory, which is typically Johannine way of bringing a section to its conclusion. Since the community is established "when he [Judas] had gone," Jesus can exclaim that the Son of Man has been glorified and will be glorified again (13:31–32).

Now that the community has been established, Jesus is in a position to leave it his testament, since he is about to depart from it. He does this not, as in Luke, with the help of sayings or incidents from the synoptic tradition,[13] but by completely restructuring the discourse. "My little children, I shall be with you only a little longer. . . . I give you a new commandment, that you love one another. . . . By this shall all know that you are my disciples: if you love one another" (13:33–35).

After an interlude in which Peter expresses a determination to follow Jesus wherever he goes, Jesus ends this section by saying that he will return to his disciples after preparing a place for them (14:1–3). Like the earlier "example" of the washing of feet, the final advice of Jesus to his followers who remain behind on earth is intended to strengthen and preserve, during his absence, the bonds uniting the disciples to him who is both absent and present.

Jesus goes on to describe the characteristic aspects of the believer's life in the present world. From 14:4 to 14:31 these last discussions have to do with the consequences of his departure; then, from 15:1 to 16:33, the perspective changes, as the glorified Christ gives a last message to his Church. But despite the variety of traditions and perspectives that are incorporated in these chapters the whole remains a farewell discourse.

The style of the whole resembles that of the *Testaments of the Twelve Patriarchs*, as, for example, in the address "my little children" or the use of the word "commandment" *(entolē)*. The same themes make their appearance: clairvoyance, intercession, imitation. Some similarities are especially clear:[14] Jesus announces his death during a final meal,[15] he recalls the example of service that he has just given,[16] he exhorts his followers to fraternal love,[17] and he predicts persecutions.[18] In addition—a new theme—he promises his consoling presence,[19] and he says that believers will be heard if they pray in his name.[20]

On this last evening, however, no mention is made of the institution of the Eucharist. Why this omission?

2. In thus substituting the testamentary tradition for the cultic tradition, does John intend to challenge the sacramental practice of his day? Critics have not been lacking who maintain this position; they are guilty, however, of some exaggeration. John is not anti-establishment; his emphasis is rather on fulfillment. He brings the synoptic tradition to its completion; by this I do not mean that he has a textual knowledge of the various recensions, but rather that he has a profound grasp of the synoptic witness and reduces it to its essentials. This is true both of the words of Jesus (his discourses here focus on faith in his person) and of his actions (most of the miracles kept by John symbolize Christian life: walking, seeing, living).

Furthermore, John, like the other evangelists, is meeting the needs of a specific community. He must ward off the danger of magical thinking that may well threaten sacramental practice in a Hellenistic environment. This may be one of the reasons why John has not included the words of institution in the account of the Supper.[21] All this does not mean, however, that John disparages the sacrament, for in his own way he gives the equivalent of the synoptic texts in his use of the testamentary genre and in his symbolic language. His special contribution is to make known the real and abiding meaning of the Eucharist. The farewell discourse may be said to focus on the "thing" or "ultimate goal" of the sacrament *(res sacramenti)*, since the ultimate purpose of the Eucharist is to intensify in this world that fraternal love which is divine in its origin.

There is an important conclusion to be drawn from the fact

that John has decided to depict the direct relation of believers with Christ as a life of charity and mutual service. The conclusion is this: that sacramental practice is only *one* way of encountering the risen Jesus, whereas the practice of mutual service is both the indispensable condition for this encounter and the indispensable expression of it.

But John is not satisfied to bring out the truth that the love Christians have for one another is the real symbol of Christ's presence in this world. He also shows that believers must constantly renew their eucharistic practice through contact with the earthly Jesus. This permanent relation to Jesus of Nazareth is a very important aspect of the fourth gospel. It applies to the practice of baptism, as can be seen from the baptismal context in which the dialogue with Nicodemus is placed in Chapter 3. Christian baptism is, of course, a baptism in the Spirit (3:5), but it must also always be related to the baptisms which Jesus himself performed (3:22): that which the Spirit effects today is and remains an act of the earthly Jesus.[22] In like manner, Chapter 6 is a eucharistic catechesis only in light of the discourse of Jesus of Nazareth on the Bread of Life. This discourse is a key for the interpretation of the fourth gospel as a whole, since it has to do with the mystery of the Lord's presence. The other eucharistic texts will enable the reader to enter more deeply into the meaning of the discourse.

II. THE BREAD OF LIFE

The "discourse on the Bread of Life" (6:26–65) follows upon the account of a miracle that Jesus performed when "the feast of Passover" was near; the date may have some symbolic value. Jesus, then, has given bread in abundance to the crowd that has been following him and now wants very much to make him king. But he withdraws into the hills, while the disciples depart in their boat for the other side of the lake. Jesus then walks on the waters and joins the disciples, who are terrified by a strong wind. Now the boat reaches shore. The Jews for their part have reached the same spot and are surprised to find Jesus there before them. After some questions and answers Jesus utters a discourse that is interrupted at times by objections aimed at making his words sound ridiculous. Let us read the text, being careful to observe how its argument advances.[23]

O. The petition (6:26–34)

Mysterious words of Jesus contrasting two foods (26–27)
[26]Truly, truly, I tell you,
you seek me, not because you have seen miracles
but because you have eaten bread and been filled.
[27]Work not for perishable food
but for the food that remains and becomes eternal life,
the food which the Son of Man will give to you,
for it is he upon whom the Father—God—has put his seal.

Dialogue on the work to be done (28–31)
[28]They therefore said to him: "What must we do to do the
    works of God?"
[29]Jesus answered them: "This is the work of God: that you
    believe in the one whom he has sent."
[30]They therefore said to him: "What sign do you give that we
    may see and believe you? What work do you do?
[31]Our fathers ate manna in the wilderness, as it is written:
'A bread from heaven he gave them to eat.' "

*Mysterious words of Jesus which lead to the petition of the
    Jews (32–34)*
[32]Jesus therefore said to them: "Truly, truly, I tell you,
it was not Moses who gave you bread from heaven;
it is my Father who gives you bread from heaven, the true
    bread;

[33]for the bread of God is he who comes down from heaven
    and gives life to the world."
[34]They said to him therefore: "Lord, give us this bread
    always."

A. The bread from heaven (6:35–47)

Mysterious words of Jesus (35–40)
[35]Jesus said to them: "The bread of life is myself.
None who come to me will ever hunger again; none who
    believe in me will ever thirst again.
[36]But as I told you, you see me but you do not believe.
[37]Everyone whom the Father gives to me will come to me,
and whoever comes to me I will not reject,

³⁸for I have come down from heaven
to do not my own will but the will of him who sent me.
³⁹This, however, is the will of him who sent me,
that I should lose nothing of what he has given to me
but should raise it up on the last day.
⁴⁰Yes, this is my Father's will
that all who see the Son and believe in him should have
    eternal life,
and I should raise them up on the last day."

Objection of the Jews (41–42)

⁴¹The Jews therefore complained about him because he had
    said: "I am the bread that has come down from heaven,"⁴²
    and they said: "Is this not Jesus, the son of Joseph, a man
    whose father and mother we know? How then can he say,
    'I have come down from heaven'?"

Revelation of the mystery of life-giving faith (43–47)

⁴³Jesus answered them: "Do not complain among yourselves.
⁴⁴None can come to me unless the Father who sent me draws
    them,
and I will raise them up on the last day.
⁴⁵It is written in the prophets:
'They shall all be taught by God.'
Whoever listens to the Father's teaching and learns from it
    comes to me.
⁴⁶No one has seen the Father, except him who is from the
    Father—he has seen the Father.
⁴⁷Truly, truly, I tell you, all who believe have eternal life."

B. The living Bread, given to be eaten (6:48–58)

Mysterious words of Jesus (48–51)

⁴⁸The bread of life is myself.
⁴⁹Your fathers ate manna in the wilderness and died.
⁵⁰But the bread coming down from heaven is such that none
    who eat it will die.
⁵¹The living bread that has come down from heaven is
    myself: all who eat of it will live for ever.
And the bread that I shall give is my flesh for the life of the
    world."

Objection of the Jews (52)

⁵²The Jews therefore argued among themselves: "How can
    this man give us his flesh to eat?"

Revelation of the mystery of the living bread (53–58)
[53]Jesus therefore said to them:

"Truly, truly, unless you eat the flesh of the Son of Man and
  drink his blood, you will not have life in you.
[54]All who eat my flesh and drink my blood have eternal life,
and I will raise them up on the last day.
[55]For my flesh is truly a food
and my blood truly a drink.
[56]All who eat my flesh and drink my blood
remain in me and I in them.
[57]Just as I whom the living Father has sent live by the Father,
  so all who eat me will live by me.
[58]Such is the bread that has come down from heaven.
It is not like the bread which the fathers ate, for they are
  dead.
All who eat this bread will live for ever."

Z. The choice (6:59–65)

Summary of the preceding discourse (59)
[59]Thus did he speak when teaching in the synagogue at
  Capernaum.

Objection of the disciples (60)
[60]After listening to him many of his disciples said:
"How hard a saying this is! Who could accept it?"

Mysterious revelation of Jesus (61–65)
[61]But, being aware that his disciples were complaining of his
  discourse, Jesus said to them:
[62]"Does that scandalize you? What if you were to see the Son
  of Man ascending to where he was before?
[63]It is the spirit that gives life, the flesh is good for nothing.
The words I have spoken to you are spirit and they are life.
[64]But there are some among you who do not believe."
Jesus had in fact known from the beginning who the non-
  believers were and who it was that would betray him.
[65]And he said: "That is why I told you that none can come to
  me unless the Father draw them."

Arrangement of the text

The arrangement of the text makes it possible to discern the
unity of the chapter, even if the organization of it is artificial.

Here, in summary form, are the literary principles that have served me as guides.

Some authors have correctly emphasized the objections of the Jews that break the discourse into sections, but in taking these objections as the point of departure they mistake their real significance. These objections are a means by which the evangelist brings out the inability of human reason to grasp the revelation of the Word: reason rejects a revelation it cannot explain or validate. Consequently the objections cannot serve as a point of departure, because they presuppose a previous revelation. Their role is to keep the dialogue going by causing Jesus to develop further the message he has just given. This literary device is characteristic of the entire gospel of John and makes it possible to grasp the movement within each dialogue.[24] The objections therefore repeat in very summary form—but in the mode of non-understanding—the revelation within which they occur.

In analyzing the arrangement of the present discourse I shall move backward from the group of verses that seems clearest: 6:48-58. In v. 52 the objection fastens on the supposed claim of Jesus that he will "give his flesh to eat." In fact, Jesus does not say this in so many words. The objection has been formulated, from a literary point of view, by joining two preceding statements of Jesus: on the one hand, that "one must eat this bread in order to live for ever" (51b) and, on the other, that "this bread is my flesh"(51c). The objection thus summarizes the preceding text, while also making it say more than it explicitly does. Moreover, in this section (48-58) as a whole, two verbs—"give" and "eat"— catch thy eye, because they had disappeared after vv. 31-33, whereas the words bread, die, life, and raising up keep recurring throughout the discourse.[25] "Give" and "eat" are to the fore in the sentences that frame the objection (vv. 53-58 and 49-51). It is therefore legitimate to regard vv. 48-58 as a literary unit.

The objection summarized by John in v. 41: "I am the bread that has come down from heaven" likewise lumps together in a single statement the words of Jesus in v. 35 ("The bread is myself") and v. 38 ("I have come down from heaven"). The whole of vv. 35-40 is thus connected with the objection of the Jews.[26] After the objection, vv. 44-47 go further into the revelation given in 36-40 by explaining the refusal of the Jews: the reason why they do not believe in Jesus is that the Father is not yet drawing them to him who alone can speak of the Father whom he has seen in person.[27]

Around the main body of the discourse as thus determined (35–47 and 48–58) the verses that precede and follow can likewise be readily grouped with the help of the objections. A detailed analysis would justify my arrangement of the opening verses (26–34). I note only that the two parts which I have distinguished within the body of the discourse are announced in the opening section both by a citation from the psalms (78:24), which I have translated in a way that respects the order of the words: "A bread from heaven (A) he gave them to eat (B)" (Jn 6:31), and by a statement of Jesus: "The bread of God is he who comes down from heaven (A) and gives life to the world (B)" (6:33).

In the closing section, the objection in v. 60 sums up the entire discourse; for this reason the answer given (60–65) provides a key to the interpretation of the whole.

The discourse on the Bread of Life, including vv. 52–58, thus proves to be very carefully structured. It is pointless to fragment it by assigning different parts to different "sources." I shall not give here a detailed exegesis of the entire passage,[28] but instead shall offer several successive readings of it.

A spontaneous reading

Let me give first the reading that might be made by Christians who regularly celebrate the Eucharist and have some little familiarity with the gospels. The story of the loaves given so generously to the crowd immediately reminds them of the generosity with which the Lord gives himself in the sacrament of the Eucharist. Furthermore, the entire story seems to have been written with an eye on the final meal of Jesus: "Jesus then took the loaves, and when he had given thanks, he distributed them to those who were seated . . . as much as they wanted" (6:11). And from the beginning, in fact, the account of the "multiplication of the loaves" has been reread in the light of the Supper.

Coming as it does directly after the reference to the manna, that is, the bread given to the Israelites from heaven, the statement of Jesus that "the bread of life is myself" further justifies a eucharistic reading of the passage. Moreover, just as in Mark's account of institution the blood of Jesus is shed "for the multitude," so here the flesh of the Son of Man is "for the life of the world" (6:51). In this v. 51 we almost have the very words of institution; so close are they that in the opinion of many critics Jesus is more likely to have used the word "flesh" (*sarx*) than "body" (*sōma*) at the Supper.[29]

The hearers of Jesus in John 6 are told that they must "eat the flesh and drink the blood of the Son of Man." How can readers fail to hear echoed in this statement the two sets of words spoken by Jesus during his final meal? John even insists that "my flesh is a real food and my blood a real drink." The discourse seems to be saying over and over that eucharistic practice ensures eternal life.

Christian readers cannot doubt the correctness of their eucharistic reading of this passage; the typically Johannine allusions make such a reading inevitable for anyone who experiences the sacrament of the Lord's Supper.

And yet such a reading runs into difficulties. A first is that while the miracle of the multiplied loaves fits in nicely with the eucharistic meal, what connection can there be between the walking on the sea and the sacrament? One may indeed answer that since the context here is quasi-biographical, every detail need not necessarily have to do with the Eucharist. And, on the other hand, the lengthy discussions of the faith required go very appropriately with the announcement of the Eucharist.

There is, however, another difficulty that seems almost insurmountable. If the teaching of Jesus here is really focused on the sacrament, then he is asking his contemporaries to make a choice they are incapable of making, since the idea of the Eucharist is completely unknown to them. It is no help to say that in speaking of the manna the Old Testament prepares the way for an understanding of this mystery, for, as I shall show, the Old Testament leads in a different direction.

A reading on critical lines

Some authors reject the previous reading and interpret the language of Jesus as metaphorical. The text says nothing of the Eucharist but speaks only of acceptance of Jesus by faith.

Both the multiplication of the loaves and the walking on the water are miracles comparable to the cures of the cripple and the man born blind. Like the latter, the former are followed by a discourse in which Jesus calls for acceptance of his words and his person on the basis of the works he has performed. In Chapter 6 he uses the standard metaphors of hunger and thirst and adds those of bread, flesh, and blood, just as elsewhere he uses the metaphors of water (of life) and light (of life). His words, he says, are "spirit and life," and are to be understood not according to the flesh but according to the spirit (6:63). Thus vv. 51–58, in which he speaks of "eating the flesh and drinking the blood of the Son of Man," have in view not a sacramental act but an act of unreserved faith in the concrete man who claims to be Savior of the world. The entire chapter can therefore be understood *without* recourse to any eucharistic interpretation. I shall develop this point, while also emphasizing the links between the passage and the sapiential writings.[30]

The crowd believes that it has found in Jesus the prophet foretold by Moses: "Your God will raise up in your midst a prophet like me: it is to him that you shall listen" (Deut 18:15). It then asks him to perform a miracle comparable to that of the manna which Moses had caused to rain down in the wilderness (vv. 30–31). Jesus tries to raise their thoughts to a higher level by correcting their idea of the manna as something earthly; the true manna in fact was nothing else than the word that came from God's own mouth and was the real sustenance of the Hebrews (Deut 8:2–3). Moreover, in the course of their long history, the Jews had reflected a great deal on this real manna, and some of their wise men had come to think of it as the "bread of angels"; by this they meant not a kind of sacrament but "the word that preserves those who believe in Yahweh" (Wis 16:26). Jesus, then, means to suggest by the miracle of the loaves that his word is this "food" par excellence and that it must therefore be received in faith. This is why he says: "The bread of life is myself."

On the other hand, when Jesus thus states that faith in his person allays hunger and thirst, he echoes the old prophetic tradition: "Behold, days are coming—oracle of Yahweh—when I will send hunger upon the land, not a hunger for bread or a thirst for water, but a hunger and thirst for hearing the word of Yahweh" (Am 8:11). This is the word of God that delighted the heart of Jeremiah (Jer 15:16); it was "eaten" by Ezekiel (Ez 3:3), and of it the psalmist could sing: "How sweet is your word to my palate, sweeter than honey in my mouth!" (Ps 119:103). At the well of Jacob Jesus tells his disciples that he has "a food of which you do not know . . . the will of him who sent me" (Jn 4:32, 34).

The entire first part of the Johannine discourse on the Bread of Life can therefore be read as a metaphor for acceptance of the word of Jesus, acceptance of the Word himself.

The meal consisting of the miraculously multiplied loaves is for its part the fulfillment of the promised feast of Wisdom: "All you who thirst, come to the water . . . even if you have no money, come . . . eat [wheat] without money" (Is 55:1–3). If, then, Jesus is the bread of life, he is so in continuity with the message of the prophets. For this reason, v. 35 should not be translated as "I am the bread," as though Jesus were issuing a proclamation; it should be interpreted rather as a response: "The bread of life is myself"; he himself is the answer to the "hunger" of human beings. The eschatological banquet he offers is the banquet of the word of Yahweh: "Wisdom has built her house . . . she has set her table. . . . Come, eat my bread and drink the wine I have prepared" (Prov. 9:1–5).[31]

Also to be located in this sapiential tradition are the passages in which Jesus announces a complete communion between himself and his disciples: "They shall all be taught by God" (6:45). The sentence: "All who eat my flesh and drink my blood remain in me and I in them" (v. 56) seems to be "an interiorization of the traditional formula of the covenant,"[32] which likewise states a reciprocity: Israel is the people of Yahweh, and Yahweh is the God of Israel.[33] This Johannine interiorization is in keeping with the character of the new covenant. To adhere fully to the word of Jesus is to enter into full communion with him and with God.

It would be an overstatement to say that this interpretation does not have its difficulties. Like it or not, vv. 51–58, for example, continue to have eucharistic overtones, not only for the unrehearsed reader but also for anyone who takes into account the life-setting in which they were redacted.

But the critics will not be fazed. Since eucharistic echoes are unmistakable in the second part of the discourse (vv. 51–58), there is no alternative but to surrender the literary unity of the discourse as a whole. The surrender has been made at various levels.

M. J. Lagrange in his day took a "biographical" approach and asked: "How could such a discourse have been understood at Capernaum?"[34] In other words: How could the mystery of the Eucharist have been set before resolute unbelievers? The question certainly deserved asking, since exegetes must always inquire into the historical probability of their texts, but Lagrange's answer seemed to be an evasion: "Vv. 51–58 were probably said to an audience of friends, an audience made up of disciples who until now seemed secure in their faith. . . . As we saw, v. 60 makes it rather clear that the duality of themes is matched by a duality of audiences." Unfortunately, the objection raised in v. 52: "How can this man give us his flesh to eat?" undermines this hypothesis, since it is placed in the mouth of Jews indistinguishable from those who had raised the previous difficulty (v. 42).

For this last reason other critics prefer to take a more radical approach to the text. If vv. 51–58 be regarded as a later Christian interpolation, the Johannine discourse regains its unity: it has to do entirely with faith in the person of Jesus.

Following the lead of various critics at the beginning of the century Bultmann called for surgery on the text; E. Schweizer added his timid assent; J. Jeremias tried to justify the operation.[35] But after the radical critique of E. Ruckstuhl this way out proved untenable, and J. Jeremias therefore fell back on another solution: vv. 51–58 are a pre-Johannine homily which the evangelist incorporates in the discourse on faith.[36] A note in *The Jerusalem Bible* seems to approve this hypothesis,[37] while D. Mollat is satisfied to say of v. 51: "A new formula which introduces the more directly eucharistic part of the discourse (51–58). But the two parts hang together: the Eucharist feeds human beings with Jesus, the divine Wisdom that has come down from heaven."[38]

These various hypotheses share a common presupposition: that vv. 51–58 have an exclusively eucharistic meaning and everything preceding them has an exclusively spiritual meaning. In order to explain the presence of two different teachings in a single discourse, some critics imagine a "eucharistic discourse" that is limited to vv. 51–58 but whose presence is difficult to explain unless it is removed from the lips of Christ and turned into a later Christian commentary. Such a hypothesis would require solid support before it could be accepted. Other critics, who are more reserved toward such a risky solution but are no less resigned to sacrificing the literary unity of the chapter, try to discover at least a thematic unity; they find it, however, only by way of considerations on the content of the successive statements made by Jesus.

Does this critical reading deserve to be called the commonly accepted one today? I think not.[39] Vv. 51–58 is neither a patch sewn into the discourse nor a pre-Johannine homily incorporated into it, but the authentic continuation of the discourse on the Bread of Life. This is what a more "Johannine" reading will seek to show: that the relation between faith and sacramental participation is asserted *simultaneously* throughout the text.

A symbolical reading

The fourth gospel is so obviously permeated by symbolism that no one would think of denying it. The reader is struck by the peculiar character of the words and actions that are reported: everything seems to be a sign of some mysterious reality. The miracles, for example, are not simply astounding incidents meant to elicit faith in the witnesses; they are "signs" which bring to light this or that hidden aspect of the person of Jesus himself. Thus when Jesus heals the man born blind or brings Lazarus back to life, he reveals himself as "light of the world" or as "the resurrection and the life." In like manner, the words of Jesus (think, for example, of the conversation with Nicodemus) bid the reader look beyond their immediate meaning for a deeper significance. This is what the critics have in mind when they say: "It cannot be doubted that many levels of thought lie under the surface of the Johannine language and presentation."[40] Some authors even see in the text nothing but an intellectual construction; in their view Christianity is simply a myth that is given a different coloring by the different evangelists in accordance with the dispositions and abilities of each; their narratives simply illustrate basic ideas, which in John's case are the ideas of light and life.[41]

I shall not stop to discuss these extreme views but shall say rather that behind John's "symbolic operation" stands his assertion that "the Word became flesh" and that consequently sensible things (light, water, bread, door, and so on), as well as the persons who revolve around Jesus, are, each in its own way, messengers of God's word for me today. Numerous examples could be given.[42]

It is more important in this context to consider how Johannine symbolism functions, for only then will it be possible to undertake the reading I propose to offer.

In one current understanding of the word, a "symbol" is "that which represents something else in virtue of an analogical relationship."[43] Contrary to a widespread view, this correspondence is not immediately forced upon us by the reality that becomes a symbol; it is only suggested by it, and the human intellect must recognize it or even establish it. It may be said that there is no such thing as a symbol-in-itself, since earthly things can have a variety of meanings. Thus water in the Bible can symbolize life but also purification from evil or terrifying destruction.[44] It is the human mind, functioning within a particular cultural or literary context, that must discover and determine the symbolic value of an external thing which it would be wrong to regard as in itself a "symbol." Furthermore it is because they share a world of ideas that interlocutors are able to recognize the relation thus brought out between two realities and that they are able to communicate such ideas to one another. For this reason, rather than speak simply of symbols, I prefer to focus on the perception of symbols, or emergence of a further meaning, and describe it as a "symbolic operation."

At the everyday level the operation consists of using the analogical relationship that may exist between two realities within a shared cultural world. Thus in the world of biblical thought bread, which means the ordinary food of human beings, can also be used to refer to their spiritual food.[45]

Like the other biblical writers John occasionally uses this simple symbolic operation. When Jesus says to his disciples: "Our friend Lazarus is sleeping" (11:11), the verb "sleep" means simply "to be dead," but it can also suggest that death is a sleep from which Lazarus will awake. In most instances, however, symbolic operations in John take a form that is much more complex and that is to some extent peculiar to him.

The language of the evangelist is intended to be doubly ambivalent (this is one aspect of his genius): it is meant to reflect, *at one and the same time,* the Jewish milieu in which Jesus lives and the Christian milieu which enlightens John in his interpretation of the past. These different milieus, which overlap in the text, make it possible for *one and the same* reality to have a twofold symbolic relationship, according as the reality (bread, for example) is seen in the Jewish tradition (which Jesus shared with his contemporaries) or in a Christian perspective. The same referent can thus be the basis of two interpretations, and the symbolism at work can be twofold. The same temple of stone, of which Jesus says: "Destroy this sanctuary, and I will rebuild it . . . "(2:19) can symbolize for his Jewish hearers the spiritual temple which the prophets of Israel had foretold and which they themselves expected from God, *and,* for Christians, the body of the risen Jesus himself.[46]

In view of this twofold symbolism informed readers might think they were being invited to undertake two different readings: a first which would discover in John the cultural and religious heritage of Judaism, that is, the heritage proper to the age in which Jesus of Nazareth lived, and a second which would reflect the Christian milieu in which the gospel was redacted.

But if the two readings were made independently of one another, both would be misleading and illusory. A first pitfall to be avoided, then, is a historicist reading that supposedly grasps the real meaning of the text. Nowadays this danger is no doubt less of a threat, but it does occur in the more subtle form of an effort to get back to the *ipsissima verba* of Jesus, as though these had greater theological value than the words as interpreted by the apostolic Church, and as though the work of exegetes was to uncover the historical rock hidden beneath John's transformations. It is true, of course, that exegetes must try to discern the past historical reality, but they must also see its contribution in an intrinsic relationship with the specifically Johannine interpretation of it.

A second and opposite pitfall awaits readers who have avoided the first: the mistake of turning the historical level into a mere springboard for getting at the Christological meaning of the Johannine text. A reading which, in seeking the deeper reality hidden in the text, would focus immediately or exclusively on the Christian meaning would turn many texts of John into mere occasions for attending solely to the post-paschal reality—which is certainly more familiar to us today and tends to bedazzle us when we read the fourth gospel.

John's purpose in fact is not to suggest *two* possible interpretations of the words and actions of Jesus, one "historical," the other post-paschal. His purpose is quite different: to lead his readers to a recognition of the essential relation *linking* the Jesus of the past to the Lord of glory: "These signs have been written down so that you may believe that Jesus the *messiah* is the *Son of God* and that by believing you may have life in his name" (Jn 20:31).

Consequently, the various double symbolizations that occur in the fourth gospel all contribute to a single major symbolic operation that subsumes them all: that of connecting Jesus of Nazareth who used to live in Palestine (and who spoke to his fellow countrymen) with the Son of God who lives today. It is the same person who is present to us before and after his death: he is *one* in *two* different manifestations which John sets before his readers without any break between them.

Is that not what the very etymology of "symbol" conveys? The Greek noun *symbolon* derives from the verb *syn-ballō*, "to put together." To recognize the *unity* of *two* separate elements is a way of becoming sensitized to the language of John. A "symbolic" reading, therefore, must maintain a dialectical relationship between the two symbolisms as they emerge, and thus respect the singularity and proper weight of the one *and* the other.

As a shorthand way of expressing the inclusive operation that directs the recurring symbolizations in John and, when all is said and done, in the gospel as a whole, I have suggested[47] speaking of "two times" that are to be discerned in the text: the time of Jesus of Nazareth and the time of the risen Christ, the two requiring to be read together "symbolically." The only valid reading is one that at every point takes into account the relation which the present time of the Spirit has, in the evangelist's eyes, to the past time of Jesus, the flesh and blood person who lived in Israel. In the final analysis it is to these two times that the text bears witness; the evangelist wants to show his readers that the first symbolizes the second *and* that without the first the second would ground only an incoherent gnosis.

The connection between the two opens the way to recognition of a language they share: the spiritual language which makes me, the reader of John, a believer and a Christian. For I cannot dissociate my present faith in the risen Christ from the history and preaching of Jesus in Palestine.

I have tried to show elsewhere how John brings out the unity of the two times and of the two milieus of life.[48] He presents himself first of all as a "coryphaeus," that is, as one who knows the outcome of the story and educates his readers by a few words of explanation as the plot unfolds.[49] "The past is present precisely as past, but in such a way that, in the light of the resurrection, it appears as the time of the first revelation, that is to say, a revelation which was to guide the contemporaries of Jesus toward a full understanding of the second revelation."

John also presents himself as a writer who is skilled in choosing words that can be understood symbolically and in organizing miracles and discourses so as to bring out the deeper meaning of the former, which he rightly calls *semeia* ("signs").

Finally—and this is especially clear in the passage on the sign of the loaves—John is a writer of dialogues. Despite appearances, dialogue never functions solely to bring out misunderstandings or a series of mistaken interpretations. Readers must therefore find in the sometimes obscure words of Jesus a meaning that could be grasped by his contemporary hearers. I suggested as much when I spoke of the twofold symbolism in the sign of the temple. But there is a further and complementary point that must be kept in mind: when his addressees cast doubt on a first revelation made by Jesus and, by ridiculing his words, close their minds to the meaning the words might have for them, he continues to maintain what he has already said, but he adds a reference—unintelligible to his addressees—to the mystery of his saving death. The end result is a refusal on the part of his listeners.

If, in the first situation, the fundamental criterion for our reading is the possibility for a Jew to understand the words of Jesus on a certain level of revelation, this is not the case for the second statement concerning [the saving] death. Here, the dialogue is cut short. It turns into a monologue, Nicodemus disappears, the Galileans cast doubt on what Jesus said, the disciples fall away. Jesus goes on with his revelation but on a level of such depth (that of unacceptable death) that his listeners balk and withdraw for good.

I have felt obliged to provide this lengthy introduction to the reading of John's texts on the Eucharist because the word "symbolic" has been given a variety of meanings and its application is therefore not a simple matter. In my view the use of the word in discussing John is based on the very purpose of the evangelist, for whom the meaning of Jesus Christ is to be found in the relation uniting two worlds (the Jewish and the Christian) or two times of revelation (that of Jesus of Nazareth and that of Christ through the Spirit). Quite simply, to read the fourth gospel "symbolically" is to read it as John wrote it.

A symbolical reading of John 6

The interpretations set forth earlier in sections 2 ("A spontaneous reading") and 3 ("A reading on critical lines") focused either on a eucharistic reading or on a "spiritualistic" reading or, finally, on a reading that is spiritualistic in its first part (26–51b) and eucharistic in its second (51c–58). My hypothesis, on the other hand, claims that the text of the discourse can be read as sacramental in its entirety *and* as spiritualistic in its entirety. If there are two successive interpretations, the succession is not in the text when we move from the first part to the second, but in the mind of the reader. The reader takes a different approach in each part of the discourse; in the first he or she recognizes a eucharistic teaching behind a teaching that is directly concerned with faith in Jesus (38–47); in the second he or she finds beneath a directly sacramental text a revelation on the person of Jesus (48–58).

I need not spend time showing that the first part of the discourse can be read in a spiritualistic manner, though with allusions to the Eucharist. Most critics, however, think the second part of the discourse has to be read as exclusively eucharistic.[50] And here indeed is precisely the difficulty with my hypothesis: Is it possible to give a reading of vv. 51c–58 that is not only sacramental *but also* spiritualistic? I admit that these verses display a primarily eucharistic vocabulary, but I remain convinced that the evangelist is bent on continuing, behind this vocabulary, a "spiritual" revelation having to do with the salutary value of the *death* of Jesus.

In order to show that this is the case, let me point out first of all that the second part of the discourse is parallel to the first. The opening (48) is the same as in 35: "The bread of life is myself"; this suggests that the teaching of the second part supposes that of the first. The ending in both parts speaks of eternal life (58 = 47), showing that the goal sought is the same in both parts. Finally, the development follows a similar pattern: the objection of the Jews regarding the fact of eating (52) is preceded by a mysterious statement (49–51) and followed by a full revelation of the mystery (53–58).

The second part, however, also advances the discourse. The key words in the passage are no longer "come to me" and "believe" (6:35), but "give" and "eat/drink." These two complementary actions, the former of God, the latter of human beings, had already been anticipated in the citation from Psalm 77 in v. 31: "A bread from heaven he gave them to eat." In the remainder of the first section the term "eat" had disappeared, except perhaps for a bare allusion lurking in "hunger/thirst" (35). The announcement of the gift' "Work for . . . the food which the Son of Man will give to you" (27) is now renewed in 51c, and we learn that what is meant is salvation through the cross. After having heard the call for faith in the Jesus who has been sent by the Father (incarnation), readers are now told that faith in Jesus as Savior of the world (redemption) is also required if they are to obtain eternal life.

Let me look at some details. V. 49 introduces the new theme of eating: "Your fathers ate manna in the wilderness and died." The manna which did not prevent death is then contrasted in 51ab with the living bread: "The living bread that has come down from heaven is myself; whoever eats of it will live for ever." This sentence sums up the first part (35–47), but it also adds the word "living" that will be characteristic of the further discussion, which reaches its climax in 57 with its reference to the living Father. Readers thus progressively enter into the mystery of the bread: Jesus is the bread of life because he is living. The giving of life is the purpose the Father intends in sending his Son; here, now, is the means by which the purpose is to be achieved. In the dialogue with Nicodemus a first part had been concerned with God's intended purpose, the gift of the Spirit who effects rebirth from on high (3:5–8); the second part had specified the means provided, namely, the "lifting up" of the Son of Man (3:9–15). The pattern is the same here:[51] it is by his sacrifice that Jesus gives life to the world. V. 51c therefore goes on to say: "And the bread that I shall give is my flesh for the life of the world."

V. 51 begins assertively, with the emphatic "myself" (egō) reminding the reader that the reference is to him who has come down from heaven. The new revelation is expressed with the help of the words "give," "flesh," and "for" (hyper). When thus brought together, these words give the statement a very precise meaning. John regularly uses the preposition hyper when he wants to say that Jesus gives his life.[52]

It is possible, then, to read these verses (48–51) without making any reference to the Eucharist. The "eating" which Jesus requires can be understood thus far as signifying only a close adherence to his person as the Savior of the world who has died for us.

But let me look more closely at the answer Jesus gives to the objection of the Jews that is reported in v. 52. The answer contains two groups of two verses each (53–54 and 56–57), with the groups being separated by a simple assertion, and a conclusion (58) that recalls the beginning of the second part of the discourse (49–51) and the end of the first (47) and thus forms a first-rate inclusion.

In the first group of verses:

[53]Jesus therefore said to them:
"Unless you eat the flesh of the Son of Man and drink his blood,
you will not have life in you.
[54]All who eat my flesh and drink my blood have eternal life,
and I will raise them up on the last day,"

the leitmotif of eternal life and the resurrection is the same as in vv. 35–40. But two new assertions show how the thought has advanced. First, Jesus calls himself the Son of Man, a title that had disappeared from the discourse after its opening (27), which also contained the word "give," a term ordinarily connected, as I have shown, with a sacrificial context. The theme of salvation through the lifting up of the Son of Man, which had been introduced in the conversation with Nicodemus (3:14), is heard again here; it will be made more explicit in the conclusion of the discourse (in 62). By calling himself "Son of Man" Jesus suggests that the mystery of the saving death crowns the mystery of his coming into the world.

The second novelty in these verses has to do with the necessity of eating the flesh and drinking the blood of the Son of Man. The point made goes beyond the general statement in v. 35b on the cessation of hunger and thirst in believers. Classical exegesis has seen in v. 53 an exclusively eucharistic meaning. I think, however, that it is possible to see beneath the sacramental terminology a statement which is directly concerned only with the sacrifice of Jesus. Two remarks will help readers to set aside their instinctive reference to sacramental language as they read this passage.

Flesh and blood are mentioned in parallel phrases. The parallelism is doubtless less close than in expressions such as "Flesh and blood has not revealed this to you" (Mt 16:17), but it is not less real, as a comparison between the formulas in this verse and those in v. 35 will show. For the verbs "eat/drink" are as parallel here as the phrases "come to me/believe in me" are there; they express in a hendiadys the act of adherence to the person of Jesus. The direct objects of the verbs, namely, "flesh/blood," strengthen the parallelism. If we today tend spontaneously to read the expressions as dissociated each from the other, it is because of the accounts of institution in which the body and the blood come at the end of two successive ritual actions. Here, on the contrary, the actions of "eating my flesh" and "drinking my blood" are in no sense distinct rites, since they can be summed up as follows in subsequent verses: "All who eat *me* will live by me" (57) and "All who eat *this bread* will live for ever" (58). "Flesh and blood" are therefore equivalent to "me" and to "bread." By means of this literary pair Jesus points to himself as a concrete, weak, perishable being.

Here is the second remark. It is clear that we cannot stop at the point just reached, for the words "flesh/blood" do not simply designate the person of Jesus but also make it clear that he will be handed over to death. Not only does the cross provide the context for these sentences, as I have pointed out in connection with 51c, but, as one exegete has sensibly observed,[53] if the blood is to be drunk it must be shed. The revelation about the flesh that is to be "given," that is, handed over to death, is thus reinforced in what is for Jewish ears a paradoxical way, by the necessity of "drinking the blood of the Son of Man."

In these words, which follow upon the audience's rejection of his announcement in 51, Jesus continues and completes his revelation, without however seeking any longer to be understood: human beings must find life not only by faith in his person but in the gift he will make of himself by dying. In the present case, therefore, it is not necessary to ask what the Jews could have understood by his statements; all that is necessary is to have shown that the text, taken in itself, can be read in a non-sacramental as well as a sacramental perspective.

V. 55 contains the simple assertion that separates the two groups of statements: "For my flesh is truly *(alēthēs)* a food and my blood truly *(alēthēs)* a drink." *Alēthēs* seems to have a different meaning here than the equivalent adjective *alēthinos*. The latter points to the heavenly nature of the realities that serve Jesus as the basis of his revelation; thus v. 32 speaks of the "true," heavenly bread in contrast to the manna, which is earthly even though it came down from heaven. *Alēthēs* emphasizes rather the effectiveness of this eating and drinking, as in v. 35 where it is said that the food and drink appease hunger and thirst and thus fulfill their function perfectly.

The second group of verses:

[56]All who eat my flesh and drink my blood remain in me and
    I in them.
[57]Just as I whom the living Father has sent live by the Father,
so all who eat me will live by me,

carries the preceding affirmation a step further by revealing the role of God in all this. In the first part of the discourse the Father was the source of faith in the person of the Son who has come into the world (6:44–45); here he is the source of the life which the Savior brings. The Living One par excellence is the Father from whom Jesus himself continually receives his life and whose will is his food (4:34).

Finally, a conclusion:

[58]Such is the bread that has come down from heaven.
It is not like the bread which the fathers ate, for they are
    dead.
All who eat this bread will live for ever,

shows the precise meaning of the metaphors "eat the flesh/drink the blood": these point to the life-giving "eating," that is, appropriation, by faith, of the saving sacrifice of Jesus.

In these words Jesus is no doubt implicitly preparing his disciples, to the extent that they have accepted his teaching, to understand what will someday be made fully intelligible in the light of the Spirit. I mean the duty of sharing sacramentally in his one sacrifice. But in the perspective I have adopted here there is no need to determine the extent to which the words of the Johannine Jesus are expressed in eucharistic language. The essential thing is that a non-sacramental reading of the text is possible; in other words, Jesus is also speaking here of faith in the saving value of his death.

The discourse on the Bread of Life is thus a revelation of the relationship that inseparably unites sacrament and faith. Readers learn that if their eucharistic practice is to be authentic, they must remain in close union with Jesus of Nazareth whose mysteries are recalled throughout the discourse.

Jesus is the eucharistic bread because he is the bread of the word of God; he is the one who has come down from heaven and has the words of eternal life. What would an encounter with Christ as sacramental bread be if it did not take place in the presence of this Jesus of Nazareth whose actions and teachings we know? I will refer to this as the "mystery of the incarnation"; it must undergird eucharistic practice.

The discourse on the Bread of Life goes further in its second part when it presents Jesus as the one who delivered himself up without reservation for the life of the world, the one whose flesh and blood have been "given" and must be "eaten" if others are to share in the gift of salvation. This is the mystery of "redemption," the mystery of the fidelity of Jesus who goes so far as to sacrifice himself completely for us.

The end of the discourse (vv. 59–65) bids the reader contemplate him who is present despite his absence, since he has been raised to heaven. This is the mystery of the "exaltation."

Finally, if it be true that "the flesh is good for nothing" and that the spirit alone gives life, the meaning is that the Holy Spirit alone can provide the meaning not only of the words of Jesus but also of eucharistic practice. What good would an external, "fleshly" practice of the sacrament be if the Spirit did not continually provide its meaning? "It is the spirit that gives life, the flesh is good for nothing. The words I have spoken to you are spirit and they are life" (6:63).

Provided readers do not judge them according to the flesh, as the Jews have just done, his words, which are filled with life by the

Spirit, become life-giving in their turn and communicate the Spirit. This assertion simply applies the principle of the two times of revelation to a particular case. Contemporaries of Jesus had to open themselves to an understanding that could reach the spiritual level, while believers of every age must in their sacramental practice be constantly going back to the person of him who lived on earth at one time and was faithful to his mission of love to the very end. Only those who have a spiritual understanding of who Christ is really receive the life that is given with his body. There is no authentic sacramental life without a personal faith that is animated by the gift of the Spirit.

John makes a very important contribution to the understanding of the Eucharist. His teaching on the sacrament is given not after but through his teaching on faith, while conversely faith in the person of Jesus is not simply the starting point of eucharistic practice but also inspires it at every moment. Believers are thus invited to taste in the Eucharist the three central mysteries of the Son of Man: the incarnation, the redemption, and the ascension; they are able to do so by the power of the life-giving Spirit.

III. OTHER "EUCHARISTIC" TEXTS

Now that I have a symbolic grill for reading the texts of John that may refer to the Eucharist, I am in a position to enrich the presentation of the eucharistic theme in the fourth gospel.

For the record, let me mention the passages which in my opinion cannot be given a eucharistic interpretation. The incident of the sellers being expelled from the temple does indeed speak of the "body" of Jesus that is symbolized by the temple; but this body is neither the Church nor the eucharistic body. Nor is there any point to bringing in here the words of Jesus: "My food is to do my Father's will" (4:31–34). Nor can the washing of the feet be given a eucharistic interpretation; it belongs to a different tradition, that of the farewell discourse which I examined earlier. Finally, it is highly doubtful that a eucharistic interpretation can be given of vv. 17–19 in the prayer (Jn 17) which Jesus utters on the point of leaving this world, as though his reference to his "sacrifice" were a reference to the words of institution.[54]

Episode of the water turned into wine (2:1–11). By this action Jesus symbolizes the fact that he is bringing the messianic age to its fulfillment: here is the joyous banquet, and the wine—a better wine—flows abundantly. But in the second time of revelation,

that of the Christian reader, the wine given in abundance can signify the blood which Jesus sheds: the blood of the Son of Man that
must be "drunk" (6:53–54), the blood that flows from the side of
Jesus on the cross (19:34).

The theme of abundance occurs frequently in the fourth gospel, in describing, for example, the bread left over, the gift of the
Spirit, and the gift of life.[55] When set beside the miracle of the
multiplied loaves, the miracle of the wine given in abundance
would, with its allusion to blood, complement the symbolism of
the loaves, which remind the reader of the body.

I am now in a position to say that the intervention of Jesus at
the wedding feast of Cana marks the celebration of his own marriage with the human race (see Rev 19:7–9). That is the point St.
Irenaeus is making so magnificently when he speaks of the *admir-*
abile vini signum ("the marvelous sign of the wine") and of the
compendii poculum ("the summarizing cup") in which Mary
wished to share ahead of time. As "the summarizing cup"—a
description that epitomizes all the mysteries of salvation and
brings them to a focus in a striking resume of the wonders of
grace—the eucharistic cup, which is prefigured by the wine of
Cana, is closely connected with the hour of the passion.[56] I may
add that this incident took place "before Passover," as did the miracle of the loaves (6:4) and the last meal of Jesus (13:1).[57]

The allegory of the vine and the branches completes what is
said in the episode at Cana by describing more fully the nature of
Christ's presence:

> [1]I am the true vine, and my Father is the vinedresser.
> [2]Every branch in me that does not bear fruit he cuts away,
> and every branch that does bear fruit he prunes so that it
> will produce more fruit. [3]You have already been pruned
> [purified] by the word which I have proclaimed to you.
> [4]Remain in me and I in you. Just as the branch cannot bear
> fruit by itself unless it remains on the vine, neither can
> you unless you remain in me. [5]I am the vine, you are the
> branches. Those who remain in me and I in them produce
> much fruit, for apart from me you can do nothing (Jn
> 15:1–5).

The meaning of the passage is clear: In order to bear fruit it is
necessary to "remain in Jesus," that is, to remain grafted onto the
vine. A comparison with the discourse on the Bread of Life is

unavoidable. Jesus had said there: "I am the bread of life"; here he says: "I am the vine" that enables the branches to bear fruit.

Believers who hear the message proclaimed here immediately connect it with the announcement of the Eucharist. In the synoptic accounts of institution does Jesus not speak of the "fruit of the vine"? Does he not utter all these words—parable of the vine and institution of the Eucharist—in the framework of his final meal at the feast of Passover? Finally, how can readers fail to hear in the invitation, "Remain in me," an echo of the promise made during the discourse on the Bread of Life: "All who eat my flesh and drink my blood remain in me and I in them" (6:56)? Consequently the disciples will bear fruit in the world by holding fast to God the Father through eucharistic communion with his Son. The Eucharist yields the fruits of love.

It yields these fruits, however, only if believers cling fast by faith to him who identifies himself as the vine. What, then, is this "vine"? As used in the Old Testament, the image of the "vine of Yahweh" refers first of all to the true Israel that must produce fruits of justice; it is subsequently applied to the coming Son of Man.[58] Jesus presents himself as the one who fulfills the expectation of Israel, just as he depicted himself in Chapter 6 as the bread of Wisdom. The close communion signified by the sharing of the Eucharist is grounded on an unreserved adherence of faith to him who is the true Israel, the Son of Man.

In other images that are complementary to those I have discussed, John continues to urge his readers to deepen their eucharistic practice by adherence to Jesus of Nazareth through an unreserved faith and love.

On the shore of Lake Tiberias the risen Lord had prepared a little meal for the fishermen who were just pulling in their nets:

> [9]Once ashore, they see a fire of coals and on it some fish and bread. . . . [The disciples bring the fish they have just caught.][13] Jesus comes and takes the bread and gives it to them; and likewise the fish (Jn 21:9–13).

In this passage John probably intends an allusion to a eucharistic meal, similar to the one the risen Lord had begun with the disciples at Emmaus (Lk 24:30–31). It was on this same shore of Lake Tiberias that the miraculous meal, followed by the discourse on the Bread of Life, had taken place. The description of Jesus' actions is almost identical with that given at the multiplication of the loaves. It is evident, however, that the traditional account of the Supper influenced the formulation of the latter text (Jn 6:11 and Mk 14:22). Why not the former as well?

It is probable, then, that there is here another allusion to the Eucharist, especially in view of the fact that most of the stories about appearances of the risen Jesus had the liturgical meals of the first Christians as their "vital setting." Ignatius of Antioch and Justin (born in Syria–Palestine) can be appealed to for this interpretation.

In these circumstances it is highly likely that the encounter with the risen Lord symbolizes the encounter with Christ in the Eucharist (or vice versa).[59]

CONCLUSION

What, then, is John's specific contribution as far as the Eucharist is concerned? I have not been able to find anything about a cultic meal; on the contrary, it is simply omitted. On the other hand, I have been able to bring to light various positive points in the farewell discourse and in a properly understood Johannine symbolism. Before attempting a summary, I would like to remind the reader of what John's attitude to public worship or cult is, and to explain his reason for not mentioning the institution of the Eucharist.

Beginning with his very first encounter with the Jews Jesus takes a position toward cult as practiced in the temple. In his version of the expulsion of the sellers from the temple (2:13–22) John has some nuances that bring out the deeper meaning of Jesus' action.

John is not satisfied to report the scene recorded by the synoptics, but adds details that are pregnant with meaning. He is careful to point out that the Passover of the Jews was at hand, thus indicating that the Christian "Passover" takes the place now of the Jewish Passover that had prefigured it. This is the solemn entrance of the high priest into his temple, for it opens the ministry of Jesus. John still has Jesus expelling the sellers, but he adds a phrase that is difficult to explain on purely stylistic grounds: "He drove them all out of the temple, together with the sheep and oxen." These last words, which are an addition to the synoptic account, teach that Jesus has not come merely to put order into the temple; he gets rid of the ancient ritual itself because it has lost its meaning now that he is present: is he himself not the place and victim of sacrifice?

Nor is John satisfied to show Jesus announcing a new temple;

rather he presents him as the very temple foretold by the prophets (see Ez 47). The body of Jesus, his flesh, is the dwelling place of God's glory. The angels ascend and descend over him as once they did over the awe-inspiring place where Jacob had seen God. The Spirit rests upon him permanently; he has been consecrated by the Father so that the Father is in him and he is in the Father; the Father makes his Name dwell in him, and in this temple worshipers will gather together and be made perfect in unity. All will share in the holiness of the temple, for "we shall come into them and make our dwelling in them."[60]

This "body" of Jesus is not the Church in the Pauline sense of the word, nor is it the eucharistic body. It is the risen body of Jesus, out of which the wellsprings of living water pour abundantly and unceasingly. The new worship of believers, a worship in spirit and in truth, is offered in this new temple.[61]

The conclusion is inescapable: the cult found in the Old Testament is abrogated. Believers are asked to pass from rite to person. Some liturgical actions still seem necessary, but they are no longer connected with a particular place or with more or less complicated rites. "Cult" has become "spiritual"; it is not eliminated but it is taken up into the very person of Jesus. John is perfectly aware that Christians have a cult consisting of baptism and Eucharist; he is aware of it, but he prefers not to speak of the institution of these, perhaps for fear he may give them an importance which they do not have but which they are always in danger of claiming.

What John is promoting, then, is not the suppression of cult but a deeper understanding of it: no authentic cult can be offered that is not mediated through the very person of Jesus of Nazareth, who alone gives it meaning. This view of cult is in keeping with John's fundamental "Christological" tendency, that is, his effort to bring everything to a focus in Jesus of Nazareth, as I noted in the discourse on the Bread of Life. The Eucharist acquires meaning only through its reference to the person of Jesus.

If then we human beings still need some form of cult because we exist as members of a community, this cult must always, even in our day, derive its meaning and function from the very life of Jesus.

John applies his principle in his way of penetrating more deeply into the Eucharist through symbolism. Let me recall some of the results of the preceding study.

In their celebration of the eucharistic meal the faithful must become increasingly conscious of the presence of Christ during the action over the bread and wine, while keeping in mind that this Christ is the man Jesus whom they must accept fully in his words and his actions. This man who came down from heaven is also the man who has brought salvation through the gift of his life for the life of the world. He is the risen Lord who is recognized in the breaking of the bread; he is present through his absence, and we must therefore not try to imprison him in anything whatsoever. He shares life and gives it in abundance. Finally, he is so intimately present that we can henceforth recognize him as dwelling in believers both by his Eucharist and by his love. John does not use the word "covenant," but has its equivalent in his formulas of immanence: "he in me and I in him," which point to the satisfaction of Israel's deepest desire.[62] Through this Eucharist believers acquire, along with life, the power to "produce fruit" in abundance.

John is not satisfied, however, to explain eucharistic practice in his own way; he also shows that he has inherited the "testamentary" tradition. Instead of reporting the words of institution he tells of the washing of the feet and how Jesus bade his followers continue on earth the service which he had just performed for them and by which he had brought into existence the community of disciples.

John brings out the goal toward which eucharistic practice is ordered, namely, mutual love. The last testament of Jesus, which enables the disciples to be his community, is: "Love one another!" The Passover context and the approach of the passion give the washing of feet and the testament of Jesus the seriousness and importance that the Eucharist requires.

PART IV

Overture

XIV
Overture

At the end of this often forbidding discussion of the biblical texts on the Eucharist readers will feel the need of a synthesis that pulls together the results progressively won. But a major difficulty immediately arises: What principle is to be used in unifying the scattered data which the analysis has produced? Does not any attempt at synthesis subordinate the data to principles extrinsic to the data? And, if so, must we be satisfied to go back to the various accounts given in the New Testament, with whatever light the analyses have shed on each? I think, in fact, that that kind of continually renewed reading is what we must settle for.

Nonetheless, by way not of a finale to my reading of the texts but of an overture to the reader's future study, I would like to set down some presuppositions for any valid reading of the eucharistic texts and to suggest three ways to an understanding of the mystery.

I. SOME PRESUPPOSITIONS OF A VALID READING

It is obvious that those who approach the texts on the Eucharist must be ready, not to cast doubt on the faith they have received from their fathers, but to question the language in which that faith has been passed on to them. Without this readiness to listen to the text as it exists in its own right, they will remain prisoners of the familiar words and the ideas these convey.

My reading of the texts has brought out two necessary presuppositions. The first is that the Eucharist is part of the Church's cultic life and is basically a *community activity*. This reminder is especially necessary for those older readers who are used to liturgical practices that emphasize the close relation between the individual and the Eucharist; I am thinking of such practices as ado-

281

ration of the Blessed Sacrament and visits to the Blessed
Sacrament. The participation of each individual in this source of
life is, of course, very important; the fact remains, however, that
it is the congregation, the one Church, which celebrates the Eucharist, and that the Eucharist is directed to the congregation, the
Church, in its entirety. The Lord is certainly present through the
Eucharist, but he is present in the form of a gift to the Church as
a whole.[1]

A second point that has emerged from my analyses is that the
"words of consecration" are not isolated utterances dealing with
an object in itself; they are part of an account which has a funda-
mentally *relational* structure. As I pointed out in Chapter VII the
words of Jesus do not simply assert the new state of the bread and
wine. Their aim is to give rise to a dialogue, and they offer at the
same time a food that is to be received and thereby lead to an existential commitment. I have therefore tried to bring out the intrinsic connection between the Eucharist and sharing.

Once these presuppositions are accepted, it is possible to proceed to a hermeneutic in the proper sense, that is, to ask what is
the meaning of *the text for me today.* If I did not raise this further
question, I would be leaving the readers to depend on their imag-
inations in their legitimate desire to relate the texts to contemporary requirements. It is worthwhile, of course, to have grasped the
meaning of New Testament teaching on the gift of Jesus or the
establishment of the ecclesial community. So too it is undoubtedly
a good thing to hear and put into practice the commandment to
"do this in memory of Jesus." But the way in which we should "do
this" is not immediately apparent, and the subsequent ecclesial
tradition has varied so widely that the choice of the model best
adapted to our age is not an easy one. I would like, therefore, to
specify the role of the exegete in this quest for the meaning the
Eucharist has for us today.

I could appeal to the author of the fourth gospel, whose intention was precisely to make the past events of Jesus of Nazareth
relevant to the Church of his day. His undertaking is certainly a
good example of evangelical hermeneutic; our situation, however,
is not comparable to his. John comes to us as an eyewitness and a
man inspired by the Spirit; exegetes cannot make such a claim.
Furthermore they are faced with several New Testament presentations which are not reducible to that of John; they must therefore keep in view all the interpretations offered by the New Testament. Finally, they must also take into account the original

event itself to the extent that they can glimpse it by the means available to them.

For these various reasons I shall try in the following sections to bring out the connections uniting the various traditions and interpretations. I shall group the results of my inquiry under three headings: to begin with, a fact which I have constantly encountered, namely, two kinds of observations that cannot be reduced to unity; second, the effort made to enter into a symbolical world; finally, attempts to formulate the mystery itself.

II. CALL TO A LIFE MARKED BY A RHYTHM

What I am alluding to in this perhaps surprising title is the fact that the New Testament constantly uses two ways of describing Christian life: that is, alongside cult, which has been the main subject of my inquiry, the New Testament over and over again sets everyday life. I have summed up this duality as the cult/life relationship. It emerges from the texts in so many places that I have felt justified in seeing in it a fundamental teaching on the nature of Christian life.

Two kinds of remembrance are required of the disciples of Jesus: remembrance by liturgical action and remembrance by an attitude of service. When the first Christians gathered around a table, they realized, to their joy, that the risen Lord was present among them; they then recalled the commandment of remembrance which the Lord had given at his last meal; they remembered what Jesus had done on that final evening as the climax of his entire life, and thus gave their own gatherings a ritual character by celebrating the eucharistic meal. On the other hand, as the fourth gospel makes clear, Jesus left something else to be commemorated: "the example I have given," namely, the washing of the feet.

Two kinds of "remembrance" were thus required of Christians: the eucharistic remembrance proper and remembrance in the form of service that was symbolized by the action of Jesus in washing the feet of his disciples. An assimilation of the two was almost inevitable, to the point that until the thirteenth century the washing of feet was regarded as a sacrament, in a broad sense of the word that is no longer used today.[2]

In both forms of remembrance Jesus transcends time. His words over the bread and cup and his action of washing feet: these are what believers are to "do in remembrance of him" or to "do in accordance with the example given." The Church is urged simultaneously to two different actions, one in its cultic life, the other in its secular existence; both, however, are focused on love of the brethren, and both have for their purpose to give life to the Church. The one uses the symbolism of food; the other finds expression in this or that form of service that is suited to the new life of Christians. Both manifest a presence despite absence, whether in the liturgical action whereby the Lord makes himself present to those to whom he gives life, or in the love-inspired action wherein Christians encounter the Lord in the least of his suffering brethren.

The New Testament has retained *two traditions about the final meal of Jesus,* but not in order to excite the curiosity of exegetes or to challenge them to determine which is the older. The reason why two traditions have been preserved is that the cultic tradition and the testamentary tradition shed light on one another.

Mark and Matthew juxtapose the cultic tradition and a remnant of the testamentary tradition which they think it imperative to keep; Luke inserts the cultic tradition into a testamentary account; John seems to retain only the testamentary form and to be satisfied with implicitly showing, in the discourse on the Bread of Life, that he is not ignorant of the cultic tradition. If neither of these two traditions can claim to be the source of the other, it becomes necessary to ask why both have been kept in the texts.

A first answer is given in the results reached in Chapter IX on "the traditions and the event." In all likelihood (I said there), Jesus celebrated a "farewell meal" which some primitive traditions quickly interpreted as a "cultic meal." When Luke and John later restored the "testamentary form," they did so in order to remind their readers of what was at the origin of their eucharistic cult, namely, the action of Jesus of Nazareth in its pre-liturgical form.

A second answer helps readers understand the relation between the cult of the early Church and the last meal of Jesus. Christians wanted to relate their cult to the life of Jesus. They wanted to show that their cultic institution was not a prolongation of Old Testament cult but was connected with the action of Jesus, who had put an end to the Old Testament cult.

The eucharistic rite is effective because it is linked to the personal sacrifice of Jesus on the cross and to his resurrection by God. But the eucharistic rite is not the only way of expressing that kind of sacrifice. When John replaces the institution of the Eucharist with the washing of feet he is telling his readers that the gift of

self which Jesus offered in order to unite us to him is also symbolized by his gesture of washing his disciples' feet, which in its
own way expresses something similar to the gift of the bread and
the cup. Both actions have for their purpose a communion (a "having part") with Jesus our Savior. When the Church gave ritual
form to the farewell meal rather than to the washing of feet, it
made it possible to actualize the memory of that meal without
omitting its basic reference to the mystery of Easter.

The point of the cult/life relationship is not only that it brings
together the gift of self symbolized at the Supper and the gift of
self made on the cross, but also that it shows what Christian life
is henceforward to be. Disciples must "serve" if their cult is to be
completely truthful. By serving they also heed the exhortations of
the prophets. Luke makes this duty of service explicit; John further defines it in terms of love. That Christians should love one
another, and do so with the very love of Jesus himself: this is the
reality symbolized by their cult; the latter signifies the divine love
that establishes and gives life to the community of Christ's disciples, a point which the classic theology of *res et sacramentum*
made in its own way.

In short, the two traditions about the final meal of Jesus bring
out two inseparable and complementary aspects of Christian
existence.

Two accounts, of the Supper and of the passion, come to us in
a meaningful relationship. The account of the passion and the
account of the Supper are like mirrors that reflect one another. In
his words over the bread and the cup Jesus tells in condensed form
what will happen on the terrible day that will soon dawn. The
account of the passion develops as it were what Jesus has said in
the upper room. The account of the Supper is like a concave mirror
that shows on a small surface the whole expanse of the passion.

Readers might of course be satisfied to read the accounts of
the eucharistic institution and the washing of feet as episodes in a
biographical narrative. In fact—to speak only of the fourth gospel—the traditional account of the Supper, in which Jesus is
shown in control of his destiny, was introduced only later into an
extended account of the passion. The purpose was to help readers
accept the baldness of the latter; this intention of the evangelist is
very important for me today. But there is more. I see that throughout the account of Christ's sufferings nothing is said of the meaning and significance of the passion for the disciples and for the
whole of humanity. Was it not necessary that this meaning and

significance should be brought out fully at some point? Jesus was not satisfied to suffer passively; not only did he turn his death into a gift of himself, but he was also fully aware that his fidelity to God and his fellow human beings would produce fruits of deliverance which would save the world.

Is this not the attitude which all disciples of Jesus must have in some degree if they are truly following in the footsteps of their Master? They must have a deep awareness that unites them to God and Jesus, and thus, paradoxically, be masters of the events which take place and of which they are the victims. In this sense, the eucharistic liturgy symbolizes the life given without reservation which Jesus lived in his day and which his disciples too must live, since they live henceforth by and in him.

Two senses of the word "koinōnia" provide confirmation of the duality that marks Christian life. The secondary tradition which Paul cites in 1 Corinthians 10:16 tells his readers: "The bread which we break, is it not a communion (*koinōnia*) in the body of Christ?" But this name for the result of the eucharistic act is also used in the Acts of the Apostles to designate what exegetes are agreed in calling "fraternal communion," that is, not only a harmony of hearts but also a sharing of goods in what is becoming the "community" of disciples.

These two meanings of *koinōnia* exemplify the New Testament practice of using words of cultic origin to name the caritative services performed by the community. Thus the word *leitourgia* and *thysia* mean either the collection or the gift of self; it is as though cultic language, stripped now of its first and proper meaning, were being used to describe the "spiritual sacrifice" that is henceforth characteristic of Christian life.

The cult/life relationship proves to be still active here, because it modifies the use of language, although in this case it is life itself that is heir to cult.

I am compelled to ask whether the same phenomenon of a double meaning is not to be equivalently found in the two names which the New Testament uses for the eucharistic liturgy, namely, "breaking of bread" and "Lord's Supper." In the former I saw reflected the "sharing of bread" which the primitive community celebrated in its *koinōnia*; in the latter, the fraternal meal pre-supposes the Lord's presence in the eucharistic rite proper. The close connection between cult and life manifests itself here again.

Two actions, one in the upper room and one on Calvary, correspond to the accounts of the Supper and the passion respectively. The connection between the two actions is the connection between two kinds of "sacrifice." On Golgotha Jesus gives his life in an act that can be called a "personal sacrifice." In the upper room he symbolizes this personal sacrifice in a liturgical action which can be described as in a sense a cultic sacrifice. But this cultic sacrifice has nothing in common with the sacrifices of the Old Testament except the fact that the praise involved in it celebrates—this time in advance—the victory of God who saves his Son from death and brings the Church into being. The Supper symbolizes the sacrifice of Christ on the cross.

The Mass likewise symbolizes the sacrifice of Christ on the cross, but it does so by way of the Supper. For the Mass repeats the rite celebrated by the first Christians as they themselves repeated and made more explicit what Jesus had done at his final meal. The Mass repeats over and over again the gestures of Jesus as received by the first Christians. In this sense there is a "repetition": not of the "meal" as Jesus might have experienced it, but of the ritual gestures and words with the meaning Jesus had given them. This is why the celebrant proclaims the eucharistic account and translates it into gestures; he pronounces the words of Jesus as tradition has reported them with variations. This independence of the tradition from the *ipsissima verba* of Jesus is extremely important, because it means that the Church exercises a freedom even as it refers back to the past event of the supper. Ecclesial tradition alone is empowered to alter these words so as to make them more pregnant or more explicit.

The Mass, like the Supper, symbolizes the life that is the fruit of Christ's sacrifice on the cross. Theologians say as much when they speak of the Mass as a "sacrament": it is the (efficacious) symbol of the covenant which Jesus established by giving his life on the cross and on which God put his seal by raising his Son from the dead. The Mass, therefore, does not represent the event of the cross, but repeats the Supper which symbolically anticipated the new world that Christ inaugurated.

Supper, cross, and Mass are seemingly three distinct and separate points of reference. In fact, however, they go together in twos. That is, the Mass is connected with the Supper, and the Supper with the cross; as a result, the Mass too is, in a way, connected with the cross. The Mass makes Calvary present again, but it does not repeat it. The situation resembles that of the earth which each morning presents itself to the sun, even though people continue to say that the sun rises each morning; so too the Church each day makes itself present to Calvary by repeating the actions of Jesus in the upper room, actions which anticipated not only his death but his resurrection.

Let me be very explicit on this point. Mass and Supper are both of them liturgical actions, and they derive their meaning from their relation to the one act of Calvary and thereby to the entire life of Jesus before and after Easter. Here again we see cult and life forming a pair; it is only when paired that cult and life each has its full meaning and value. As I said earlier, there is a "dialectical" relation between the two; in other words, neither pole of the relation can be surrendered.

Christian life therefore has a rhythm of its own, as does all authentic life. This truth has a value for my personal life. What place does the Eucharist have in my life since it is counterbalanced by the teaching of the testamentary tradition, namely, the supreme value of fraternal love and of the pursuit of justice among human beings? I do not choose between the two but cling to both by establishing a rhythm between them.

My entire life is conditioned by the rhythm linking day and night or waking and sleeping. Modern civilization does no doubt tend to blur the boundary between the two; electric light or night-time work might give the impression that we moderns live in constant wakefulness. But the same cannot be said of individuals, experiencing, as they do, the human condition, for if they do not sleep, their efforts to keep on working will be in vain.

Through baptism I have been born a second time, and the new life thus acquired needs a special food to sustain it, or else I shall be quickly weakened. I take part in the eucharistic liturgy because I have a vital desire for it. Admittedly, the eucharistic liturgy seems to complicate my life, since instead of simply devoting myself to my daily tasks I must set aside a little time for this occupation that seems useless but is in fact indispensable if I wish to bear witness to my Christian faith. The truth of this statement becomes inescapably clear once I look upon the Eucharist not as a "means" of obtaining graces but as an exercise of my Christian language. If I am to exist fully, I need to express myself in this way.

These remarks doubtless apply also to prayer. But there is something more in the Eucharist, since it is a communal act, the action of a community. In addition to the alternations already mentioned—day and night, waking and sleeping—there is another of which I must be aware: the alternation imposed by the relationship of person and community. I am not in the world as an isolated individual but am part of a network of solidarities and dependences, and this is true in the spiritual world as well as in the secular. The Eucharist is the place par excellence where I draw breath as member of a community; in and through the Eucharist I live at the level of the universal Church and thus of the entire human race, that "multitude" which Jesus had before him at his final meal.

III. ENTRANCE INTO A WORLD OF SYMBOLS

The words "symbolize" and "symbolic" have occurred repeatedly in this book. The reason is that the universe which the Bible bids us enter is a universe of symbols, and we must understand it as such if we are to understand and properly situate our faith in the eucharistic mystery. A moment ago, I was emphasizing the rhythm that characterizes our lives. Now I must unify in a paradoxical way the seemingly incompatible elements in the eucharistic texts.

The eucharistic expression of Christian life belongs essentially to the order of symbols. Liturgical action is located on an intermediate plane between secular realities and purely heavenly realities; that plane is often called the "sacramental" plane. Let me try to define its nature on the basis of the data supplied by the Bible.

My general impression is that the classical presentation of a sacrament as an "effective sign of salvation" does not express very well the data I have uncovered. I mention it, however, because the Eucharist is usually placed in that category. We are taught—and quite legitimately—that a sacrament is an instrument of salvation. Baptism causes us to be reborn through purification and incorporation into the Church; throughout our lives the Eucharist gives us a share in the fruits of redemption that were won by Jesus Christ. A sacrament is therefore a rite which effects grace, a cause which produces what it signifies. This theology of the sacraments is based on a concept of sign according to which the signified (salvation) is distinct from the signifier (the material object or action that is used): two different worlds are thus brought together in the sacrament as mediator of grace.

This approach can hardly be said to reflect the biblical way of thinking. The biblical writers do not link things to each other as causes and effects; they prefer to think in terms of integration.

Thus the actions of the fathers have repercussions in their children, not because of any causal link but because children are in a sense present in the loins of their fathers. In taking this approach the Bible is not rejecting the category of causality; it is simply adopting a different point of view.

This same point of view was adopted by another ecclesial tradition that originates not in St. Augustine but in Dionysius the Areopagite (5th/6th century).[3] In this tradition, which remains alive in the Eastern world, the term "mystery" is preferred to the term "sacrament." As seen in this perspective the sensible world encountered in the liturgy is not strictly speaking a springboard that launches us into an intelligible world distinct from it; rather it is an epiphany of God the Creator and Redeemer. The liturgical mysteries are therefore looked upon not as "instruments " of salvation but as actions which symbolize, each in its own way, the one mystery of God as manifested in the man who is Christ.

When the Church celebrates God in the Eucharist it produces much more than an instrument or means of salvation; it performs a saving act or what we today might call a "speech act." In this act the Church gives symbolic expression to the mystery from which it draws its existence. Such an approach presupposes that I am setting aside the categories of causality for the time being and using the categories of symbolism: the eucharistic action *is and is not* the mystery of Jesus as celebrated in the form of thanksgiving to God.

This view of the Eucharist has several advantages. A first is that it makes immediately clear the continuity between Mass and Supper. The Mass, as I said earlier, actualizes the words of Jesus, for it is still Jesus who acts through the Spirit. At the Supper he anticipated in a symbolic manner his passage or saving paschal event; today he gives expression, with the Church, to the passage which the Church accomplishes in him. The agent is the same, the action is the same. The passage is not strictly an "effect" of the liturgical action; it is that very action itself. By means of its eucharistic language the Church experiences what Jesus experienced.

Another advantage is that we do not reduce the Eucharist to a seemingly secondary role as an external means, but make it instead the heart and source of Christian life. The Eucharist is Christian life in a symbolic state. If attendance at Mass is obligatory for us, the reason is not that we may profit by the cross, the sole means of salvation, for by their baptism Christians are already united to the saving cross. The reason is rather that life demands expression and nourishment. Liturgical action is one aspect of our common life in Christ.

Jesus is symbolically present despite his absence

Recourse to symbolism makes it possible to express in a more satisfactory way the mystery of the real presence of Jesus in the Eucharist.

What does "presence" mean? God is always present to our world, which he carries in his hands and makes to exist as though he were within it, but in a manner which we are incapable of detecting. The mystery of God and his presence is incomprehensible. In like manner, the risen Lord is at work in the world; he continues his struggle there to the end.[4] The saints and the humble know that he is present, not as one who stands alongside us but as one who is more truly ourselves than we can ever be. How, then, are we to understand his eucharistic presence?

The word "presence" has in fact a wide range of meanings. There are two extremes to be avoided. One consists in likening the eucharistic presence to a material presence, like the presence to me of the sheet of paper on which I write these lines. The problem of real presence took the form at one time of asking how Jesus could be present simultaneously in heaven and here on earth in the Eucharist. In those days people were not embarrassed by the idea of a heaven located in a particular place; as a result, they created for themselves traps from which there was no escaping. Many theologians of the ninth century fell into these traps and adopted a materialistic view of the Eucharist that led by reaction to the exaggerated spiritualism of Berengarius of Tours. The entire intellectual approach was no longer that of the Fathers.[5]

The opposite extreme is to "spiritualize" the Eucharist to such an extent that it embodies no more than an awareness of an abiding reality: the reality of the salvation offered to us and of Christ living through the centuries. In the Eucharist there is no longer any real sacramental encounter.

Is it possible to find a mean between these two extremes and to define the real presence on the basis of what the Bible tells us?

In the Eucharist our encounter with the God of the covenant takes place through the mediation of bread and wine, within the Church's communal celebration. As I pointed in Chapter VII, the bread *is and is not* the body of Christ. It is not I who give rise to the mystery, it is not I who bring about the presence of Christ; in this sense the body of Christ is objectively present. At the same time, however, I must enter into the dialogue which God establishes with me, and recognize this presence; without faith I remain outside the mystery. It is legitimate, of course, to adopt the viewpoint of someone on Sirius and ask what the bread is apart from this recognition. That question does not, however, reflect the data provided in the text: Jesus is speaking there not to all and sundry but to the twelve and his faithful disciples. His assertion has meaning, therefore, only within the relationship between him and them.

Is not the situation of the Eucharist comparable to that of the risen body of Jesus which the disciples saw before them? People often think that the objectivity of the risen body of Jesus is due to the fact that it can be "touched," "seen," and so on. I have shown,[6] however, that the real objectivity of the appearances resides in the fact that they were not subjective; that is, they were the result of an initiative on the part of the risen Jesus and not of the disciples' imagination. The appearances, I said, were objective because they were not subjective. The same holds true for the Eucharist. The presence of Jesus is objective because I am not its author. It is not I who create the identity between the bread and Jesus; it is, however, I who, with the Church, confess that the bread has become Jesus who offers us his life.

Let me put it differently. We often speak of the Eucharist as a reality independent of those who receive it, as if the action of Jesus terminated in the transformation of the bread into his body. The biblical texts, on the other hand, constantly make it clear that the Eucharist is connected with a dialogue which Jesus wishes to carry on with his disciples. We have to restore the role of faith in the eucharistic mystery: in the eucharistic bread I perceive Jesus, the Bread of Life. If, however, I abstract from all this and ask what the bread is, as though I were an unbeliever, I can only describe it in terms of its nutritional function.[7]

A further step has to be taken. The encounter with Jesus through the eucharistic bread leads me first of all to God. The reason is that the intention of Jesus is identical with the intention of God himself. In Jesus I share in this intention. Therefore I immediately begin to praise God for what he did in Jesus; I thank and praise him also for the Church, since in Jesus the Church lives in love and receives the Holy Spirit.

This sharing in the intention of Jesus leads me to action. The sequence here is the same as in the appearances of the risen Lord. After recognition ("It is indeed I," says the risen Lord) comes mission ("Go!"). The cultic encounter with Jesus sends me out into the world; the Eucharist leads to service of the brethren. The eucharistic remembering leads to existential remembering.

The eucharistic "presence," therefore, is not something static, but is directly active. It is a "synergy," to use an expression from the Orthodox theologians. It is like the presence of Jesus that is produced by the "example" of the washing of feet, an example wholly ordered to effective service.

According to the teaching in the account of the Supper, the eucharistic body gives life to the Church: by making himself present to his disciples and the whole vast multitude of human beings Jesus symbolically transforms his relationship with them.[8] The paradox is that he remains over against his disciples and yet at the same time becomes their food.

On the one hand, Jesus is irreducibly set over against his disciples. He alone is active, while they seem "passive," as we saw in Chapter III. It is Jesus who calls them together; it is he who speaks and gives the bread, the cup, and a command. From this point of view, he is completely distinct from his disciples.[9]

On the other hand—and this is the second aspect of the situation—Jesus gives his disciples a share in his own life, thus transforming their group into a community that exists only through and in him. That is God's intention in Jesus, namely, to bring all human beings together in him and through him.

Here again, the mystery of the two-in-one can be expressed in the language of symbol. In the account of the Supper the disciples symbolize the multitude to which Jesus refers. He who speaks is at the same time the Church's food; he is the *corpus mysticum*, a term that in times past meant the Eucharist but today means the Church, the mystical body of Christ.[10] The Church *is and is not* the body of Christ.

The circumstances of the eucharistic action

The Eucharist is not celebrated only on Easter but daily. This means that without losing its character as the paschal feast the new passover can become a daily celebration because it is always linked to the parousia, that is, the last day. In a sense, the Mass actualizes the feast of Easter with its accompanying ideas and hopes; but at the same time it is wholly focused on the definitive victory of God at the end of time. The tension between Easter and parousia, however, is absorbed into the unity of the eucharistic action, which is both the one and the other. It might be said that in the Mass eternity shows through during the time of the celebration and reduces Easter and parousia to unity in itself, without thereby eliminating their fundamental and necessary duality.

In addition to time, space plays a part. The Eucharist is not celebrated only in a single set place: the temple in Jerusalem, but can occur anywhere on earth. At the same time, however, it must remain rooted in a precisely defined soil. In it the particular and universal are brought into unity without losing their radical distinctness. The result is a symbolic place which *is and is not* the entire world.

The elements of the eucharistic action

These likewise take on a symbolic value. The *meal* symbolizes the heavenly banquet because of its intrinsic relation to the Last Supper, the basic words and gestures of which it repeats. At the level of the created world, a meal already symbolizes the brotherhood and sisterhood of the participants; in the Eucharist it also symbolizes the union which believers have with Christ thanks to his sacrifice.

Bread and wine constitute a two-part whole, the significance of which it is important to understand. Why the twofold action? A first answer comes from scholars familiar with the ancient mentality; they tell us that teachings were usually given in twos. I do not lay great stress on this obvious point, though it is worth recalling.

There is another motif that can account for the twofold action of Jesus over bread and cup. The bread represents everyday food that is necessary in the way that the manna was necessary; the wine, on the other hand, is connected with the festive atmosphere of banquets. The daily and the festive are two dimensions of human life that are brought into unity in the primitive liturgy.

The fact that bread is used certainly suggests an emphasis on the "food" aspect and thus on the increase of life both individual and communal. Should an ordinary sustaining meal be therefore added to the eucharistic rite? The history of the Corinthian Church warns us against this kind of dangerous mixture; was the Eucharist not gradually separated from the fraternal love-feast or agape?

The fact that wine, customary at banquets, is used suggests an emphasis on the festive character of the meal, which is celebrated in an atmosphere of joy, as the Acts of the Apostles show.

Finally, and more generally, the *food* as such, being the source of increased life, symbolizes the life newly given to the community. The Eucharist is above all else a way in which Jesus communicates the life of God to the community; this life consists in adopting toward the Father the filial attitude so characteristic of Jesus himself, an attitude of complete self-giving and cooperation with the plans of God.

As the reader can already see, this "symbolical" interpretation is rich in meaning, provided it has its basis in the symbolic universe of Jesus himself. But is it possible to universalize a set of symbols? Yes, if it be recognized that Jesus was heir to Israel and via Israel to the human world and that his actions have their roots in the inmost depths of humanity. It is only the specific materials, bread and wine, that come from a particular civilization. Let me make one point, however, with regard to these materials: If we try to disregard the particular materials and retain only their significance as daily and festive foods, we risk depriving the celebration of any historical connection with Jesus of Nazareth.[11] Is not the use of bread and wine the only way of keeping the Eucharist connected with past history? Since the symbolism is the most important thing, this question needs to be asked. I leave it to contemporary liturgists to supply an answer.

IV. APPROACH TO THE MYSTERY

Rhythmic pattern and symbolism provide ways of speaking of the eucharistic mystery. But at a deeper level the eucharistic mystery refers us in turn to the mystery of the relation between God and human beings in creation and in history. Covenant, shed blood, and sharing are three things that help us come to grips with this mystery of God in his relationship with the human race.

The mystery of the covenant

When the attempt is made to say how God has entered into a relationship with human beings, "covenant" (word and reality) proves to be the best way of describing the mystery of what we sometimes call the "grace" of God who wills to divinize human beings. The eucharistic liturgy therefore proclaims that in the person of Jesus the covenant between God and the people has taken its definitive form. I shall not reexamine the history of this covenant, which was briefly reviewed in Chapter VIII. The anthropomorphic language of covenant provides a way of understanding the mysterious reality of the God/humanity relationship, namely, the "synergy" of God and human beings.

The "synergy" that is meant here corresponds, in biblical terms, to the action of *remembrance*. What is it precisely that happens when one "remembers"? In the Eucharist "remembering" means that a contact with a living person is regained or intensified or expressed (or all three at once). The risen Lord is present, and in him we recognize Jesus of Nazareth, who enables us to share in his intentions. As I explained in Chapter VI, to remember is to go back to the very source of life and, having there come in contact with God, to be carried into the future by his intentions.

In this "re-cognition" we see that God is at work in Jesus and in us; as a result we enter into the divine work and make the covenant produce its fruits of grace.

The mystery of the shed blood

The shed blood makes it immediately clear that the covenant is not established and maintained apart from the victory of life over death. That is what is rightly asserted in the word "sacrifice," on which I think it necessary to dwell for a moment.

The Eucharist is a "sacrifice." Unfortunately, the proper meaning of the word has been obscured by the controversies which raged between Luther and the Catholicism of his day, since it is difficult for later generations not to be influenced by these.

According to historians of religion and psychologists, "sacrifice" reflects a structure of exchanges between human beings and their divinities. The very idea of exchange supposes awareness of a distance, which is sometimes identified with a radical indebtedness for existence itself,[12] an indebtedness that goes deeper even than the sins from which human beings seek to be delivered. By means of sacrifice human beings try to bridge this distance. They symbolize the desired union by offering something of which they deprive themselves; they thereby renounce the immediate possession of things in order to reach the Giver of them.

The sacrifice of Jesus on the cross adds the gift actually given to the gift symbolized at the supper and puts an end to earlier sacrifices. The desired union is fully attained and the "distance" is abolished, not only between Jesus and God but between the new Human Being and the Father.

By symbolizing this sacrificial act at the Supper Jesus created the possibility of having his sacrifice remembered in a "sacramental" form. The Eucharist is a sacramental action that recalls the action of Jesus at the Supper and thereby refers ultimately to the cross; it adds nothing, however, to the sacrifice of Calvary. It expresses in the course of time what Jesus signified at his final meal.

In what sense is the Eucharist a "sacrifice"? It is not one in the sense that it is a means of establishing the covenant, for the covenant was brought into existence on the cross and is actualized, or made efficaciously present, in baptism, which gives the members of the Church their new being. In the Mass these persons made newly alive express their faith, their gratitude, and their longing for fulfillment.

The Mass can nonetheless be called a "sacrifice," because although the Church is already the body of Christ and is already united to its Lord, it is not yet fully his body, not yet fully united. It must still "pass" from death to life, and do so unceasingly; its eucharistic action thus symbolizes a passage that is going on at every moment. If there is still a distance to be bridged, then there is, in a sense, a sacrifice. The Church is not yet fully the body of Christ but must become it.

Like the Supper, the Mass *is and is not* the sacrifice of Jesus on the cross, the sacrifice which established Christ in his new mode of being. It *is* that sacrifice in the sense that it symbolizes the passing of the entire ecclesial community into the new and definitive covenant; it thus asserts the new being, challenges the past, acknowledges the removal of the distance, and expresses the new way of existing. The Mass *is not* that sacrifice, however, since, just as Jesus was not yet dead during the Supper, the Church analogously is not yet really dead to sin and distanced from it. Just as during the Supper Jesus still had to die, so the Church must translate its new mode of being into everyday reality. There is thus a true "sacrifice," but it is entirely "spiritual," since it is the self-giving of the Church insofar as it lives through Jesus; it gives itself by receiving the Father's gift.

The Mass is a "sacrifice of praise." This phrase connects two words which modern ears find it difficult to associate: does "sacrifice" not suggest immolation, while "praise" refers rather to a joyous exclamation inspired by thanksgiving at having received something from Another? But it is precisely here that we must revise our understanding of sacrifice and realize that it does not necessarily involve suffering or immolation. I will only mention that in the phrase "sacrifice of praise" the word "sacrifice" is being used in its original meaning (recovered as the result of a slow development), namely, that which "makes sacred" or restores a relationship with God. Thus when Jesus says: "I consecrate myself so that they too may be consecrated," he uses the verb *hagiazō*, which also means "to sacrifice," but he uses it to mean that he takes his proper place as the Son.[13]

The Mass proclaims the praise of God, of him who rescued his Son from death and brought the community of believers into existence. It is obvious that expiation from sin is also connoted, provided we understand expiation as meaning not a punishment for a sin but a reconciliation after an estrangement.

The mystery of gift and sharing

The covenant from God is a gift, the blood shed by Jesus is a gift, and the Eucharist is the gift par excellence. If, then, there is a single word which captures the reality of God as he expresses himself in human history, it is the word "gift."

In the Introduction to this book I gave a preliminary description of how God sought without wearying to become ever more present to human beings, and I ended by speaking of love and the Holy Spirit. Now, in fidelity to the texts of scripture, I would prefer to speak of "gift." In giving the bread and the cup Jesus gives himself to us as food in order to transform us into himself.

The Church in turn gives what it itself continuously receives from the Lord. More accurately, it "distributes" or "shares" the bread. That is why I think the name "breaking of bread" which described the Eucharist at the beginning can be rephrased as "sharing of bread." The sharing goes on endlessly, just as there was bread to spare at the multiplication of the loaves.

The "sharing of bread" is a name that applies to life in community as well as to the liturgy and thus bids us closely associate the liturgy and the life of real communion that Christianity is meant to be. To say "communion" is to say "union with Jesus in his gift of his own life" and therefore also "union with the brethren and openness to the multitude."

By deliberately relating eucharistic cult to service in everyday life, the testamentary tradition in Luke tells believers that they too must relate their liturgical activity to their life as brothers and sisters.

In point of fact, the two elements used in the Eucharist already symbolize the twofold relationship which believers have with God and neighbor: since there is but one loaf we form a single body, while the one cup expresses the unity of those who drink from it with Jesus and among themselves. To celebrate the Eucharist is already to affirm the fraternal unity of all human beings.

The conclusions to be drawn from the celebration of the Eucharist are obvious. According to the authentic tradition of the prophets and the teaching of Jesus, dialogue with God both supposes and promotes justice among brethren. Cult is therefore not an end in itself but a symbolic expression of the existence of love both in its origin (Jesus) and in its outcome (the Church).

Liturgical action should therefore be prolonged in the form of sharing bread, that is, promoting justice, fighting against hunger in the world, and delivering the oppressed from every evil. Cult may be at the heart of the life of brotherhood and sisterhood, but it is not therefore a "higher" degree of that life or its "summit"; that is, it is not above the life of charity but within it as its source of inspiration. Once believers realize this, they will approach the mystery of the Eucharist in the right way.

Envoi

"Let us cross over to the other shore," says Jesus after a long day of teaching in parables (Mk 4:35). The people have asked no questions of this teller of astonishing parables, and he seems to be hoping for a better reception among the pagans on the far side of the lake; or does he simply want to extend his activity to them? The gospel says nothing of his intention. The one thing certain is that the storm on the lake seems to resist such an extension and that the pagans, disturbed by the exorcism Jesus performs in their midst, ask him to return to his own country. The hour for a mission to the pagans has not yet come; it must wait until by his death and resurrection Jesus has once and for all forced his contemporaries to abandon their narrow views.

In his desire to cross to the farther shore Jesus shows himself a true son of Abraham, at least according to a recent author, André Néher.[1] In Néher's view, contradiction is at the heart of Jewish existence: a Jew is a "Hebrew," a word which etymologically means to "pass over" and "cause to pass over"; at the same time, however, the Jew is Israel who settled in the land that had been promised and then actually given to him. Jews must therefore keep a vital balance between the urge that impels them to abandon every form of settled existence and their instinct to enjoy what they have.

Let us cross over to the other shore! This describes the situation of the disciples of him who willed to die during Passover, the feast that effects a passage from one place to another. Abraham had long ago left behind the great civilization of Ur in Chaldea; Moses could not be satisfied with the wealth of Egypt; the people crossed the wilderness: all of them had to go elsewhere.

Those who would dream of crossing to the other shore must be constantly open to an always possible better existence; this openness is inspired by the living God to whom Jesus prayed in

300

the night. Jesus threw down the barriers behind which too many of his contemporaries enclosed themselves. His action in the upper room signifies his own final and definitive passage.

The Eucharist is by its nature a challenge. To the early Christians it was not simply a part of a well-organized cultic life such as we tend to establish and then regulate down to the last detail. It was anything but that at a time when the Church had not yet received the stamp of approval from the public authorities but was still weak and even persecuted. Let me look for a moment at those early Christians, as I allow my imagination to project a probable picture of their life in the first centuries.

I see myself praying with my fellow believers in the silent catacombs, cut off from the outside world. In descending into the depths of earth I leave behind the world of business, of ambitions, of injustice and money, the world too in which human beings suffer. I go down into the haven of peace. Yes, I am tempted to stay there and flee that world, but I resist the temptation, for I know that I must soon go back up into a turbulent and even hostile environment.

Here I am, then, in a community of men and women who have cast their lot with Jesus Christ and who are desirous of living and proclaiming the good news of justice and love. For them the eucharistic assembly is not a time of escape into a dream world; it is a time when the community receives strength to face testing of one or other kind: the same corruption, torture, violence, and wretched conditions with which we are familiar today. Yes, the Mass is essentially a challenge.

I recapture in spirit the climate in which the Jews used to live: oppressed first by the Egyptians, then the Greeks, then the Romans, but longing meanwhile with all their hearts for a deliverance that doubtless had its political side but was above all religious. This situation came home to them with special intensity at Passover time, for Passover was basically a challenge issued by God himself to an unjust order.

The Eucharist is of course not the moment to prepare for revolution with weapons in hand; it sets a table at which the witnesses to God's love and to justice can nourish and sustain themselves.—I know little of the actual rite followed in those catacomb services, but what difference does that make? The essential thing was not the ritual but the power which the leaven had of making the bread of this world rise.

Does this backward glance at the early Christian Eucharist have meaning outside of countries in which justice is frustrated? But it is frustrated in every land! I have simply gotten used to injustice and I tolerate all sorts of compromises with it. If, however, the Eucharist breaks down my habitual attitude, not only because I hear the good news proclaimed there but also because I find myself united, as a member of community, with him who gave his life for the reign of justice and love, then this cultic intermission in my secular life will produce its intended effects, since it will make me ready to risk what I have won in life and even life itself.

I have already heard this invitation because I have seen how Jesus behaved in the face of death. But now, in the eucharistic liturgy, I no longer receive a mere command or even a model for my imitation; rather I enter into a communion, and a "synergy" makes its dwelling within me.

It is precisely this that distinguishes me from a Jewish believer. The passage that I experience is not a simple movement from one point to another, but is at the same time a constantly deepening presence. I am united with the mystery of the eternal that makes time fruitful. If God were not God, he would be satisfied to issue orders; but in fact he always accompanies those whom he has chosen for the passage from one shore to the other: he comes and is present, with the active presence that is his intention for a human race which is at last reconciled with him and at peace with itself. Israel caught a glimpse of all this. The disciples of Jesus know that the Spirit has been given to them even now in order to help them cross over to the other shore.

Appendix

I. SOLEMN JEWISH MEALS

Among the Jewish meals that were marked by a degree of solemnity two are relevant to the subject of this book: the Passover meal and the brotherhood meal. I shall explain in section II of this appendix why I think that Jesus ate his final meal in a Passover atmosphere but not according to the strict Jewish Passover rite.

The Passover meal

Although the documentation for the Passover meal dates from the second century A.D. at the earliest, experts in matters rabbinical think it possible to establish the organization of the meal as celebrated in the time of Jesus and to avoid major errors in doing so.[1] First, then, the preparations for the meal; then the celebration proper.

(a) Preparations

1. A room, usually located in the upper part of a house, had to be prepared for the celebration of the meal. It had to be large enough for at least ten persons to recline on couches, and it had to have the necessary furnishings.

2. A lamb had to be obtained for the meal: one year old, without defects (see 1 Pet 1:19; Ex 12:5), large enough for each guest to have a piece the size of an olive or about ten grams in weight. It could be obtained between the 10th and the 14th of Nisan.

3. The guests had to be selected: the family or a group of friends. Others could be added, but any additions had to be made before the moment when the lamb was to be sacrificed in the temple.

4. The father of the family or his delegate took the lamb to the temple, where its throat was cut in the inner court at about 2:30

p.m. Its blood was collected in cups and carefully poured out at the foot of the altar. The animal was skinned and prepared in such a way that it could be easily roasted.

5. The house had been carefully cleansed of every trace of yeast, or leavened bread (Ex 12:15, 19; 1 Cor 5:7); from this point on only unleavened bread was to be eaten, in memory of the "bread of affliction" that had been hastily prepared before the exodus from Egypt (Deut 16:3). After being brought back to the house the lamb was roasted over a fire, on a grill shaped in the form of a cross. It had to be roasted in its entirety, with none of it boiled (Ex 12:9), and with none of its bones being broken.

6. There was to be a strict fast during the day of 14 Nisan.

(b) The celebration of the Passover meal

The meal could be begun when darkness had fallen on the evening of 14 Nisan, and it had to end by dawn on the 15th. A passage in the Mishnah clearly explains the stages of the meal.[2]

1. *Hors d'oeuvres* were served in a room separate from the dining room; the guests sat while eating them. They were abundant and were meant to allay hunger, so that the lamb would be simply the crowning part of the meal (the amount of lamb served to each individual was usually very small).

There was a consecration or dedication of the feast day and the first cup (called the "*Qiddush* or dedication cup").

The hors d'oeuvres or preliminary dish consisted of green herbs (lettuce), bitter herbs, a fruit puree *(haroseth)* of various squeezed and grated fruits (dates, figs, grapes, apples, almonds), seasoned with spices and vinegar.

2. The *meal proper* then began in the dining room. It was served, but left untouched. A second cup was distributed, but not yet drunk. Then a child questioned the head of the household.

The question elicited the *haggadah*, which was read in Aramaic (Deut 26:5–11) by the father of the family, who also explained the rites, for example, the unleavened bread (Ex 12:39) and the bitter herbs (Ex 12:8). The guests were thus all reminded of the deliverance from Egypt (Ex 12:27).

The first part of the *hallel*—Ps 113 to v. 9, or 113 to 114:3— was recited (in Hebrew) by a single voice, with everyone joining in the refrain.

Finally, the second cup—the Haggadah cup—was drunk.

After this specifically Passover ritual, the *meal* began. There were no plates, and the bread (a flat piece) was used to scoop food from the serving dish. The *blessing of the unleavened bread* was recited by the father of the house, who stood with his hands empty. The guests answered "Amen." Then, holding the loaf in his left hand, the president used his right hand to break off (not cut) a piece for each guest and distribute it; when he had completed the distribution, all ate the piece given to them.

The guests then ate the Passover lamb as well as the unleavened bread, bitter herbs, and *haroseth,* and drank wine.

Finally, a *thanksgiving (birkat ha-mazon)* was said over the third cup or cup of blessing.

As a close to the meal, a fourth cup (the Hallel cup) was poured, and the second part of the *hallel* (Ps 114-18) was recited (in Hebrew) in praise of God.

A brotherhood meal

In the time of Jesus there were brotherhoods *(haburoth)* which used to give solemn expression to their fellowship by celebrating a meal together almost every week. The order followed at these meals seems to have been that of the Passover meal, except for the omission of the specifically Passover liturgy.[3] Here are the main parts of such a meal.

(a) Preliminaries

Hors d'oeuvres consisting of fish, chicken, herbs, mustard, and wine. Each guest blessed his own food.

When the guests had finished, they washed their hands.

(b) The meal

Blessing over the bread.
Ritual blessing over each dish and over the various cups.
Blessing of the lamp.

Second washing of hands.
Ritual blessing of the final cup by the president.

*

Here is the text for the president's blessing of the final cup:

Blessed be you, Lord our God, eternal king, who feed the whole world in your kindness and graciousness, your mercy and tender compassion. You give all flesh its food, for your mercy endures for ever. In your great kindness we have never lacked for food; for love of your great name may we never lack it, for you support and sustain all living things; you do good to all of them; you provide food for everything you have made. Blessed be you, Lord, who give all things their food!

We thank you, Lord, for giving our fathers a broad, good, and lovely land as an inheritance; for delivering us, Lord our God, from the house of bondage and leading us from the land of Egypt; for your covenant, which you have sealed in our flesh; for your law, which you taught us, and your statutes, which you made known to us; for the life, favor, and mercy which you have poured out upon us; and for the food with which you nourish and constantly sustain us, every day and every hour of every season. For all this, Lord our God, we thank and bless you. May your name be blessed by the mouths of all living creatures, continually and for ever, as it is written: "You shall eat and be filled, and you shall bless the Lord your God for the good land he has given you." Blessed be you, Lord, for food and for the land!

II. THE LAST SUPPER AND THE JEWISH PASSOVER MEAL

In telling the story of the Supper the synoptic evangelists show it being held on the feast of Passover. Does it follow that this final meal of Jesus was celebrated according to the Passover rite? If the answer is yes, more light is thrown on this meal.

An affirmative answer was in fact standard for a long time, and anyone who dared question it was regarded with suspicion. Back in 1720, indeed, Dom Calmet had written a fine study of the subject in which he concluded that the last meal of Jesus was not a Passover meal.[4] His hypothesis did not win universal approval, however, for in 1760 J. D. Mansi thought it necessary to add an appendix to the Latin translation of Calmet's work (which some would have liked to see simply disappear) in order to explain the contrary view and thus "make the study questionable."[5]

Even today the question is not finally settled. One might generalize (with some simplification) and say that German critics believe the Last Supper to have been a Passover meal,[6] while English-language authors incline rather to say that it was not.[7] Among the authors writing in French some have opted for a non-Passover meal, but they remain divided among themselves.[8] The problem is not a trivial one, since the answer given often determines the interpretation of the Last Supper, as is clear from J. Jeremias.

Let me be more specific. No one denies the Passover atmosphere in the account of the Supper; some critics add, however, that the meal celebrated by Jesus followed the Jewish Passover ritual, and on this fact they base their theological interpretaion of the meal. In my opinion, exegetes can legitimately be dubious about this identification, for the arguments advanced by Jeremias do not prove his thesis. Since the English-reading public may have been swayed by his chapter on the subject,[9] I think it useful to comment here on the fourteen arguments he offers, although I shall leave aside those which have little relation to the subject, namely, arguments 2, 6, 10, 11, and 13.

1. If Jesus remained in Jerusalem, contrary to his habit of leaving the Holy City, the reason was that he had to eat the Passover lamb within the city walls (pp. 42–43).

Answer: This may have been his reason, but the argument is not compelling.

3. Contrary to the usual practice, the meal began when evening had come and continued until late in the night; therefore it was a Passover meal (pp. 44–46).

Answer: Solemn meals were often held at that time.

4. Contrary to his custom (of eating with a crowd of people who wanted to hear him?), Jesus was here accompanied only by the twelve, a number which met the requirement of the Passover meal (that there had to be at least ten people at table) (pp. 46–47).

Answer: How does this prove that the meal was a Passover meal?

5. Contrary to the usual practice of sitting for meals, Jesus reclined at table, a posture that symbolized the freedom won by the exodus from Egypt (pp. 48–49).

Answer: Jesus is said to have reclined at other meals which were out of the ordinary (multiplication of the loaves, banquets). Why not here as well, as a way of lending greater solemnity to this final meal?

7. The breaking of bread took place during the meal, but this practice was peculiar to the Passover meal (pp. 49–50).

Answer: At solemn meals, too, a distinction was made between the hor d'oeuvres or appetizers and the meal proper. The breaking of bread began the meal proper.

8. Wine was drunk only on festive occasions, while it was obligatory at the Passover meal (pp. 50–52).

Answer: Therefore it was not limited to the Passover meal.

9. Red wine symbolizes blood (p. 53).

Answer: The rabbinical testimonies are late, and the claim is unfounded.

12. The Hallel indicates the end of a Passover meal (pp. 54–55).

Answer: But the Therapeutae in Egypt sang it after their meals.

14. The decisive argument: The words of explanation spoken by Jesus over the bread and the cup correspond to the explanation given by the father of the family in the Passover Haggadah: "This is the bread of affliction" (pp. 55–61).

Answer: This is a questionable hypothesis. Jesus explains his action in a prophetic manner; his explanation does not refer to the past.

None of the fourteen arguments which Jeremias gives for the identification of Supper and Passover meal is probative. In fact, Jeremias himself is not fully persuaded, since after trying to refute objections to this identification he concludes:

> We shall see that Jesus' avowal of abstinence, the words of interpretation and the command to [sic] repetition first become fully understandable when they are set within the context of the passover ritual. It should also be emphasized, however, that the Last Supper would still be surrounded by the atmosphere of the passover even if it should have occurred on the evening before the feast.[10]

In the final analysis, Jeremias' proof is based on a false dilemma: either an ordinary meal or a Passover meal. The fact is that there were other kinds of solemn meals, which can explain the solemn character of Jesus' final meal.

In my opinion, the only datum that tips the balance in favor of a Passover meal is the fact that the synoptics seem to say that the Supper was in fact a Passover meal. Do they not tell how Jesus sent disciples to "prepare the Passover" which he is to celebrate? But this is not an insurmountable difficulty once we understand the evangelists' way of presenting not the Passover of the Jews but the Passover *of Jesus*.[11]

Abbreviations

Bib	*Biblica*
BZ	*Biblische Zeitschrift*
DBS	*Dictionnaire de la Bible: Supplément*
DBT	*Dictionary of Biblical Theology*, ed. X. Léon-Dufour, 2d ed., rev. and enl., trans. under the direction of P. Joseph Cahill (New York, 1973).
DC	*Documentation catholique*
DSp	*Dictionnaire de spiritualité*
DTC	*Dictionnaire de théologie catholique*
ETL	*Ephemerides Theologicae Lovanienses*
ETR	*Etudes théologiques et religieuses*
EvT	*Evangelische Theologie*
GL	*Geist und Leben*
HTR	*Harvard Theological Review*
Irén	*Irénikon*
Ist	*Istina*
JB	*The Jerusalem Bible*
JBL	*Journal of Biblical Literature*
JTS	*Journal of Theological Studies*
LAB	Pseudo-Philo, *Liber antiquitatum biblicarum*
MD	*La Maison-Dieu*
MTZ	*Münchener theologische Zeitschrift*
NRT	*Nouvelle revue théologique*
NT	*Novum Testamentum*
NTS	*New Testament Studies*
QLP	*Questions liturgiques et paroissiales*
RB	*Revue biblique*
RevSr	*Revue des sciences religieuses*
RGG	*Die Religion in Geschichte und Gegenwart* (3d ed.)
RHR	*Revue d'histoire des religions*
RivB	*Rivista biblica*

RSPT	Revue des sciences philosophiques et théologiques
RSR	Recherches de science religieuse
SBT	Studies in Biblical Theology
SC	Sources chrétiennes
TDNT	Theological Dictionary of the New Testament
TLZ	Theologische Literaturzeitung
TOB	Traduction oecuménique de la Bible
TS	Theological Studies
TZ	Theologische Zeitschrift
ZKT	Zeitschrift für katholische Theologie
ZNW	Zeitschrift für die alttestamentliche Wissenschaft und die Kunde der alteren Kirche
ZTK	Zeitschrift für Theologie und Kirche

Bibliography

From the vast literature on the Eucharist I have selected for the most part recent exegetical studies; but I have also included a few books or articles on the dogmatic, pastoral, and ecumenical aspects of the Eucharist, as well as the principal documents of the International Eucharistic Congress held at Lourdes. The first list contains works of which I have made particular use in this book, together with a short form of reference to them if I have used one.

A. WORKS FREQUENTLY CITED

Betz, J., *Die Eucharistie in der Zeit der griechischen Väter* II/1. *Die Realpräsenz des Leibes und Blutes Jesu im Abendmahl nach dem Neuen Testament* (Freiburg—Basel—Vienna, 1961). (= Betz)

Billerbeck, P., *Kommentar zum Neuen Testament aus Talmud und Midrasch* (6 vols.; Munich, 1922–61). (= Billerbeck)

Cazelles, H., "Eucharistie, bénédiction et sacrifice dans l'Ancien Testament," *MD* no. 123 (1975) 7–28. (= *MD* no. 123)

Chauvet, L. M., "La dimension sacrificielle de l'eucharistie," *MD* no. 123 (1975) 47–78. (= *MD* no. 123).

——————, "L'eucharistie parmi les sacrements," *MD* no. 137 (1979) 49–72. (= *MD* no. 137).

Dalman, G., *Jesus-Jeshua. Studies in the Gospels,* trans. P. P. Levertoff (New York, 1929; reprinted, 1971), 106–84. (= Dalman)

Dupont, J., "Ceci est mon corps, Ceci est mon sang," *NRT* 80 (1958) 1025–41.

——————, "L'union entre les premiers chrétiens dans les Actes des Apôtres," *NRT* 91 (1969) 897–915.

Feneberg, R., *Christliche Passafeier und Abendmahl* (Munich, 1971).

311

Gerken, A., *Theologie der Eucharistie* (Munich, 1973).

Gese, H., "Die Herkunft des Abendmahles," in idem, *Zur biblischen Theologie. Alttestamentliche Vorträge* (Beiträge zur evangelischen Theologie 78; Munich, 1977), 107–27.

Giraudo, C., *La struttura letteraria della preghiera eucaristica. Saggio sulla genesi letteraria di una forma. Toda veterotestamentaria, Bᵉraka giudaica, Anafora cristiana* (Analecta biblica 92; Rome, 1981).

Hahn, F., "Die alttestamentliche Motive in der urchristlichen Abendmahlsüberlieferung," *EvT* 27 (1967) 337–74. (= "Motive")

————, "Zum Stand der Erforschung des urchristlichen Abendmahles," *EvT* 35 (1975) 553–63.

Jeremias, J., *The Eucharistic Words of Jesus*, trans. N. Perrin from 3d German ed., with corrections to 1964 (New York, 1966). (= Jeremias)

Leenhardt, F. J., "Ceci est mon corps. Explication de ces paroles de Jesus-Christ" (1955), in *Parole—Ecriture—Sacrements* (Bibliothèque théologique 41; Neuchâtel, 1968), 136–84.

————, "La présence eucharistique," *ibid.*, 185–203.

Ligier, L., "De la Cène de Jésus à l'anaphore de l'Eglise," *MD* no. 87 (1966) 7–49.

————, "Les origines de la prière eucharistique: de la Cène à l'eucharistie," *Questions liturgiques et pastorales* (Mont César, Louvain) 3 (1972) 181–202.

Lubac, H. de, *Corpus Mysticum. L'Eucharistie et l'Eglise au Moyen Age* (Théologie 3; Paris, 1944).

Merklein, H., "Erwägungen zur Überlieferungsgeschichte der neutestamentlichen Abendmahlstraditionen," *BZ* 21 (1977) 88–101, 235–44. (= "Überlieferungsgeschichte")

Michel, H. J., *Die Abschiedsrede des Paulus an die Kirche (Apg 20, 17–38)* (Munich, 1973).

Neuenzeit, P., *Das Herrenmahl. Studien zur paulinischen Eucharistieauffassung* (Studien zum Alten und Neuen Testament 1; Munich, 1960). (= Neuenzeit)

Panikulam, G., *Koinonia in the New Testament. A Dynamic Expression of Christian Life* (Analecta Biblica 85; Rome, 1979). (= Koinonia)

Patsch, H., *Abendmahl und historischer Jesus* (Stuttgart, 1972). (= Patsch)

Perrot, C., "Le repas du Seigneur," *MD* no. 123 (1975) 29–46.

——————, "L'eucharistie comme fondement de l'identité de l'Eglise dans le Nouveau Testament," *MD* no. 137 (1979) 109–25; reprinted in idem, *Jésus et l'histoire* (Paris, 1979), 291–322.

Reicke, B., *Diakonie. Festfreude und Zelos in Verbindung mit der altchristlichen Agapefeiern* (Uppsala, 1951). (= *Diakonie*)

Schenke, J., *Studien zur Passionsgeschichte des Markus. Tradition und Redaktion in Markus 14, 1–42* (Forschung zur Bibel 4; Würzburg, 1971), 152–347. (= *Studien*)

Schürmann, H., *Der Paschamahlbericht Lk 22, (7–14.) 15–18* (= I); *Der Einsetzungsbericht Lk 22, 19–20* (= II); *Jesu Abschiedsrede Lk 22, 21–38* (= III) (Münster, 1953, 1955, 1956). (= II, for vol. 2)

——————, *Le Récit de la dernière Cène. Luc 22, 7–38* (German original: 1955) (Le Puy, 1965). (= *Récit*)

——————, "Die Gestalt der urchristlichen Eucharistiefeier," in idem, *Ursprung und Gestalt. Erörterungen und Besinnungen zum Neuen Testament* (Düsseldorf, 1970). (= *Ursprung*)

——————, "Jesus' Words in the Light of His Actions at the Last Supper," *Concilium* no. 40 (1968) 119–38.

Talley, T. J., "De la 'berakah' à l'eucharistie. Une question à réexaminer," *MD* no. 125 (1976) 11–39.

Vaux, R. de, *Ancient Israel: Its Life and Institutions*, trans. J. McHugh (New York, 1961), 415–56.

——————, *Studies in Old Testament Sacrifice* (Cardiff, 1964).

B. OTHER WORKS

Allmen, J. J. von, *Essai sur le Repas du Seigneur* (Neuchatel, 1966).

Andriessen, P., "L' eucharistie dans l'Epître aux Hébreux," *NRT* 94 (1972) 269–77.

Audet, J. P., "Esquisse historique du genre littéraire de la 'Bénédiction juive' et de l' 'Eucharistie chrétienne,' " *RB* 65 (1958) 371–99.

Baciocchi, J. de, "Présence eucharistique et transsubstantiation," *Irén* 32 (1959) 139–61.

——————, *L'Eucharistie* (Tournai, 1964).

Barosse, T., "The Passover and the Paschal Meal," *Concilium* no. 40 (1968) 23–34.

Beguerie, P., *Eucharistie* (Paris, 1975).

Benoit, P., "The Holy Eucharist," *Scripture* 8 (1956) 97–108; 9 (1957) 1–14.

Betz, J., "Eucharistie als zentrales Mysterium," in *Mysterium salutis* IV/2 (Einsiedeln, 1973), 185–313.

Boismard, M. E., "L'eucharistie selon saint Paul," *LV* no. 31 (1957) 93–106.

Bornkamm, G., "Lord's Supper and Church in Paul," in his *Early Christian Experience*, trans. P. L. Hammer (New York, 1969), 123–60.

Bouyer, L., *Eucharist: Theology and Spirituality of the Eucharistic Prayer*, trans. C. U. Quinn (Notre Dame, 1968).

Casel, O., *Faites ceci en mémoire de moi* (Paris, 1964).

Cazelles, H., "L'anaphore et l'Ancien Testament," in *Eucharisties d'Orient et d'Occident* I (Paris, 1970), 11–21.

Chauvet, L. M., *Du symbolique au symbole. Essai sur les sacrements* (Paris, 1979).

Cangh, J. M. van, *La Multiplication des pains et l'Eucharistie* (Lectio divina 86; Paris, 1975).

Coppens, J., "L'eucharistie néotestamentaire," in *Exégèse et théologie. Les saintes écritures et leur interprétation théologique*, ed. G. Thils and R. E. Brown (Bibliotheca ETL 26 = Donum natalicium Iosepho Coppens 3; Gembloux, 1968), 262–81.

———, "L'eucharistie, sacrement et sacrifice de la Nouvelle Alliance, fondement de l'Eglise," in *Aux origines de l'Eglise* (Paris, 1965), 125–58; see *ETL* 50 (1974) 269–72.

Deiss, L., *It's the Lord's Supper: The Eucharist of Christians*, trans. E. Bonin (New York, 1976).

Delorme, J., "The Last Supper and the Pasch in the New Testament," in J. Delorme *et al.*, *The Eucharist in the New Testament. A Symposium*, trans. E. M. Stewart (Baltimore, 1964), 21–67.

Dequeker, L., and W. Zuidema, "The Eucharist and St. Paul (1 Cor. 11, 17–34)," *Concilium* no. 40 (1968) 48–59.

Descamps, A., "Les origines de l'Eucharistie," in *L'Eucharistie, symbole et réalité* (Gembloux, 1970), 57–125.

Didier, R., "Théologie de l'eucharistie," in *L'Eucharistie. Le sens des sacrements* (Lyons, 1971), 15–76.

———, "Mythe et rite," *ibid.*, 172–80.

Dix, G., *The Shape of the Liturgy* (Westminster, 1945).

Duchesnau, C., *La célébration dans la vie chrétienne* (Paris, 1975)

Dupont, J., "The Meal at Emmaus," in J. Delorme *et al.*, *The*

Eucharist in the New Testament. A Symposium, trans. E. M. Stewart (Baltimore, 1964).

―――――, "La *koinonia* des premiers chrétiens dans les Actes des Apôtres," in *Communione interecclesiale,* ed. d'Ercole (Rome, 1972), 41–61.

Duquoc, C., "Signification sacramentelle de la présence," *RSPT* 53 (1969) 421–32.

Durand, G., *L'imagination symbolique* (Paris, 1964).

Durrwell, F. X., *The Eucharist: Presence of Christ,* trans. S. Attanasio (Denville, N.J., 1974).

―――――, *L'Eucharistie, sacrement pascal* (Paris, 1980).

Dussaut, L., *L'Eucharistie, Pâques de toute la vie. Diachronie symbolique de l'eucharistie* (Paris, 1972).

Feuillet, A., "The Principal Biblical Themes in the Discourse on the Bread of Life," in his *Johannine Studies,* trans. T. E. Crane (Staten Island, N.Y., 1965), 53–128.

Fraigneau-Julien, B., "Bénédiction . . . sacrifice . . . communion," *RevSR* 34 (1960) 35–61; 37 (1963) 321–44; 40 (1966) 27–47.

Füglister, N., *Die Heilsbedeutung des Pascha* (Munich, 1963).

Gaugler, E., in *La Sainte Cène* (Neuchâtel, 1945).

Gelineau, J., *The Liturgy Today and Tomorrow,* trans. D. Livingstone (New York, 1978).

Ghysens, D. H., "Présence réelle eucharistique et transsubstantiation dans les définitions de l'Eglise catholique," *Irén* 32 (1959) 420–42.

Guillet, J., "Le langage spontané de la Bénédiction dans l'Ancien Testament," *RSR* 57 (1969) 163–204.

Hahn, F., *The Worship of the Early Church,* trans. D. E. Green (Philadelphia, 1973).

Higgins, A. J. B., *The Lord's Supper in the New Testament* (London, 1952).

Hruby, K., "L'action de grâces dans la liturgie juive," in *Eucharisties d'Orient et d'Occident* I (Paris, 1970), 23–51.

Huber, W. *Passa und Ostern. Untersuchungen zur Osterfeier der alten Kirche* (Berlin, 1969).

Isambert, F. A., "Magie, religion, symbole. A propos de la session 'Magie et sacrements,'" *MD* no. 133 (1978) 147–56.

Jaubert, A., *The Date of the Last Supper,* trans. I. Rafferty (Staten Island, N.Y., 1965).

Johanny, R., *L'Eucharistie, chemin de résurrection* (Paris, 1974).

John-Paul II, Letter *Dominicae cenae* on the Mystery and Veneration of the Eucharist (February 24, 1980), in *The Pope Speaks* 25 (1980) 139–64.

Jong, J. P. de, *L'Eucharistie comme réalité symbolique* (Paris, 1972).

Kehl, M., "Eucharistie und Auferstehung. Zur Deutung der Ostererscheinungen beim Mahl," *GL* 24 (1970) 90–125.

Kertelge, K., "Das Abendmahl Jesu im Markusevangelium," in *Mélanges Zimmermann* (Bonn, 1980), 67–80.

Kilmartin, E., "The Last Supper and the Earliest Eucharists of the Church," *Concilium* no. 40 (1968) 35–47.

Koulomzine, N., "La sainte Cène dans le Nouveau Testament," in *Eucharisties d'Orient et d'Occident* I (Paris, 1970), 53–64.

Kuhn, K. G., "Die Abendmahlsworte," *TLZ* 75 (1950) 399–408.

Lebeau, P., *Le Vin nouveau de Royaume. Les paroles eschatologiques de Jésus à la Cène* (Paris, 1966).

Lecuyer, J., *Le Sacrifice de la Nouvelle Alliance* (Le Puy, 1962).

Léon-Dufour, X., "Le mystère du Pain de vie (Jean VI)," *RSR* 46 (1958) 481–523.

————, "Jésus devant sa mort à la lumière des textes de l'institution eucharistique et des discours d'adieu," in J. Dupont (ed.), *Jesus aux origines de la christologie* (Louvain, 1975), 141–68.

————, "Jesus face à la mort imminente, lors de son dernier repas," in his *Face à la mort: Jésus et Paul* (Paris, 1979), 101–13.

————, "Faites ceci en mémoire de moi," *Etudes*, no. 354 (June, 1981), 831–42.

————, "Das letzte Mahl Jesu und die testamentarische Tradition nach Lk 22," *ZKT* 103 (1981) 33–35.

Lies, L., "Eulogia. Überlegungen zur formalen Sinngestalt der Eucharistie," *ZKT* 100 (1978) 69–97, with many reviews, 98–121.

Lietzmann, H., *Mass and Lord's Supper. A Study in the History of the Liturgy*, trans. with appendixes by D. H. G. Reeves; introduction and supplementary essay by R. D. Richardson (Lewiden, [1953–] 1979). German original: *Messe und Herrenmahl* (Bonn, 1926).

Ligier, L., "Autour du sacrifice eucharistique," *NRT* 82 (1960) 40–55.

Lyonnet, S., "La nature du culte dans le Nouveau Testament," in *La Liturgie apres Vatican II* (Paris, 1967), 357–84.

Manaranche, A., *Ceci est mon corps* (Paris, 1975).

Martelet, G., *The Risen Christ and the Eucharistic World*, trans. R. Hague (New York, 1976).

Marxsen, W., *The Lord's Supper as a Christological Problem*, trans. L. Nieting (Philadelphia, 1970).

Menoud, P. H., "Les Actes des Apôtres et l'eucharistie" (1953), reprinted in *Jésus Christ et la foi* (Neuchatel, 1975).

Montcheuil, Y. de, "Signification eschatologique du repas eucharistique," *RSR* 33 (1946) 10–43.

————, "L'unité du sacrifice et du sacrement dans l'eucharistie," in his *Mélanges théologiques* (Théologie 9; Paris, 1951), 49–70.

Mouroux, J., *Do This in Memory of Me*, trans. S. Attanasio (Denville, N.J., 1974).

Neunheuser, B., *L'Eucharistie* I. *Moyen Age et époque moderne* (Paris, 1966).

Nussbaum, O., "Die Eucharistie als Anamnese (Opfer und Mahl)," *BLit* 44 (1971) 2–16.

————, "Herrenmahl und Brudermahl," *BLit* 47 (1974) 139–64.

Patsch, H., "Abendmahlsterminologie ausserhalb der Einsetzungsberichte. Erwägungen zur Traditionsgeschichte der Abendmahlsworte," *ZNW* 62 (1971) 210–31.

Paul VI, Encyclical *Mysterium fidei* on the Doctrine and Worship of the Eucharist (September 3, 1965), in *Documents on the Liturgy 1963–1979: Conciliar, Papal, and Curial Texts*, ed. International Commission on English in the Liturgy (Collegeville, 1982), nos 1145–1220 (pp. 378–92).

Perrot, C., "L'eau, le pain et la confession du Seigneur crucifié," in J. Doré (ed.), *Sacrements de Jesus Christ* (Paris, 1982).

Pesch, R., *Das Abendmahl und Jesu Todesverständnis* (Quaestiones Disputatae 80; Freiburg, 1978).

Pousset, E., "L'eucharistie: présence réelle et transsubstantiation," *RSR* 54 (1966) 177–212.

————, "L'eucharistie: sacrement et existence," *NRT* 88 (1966) 943–65.

Rahner, K., *The Christian Commitment: Essays in Pastoral Theology*, trans. C. Hastings (New York, 1963), 136ff., 171ff.

————, "The Word and the Eucharist," in *Theological Investigations* 4, trans. K. Smyth (Baltimore, 1966) 253–86.

————, "The Presence of Christ in the Sacrament of the Lord's Supper," *ibid.*, 287–311.

————, "On the Duration of the Presence of Christ after Communion," *ibid.*, 312–20.

Ratzinger, J., "De la Cène de Jésus au sacrement de l'Eglise," *Communio* 2 (1977) 21–32.

Rordorf, W., "Les prières eucharistiques de la Didachè," in *Eucharisties d'Orient et d'Occident* I (Paris, 1970), 65–82.

Ruckstuhl, E., "Neue und alte Überlegungen zu den Abendmahlsworten Jesu," in *Studien zum Neuen Testament und seiner Umwelt*, Series A. vol. 5 (Linz, 1981), 79–106.

Sagne, J. C., "L'interprétation analytique de l'eucharistie," in *L'Eucharistie. Le sens des sacrements* (Lyons, 1971), 153–64.

————, "Le repas comme acte d'alliance," in *Recherches et Documents du Centre Thomas More* (L'Arbresle), 7, no. 26 (1980), 15–32.

Sandvik, E., *Das Kommen des Herrn beim Abendmahl im Neuen Testament* (Zurich, 1970).

Schenker, A., *Das Abendmahl Jesu als Brennpunkt des Alten Testaments. Begegnung zwischen den beiden Testamenten—eine bibeltheologische Skizze* (Fribourg, 1977).

Schillebeeckx, E., *The Eucharist*, trans. N. D. Smith (New York, 1968).

Schoonenberg, P., "Transubstantiation: How Far Is This Doctrine Historically Determined?" *Concilium* no. 24 (1967) 78–91.

Schweizer, E., "Das Herrenmahl im Neuen Testament. Ein Forschungsbericht" *TLZ* 79 (1954) 577–92. Reprinted in his *Neotestamentica* (Zürich—Stuttgart, 1963), 344–70.

Seidensticker, P., *Lebendiges Opfer (Rm 12, 1)* (Münster, 1954).

Sesboüé, B., "Eucharistie: deux générations de travaux," *Etudes* no. 355 (July, 1981) 99–115.

Süss, T., *La Communion au corps du Christ. Etudes sur les problèmes de la sainte Cène et des paroles d'institution* (Neuchâtel, 1968).

Theissen, G., "Social Integration and Sacramental Activity: An Analysis of 1 Cor. 11:17–34," in his *The Social Setting of Pauline Christianity. Essays on Corinth*, trans. J. H. Schütz (Philadelphia, 1982), 145–74.

Thurian, M., *The Eucharistic Memorial*, trans. J. G. Davies (2 vols.; Ecumenical Studies in Worship 7–8; Richmond, Va., 1960).

Tillard, J. M. R., *The Eucharist: Pasch of God's People*, trans. D. L. Wienk (Staten Island, N.Y., 1967).

Trooster, S., "L'eucharistie, approche théologique," in *Exégèse et théologie. Les saintes écritures et leur interprétation théolo-*

gique, ed. G. Thils and R. E. Brown (Bibliotheca ETL 26 = Donum natalicium Iosepho Coppens 3; Gembloux, 1968), 247–61.

Vatican II, Constitution *Sacrosanctum Concilium* on the Liturgy (December 4, 1963), Chapter 2 (nos. 47–58), in *Documents on the Liturgy 1963–1979: Conciliar, Papal, and Curial Texts*, ed. International Commission on English in the Liturgy (Collegeville, 1982), nos. 47–58 (pp. 14–16).

Vergote, A., "Dimensions anthropologiques de l'eucharistie," in *L'Eucharistie, symbole et réalité* (Gembloux, 1970), 7–56.

Vonier, A., *A Key to the Doctrine of the Eucharist* (London, 1925).

Wanke, J. *Beobachtungen zum Eucharistieverständnis des Lukas* (Leipzig, 1973).

Warnach, V., "Symbol and Reality in the Eucharist," *Concilium* no. 40 (1968) 82–105.

Watteveille, J. de, *Le sacrifice dans les textes eucharistiques des premiers siècles* (Neuchâtel, 1966).

C. COLLECTIVE WORKS

"Autour de l'eucharistie," *MD* no. 141 (1980).

"The Breaking of Bread," *Concilium* no. 40 (1968).

"L'eucharistie," *Catéchèse* no. 71 (April, 1978), 131–91.

"L'eucharistie," *Communio* 2, nos. 5 and 6 (1977).

"L'eucharistie dans la Bible," *Cahiers Evangile* no. 37 (1981).

Eucharisties d'Orient et d'Occident I (Lex orandi 46; Paris, 1970).

"L'Eucharistie, repas du Seigneur ou sacrifice?," *MD* no. 123 (1975).

L'Eucharistie. Le sens des sacrements (Recherche pluridisciplinaire sous la direction de R. Didier) (Lyons, 1971).

L'Eucharistie, symbole et réalité by A. Descamps, A. Houssiau, and A. Vergote (Gembloux, 1970).

The Eucharist in the New Testament: A Symposium by J. Delorme et al., trans. E. M. Stewart (Baltimore, 1964).

The Eucharist of the Early Christians, ed. R. Johanny, trans, M. J. O'Connell (New York, 1978).

"Problématique théologique de l'eucharistie (Colloque de la section des Sciences théologiques et religieuses de l'Institut catholique de Paris, 24–26 janvier 1979)," *MD* no. 137 (1979).

"Le sens vécu de l'eucharistie," *Spiritus* no. 80 (September, 1980) 225–327.

D. THE EUCHARISTIC CONGRESS OF LOURDES (1981)

I. *Jésus-Christ, pain rompu pour un monde nouveau. Document de réflexion théologique et spirituelle pour le Congrès eucharistique international*, Lourdes, 1981 (Paris, 1980).
II. Episcopal documents: *DC* 78 (1981) 289–97 and 631–48.
III. International Symposium in Toulouse: *DC* 78 (1981) 717–29.
IV. The Eucharistic Congress of Lourdes: *DC* 78 (1981) 730–81.

E. SOME ECUMENICAL TEXTS

Das Abendmahl des Herrn. Tagungsbericht über ein interkonfessionelles Gespräch (1959) (Rottenburg, 1960).
T. Sartory, *Die Eucharistie im Verständnis der Konfessionen* (Recklinghausen, 1961).
K. Kertelge, "Abendmahlsgemeinschaft und Kirchengemeinschaft im Neuen Testament und in der alten Kirche," in *Interkommunion–Konziliarität*, Supplement to *Okumenisches Rundschau* 25 (1974) = F. Hahn, K. Kertelge, and R. Schnackenburg, *Einheit der Kirche* (Freiburg, 1979), 94–132.
Group of Les Dombes, "Towards a Common Eucharistic Faith? Agreement between Roman Catholics and Protestants," trans. P. Gaughan, in *Modern Eucharistic Agreement* (London, 1973), 51–78. On this document see *DC* 69 (1972) 126–29; 77 (1980) 421–36.
Anglicans and Roman Catholics: The Windsor Statement on Eucharistic Doctrine (September, 1971) by the Anglican-Roman Catholic International Commission, in *Growth in Agreement. Reports and Agreed Statements of Ecumenical Conversations on a World Level*, ed. H. Meyer and L. Vischer (Ecumenical Documents II; New York: Paulist, 1984), 69–72.—Comments on the Windsor Statement by the Theological Commission of the Anglican Episcopate, in *DC* 69 (1972) 346–47.—Elucidations of the Windsor Statement, by the Anglican-Roman Catholic International Commission (1979), in *Growth in Agreement*, 72–77.
Reformed Churches and Roman Catholic Church: "The Presence of Christ in Church and World: Final Report of the Dialogue between the World Alliance of Reformed Churches and the Secretariat for Promoting Christian Unity, 1977," in *Growth in Agreement*, 434–63.

Lutherans and Roman Catholics: "The Eucharist: Final Report of the Joint Roman Catholic-Lutheran Commission, 1978," in *Growth in Agreement*, 192–214.—Declaration of the Standing Luther-Reformed Commission of France (1981), in *DC* 78 (1981) 512–13.

Notes

INTRODUCTION

1. The noun *eucharistia* occurs once with the meaning of "thanks" given to other human beings: Acts 24:3 (see Lk 17:16; Rom 16:4). It usually means a prayer of thanksgiving to God: 1 Cor 14:16; 2 Cor 4:15; 9:12; Eph 5:4; Phil 4:6; Col 2:7; 4:2; 1 Thess 3:9; 1 Tim 2:1; 4:3f.; Rev 4:9; 7:12. According to Schürmann, *Ursprung* 88, in two passages (Eph 5:15–20 and Col 3:12–17) the verb *eucharistein*, occurring as it does in the context of an assembly, a meal, and prayers, may refer to the Eucharist in the proper sense.

2. Ignatius of Antioch, who is also familiar with the word in its general sense of a prayer (*Eph.* 13, 1 = SC 10, 83), uses it several times for the Eucharist: "Be careful to take part only in the one Eucharist, because . . . " (*Phld.* 4, 1 = SC 10, 142–45); "They abstain from the Eucharist and the prayer because they do not confess that the Eucharist is the flesh of our Lord Jesus Christ" (*Smyrn.* 7, 1 = SC 10, 160f.); "Let that Eucharist be regarded as secure which is celebrated under the presidency of the bishop or someone to whom the bishop entrusts it" (*Smyrn.* 8, 1 = SC 10, 162f.). See M. Jourjon, "Textes eucharistiques des Pères anténicéens," in R. Didier (ed.), *L'Eucharistie. Le sens des sacrements* (Lyons, 1971), 98–100; R. Johanny, "Ignatius of Antioch," in R. Johanny (ed.), *The Eucharist of the Early Christians*, trans. M. J. O'Connell (New York, 1978), 48–70.

3. Justin says: "This food we call 'eucharist'" (*Apol. I* 66) and describes the practice of his day; see M. Jourjon, "Justin," in *The Eucharist of the Early Christians*, 71–85.

4. "With regard to the eucharist, give thanks in this manner"

322

(*Did.* 9, 1; disputed text); "Come together on the dominical day of the Lord to break bread and give thanks, after having also confessed your sins so that your sacrifice may be pure" (14, 1). According to authoritative commentators such as M. Jourjon, in *L'Eucharistie. Le sens des sacrements,* 102–7, or W. Rordorf, in *The Eucharist of the Early Christians,* 1–23, the reference to Mal 1:11 suggests a contrast between the "sacrifice of thanksgiving" and the blood sacrifices of the Jews or the pagans.

I. THE EUCHARISTIC ASSEMBLIES OF THE EARLY CHRISTIANS

1. Luke's "summaries" (Acts 2:42–47; 4:32–35; 5:12–16) have been the subject of numerous studies, among them those of L. Cerfaux, *ETL* 12 (1936) 673–80; P. Benoit, *Mélanges Goguel* (1950), 1–10; H. Zimmermann, *BZ* 5 (1961) 71–82; E. Rasco, *Actus Apostolorum* (Rome, 1968²), 271–330.

2. The text of Paul is examined in detail below in Chapter XI, sect. II. The name "Lord's Supper" occurs only here in the New Testament. See "the wedding feast of the Lamb" (Rev 19:9; see Mt 22:3; Lk 14:15, 17).

3. See C. Perrot, *MD* no. 123 (1975) 29–46, and *MD* no. 137 (1979) 109–25.

4. It is difficult to say with certainty that brotherhoods *(habbourot)* celebrated meals in the first century after the manner of the sectaries of Qumran (see Perrot, *MD* no. 23, 34). See below, 305.

5. According to Philo, *De vita contemplativa* 64–65 these meals were marked by a discourse.

6. This meal has been reconstructed on the basis of a Jewish novel, *Joseph and Aseneth* (ed. M. Philonenko, Leiden, 1968), which dates from the first century A.D.; see 8, 5 and 11; 15, 4. K. G. Kuhn, in his *Les Manuscrits de la Mer Morte* (Paris, 1957), 90, compares it with the meals not of the Essenes but of the Therapeutae; Philonenko compares it with "the sacred meal of the mystery cults" (98); but T. Holtz, "Christliche Interpretationen in 'Joseph und Aseneth,'" *NTS* 14 (1968) 482–97, finds that the passage has been twice interpolated, by Christians and by gnostics.

7. Perrot, *MD* no. 137, 111.

8. See C. Lécrivain, "Thiasos," in Daremberg and Saglio (eds.), *Dictionnaire des antiquités grecques et romains* 9 (1912) 257–66.

9. See below, 204–208.

10. See below, n. 28 of this chapter.

11. See below, 217.

12. See Perrot, *MD* no. 123, 34.

13. Perrot, *ibid.*, 35–35, and *MD* no. 137, 114–15; he cites in support *m. Pe'a* 8, 7; *m. Pesah.* 10, 1; *b. B. Bat.* 8a–9c, and admits that such a custom is difficult to date; see *ZNW* 63 (1972) 271–76; *JTS* 29 (1978) 140–43; and J. Jeremias, *Jerusalem in the Time of Jesus*, trans. F. H. and C. H. Cave (Philadelphia, 1969), 130–34.

14. See below, 216.

15. Jer 16:7.

16. See Jeremias, *Eucharistic Words*, 120. n. 1.

17. *Ibid.*, 232. See Th. Schermann, "Das Brotbrechen im Urchristenum," *BZ* 8 (1910) 42, who is followed by J.-M. Nielen, *Gebet und Gottesdienst im Neuen Testament* (Freiburg im B., 1937), cited in Betz, *Eucharistie*, 5.

18. Mt 14:19 par; 15:36 par; Jn 6:11.

19. Lk 24:30. The term "breaking of the bread" occurs once in isolation, Lk 24:35, but it refers back to the story as previously told in detail (24:30). One may share the doubt of TOB (418 and 436) on the eucharistic character of Paul's "breaking of bread" after the storm (Acts 27:35). According to the JB, the terms used by Luke suggest the Eucharist, but Schürmann, *Ursprung* 82, n. 36, denies this. In my opinion, even if Luke intended to suggest a Eucharist of a "prophetic" kind, the description of Paul's series of actions reflects rather the way a good Jew went about his meal.

20. With Schürmann, *Ursprung*, 82; see Jeremias, 119–20, citing in support J. H. Lightfoot's commentaries on Acts 2:42 in his *Horae hebraicae et talmudicae* (= *Opera omnia* 2 [Rotterdam, 1686], 696f., 768), as well as *b. Ber.* 47a and *Tg* 1 Sam 9:13.

21. For example, by O. Nussbaum, "Herrenmahl and Brudermahl," *BLit* 47 (1974) 142.

22. On the historical value of the passages in Acts in which Luke indicates by saying "we" that he was with Paul at that time (the "We-sections"), see C. Perrot, in A. George and P. Grelot (eds.), *Introduction à la Bible. Nouveau Testament* III/2 (Paris, 1976), 281–86.

23. Rev 1:10. In Latin *dominica dies; dominica* would become the word for Sunday in the Romance languages (*dimanche, domenica, domingo*).

24. See Mt. 28:1 par; Mk 16:9. Among the Jews the legal day began on the eve at sunset.

25. See below, 27.—We may find it surprising that in the Troas story the others present are not also said to have eaten the

bread. It may be said, however, that Luke is interested not in giving a direct description of the liturgical action but in highlighting the actions of Paul, the hero of this part of his book.

26. Despite the doubts of O. Nussbaum, "Herrenmahl and Brudermahl" (above, n. 21), this is the view held by most critics today (see Jeremias, 119–20; Schürmann, *Ursprung* 85–91; G. Panikulam, *Koinonia*, 122).

27. See the thoughtful discussion in F. A. Hahn, *The Worship of the Early Church*, trans. D. E. Green (Philadelphia, 1973), 12–31.

28. Luke takes care to give the names of the owners of houses in which Peter or Paul stayed and in which they probably gathered their fellow believers around them: Judas in Damascus (Acts 9:11), Simon the tanner in Jaffa (9:43), Lydia in Philippi (16:15), Jason in Thessalonica (17:5), Titus Justus in Corinth (18:7), Philip the evangelist and Mnason in Caesarea (21:8, 16). Paul likewise carefully notes the names of Christians with whom he has stayed or in whose homes the assemblies were held: "The household of Stephanas were the first converts in Achaia, and they have devoted themselves to the service of the saints" (1 Cor 16:15); "Aquila and Prisca, together with the church in their house" (1 Cor 16:19; see Rom 16:5); "Gaius, who is host to me and to the whole church" (Rom 16:23); "to Philemon our beloved fellow worker . . . the church in your house" (the house of Philemon or Apphia or Archippus; Phlm 2); "Nympha and the church in her house" (Col 4:15) in Laodicea.

29. Even when such places are acquired later on, in the third century, they will not be former sacred buildings but "basilicas," i.e., public buildings for secular uses.

30. See below, 305–306.

31. Schürmann, *Ursprung*, 89–91.

32. As R. Bultmann, "Agalliaomai," *TDNT* 1 (original: 1933) 19–21, has clearly shown, the term *agalliasis* has essentially an eschatological meaning: it is the jubilation that flows from the experience of definitive salvation (see Rev 19:7; 1 Pet 4:13); this gives Acts 2:46 its cultic tonality (see 16:34).

33. Acts 2:41–47.

34. The verb *prokarterein* is found in Jewish inscriptions to refer to regular attendance at the synagogue; see J. B. Frey, *Corpus Inscriptionum Judaicarum* I, 495f, no. 683, lines 13–15, cited (from Moulton-Milligan) in Jeremias, 118, n. 6.

35. Jeremias, 119, wrongly assigns *koinōnia* the meaning of "table fellowship."

36. I disagree with authors who regard these prayers as "specifically Christian": TOB 368, n. z. See Acts 2:46; 3:1, 4:25, where Ps 2 is used to voice the prayer of the persecuted Church.

37. The verb *dielegeto* could mean "he dialogued" or conversed with the others present (see 13:1–4). However, the writer seems impressed here rather by the abundance of Paul's discourse.

38. A targum was a paraphrase in Aramaic (the language of first-century Palestine) of the Hebrew text of the Bible; it had been introduced long ago to facilitate understanding of the scriptures by Jews who had returned from exile.

39. See my *Les Evangiles et l'Histoire de Jesus* (Paris, 1963), 266–69; the English translation by J. McHugh, *The Gospels and the Jesus of History* (New York, 1967), is a shortened version; see 180–82.

40. See my *Resurrection and the Message of Easter*, trans. R. N. Wilson (New York, 1974), 92–93 and 163.

41. Jeremias, 120, n. 3, shows that if Luke had wanted to say that "they recognized him *by* the breaking of the bread," he would have used, as he does elsewhere, the preposition *ek* (6:44) or *kata* (1:18). *en* is therefore to be translated as "at" or "during."

42. S. Lyonnet has rightly objected to this translation which has been popularized by Segond, Goguel, and the Crampon and Maredsous versions; see "La nature du culte chrétien," *Studia missionalia* 23 (1974) 241.—On *koinōnia* see below, Chapter XI, n. 17.

43. Thus Jeremias, 119; see above, n. 35.

44. Thus F. Mussner, "Die Una Sancta nach Apg.," in idem, *Praesentia Salutis* (Düsseldorf, 1967), 212–22.

45. Thus E. Haenchen and H. Conzelmann. On the whole subject see G. Panikulam, *Koinonia*, 122–25.

46. Other text: Phil 1:27, 2:2. The Greek phrase *epi to auto* (Acts 1:15, 2:1, 44, 47; 4:26) is translated as "together" (JB) or "were gathered" (TOB). See Panikulam, 76 and 125f.

47. Acts 2:41, 46; 5:12; see 1:4; 4:24; Rom 15:5f.

48. Acts 4:37; 5:4.

49. Acts 2:12. Luke generalized from the example of Barnabas: see Lk 5:11, 28; 14:33; 18:22. See J. Dupont, "L'union entre les premiers chrétiens dans les Actes des Apôtres," *NRT* 91 (1969) 901, n. 10. This picture is sometimes attributed to a desire on Luke's part to imitate what was practiced at Qumran (1 QS I, 11f.; VI, 18–25) by the Essenes whom Philo praises for "their spirit of fellowship that beggars description" (*Quod omnis probus* 84,

trans. David Winston in *Philo of Alexandria. The Contemplative Life, the Giants, and Selections* [Classics of Western Spirituality; New York, 1981], 251) and whom Josephus admires as "communists to perfection" (*The Jewish War* II, 122, trans. G. A. Williamson [Baltimore, 1959], 125). Reference has also been made to the Pythagoreans who had dreamed of such a society; but the point of this reference was to show that Christians had been able to turn the ideal into reality; see L. Cerfaux, *La communauté apostolique* (Paris, 1953²), 47.

On the other hand, it is appropriate to compare the attitude of the early Christians with the Greek ideal of friendship: "Everything is shared by friends. . . . There is no authentic friendship between two people if each does not put all possessions at the disposal of the other" (Aristotle, *Nic. Eth.* VIII, 11 [1159b, 31]). See J. Dupont, *Etudes sur les Actes des Apôtres* (Paris, 1967), 505–09, 513–14; idem, *NRT* 91 (1969) 902. The fact that the ideal is shared in this way proves that it is written in the human heart; the fact that it was realized in Jerusalem cannot have been the result of friendship alone but was a fruit of faith. The Christian community is not a gathering of friends but a brotherhood and sisterhood of believers (see Acts 4:34 which shows the community fulfilling the ideal dreamed of in Deut 15:4). "A church of God is to be recognized by the fact that none of its members are in need" (J. Dupont, *NRT* 91 [1969] 903; and see A. Négrier and X. Léon-Dufour, "Brother," in *DBT* 60–62).

50. This exemplary mutual help (Rom 15:25–32; 1 Cor 16:1–4; 2 Cor 8–9) is called *diakonia* (service: Acts 11:29; Rom 15:31; 2 Cor 8:4), *koinōnia* (communion: Rom 15:26), and *leitourgia* (ministry: 2 Cor 9:12).

51. See St. Thomas, *Summa theologiae* II-II, 66, 2: "In regard to this [the use and management of the world's resources] no man is entitled to manage things merely for himself, he must do so in the interests of all" (trans. M. Lefebure, in Saint Thomas, *Injustice* [*Summa Theologiae* 28; New York, 1975], 64).

52. See my *Resurrection* 86 and 234–36.

53. A. Tevoedure, a Zairean, put it well at the Lourdes eucharistic congress in 1981: "We can legitimately offer the bread of sacrifice to God only if we offer ourselves as food to our fellow human beings. We must consent to 'be eaten' by all the peoples of the world if we are to be attuned to our own eucharistic food; we must be capable of giving our lives for the brethren if we are to drink worthily from the Lord's cup" (cited by H. de Soos in *La Croix*, August 19, 1981, 16).

II. MEAL AND CELEBRATION OF THE LORD

1. 1 Cor 11:34. O. Nussbaum, "Herrenmahl und Brudermahl," *BLit* 47 (1974) 153f. shows that the Eucharist need not be completed by a fraternal meal in order to have its proper meaning.

2. For the meaning of the expression "is and is not" see below, 123–129.

3. On fasting see, e.g., *RGG* 2 (1958³) 881f., and below, n. 9 of this chapter.

4. Lk 8:55; 24:41; see 5:34f.; Mt 9:14f.; Acts 2:46.

5. Prov. 30:8f.

6. Mt 3:4.

7. Mt 4:4. Jesus cites the Bible (Deut 8:3) to refute Satan's specious argument.

8. Mt 14:13–21 par; 15:32–38 par; Jn 6:1–15.

9. See R. Gerard, "Fasting," in *DBT* 166–67. Jesus warns against practices of fasting that call attention to oneself (Mt 5:17–20; 6:1, 16–18); unlike the Baptist, he hardly encouraged his disciples to fast (Mk 2:18–20). It was the early community that revived the practice (Acts 13:2f.; 14:23; see 2 Cor 6:5; 11:27; in Mt 17:21 and Mk 9:29 the mention of fasting is not certainly authentic).

10. Jn 6:25–59.

11. Certain of Jesus' sayings have to do with the social character of meal. Thus one of his parables has to do with invited guests who choose the first places (Lk 14:7). Again, when he distributes bread in abundance he does not ask those present to serve themselves but has the people "sit down by companies ... in groups, by hundreds and by fifties" (Mk 6:39–40), thus forming parties; this done, a real meal can begin.

12. A thanksgiving brings the Passover liturgy to an end. See below, 305.

13. See J. Döller, "Der Wein in Bibel und Talmud," *Bib* 4 (1923) 143–67, 267–69 (at 274); he refers to Josephus, *Ant. Jud.* 19, 9, 1.

14. E.g., Lk 14:1–24. See X. de Meeus, "Composition de Luc 14 et le jeûne symposiaque," *ETL* 37 (1961) 847–70; J.-Cl. Sagne, "Le repas comme acte d'alliance," *Recherches et Documents du Centre Thomas More* (l'Arbresle) 7, no. 26 (1980) 15–32.

15. Gen 26:30; 31:54.

16. Ex 24:9, 11.

17. 2 Kgs 25:27–30; Josephus, *Ant. Jud.* 19, 321.

18. Lk 15:23f.

19. Acts 16:34.

20. Acts 1:4; 10:41; see Jn 21:13 and (?) Lk 24:30, 35, 43. See Prov 15:27; 25:21f.; Jer 16:6f.

21. Acts 11:2; my interpretation differs from that of TOB *in loc.*, n. *d*; see Acts 10:28.

22. Jn 2:2–11; 12:2; Lk 10:38–42.

23. Mt 4:17 par.

24. Mk 2:17; Lk 19:9; see Lk 7:36–50; 15:2; 19:2–10.

25. Lk 14:21; Mt 22:10 (although there is then a sorting out: 22:11-13).

26. Lk 22:30; see Is 55:1f.

27. Lk 12:37; see 22:27.

28. Mk 14:24; Mt 26:28; see below,

29. "Religion (from the Latin *religare*, 'bind') consists of a set of ritual actions that are connected with the idea of a sacral sphere distinct from the profane and are intended to establish a relation between the human soul and God" *(Dictionnaire Robert)*. I prefer the designation "religious meal" to "cultic meal," because the latter too readily calls to mind the sacrificial meals of the period, and to "sacred meal," because "religious," while including the element of the sacred, lays greater emphasis on the idea of a link with God.

30. See the charts giving the texts in parallel columns, below, 101, 137.

31. See O. Cullmann, *Early Christian Worship*, trans. D. J. Greenwood (SBT 10; Naperville, Ill., 1953), 15ff.; Y. de Montcheuil, "Signification eschatologique du repas eucharistique," *RSR* 33 (1946) 10–43; W. Rordorf, *Sunday. The History of the Day of Rest and Worship in the Earliest Centuries of the Christian Church*, trans. A. A. K. Graham (Philadelphia, 1968), 221ff.

32. Lk 24:30, 41, 43; Jn 21:9–13; Acts 1:4; 10:41.

33. Mk 16:14.

34. See M. Kehl, "Eucharistie und Auferstehung," *Geist und Leben* (1970) 90–125; and see my *Resurrection* 92.

35. See above, 37.

36. See H. Patsch, "Abendmahlsterminologie ausserhalb der Einsetzungsberichte. Erwägungen zur Traditionsgeschichte der Abendmahlsworte," *ZNW* 62 (1971) 210–31; J. W. van Cangh, *La Multiplication des pains et l'Eucharistie* (Paris, 1975).

37. The English word "sacrifice" covers a great variety of Hebrew or Greek terms; the Greek word *thysia*, for example, has

a different etymology than the Latin *sacrificium*. On the whole problem of sacrifice see R. Bastide, "Sacrifice," *Encyclopedia Universalis* 14 (1972) 583–85. It is therefore risky to speak in general terms of "sacrifice," even in the Jewish world. On the latter the basic work is still R. de Vaux, *Studies in Old Testament Sacrifice* (Cardiff, 1964); this book develops some chapters (10–13) in the same author's *Ancient Israel: Its Life and Institutions*, trans. J. McHugh (New York, 1961), 416–56. See also R. Schmid, *Das Bundesopfer* (Munich, 1964).

38. Since the victim was entirely consumed by fire on the altar, there could be no question of a sacrificial meal.

39. Unlike the "communion" that followed the *s*ᵉ*lamîm*, expiatory sacrifices were distinguished by their purpose, which was to make reparation for sins committed.

40. Another type of sacrifice—vegetable offerings—might be of interest here, inasmuch as bread and wine are the offerings used in the Eucharist (see de Vaux, *Ancient Israel* 430). But this fact is of secondary importance in determining the type of Jewish sacrifice that provides for the Eucharist.

41. See the Appendix below, 303–306, 306–308.

42. *LAB* 21, 8; 23, 14; 26, 7; 49, 8; 2 QS 24, 4.

43. See C. Perrot, *La Lecture de la Bible dans la Synagogue. Les lectures palestiniennes du shabbat et des fêtes* (Hildesheim, 1973), 238–58. See also J. Potin, *La Fête juive de la Pentecôte* (Paris, 1871).

44. Ex 24:8. The passage from Exodus is given below, 145.

45. On the difference between eucharistic "communion" and Greek mysticism see below, 210–211. Let me say a word here on the character of cultic meals in Israel. Some scholars have inferred from various biblical phrases that these meals were "meals taken by God" himself. The texts do speak of the table or food of Yahweh (Ez 44:7–16; Mal 1:7, 12; Lev 21:6, 8; 22:25; Num 28:2), of "loaves of permanent offering" given to Yahweh each sabbath (Lev 24:5–9), of God breathing in the pleasing smell of sacrifices (an expression taken from the Babylonian world—with which the Jews became familiar during the exile—then purified and used: see the Epic of Gilgamesh, XI, 155–61). The texts also speak of oil that gives honor to the gods and of wine that cheers gods and men (Jgs 9:9, 13, but compare with Ps 104:15, which refers only to human beings). The anthropomorphism is pushed to the extreme in the story of Abraham's three mysterious visitors, among whom Yahweh is hidden (Gen 18): for these three "men" Abraham prepares

a meal and "they ate." But this meal, which is not a sacrifice, is unique in its kind (see de Vaux, *Ancient Israel* 450). Most of the time the idea that God could derive sustenance from sacrifices is rejected (Jgs 6:18, 22; 13:15–20). The psalmists fight against popular tendencies in that direction: "If I were hungry I would not tell you" (Ps 50:12f.; see Deut 32:38). Jewish cultic meals did not supply God with food.

These cultic meals are celebrated not "with" but "in the presence of" God, as at the covenant meal on Sinai (Ex 24:11; see 18:12). God does not eat but he is present to his people; eating together becomes a "rejoicing in the presence of the Lord your God" or "in the place the Lord your God chooses" for the commemoration of his action in history (see Deut 12:7, 12, 18; 16:10–17; Neh 12:27–43). When human beings join in acknowledging him from whom every gift comes, they even "make the Lord dance with them" (see Zeph 3:14–17).

46. Thus L. Ligier, "De la Cène à l'anaphore de l'Eglise," *MD* no. 89 (1966) 82–118; H. Cazelles, "L'anaphore et l'Ancien Testament," in *Eucharisties d'Orient et d'Occident* I (Paris, 1970), 11–21; L. Ligier, "Les origines de la prière eucharistique. De la Cène à l'Eucharistie," *QLP* 57 (1972) 181–201; H. Cazelles, "Eucharistie, bénédiction et sacrifice dans l'Ancien Testament," *MD* no. 123 (1975) 7–28; C. Perrot, "Le repas du Seigneur," *MD* no. 123 (1975) 29–46; T. J. Talley, "De la Berakah à l'Eucharistie. Une question à réexaminer," *MD* no. 125 (1976) 11–39; H. Gese, "Die Herkunft des Abendmahls," in his *Zur biblischen Theologie* (Munich, 1977), 107–27; finally and above all, C. Giraudo, *La struttura letteraria della Preghiera eucaristica. Saggio sulla genesi letteraria di una forma. Toda veterotestamentaria, Bᵉraka giudaica, Anafora cristiana* (Analecta biblica 92; Rome, 1981).

47. See above, 26–27.

48. From the root *ydh*, meaning "to know," comes the causative "cause to know." See C. Westermann, *"ydh," Theologisches Handwörterbuch zum Alten Testament* 1 (Munich, 1971), 674–82, and B. Lang, *"zabah," Theologisches Wörterbuch zum Alten Testament* 2 (Stuttgart, 1977), 528–31.

49. Giraudo's book is intended as a study of the eucharistic anaphora, but to this end he analyzes at length the Old Testament *tôdâ* and the Jewish blessings, which (he says) provided the anaphora with its literary form (11-269).

50. This phrase occurs in Lev 7:12–15; see Jer 17:26; 33:11; Ps 50:14, 23; 107:22; 116:17.

51. According to P. Joüon, "Reconnaissance et remerciement en hébreu biblique," *Bib* 4 (1923) 384.

52. TOB, *Ancien Testament*, 215, n. z.

53. See Giraudo (n. 46) 267, where he criticizes the tendency expressed in H. Cazelles, "L'Anaphore et l'Ancien Testament" (n. 46), 16–20.

54. For example, Is 51:3; Jer 30:19; Ps 42:5, and even Ps 50:14, 23, or Ps 26:6f. and 116:17, which clarify the meaning by invoking the name of God or proclaiming his wonderful deeds.

55. On the spiritualization of the cult see H. Wenschkewitz, *Die Spiritualisierung der Kultbegriffe Tempel, Priester und Opfer im Neuen Testament* (Leipzig, 1932); P. Seidensticker, *"Lebendiges Opfer": Rom 12, 1* (Münster, 1954); G. Klinzing, *Die Umdeutung des Kultus in der Qumrangemeinde und im Neuen Testament* (Göttingen, 1971).

56. Heb 13:15: "Through him let us continually offer up a sacrifice of praise to God, that is, the fruit of lips that acknowledge his name," citing Ps 50:14, 23, and Hos 14:3. See 1 QS IX, 3–5.

57. 1 QS IX, 4–5, and *Temple Scroll* 52, 14f.; see *ETR* 53 (1978) 443–500.

58. As a result, the keeping of the Feast of Unleavened Bread or the Feast of Weeks became widespread.

59. The legislation says that if the communion sacrifice is offered as a sacrifice with praise, the sacrifice proper is to be supplemented by an offering of unleavened wafers spread with oil and of wheaten flour (Lev 7:12f., and *Menahot* 7). To some authors this suggests a comparison with the eucharistic liturgy and its bread and wine, but the basis of such a comparison seems difficult to establish.

60. P^e*siqta* 79a (ed. B. Mandelbaum [1962] I, 159); Billerbeck IV, 936 aō; see *LvR* IX, 7. The tradition goes back to R. Menahem de Gallia, a second-century Tannaite.

61. Acts 2:46. See above.

62. Schürmann, *Ursprung* 88 cites Eph 5:15–20 and Col 3:12–17.

63. I refer the reader to the writings of L. Ligier, T. J. Talley and C. Giraudo, listed above in n. 46.

III. THE ACCOUNT OF THE LAST SUPPER OF JESUS

1. Mt 26:26–29 = Mk 14:22–25 = Lk 22:14–20 = 1 Cor 11:23–25. The texts are given in synoptic form on the facing page.

For the moment I leave aside the problem raised by the fourth gospel in regard to the final meal of Jesus: instead of the account of institution this gospel has the episode of the washing of feet (Jn 13). See below, Chapters IV and XIII.

2. Chapters IV and V examine the traditions behind the present recensions.

3. See below, 186.

4. The meal, for which formal preparations have been made, begins in Mk 14:17 = Mt 26:20 and ends in Mk 14:26 = Mt 26:30 with the Hallel and the departure for Mount Olivet.

5. Mk 14:21 (= Mt 26:24 = Lk 22:22).

6. Mk 25 = Mt 29 = Lk 18. The fact that this saying is part of the structure of the account tells us nothing as yet about its origin. In my opinion it comes from a tradition that is testamentary and not cultic (see below, Chapter IV). The definition of the boundaries of the text is accomplished by methods proper to literary criticism.

7. See the synoptic arrangement of the texts, 48–49. In referring to it I shall henceforth give only the verse number (as I have in n. 6, above) of the passage; e.g., Mk 25 stands for Mk 14:25.

8. Paul omits the verb "give"; see below, 222.

9. Paul and Luke are content to sum up the gestures of Jesus with the words "likewise the cup."

10. The command of remembrance is omitted in Mk/Mt because the account itself is liturgical (see below, 199); it may therefore be regarded as implicitly present in their recensions.

11. Mt 9:11; Mk 2:16; Lk 5:30; 15:2; etc. See above, 37–38.

12. "Table" (Lk 21), "dip his hand in the dish" (Mk 20 = Mt 23), "eat" (Mt 26c; Lk 15, 16), "drink" (Mk 23, 25; Mt 27, 29; Lk 18), "bread" (Mk 22; Mt 26; Lk 19), "cup" (Mk 23; Mt 27; Lk 17, 20a, c), "fruit of the vine" (Mk 25; Mt 29; Mk 18).

13. Either Jesus is at table with (meta) the disciples (Mk 17 = Mt 20) or the disciples are at table with (syn) him (Lk 14).

14. See above, 33. Thus after her resuscitation the little daughter of Jairus is told to eat (Mk 5:43 par.), and after his resurrection Jesus himself asks for something to eat (Lk 24:41; see Jn 21:12f.): to take food is a sign that one is truly alive.

15. See, e.g., the call to follow Jesus that is given to Simon and Andrew (Mt 4:19f. par.), to Levi (Mt 9:9 par.), to the rich man (Mt 19:21f.); the order to throw in the nets (Lk 5:4–6; see Jn 21:6), to leave and say nothing after the transfiguration (Mk 9:9f., par.); the

sending as missionaries (Mk 6:10–12 par.; see Lk 10:17); the invitation to Peter to come to Jesus on the water (Mt 14:29); the instructions in connection with the entry into Jerusalem (Mt 21:2–6 par.) and with the Passover meal (Mt 26:18f., par.); the invitation to stay, watch and pray in Gethsemane (Mt 26:38, 41 par.); etc.

16. For example, when Jesus asks to be shown the coin used for tribute (Mt 22:19).

17. See, e.g., "Lend, expecting nothing in return" (Lk 6:35); "Let the children come to me" (Mt 19:13 par.); "Pray for those who persecute you" (Mt 5:44); "Watch therefore" (Mk 13:35 par.); and Lk 11:9, 35, 41; 12:15, 24, 27; 16:9, 20, 46; etc.

18. Irenaeus, Adv. haer. III, 11, 5. The Bible sees all of creation as "a vast stem on which the human race is the flower" (J. Huby, Epître aux Romains [Paris, 1957], 297).

19. T. J. Talley (above, Ch. II, n. 46), 11–39, criticizing the hypotheses of J.-P. Audet.

20. At creation "God blessed them, saying to them, 'Be fruitful, multiply . . . '" (Gen 1:28).

21. In order to be able to bless his son, Isaac must recoup his strength by a large and tasty meal (Gen 27).

22. For the meaning I assign to this word see below, 127–129, on the words over the bread.

23. See above, 33–34; see Am 4:6; Mk 3:20; Mk 11:5; 15:17.

24. See Ex 23:25; Ps 78:20; 132:15; 146:7; Mt 6:11 par.; and see D. Sesboüé, "Bread," in DBT 58–60.

25. Among the crops characteristic of the promised land wheat heads the list (see Deut 8:8f.; 11:14). The same is true in the promises of future consolation that are repeated during Israel's trials (see Ez 36:29); in addition, see 2 Kgs 18:32; Is 36:17.

26. Is 58:7; Ez 18:7.

27. Ex 16; Num 11:7–9; Ps 78:23–25; Rev 2:17.

28. Cultic uses of bread do not seem to have figured in Jesus' thinking (except in Mt 12:4 par., in the context of debate over the sabbath). In the Judaism of the day, the role of the bread was not to provide God with food in return for his gift (the "loaves of permanent offering" that were set before Yahweh: Lev 24:5–8; 1 Sam 21:5–7; Mt 12:4 par., and the loaves from the first fruits: Lev 23:17), but to signify gratitude for the fruitfulness God had given the soil or, in the case of unleavened loaves, remembrance of the deliverance from Egypt, which was the model of every deliverance (Ex 12:8, 11, 39; 1 Cor 5:7f.).

29. Life (Sir 31:27), friendship (Sir 9:10), love (Cant 1:2; 4:10; etc.), joy (Eccl 10:19; Zech 10:7), music (Sir 32:6; 40:20; Is 5:12). Wine also had negative connotations, e.g., the divine wrath (Ps 60:5; Rev 16:19). See on this point D. Sesboüé, "Wine," in *DBT* 656–57.

30. See Am 9:14; Hos 2:24; Jer 31:12; etc. "New" wine makes old wineskins burst (Mt 9:17 par.). In the new heavens and the new earth (Rev 21:1) the wine will be different from the "fruit of the vine" that is Israel and that has not borne fruit (Is 51:1–7; Mk 12:1–9 par.). On "new" see below, 72 and 200.

31. Ps 104:15. Archeology seems to confirm the claim that wine was usual only at meals that were both complete and festive. See G. Dalman, *Arbeit und Sitte in Palästina* (Gütersloh, 1935), IV, 388f.; *RGG* 6 (1962) 1573.

32. The deprivation of wine is a typical trait in predictions of punishment (Am 5:11; Mic 6:15; etc.), just as the presence of a vine indicates that God has not totally cursed the soil as a result of human sin (Gen 5:29). Wine had a more important place than bread in the ritual sacrifices of the temple (Ex 29:40; Num 15:5, 10; Deut 18:4; 1 Sam 1:24; Hos 9:4).

33. Ps 23:5; 16:5; 116:13. See below, 140–141.

34. These movements are to be found in the account of Gethsemane, which I have studied elsewhere; see my *Face a la mort: Jesus et Paul* (Paris, 1979), 113–43.

35. A. Gerken, a dogmatic theologian, emphasizes this aspect of the Supper in his *Theologie der Eucharistie* (Munich, 1973). He urges his colleagues to develop a "theology of relations" that will enable them to break out of the aporias encountered in the classical theology of the Eucharist.

36. Ex 24:8; see below, 146.

37. See below, 109–115.

38. A comparable literary device is found in John when Jesus says: "All who eat *my flesh* and drink *my blood*. . . . All who eat *me* will live by me" (Jn 6:56f.).

39. The existence of the Supper text in the synoptics and Paul can be regarded as in a sense a de facto response to Jesus, not from the twelve but from the entire early community, since it bears witness to an ecclesial liturgy that was celebrated because the Lord had instituted it. See below, 82–84.

40. See below, 189–193.

41. See below, 291–293.

42. See below, 200.

43. The term "transubstantiation" belongs only in a theological context which I cannot take space to explain here. See J. Baciocchi, "Présence eucharistique et transsubstantiation," *Irén* 32 (1959) 139–61, and B. Neunheuser, *L'Eucharistie* (Paris, 1966). A. Gerken (above, n. 35), 157–227, gives an excellent explanation of the different mentalities at work in the Fathers of the Church and in the Council of Trent. See below, 133–135.

44. See X. Léon-Dufour (ed.), *Les miracles de Jésus selon le Nouveau Testament* (Paris, 1977), 302–4.

45. See H. de Lubac, *Corpus Mysticum* (Paris, 1944), 292; idem, *The Splendour of the Church*, trans. M. Mason (New York, 1956), chapter 6 (87–113).

Notes for part II

INTRODUCTION

1. J. Jeremias and H. Schürmann. The latter published his dissertation in three volumes totaling almost 450 pages (1953–57), in the collection Neutestamentliche Abhandlungen, XIX/5, XX/4, and XX/5 (Münster, 1953–56); but see his letter of March 25, 1959, to which Jeremias refers, 190.

2. Every tradition supposes a living milieu in which a teaching or a reading of the memory of an event is passed on. A tradition is expressed and transmitted in well defined "forms": thus in my opinion the "testamentary form" and the "cultic form" are the ways in which recollections of the last meal of Jesus were recorded. Strictly speaking, since I cannot precisely describe the character of the milieus from which these forms came, I should keep on using the terms "testamentary form" and "cultic form." However, since I suppose that there were different milieus at the origin of these "forms," I can use the word "tradition" in a broader sense and speak of "testamentary tradition" and "cultic tradition." On the other hand, the two developments of the cultic form can be located in milieus—the Markan and the Antiochene—that are known to us; whence the terms "Markan tradition" and "Antiochene tradition" which I use below in Chapter V and *passim*.

IV. CULTIC TRADITION AND TESTAMENTARY TRADITION

1. In 1 Cor 15:3 as in 11:23 the words "receive" (*paralam-bano*) and "pass on" (*paradidomi*) correspond to the technical rabbinical terms *kibbel mîn* and *masar l*, which describe the chain of tradition. See Neuenzeit 77-89. On 1 Cor 11:17–34 as a whole see below, 213–227.

2. The Pauline account of the Supper has several turns of phrase that are not part of Paul's vocabulary or style: the absolute use of *paradidomi* and *eucharisteo*, the words *anamnesis* and *klao* without a complement, and, above all, *to soma* as referring to the individual, personal body of Jesus. The whole account is undoubtedly pre-Pauline (see Jeremias 104; Neuenzeit 86).

3. L. Schenke, *Studien* 312, n. 5, lists about twenty names. See also J. Betz, *Mysterium salutis* IV/2 (Einsiedeln, 1973), 188.

4. "Etiological" (from the Greek *aitia*, "cause") means "explanatory of the origin of something." On the whole question see Neuenzeit 96–100 (despite the reservations of Schürmann II, 145f.). I pass over the distinction made by L. Schenke, *Studien*, 313f., between an account which is simply intended to provide a basis for a cultic act and is not itself used in the celebration (*kult-begründend*—the account of institution as transmitted by Paul) and an account that is part of the cultic action (*kultbegleitend* or *Kultanamnese*—the account as transmitted by Mark).

5. The words "the Lord Jesus" are pre-Pauline, contrary to Schürmann II, 50-56, and in agreement with Neuenzeit 103–5, W. Popkes, *Christus traditus* (Zürich, 1967), 205f., and H. Patsch, *Abendmahl*, 104f.

6. To describe a text as "etiological" does not pre-judge the question of the historicity of the foundational event thus narrated, especially since the Christian community celebrated the Eucharist from a very early date and it is unlikely that this celebration reflected nothing but the creativity of believers. In addition to what I shall go on to say here about the historical problem, see below, 157–179.

7. The passion proper begins with the arrest of Jesus; see X. Léon-Dufour, "Passion (Recit de la)," *DBS* 6 (1960) 1424f., and below, 186. According to Patsch 61, n. 22, the cultic account replaced another of which *hymnesantes* (Mk 14:26) is a remnant (63).

8. The Greek words are *kai esthionton auton*. According to R. Pesch, *Das Abendmahl und Jesu Todesverständis* (Freiburg,

1979), 71, the genitive absolute in 14:22 is a naive repetition of 14:18; in keeping with his usual style, Mark thus indicates that a new situation is beginning. Despite the approval given to Pesch by a very few authors, such as R. Daly in *Biblical Theology Bulletin* 11 (1981) 21–27, I side with those who vigorously disagree with his position: e.g., E. Ruckstuhl, "Neue und alte Überlegungen zu den Abendmahlsworten Jesu," in *Studien zum Neuen Testament und seiner Umwelt* (series A, vol. 5; Linz, 1981), 76–106 (at 95), and K. Kertelge, "Das Abendmahl Jesu im Markusevangelium," in *Mélanges H. Zimmermann* (Bonn, 1980), 67–80.

9. The remembrance command is studied below, 109–116.

10. On this point Schürmann's various works are excellent; see, in particular, "Das Weiterleben der Sache Jesu im nachösterlichen Herrenmahl," in *Jesu Abendmahlshandlung als Zeichen für die Welt* (Leipzig, 1970), 63–101; reworked in *BZ* 16 (1972) 1–23.

11. With Schürmann, "Weiterleben . . . ," 95 (= *BZ* 6); against Dalman 140 and Jeremias 69–70; see below, 164.

12. See Schürmann, *ibid.*, 90.

13. See *Ber* 46a; Dalman 126; Billerbeck IV, 616; Jeremias 173ff.; L. Ligier, *MD* n. 87, 66; Schürmann, *Ursprung* 77–79.

14. Despite Jeremias 220ff.

15. See S. Dockx, "Le récit du repas pascal: Marc 14, 17–26," *Bib* 46 (1965) 445–53.

16. See below, 165–166, for the justification for this statement.

17. H. Merklein, "Überlieferungsgeschichte," 236.

18. Patsch, "Abendmahl," 100–02.

19. *Qiddush*, a Hebrew word meaning "sanctification" and therefore a blessing said over a cup of wine to mark the beginning of each sabbath and feast day.

20. I shall show this in an appendix, 306–308.

21. Schürmann II.

22. Schürmann, *Récit*, 29, n. 3. On the various cups at the Passover meal see below, 303–304.

23. There is likewise no point in supposing that the ritual of the cup replaced the traditional meal, since we have no information on any ancient Passover ceremony (with Patsch, *Abendmahl*, 97, vs. F. Hahn, "Motive," 353f.).

24. Jeremias 122–25.

25. B. Lohse, *Das Passafest der Quartadecimaner* (Gütersloh, 1953). His hypothesis is challenged by W. Huber, *Passa und*

Ostern (Berlin, 1969), 12–31. See K. G. Kuhn's review of Lohse in *TLZ* 81 (1956) 682–84.

26. Acts 12:3; 20:6 speak, however, of "the days of Unleavened Bread." See n. 10 in Chapter X.

27. H. Lietzmann, *Messe und Herrenmahl. Eine Studie zur Geschichte der Liturgie* (Bonn, 1926), 252; ET: *Mass and Lord's Supper. A Study in the History of the Liturgy*, trans. with appendixes by D. H. G. Reeves; introduction and supplementary essay by R. D. Richardson (Leiden, 1953–79), 206.

28. In particular, the fact that the long reading of Lk, which includes 22:19b–20, is original, while the short reading (without 19b–20) is an abbreviation (for which various explanations are given). See H. Schürmann, "Lk 22, 19b–20 als ursprüngliche Textüberlieferung," *Bib* 32 (1951) 522–41 (= *Traditionsgeschichtliche Untersuchungen zu den synoptischen Evangelien* [Dusseldorf, 1968], 152–92); Jeremias 139-60; E. Schweizer, "Das Herrenmahl im Neuen Testament. Ein Forschungsbericht" (1954), in his *Neotestamentica* (Zürich-Stuttgart, 1963), 344–47.

29. K. G. Kuhn, review of Jeremias' *Die Abendmahlsworte* in *TLZ* 75 (1950) 399–408; similarly E. Schweizer (n. 28), 355f.

30. X. Leon-Dufour, "Passion (Récits de la)" (n. 7), 1456f.

31. Some studies of the subject: J. Munck, "Discours d'adieu dans le Nouveau Testament et dans la littérature biblique," in *Aux sources de la tradition chrétienne (Mélanges M. Goguel)* (Neuchâtel, 1950), 155–70; E. Cortes, *Los Discursos de Adios de Gn 49 a Jn 13–17* (Barcelona, 1973); J. Becker, *Untersuchungen zur Entstehungsgeschichte der Testamente der Zwölf Patriarchen* (Leiden, 1970). I have also been aided by the work which R. Guého, one of my students, did under my direction in 1968.

32. Gen 49; Deut 33; 1 Sam 12; 1 Kgs 2; 1 Mac 2:49–70; Tob 4:14.

33. *Jub.* 7; 20; 35; 26; *1 Enoch* 91-93; *T. Job; 2 Apoc. Bar.* 31–34, 43–46; *T. 12 Patr.; T. Mos.; 2 Enoch;* Coptic *T. Jacob;* Coptic *T. Isaac; T. Adam.*

34. Acts 20:17–38; 1 Tim 4:1; 2 Tim 3:1–4:10; Jn 13–17.

35. H. J. Michel, *Die Abschiedsrede des Paulus an die Kirche. Apg 20, 17-38* (Munich, 1973), 47–54.

36. Gen 27:2–4; 1 Sam 12; *Jub.* 22; 35:27; 45:5; *T. Neph.* 1, 1–4.

37. Abraham will die during the Feast of Weeks (or firstfruits of the harvest) (*Jub.* 22). Greek *T. Neph.* is dated on the first

day of the seventh month (feast of Booths). 1 Sam 11:15 mentions a preparatory sacrifice.

38. Gen 27; *Jub.* 22.
39. *Jub.* 35, 27 and 36, 17.
40. *Jub.* 45, 5.
41. *Jub.* 22.
42. *Adam and Eve* 30–46; *T. Jos.*; *T. Judah.*
43. *Jub.* 20; 21; 22; 36; *LAB* 33; *T. Asher.*
44. Tob 14:3–11; *As. Mos; 1 Enoch* 91.
45. For further details see Michel (n. 35).
46. 2 Tim 1:11–14; 2:2, 8-13; 3:10–12.
47. 2 Tim 1:5; 2:14–18, 23; 3:1–9, 13; 4:3f.
48. See below, 249–252.
49. See below, 125–128.

V. THE TWO TENDENCIES IN THE CULTIC TRADITION

1. Mark's statement, "They all drank of it" (line 40), becomes in Matthew, "Drink of it, all of you" (line 42); see above, 83. Matthew also shows himself more recent than Mark in that he makes two additions: "Eat" (line 30) and "for the forgiveness of sins" (lines 49–50).

2. See above, Chapter III, n. 2.

3. Jeremias 186-96. Many have followed in his steps: A. J. Higgins (1954), E. Lohse (1955), P. Benoit (1957), J. Delorme (1957), J. Dupont (1958), H. Patsch (1972), C. Perrot, earlier work (1975), R. Pesch (1978).

4. And even more specifically in favor of Lk (see II, 132). He is joined by H. Merklein, "Überlieferungsgeschichte," 98. Today, however, Paul is often regarded as the more faithful representative of the primitive tradition; thus, with many critics, Neuenzeit 103-20.

5. They are not such in every instance, despite Jeremias 173–86. See Schürmann, *ZKT* 73 (1951) 750; N. Turner, "The Style of Mark's Eucharistic Words," *JTS* 8 (1957) 108-11; L. Schenke, *Studien* 308f.

6. Especially F. Hahn, "Motive," 358-66.

7. Schürmann II, 17–30, relying on Dalman 132f.; see Neuenzeit 108f.

8. See Neuenzeit, *ibid.*; J. Betz, 15, is hesitant.

9. See Jeremias 175 and 177–78.

10. Thus Jeremias 172.

11. With Schürmann II, 76f. and Neuenzeit 110f. The relative clause "which is for you" is intended not to explain but to specify the character of the subject of the clause.

12. See below, 211.

13. Schürmann II, 118.

14. Following A. Oepke, *TLZ* 80 (1955) 134f., Jeremias 194-95; see Patsch 90, nn. 208-10, and Betz 20, n. 77. Recently A. Diez Macho has provided authoritative confirmation of Jeremias' hypothesis by pursuing the inquiry into Aramaic literature on the basis of earlier studies of J. A. Emerton, *JTS* 6 (1955) 238-401; 13 (1962) 111-17; 15 (1964) 58f., of J. E. David, *Bib* 48 (1967) 291f., and of M. McNamara, *Targum and Testament* (Shannon, Ireland, 1972), 127s. Diez Macho cites passages from Neofiti such as 49, 2: "Blessed be *his* name of *his* glory of his reign," *RevSR* 47 (1973) 209s. (= *Exégèse biblique et Judaïsme* [Strasbourg, 1973], 55f.).

15. Thus Merklein, "Überlieferungsgeschichte," 98, thinks he can establish an original form (*Ursprungsform*) of the sayings; "touto estin to sōma mou to hyper pollōn didomenon" and "touto to potērion hē kainē diathekē en tō haimati mou." He says a similar version is proposed by G. Bornkam (154), W. Marxsen (296-99), H. Schürmann (II, 131f.), E. Schweizer (*RGG* I, 13f.), J. Betz (12, 25), P. Neuenzeit (101-20), and L. Schenke (307-19). But each of these critics introduces so many nuances into the text as compared with that of Merklein that it is risky to speak of agreement among them.

VI. THE WORDS ON REMEMBRANCE

1. Above, 69-71. On the absence of the command of remembrance in the Markan tradition see above, Chapter III. n. 10.

2. Justification of the very brief remarks that follow would require an entire book on the biblical understanding of time and memory. I refer the reader to three essays of my own: "Das Letzte Abendmahl: Stiftung und kultische Aktualisierung," *BLit* 46 (1973), 167-77; "En mémoire de moi," *Christus* 24, no. 95 (1977), 200-8; and "Faites ceci en mémoire de moi," *Etudes* 354 (1981) 831-42. One of the outstanding works on the subject is M. Thurian, *The Eucharistic Memorial*, trans J. G. Davies (Ecumenical Studies in Worship 7-8; Richmond, Va., 1961). A recent article provides a very good overview of the subject: O. Nussbaum, "Die Eucharistie als Anamnese (Opfer und Mahl)," *BLit* 44 (1971) 2-16.

3. A trace of this link remains in modern English: at times, when a person is asked to remember someone, he is being asked to act in that someone's behalf or favor; to be mindful of advice received means to act in accordance with the advice.

4. See O. Michel, "mimnēskomai," *TDNT* 4 (original, 1942) 675: "God's remembering is thus an efficacious and creative event"; see Gen 8:1; 19:29; 30:22. Some specialized studies of memory in the Bible: W. Schottroff, *"Gedenken" im Alten Orient und im Alten Testament. Die Wurzel zakar im semitischen Sprachkreis* (Neukirchen, 1964); H. Zirker, *Die kultische Vergegenwärtigung der Vergangenheit in den Psalmen* (Bonn, 1964). Among the available articles, A. Darlapp, "Anamnesis," *ZKT* 97 (1975) 80–86.

5. A complete list of references would be endless. Here are a few examples: "Remember me . . . and strengthen me," cries Samson (Jgs 16:28), a plea that the psalmists repeat in their laments, whether individual (Ps 25:7; see 1 Sam 1:11; Jer 15:15) or collective (Ps 74:2; 106:4). May God remember the weakness of human beings (Ps 78:39; 89:48; 103:14) and their humiliations (Ps 89:51)! Above all, may he remember his promise (Ex 32:13; Deut 9:27), his covenant (Jer 14:21), his merciful graciousness (Hab 3:2; Ps 25:6)! May he forget the sins of human beings (Is 64:8; Ps 79:8) and remember only their good actions (Is 38:3; Jer 18:20)! Finally, may he deign to recognize his twelve tribes in the twelve precious stones which the high priest wears on his breastplate when he enters the sanctuary (Ex 28:17–20). And if this appeal is heard, there is an outburst of gratitude and praise of the Lord: God has remembered (Ps 136:23); in particular, he has remembered his covenant (Ps 105:8).

6. Mic 6:5; Is 17:10; 44:21f.; 46:8; 57:11; Jer 51:50; Ez 16:22, 43; etc.

7. Deut 5:15; 7:18; 8:2, 18; 9:7; 15:15; 24:9, 18; etc.

8. As does R. Bultmann, *Theology of the New Testament*, trans. K. Grobel (2 vols.; New York, 1951, 1955), I.

9. See Ps 104; 139; etc.

10. When God "remembers" Hannah he makes the action of her husband fruitful and gives her a child: "Elkanah knew his wife, and the Lord remembered her" (1 Sam 1:19).

11. On the spiritualization of the cult see above, Chapter II, n. 55.

12. This was true even when the feasts were agricultural in origin: the feasts of the first sheaf of grain, harvest, and vintage became Passover, Shelters, and Pentecost.

13. Lev 23:33-44. Also of interest is the account of the institution of the Feast of Purim ("Lots") in Est 9:18-28.

14. Ex 20:8-11.

15. I mention further on in this chapter the abbreviated equivalents the Israelites found for the cultic commemoration.

16. This is in keeping with biblical anthropology; see J. De Fraine, *Adam and the Family of Man*, trans. D. Raible (Staten Island, N.Y., 1965).

17. Ex 12:26; 13:14; Deut 6:20f.; 29:21; Jos 4:6, 21.

18. See Ex 20:24, cited earlier in this chapter.

19. Ps 44:2 JB; 78:3f.

20. Among the many prophetic oracles that call for social justice are Am 4:1-3; 5:10-13; etc. There is a short discussion in my *Etudes* article (above, n. 2), 839-42.

21. See H. Haag, "Kult," *LTK* 6 (1961) 662.

22. Ps 26:12; 35:18.

23. Ps 22:23.

24. Ps 22:27; 34:3; 69:33.

25. Ps 47:2; 48:11.

26. Ps 9:12. See Ps 57:10, 12.

27. See n. 16.

28. On the literary genre and significance of genealogies in the Bible see my *Etudes d'Evangile* (Paris, 1965), 51-63.

29. See H. Leitzmann, *Messe und Herrenmahl. Eine Studie zur Geschichte der Liturgie* (Bonn, 1926), 223; ET: *Mass and Lord's Supper. A Study in the History of the Liturgy*, trans. D. H. G. Reeves (Leiden, 1953-79) 182.

30. 1 Cor 11:26f. Thus many authors, especially O. Nussbaum, "Die Eucharistie . . . " (above, n. 2), 8f. Nussbaum refers to H. Schürmann, *Ursprung*, 77-100, who shows that the eucharistic liturgy must be in conformity not with the "original form" *(Urgestalt)* but with the "basic form" *(Grundgestalt)* of the Supper (98). Consequently, though the Eucharist may have been linked in the beginning to a fraternal meal, just as it was at the Last Supper, it was not by its nature connected with such a meal and in fact was very soon separated from it, perhaps as a result of abuses such as Paul found at Corinth (see below, Chapter XI).

31. Note that the Greek does not say *eis tēn mou anamnēsin* but instead puts the emphasis on the personal pronoun: *eis tēn emēn anamnēsin*. To achieve the same effect in English, the procedure must be reversed: not "in my memory" but "in memory of me." On the other hand, the two formulations seem to be equivalent in that both signify an objective commemoration "of me"

(see F. W. Blass and A. Debrunner, *A Greek Grammar of the New Testament and Other Early Christian Literature*, trans. and rev. R. W. Funk [Chicago, 1961], §§ 284, 1 and 285, 1; see Rom 10:1; Gal 1:13; Phil 1:26), whereas "Do this in my action of recalling" would be meaningless in the context.

32. P. Chantraine, *Dictionnaire étymologique de la langue grecque. Histoire des mots* (Paris, 1974), 702f.

33. Some equivalent formulas: "Do this while recalling my presence" or, more simply, "Do this while recalling my Name." It must be realized, however, that to remember the "name" is to remember the full reality of the person, as we are told in the revelation of the divine Name in Ex 3:15; it is to remember that this Name is God and to remind God to remember human beings. Another equivalent formula would involve a shift in the relation between the various words: "Do this in order that I may always be present to human beings"; but such a formulation would presuppose an understanding of Is 49:1, 3: "The Lord called me from the womb, from the body of my mother he named my name. . . . He said to me, 'You are my servant, Israel, in whom I will be glorified.' " Through the Eucharist Jesus extends his presence in history.

For completeness' sake, let me mention the novel hypothesis of J. Jeremias (251–55). According to Jeremias the command of remembrance should be translated: "This do, that God may remember me" (252; see Ps 131:1 LXX). Through the eucharistic action the sacrificial act of Jesus continues to be present to God and to obtain the redemptive effects that are its fruit. The eucharistic action (in Jeremias' explanation) consists in transferring into the divine world the past action of Jesus' sacrifice. The Eucharist would thus be, in the proper sense of the word, a "memorial": something that serves to keep alive the memory of something; in this instance, it keeps the memory of Jesus' sacrifice alive in God himself. By celebrating the Eucharist believers set up a memorial of Jesus in the presence of God. For, according to the Bible, when a believer makes an offering to God, the priest "makes the memorial smoke on the altar" (Lev 2:2); here the offering is described by a word that has the same root as remembrance: *'azkarah*. The function of the eucharistic offering is to remind God of Jesus who offers himself.

Despite the biblical link I join the majority of critics in rejecting this hypothesis. First, for linguistic reasons: a "memorial" would be *mnēmosynon* in Greek, not *anamnēsis*. Moreover: it is true enough that in the case of the Old Testament sacrifices or of the prayers and alms of Cornelius (Acts 10:4, 31), human actions bring into existence a treasure that is of great value in God's sight; but how could an action of the disciples set up a memorial of Jesus in God's sight? Such a charge would surely be beyond human powers and represent a failure to understand the unique relationship of Jesus and his Father.

34. Thus H. Leclercq in his article "Agape" (written in 1903), in *DACL* 1 (1907) 786; Lietzmann, *Messe und Herrenmahl* 222 (ET: 181–82); and B. Reicke, *Diakonie* 260–63.

35. There is a good refutation in Jeremias 238–43.

36. The following remarks draw upon the excellent work of C. Giraudo (see above, Chapter II, n. 46), 174.

37. If we keep these points in mind, we will avoid reducing the eucharistic action to a sacrificial rite that supposedly repeats the past event. On the positive side, we will find ourselves drawn into a dynamic following of the faithful Jesus of Nazareth. I refer the reader to my *Face à la mort: Jésus et Paul* (Paris, 1979), especially 168–71 and 285–89.

38. Lev 24:7.

39. Jos 4:7. Votive offerings in sanctuaries likewise had for their purpose to bear witness to some historically transient action.

40. Num 15:38–41.

41. Deut 6:8; Mic 23:5.

42. I take this word from the Eastern tradition so finely described by Madam Lot-Borodine, "La doctrine de la déification dans l'Eglise grecque jusqu'au onzième siècle," *RHR* 105 (1932) 5–43; 106 (1932) 525–74 (at 541); 107 (1933) 8–55 (see *RSR* 33 [1946] 156f.).

VII. THE WORDS OVER THE BREAD

1. See above, 99.

2. See above, 60–62.

3. The neuter *touto* in place of the masculine *houtos ho artos* sums up all that precedes. Some critics believe that an appeal to Greek usage will explain the difference between the Markan and Antiochene formulations. Thus E. Lohmeyer, *Das Evangelium des Markus* (Göttingen, 1957), 304f., says that when a word that seems to be in an attributive position has no modifier it is in fact the subject of the sentence; the words of Jesus could therefore be translated "My body, here it is!" This translation might be valid for the Aramaic substratum; see D. Lys, "Mon corps, le voici,"

ETR 45 (1970) 389f. It definitely allows the reader not to identify the body of Jesus with the material bread as such; the neuter *touto* serves to sum up the preceding action and to give the bread a special meaning.

4. J. Pedersen, *Israel, Its Life and Culture* (Oxford, 1926); K. Grobel, "Soma as Self, Person in the Septuagint," in *Mélanges Rudolf Bultmann* (Berlin, 1954), 52–59; J. A. T. Robinson, *The Body. A Study in Pauline Theology* (SBT 5; London, 1961); R. H. Gundry, *Soma in Biblical Theology with Emphasis on Pauline Anthropology* (Cambridge, 1976), 3–8; R. Jewett, *Paul's Anthropological Terms. A Study of Their Use in Conflict Settings* (Leiden, 1971); E. Schweizer, "Soma," *TNDT* 7 (original = 1964) 1024–94. See X. Léon-Dufour, "Flesh," in *DBT* 185–88; idem, "Body," *DBT* 73–75. Some modern philosophers—Merleau-Ponty, for example—would find biblical anthropology quite congenial.

5. For example, two modern studies of the subject: J. Bonsirven, "*Hoc est corpus meum.* Recherches sur l'originel araméen," *Bib* 29 (1948) 217; and Jeremias 198–201. In fact, in the second century Ignatius of Antioch (*Smyrn.,* 7, 1; *Rom.,* 7, 3f.; *Phld.,* 4, 1; *Trall.,* 8, 1) and Justin (*Apol. I* 66, 2) use the word *sarx* in a eucharistic context, just as John had in the discourse on the Bread of Life (Jn 6:51–56).

6. In favor of *gûph* (following Dalman 141ff.) are W. G. Kümmel, *Promise and Fulfillment: The Eschatological Message of Jesus,* trans. D. M. Barton (SBT 23; Naperville, Ill., 1961), 120; E. Schweizer, *TDNT* 7:1059; F. Hahn, "Zum Stand der Erforschung des urchristlichen Herrenmahls," *EvT* 35 (1975) 553–63 (at 558). A back-translation into Aramaic would yield something like this: *den hû' bisari* or *den hû' gûphi,* and into Hebrew, *zeh hû' b^esari* or *zeh hû' gûphi.* It is better to retain the pronoun *hû',* with Delitzsch and Dalman and against Jeremias 201, n. 5. Schürmann II, 119, n. 416, has a good presentation of the problem.

7. See Schweizer, *TDNT* 7:1045–46. Among the passages cited in support are: Gen 36:6 (= persons); 1 Kgs 14:9 and Ez 23:25 (= the back); Prov 11:17 (= the self); Dan 7:11. In the New Testament: Mt 27:59 par.; Lk 23:55; Jn 20:12.

8. See Is 53:12.

9. Betz 21, n. 80, sharply refutes the statements of Jeremias 221–22: the passages from the Septuagint and Philo which Jeremias cites do not speak of sacrifice. See also Schweizer, *TDNT* 7:1048.

10. H. Riesenfeld, "Hyper," *TDNT* 8 (original = 1968) 511.

11. As Riesenfeld correctly points out, the only examples in the New Testament are Phlm 13 and, perhaps, 1 Cor 15:29; 2 Cor 5:14f.

12. Mk 9:40.

13. Phil 1:7; 4:10.

14. 2 Cor 12:15; see 1 Cor 4:6; 2 Cor 7:7, 12; 8:16.

15. Rom 9:3.

16. Col 1:24.

17. 1 Thess 5:10.

18. Rom 5:6.

19. 1 Cor 15:3; see 2 Cor 5:21; 1 Pet 3:18.

20. Lev 4:1–5:13; see R. de Vaux, *Ancient Israel: Its Life and Institutions*, trans. J. McHugh (New York, 1961), 418–20. The preposition *peri* is usually used in the Old Testament to designate those for whom forgiveness is obtained; for example: "when the priest performs the rite of absolution *(kippur)* for *(peri)* the people, they are forgiven" (Lev 4:20). As a result sacrifice for sin is sometimes referred to as *peri hamartias*, an expression that occurs in Rom 8:3. The preposition *peri* is rarely used in the New Testament: it occurs in Heb 5:3 (= Lev 16:17) and Heb 10:6 (= Ps 39:7 LXX) and again in Mt 26:28, where an effort is made to reproduce the Greek of Is 53:10. The replacement of *peri* with *hyper* is consonant with the evolution of the Greek language which, in the time of Jesus, did not distinguish between these two prepositions: thus Eph 6:18f. uses them one after another, with the same meaning, simply for the sake of variety (see also 1 Pet 3:18 and 1 Thess 5:10 in the Vetus Latina).

21. The best known of these sacrifices is the Kippur. On "expiatory sacrifice" see below, 145–146.

22. Thus Riesenfeld (n. 10), 510f.

23. See my *Face à la mort: Jésus et Paul* (Paris, 1979), 182–212.

24. See Rom 5:6, 8; 1 Cor 15:3; Gal 1:4; Eph 5:2; 1 Tim 2:6.

25. Rom 5:7.

26. Gal 2:20; Rom 5:8.

27. Jn 15:13JB; see 13:37f. Why not cite Plato, *Symposium* 179b: "Only those who love are willing to die for *(hyper-apothnēskein)* another"?

28. Jn 17:19; see the excellent study by I. de la Potterie, which is revised in his *La Vérité dans saint Jean* (Rome, 1977), 706–85 (at 758–75). See also J. T. Forestell, *The Word of the Cross* (Rome, 1974), 42.

29. See above, 33.

30. On "substance," for example, see below, 133–134.

31. J. Dupont's explanation in his "'Ceci est mon corps, Ceci est mon sang,'"*NRT* 80 (1958) 1025–41, is representative of the common view of Catholic exegetes. See also P. Benoit, "The Holy Eucharist," *Scripture* 8 (1956) 97–108; 9 (1957) 1–14 (at 4).

32. Dupont 1034f.

33. There is a vast literature on the subject and I shall list only a few works: E. Ortigues, *Le Discours et le Symbole* (Paris, 1962); J. L. Austin, *How To Do Things With Words* (New York, 1962); A. Vergote, "Dimensions anthropologiques de l'Eucharistie," in the collective work *L'Eucharistie: Symbole et réalité* (Gembloux, 1970), 7–56; J. Ladrière, "The Performativity of Liturgical Language," in H. Schmidt and D. Power (eds.), *Liturgical Experience of Faith* (Concilium 82; New York, 1973), 50–62; L. M. Chauvet, *Du symbolique au symbole* (Paris, 1979).

34. "The primary elements constituting a process of enunciation are the *speaker*, who produces the utterance, and the *hearer* (or addressee), to whom the utterance is addressed (both are called *interlocutors*)" (T. Todorov, in O. Ducrow and T. Todorov, *Encyclopedic Dictionary of the Sciences of Language*, trans. C. Porter (Baltimore, 1979), 324. To simplify the terminology I use the term "interlocutor" only for the "addressee."

35. I take this terminology from J. L. Austin, having modified it as he himself does in his later studies. "An expression is called *constative* if it tends only to describe an event. It is called *performative* if (1) it describes a certain action performed by its speaker and (2) producing this expression amounts to accomplishing that action. A sentence beginning 'I promise you that . . . ' is said to be performative, since by using it, we accomplish the act of promising; not only do we say that we are promising but, by so doing, we are promising. . . . The performatives thus have as a property that their intrinsic meaning cannot be grasped independently of a certain action that they allow us to accomplish" (Todorov 342). Let me add a word about the term "speech act," which is often identified with "speech in action." Austin distinguished between a *locutionary* act (the act of combining sounds and linking the notions represented by the words), a *perlocutionary* act (the act of enunciations serves further ends that are consequences of the utterance), and an *illocutionary* act (the enunciation of the sentence changes relations between the interlocutors; the act is accomplished by the utterance itself and is not simply a consequence of the latter; such an act can take the form of a performa-

tive utterance). An illocutionary act "is always conventional," since "it is only actualized through the existence of a sort of social ceremonial, which attributes a particular value to a given formula used by a certain person in specific circumstances" (Todorov 343). An example: "The Olympic Games are open."

36. "The *competence* of a speaker of English . . . is the set of possibilities given the subject owing to the fact—and to this fact alone—that he has mastered the English language" (Todorov 120). *Performance* consists in actualizing these linguistic possibilities, as well as the person's knowledge of the world and his or her human relations (*ibid.,* 120ff.).

37. I am indebted here especially to G. Durand's lucid little book, *L'Imagination symbolique* (Paris, 1976³). In keeping with its etymology, a symbol (from Greek *syn* = with, together, and *ballō* = throw, place) effects a union (and not simply a juxtaposition, as in the case of allegory) between a sensible image and a reality that cannot be grasped by or confined within discursive language, but can only be experienced. In the sensible image the mind reaches a reality of a different order, something that cannot be expressed or formulated, either because it transcends the rational order (e.g., love) or because it is too concentrated, profound, and rich to be completely grasped by direct thought. In an allegory human thought moves from representation to idea; in a symbol a reality not reducible to concepts makes itself present in and through an image, nor can it bypass the image and communicate itself directly. A symbol signifies only itself; it *makes present* a reality not attainable in any other way, a reality which is at once near *and* distant. A symbol is not a way of access to something else, or a passageway to it, or something that refers to it, but the emergence in an image of a reality that comes to meet us.

"A symbol is a representation that brings to light a hidden meaning; it is the *epiphany* of a mystery . . . a sign which leads the mind to a signified that is ineffable and invisible, and which is therefore compelled to embody in a concrete way what it cannot grasp directly" (Durand 13, 18).

38. Jeremias 224.

39. B. Sesboüé, "Réflexions sur la présence réelle de l'eucharistie," *Note inédite,* 1981.

40. J. de Baciocchi, "Présence eucharistique et transsubstantiation," *Irén* 32 (1959) 155.

41. According to E. Pousset, "L'Eucharistie: présence réelle et transsubstantiation," *RSR* 54 (1966) 177–212.

42. Baciocchi 157.

43. Group of Les Dombes, "Towards a Common Eucharistic Faith?: Agreement Between Roman Catholics and Protestants," trans. P. Gaughan, in *Modern Eucharistic Agreement* (London, 1973), no. 18 (p. 60).

44. *Ibid.*, no. 19 (p. 60).

45. See E. Schillebeeckx, *The Eucharist*, trans. N. D. Smith (New York, 1968), 36–39.

46. B. Sesboüé, "L'accord eucharistique des Dombes. Réflexions théologiques," *Ist* 18 (1973) 219, n. 9. See also K. Rahner, "The Presence of Christ in the Sacrament of the Lord's Supper," in his *Theological Investigations* 4, trans. K. Smyth (Baltimore, 1966), 287–311.

47. The people in their devotions should avoid thinking of the eucharistic elements in a material way, as they think of the corporeal realities of their world. Yet that is the kind of thinking sometimes found even in statements by those who should know better. Thus the effects of communion are said to be connected "with the duration of the bodily presence of our Lord in the recipient: fifteen, twenty, thirty minutes" (F. Cuttaz, "Communion," *DSp* 2 [1953] 1204); or again: thanksgiving after Mass "should last as long as the eucharistic presence within us, that is, about a quarter of an hour" (M. Viller, *ibid.*, 1232). And what response should one make to what a Greek archimandrite told me on November 22, 1981: in the countryside old women urge boys not to play in the street on the day when they receive communion, because they might scrape their knees and, in bleeding, risk profaning the blood of the Lord. Such advice seems to apply to males a prescription directed at menstruating women by St. Gregory in the sixth century (*Ep.* 2) and, in 1979, by Pantaleimon C. Caranicolas, Bishop of Corinth, in the article "Emmena" of his *Kleis orthodoxōn kanonikōn Diataxeōn* (Athens, 1979), regarding the reception of communion by women at their wedding. Such counsels not only echo the Old Testament regulations on cleanness but seem also to reflect a belief in a kind of symbiosis between the blood of Christ and the blood of the recipient.

48. Schillebeeckx, 143f., points out the outdatedness of certain rubrics dealing with the "purification" of cultic instruments or the fear of profanation in cases of indeliberate accidents.

49. See Group of Les Dombes (n. 43), no. 20 (p. 60): "We ask that: (i) On the Roman Catholic side it be pointed out . . . that the primary purpose of reserving the eucharist is for its distribution to the sick and the absent; (ii) On the Protestant side the best

means should be adopted of showing the respect due to the elements that have served for the celebration of the eucharist, which is to consume them subsequently, without precluding their use for the communion of the sick."

VIII. THE WORDS OVER THE CUP

1. See my *Face à la mort: Jésus et Paul* (Paris, 1979), 61–72.

2. *Eucharistēsas:* this term is already used in the A tradition in the words over the bread, perhaps as a properly Greek equivalent of the semitic *eulogēsas*, perhaps in order to have the entire eucharistic action performed under the sign of thanksgiving.

3. On the *tôdâ* see above, 42–44.

4. On the different meanings that "body" and "blood" can have when paired see below, 209.

5. It was customary at meals for the head of the family to give each person at table a cup already filled; consequently, to drink from a single cup symbolizes a communion among those present (Ps 16:5; 1 Cor 10:20). The table custom is also the origin of the metaphorical use of "cup" to signify a person's fate or lot (Mk 10:38f.) or trial to be endured (Num 5:12–28; Mk 14:36) or a punishment to be undergone (Is 51:17; Jer 25:15; Rev 14:10). The "cup of salvation" (Ps 116:13) was offered and drunk in the temple, and it signified communion with God. An analogous rite existed in idolatrous cults (1 Cor 10:21). See my *Dictionary of the New Testament*, trans. T. Prendergast (San Francisco, 1980), 153, and *Face à la mort* 127, n. 61; see also above, 59.

6. With Schürmann, *BZ* 16 (1972) 67, against Dalman 153 and Jeremias 69–70.

7. See Num 4:14. Sacrificial usage had, of course, prepared the way for the association of cup and blood, but the eucharistic situation is new in relation to Jewish sacrifices.

8. The cup of God's wrath (Ps 11:6, Is 51:17; Jer 25:15; Rev 14:10; 15:7–16:19) appears only in well-defined contexts. On the appalling statements prompted by a false interpretation of the cup see my *Face à la mort*, 152f.

9. On the covenant see the presentation and bibliography in E. Kutsch, "Bund," *Theologische Realenzyklopädie* 7 (1980) 397–403. There are many studies of the theme, but I shall cite only a few: D. J. McCarthy, *Treaty and Covenant* (Rome, 1963), with two supplementary notes: "The Symbolism of Blood and Sacrifice," *JBL* 88 (1969) 166–76, and 92 (1973) 205–10; P. Beauchamp,

"Propositions sur l'alliance de l'Ancien Testament comme structure centrale," *RSR* 58 (1970) 161–94; P. Buis, *La notion de l'alliance dans l'Ancien Testament* (Paris, 1976).

The Greek word *diathēkē* translates the Hebrew *berît*, which probably derives from Akkadian *birtû*, meaning "to bind together in a community" (see the nuanced explanation in Buis 42–44). The word signifies a treaty or contract between two nations (Jos 9:11–15; 1 Sam 23:18), two families (Gen 26:28), or two individuals (Gen 31:44f), who pledge themselves to maintain a union under certain conditions. In Israel such a treaty can unite human beings with one another or God with human partners; in the latter case it acquires a special character. The rites mediating relations among human beings can vary: a gift (Gen 21:27), a meal (Gen 26:28–30; 31:46, 54), etc.

10. Modern excavations at Mari brought to light a number of Hittite treaties that probably served as models for the Hebrew covenant treaty; see McCarthy, or Buis 65, 112–20, with the texts in 193–205.—In the Israelite covenant with God the partners are never equal, as they are in secular treaties (Gen 21:27, 32; 26:28, 31; 31:44–54; 1 Kgs 5:26). In order to keep the covenant from being regarded as an ordinary contract, the Greek translators translated *berît* not as *syn-thēkē* (*syn*, "with," and *tithēmi*, "place"), which suggests equality between the two parties, but as *dia-thēkē* (*dia*, "by, through," and *tithēmi*, "place"), which emphasizes the element of gift or "testament" made by God and appears in the modern names, "Old Testament" and "New Testament."

11. The first covenant was with Abraham, our father in the faith (Gen 15:17), and was renewed subsequently (Deut 4:31; 7:12; 8:18) with David (2 Sam 7:12) and with the Servant (Is 42:6; 46:9).

12. Paul does not have the words "shed for you," but this is due to his perspective; he has the equivalent of them when he adds to the words of institution the sentence: "You proclaim the *death* of the Lord . . . "; see below, 224–227.

13. Lev 17:11, 14.

14. Gen 9:6; Mt 27:4, 25; Acts 5:28.

15. Deut 12:23f.; Acts 15:20, 29. See below, n. 26.

16. Mt 23:30, 35f. = Lk 11:50.

17. Mt 27:4, 6, 8, 24f.; see *Face à la mort*, 82–86. Paul has the equivalent in Phil 2:17: "Even if I must shed my blood as a libation on the sacrificial service of your faith"; he likens the "service of faith" to a sacrifice to which is added a libation of blood that is shed, that is to say, his own violent death.

18. In the Old Testament, ritual sprinkling was done with water (Num 19:2–10) or with oil (Lev 8:11) or, especially on the feast of Kippur, with blood (Lev 16). In all these cases, the people were seeking purification from sin, so that the verb "sprinkle" came to be used metaphorically (Ps 51:9; Ex 36:25). In the New Testament the verb occurs especially in Heb 9:13f., 18–21; 12:24. See C. Hunzinger, "Rhantizō," *TDNT* 6 (original = 1959) 976–84.

19. 1 Pet 1:2 and Heb 10:22 use the word in connection with baptism.

20. On "expiatory" sacrifice see below, 145–146.

21. *Face à la mort,* 73–90.

22. See above, 120–123.

23. Ex 20:1–17.

24. Ex 20:22–23:19.

25. The only explicit reference to it in the Old Testament is in Zech 9:11. The other reference is in Heb 9:16–21, which is a commentary on the account.

26. At the consecration of Aaron and his sons the blood is brought in contact with certain parts of the body (Ex 29:21; Lev 8:23, 30). At Sinai the entire people is consecrated by sprinkling. In other cases of sacrifice the blood is simply poured on the altar, that is, it is given back to God himself. At Sinai, and only there, it is the people who are sprinkled with the blood and thereby consecrated to God in a special covenant.

27. This is, more accurately, a "renewal" or "actualization" of the covenant; see H. Cazelles, "Alliance du Sinaï, alliance de l'Horeb et renouvellement de l'alliance," in *Mélanges W. Zimmerli* (Göttingen, 1977), 69–79. For in fact the covenant with Abraham remains forever and is renewed here.

28. On the theme of sacrifice see above, Chapter II, n. 37.

29. Leviticus distinguishes three types of communion sacrifices *(sᵉlamîm)*: praise *(tôdâ)*, spontaneous thanksgiving, and votive offering (Lev 7:12–16). See above, 42.

30. Translated by R. Le Déaut in SC 256 (1979), 201, from ms 27031 in the British Museum in London. Note that Neofiti I does not have the italicized words. The same interpretation is given in *Jub.* 6, 2. 11. 14. Finally, see A. Charbel's article with its significant title, "Virtus sanguinis non expiatoria in sacrificio selamim," in *Sacra Pagina* I (Gembloux, 1959), 366–76.

31. See Part IV of the present book,

32. See A. Vanhoye, "Il sangue di Cristo nell'Epistola agli Ebrei," in *Sangue e Antropologia Biblica* II (Tome, 1981), 819–29.

33. Rom 12:1; see *Face à la mort*, 203, 210, 212.

34. A. Vanhoye, *Prêtres anciens, Prêtre nouveau* (Paris, 1980), 204-34.

35. *Ibid.*, 202.

36. See, among others, L. Chauvet, *Thèmes de réflexion sur l'eucharistie* (Lourdes, 1981), 47f.

37. Is 53:12. The Greek word *polloi,* which translates the Hebrew *rabbîm,* means not "a large number," but the multitude in its entirety. See J. Jeremias, "Polloi," *TDNT* 6 (original = 1959) 536-45. Is 53:10 uses cultic language—"If he offers his life in expiation *('asam),*" the last word meaning approximately "sacrifice of expiation"—in order to make the point that the Servant's personal sacrifice has universal significance.

38. Rom 5:12-21; see *Face à la mort,* 223-29.

39. Thus Mt. 26:38 replaces *hyper* with *peri* in order to reproduce more closely the Greek of Is 53:10: "ean dōte peri hamartias," and 53:12: "kai autos hamartias pollōn anēnegken kai dia hamartias autōn paredothē." See Heb. 9:22: "Without the shedding of blood there is no forgiveness."

40. The "former" prophets (as the historians of the books of Kings are called) and the Chronicler after them made this repeated breaking of the covenant and repeated attempt to renew it an organizational principle of their work. So for Asa (1 Kgs 15:12f.), Jehoash (2 Kgs 11:17), Hezekiah (2 Chr 29:5-10), and especially Josiah.

41. 2 Kgs 22:8-23:24.

42. Jer 11:1-10.

43. Is 24:23; 54:8-10. See A. Jaubert, *La notion de l'alliance dans le judaïsme aux abords de l'ère chrétienne* (Paris, 1963), 58.

44. Jer 31:32a echoes Ex 24:8.

45. See Neh 10; Ezr 10:3.

46. *Dam.* 6, 19; 8, 21; see Jaubert 209; J. Carmignac, *Les textes de Qumrân* II (Paris, 1963), 169, n. 24.

47. 1QS 5, 5f.; 1QpH 2, 3.

48. See J. Starcky, "Qumrân," *DBS* 9 (1978) 1003.

49. *Ibid.,* 996-99. Certain similarities catch the eye first, especially the name "community of the new covenant" and the practice of ritual community meals. Blood rites had been replaced by ritual meals, described as follows: "They shall eat in common, bless in common, and deliberate in common. And in every place where there are ten persons of the Council of the Community, let there not lack among them a man who is a priest. And let them sit before him, each according to his rank, and in the same order ask

their advice in everything. And when they set the table to eat, or (prepare) the wine to drink, the priest shall first stretch out his hand to pronounce a blessing on the first-fruits of the bread and wine" (1QS 6, 2–6, in A. Dupont-Sommer, *The Essene Writings from Qumran*, trans. G. Vermes [Oxford, 1961; repr., Gloucester, Mass., 1973], 85).

But the important things in these meals are a very strict ritual cleanness, the presidency of a priest, and eschatological forgiveness. As a result, the differences between Qumran and Christian belief and practice are greater than the similarities. The Messiah does not give himself, but is awaited; the food has no connection with the person of the Messiah, but consists of ritually determined viands. Finally, the "unclean" are excluded.

50. Ex 19, 5f.

51. The Servant is *bᵉrît 'am*, a "covenant for the people" (Is 42:6; 49:8). See Betz 63f., who judiciously emphasizes the connection of the Antiochene tradition with the prophecy regarding the Servant. Similarly, G. Dalman, G. Kittel, W. Manson, E. Lohmeyer, W. W. Wolff, O. Cullmann, H. Schürmann, and, recently, P. Massi, "Legami tra i racconti della Cena e i carmi del Servo di Jahweh," *RivB* 7 (1959) 95–125, 193–207.

52. Is 49:4, 7.

53. Is 53:3.

54. Is 53:12 (LXX). The text speaks not of "shedding his blood" but of "giving his soul" *(nephesh)*, which is identical with the blood (Lev 17:11, 14).

55. Is 53:12.

56. Is 53:11f.

57. According to the text of Isaiah found at Qumran, which repeats Is 52:15; see Betz 77; and see Heb 12:24.

58. Is 53:10.

59. The way is thus prepared for the New Testament use of cultic terms—pour, libation, offering, etc.—to express existential realities.

60. "I shall make with them an everlasting covenant" (Jer 32:40). "The new covenant of Jeremiah is therefore the everlasting covenant viewed in its eschatological aspect" (Jaubert 65).

61. Jer 33:19–26; Is 55:3.

62. 2 Cor 3. Note that the word "covenant," which is absent from the gospels (except in the account of the Supper and in Lk 1:72), is used in its Jewish meaning by Paul in Rom 9:4; 11:27; Gal 4:24; Eph 2:12. The word occurs frequently in Hebrews.

63. See P. Grelot, *Les Poèmes du Serviteur* (Paris, 1981).

64. This is why, as I pointed out earlier, Paul repeats the command of remembrance: it is thus that believers receive the event even now.

65. For example, Merklein, "Überlieferungsgeschichte," 96.

66. The structure of the text has already made this clear; see above, 60–63.

67. One deplorable consequence of this step backward was a general continuation along Old Testament lines, with the priests of the new covenant being turned into "new old priests," as A. Vanhoye aptly puts it in his *Prêtres* (above, n. 34), 348. Vanhoye criticizes A. Feuillet, *The Priesthood of Christ and His Ministers*, trans. M. J. O'Connell (New York, 1975), Chapters 1 and 2.

IX. THE TRADITIONS AND THE EVENT

1. I repeat here in summary form what I have tried to explain more fully in previous publications: *Les Evangiles et l'Histoire de Jésus* (Paris, 1963), 29–32, 320–24 (ET: 28–30, 204–6); *Etudes d'Evangile* (Paris, 1965), 20–29; *Resurrection and the Message of Easter*, trans. R. N. Wilson (New York, 1974), 195–200; *Face à la mort*, 19–22.

2. I repeat what I have already proposed in various contexts, especially at the Louvain Congress of 1974: "Jésus devant sa mort à la lumière des textes de l'institution eucharistique et des discours d'adieu," in J. Dupont (ed.), *Jésus aux origines de la christologie* (Louvain, 1975), 142–44.—Since that time various studies of the subject have appeared: e.g., R. Latourelle, *Finding Jesus through the Gospels: History and Hermeneutics*, trans. A. Owen (Staten Island, N.Y., 1979); C. Perrot, *Jésus et l'histoire* (Paris, 1979).

3. See two earlier studies of mine: "Der Exeget im Dialog mit dem Ereignis Jesus Christus," *BZ* 10 (1966) 1–15, and "L'exégète et l'événement historique," *RSR* 58 (1970) 551–60.

4. This criterion is sometimes attributed to E. Käsemann (1953) in his "The Problem of the Historical Jesus" (1953), reprinted in his collection, *Essays on New Testament Themes*, trans. W. J. Montague (London, 1964), 34–37; see C. Perrot (n. 2), 64, 67, and, after him, J. Guillet, *RSR* 68 (1980) 567f. In fact, M. Goguel proposed it as early as 1950; see my *Les Evangiles et l'Histoire de Jésus* (Paris, 1963), 323 [the English edition—n. 2, above—omits the reference.—Tr.]

5. See H. Schürmann, "Wie hat Jesus seinen Tod bestanden

und verstanden?" in *Mélanges J. Schmid* (Freiburg/Br., 1973), 325–63, developed and translated in H. Schürmann, *Comment Jésus a-t-il vécu sa mort?* (Paris, 1977). Dogmatic theologians say something similar: K. Rahner and W. Thüsing, *Christologie systematisch und exegtisch* (Freiburg/Br., 1972), 33 (see 48f.)

6. H. Schürmann, "Le problème fondamental posé à l'herméneutique de la prédication de Jésus. Eschato-logie et théo-logie dans leur rapport mutuel" (1964), translated into French in *Le message de Jésus et l'interprétation moderne* (Paris, 1969), 115–49.

7. See above, Chapter IV, n. 4.

8. See *Neuenzeit* 96–100. See also Betz 20f.; Hahn, "Motive," 340; Merklein, "Überlieferungsgeschichte," 99–101.—An opposing view in R. Pesch, who is refuted by K. Kertelge, "Das Abendmahl Jesu in Markusevangelium," in *Mélanges H. Zimmermann* (Bonn, 1980), 47–80, and E. Ruckstuhl, "Neue und alte Überlegungen zu den Abendmahlsworten Jesu," in *Studien zum Neuen Testament und seiner Umwelt*, series A, vol. 5 (Linz, 1981), 79–106.

9. There seems to be no point in insisting on the arbitrariness with which, following W. Heitmüller, *Taufe und Abendmahl im Urchristentum* (1911), 67f., R. Bultmann apodictically asserts that the idea of a sacramental meal was possible only in a Hellenistic milieu; only there, he claims, did people enter into communion with a divinity who had died and returned to life: only there did they share his fate, as in the mysteries of Attis and Mithras (*Theology of the New Testament*, trans. K. Grobel [2 vols.; New York, 1951, 1955], I, 148). Rather than let oneself be dazzled by such generalizations, it is better to look more closely at the various types of sacramental meal practiced at that time, even if the documentation is incomplete and similarities are often superficial. This is what H. Patsch, 19–34, has done.

10. See above, 84.

11. Paul himself tells us so when he introduces the traditional text: "This is what I received from the Lord and handed on to you" (1 Cor 11:23 JB). Recognizable here are the technical terms for the transmission of tradition (see above, Chapter IV, n. 1), and an introduction similar to the one that prefaces the tradition about the resurrection of Jesus (1 Cor 15:1).

12. The death of Jesus is usually dated in A.D. 33. See my *Dictionary of the New Testament*, trans. T. Prendergast (San Francisco, 1980), 133–34.

13. Thus Merklein, "Überlieferungsgeschichte," 101, citing W. Marxsen, "Der Ursprung des Abendmahls," *EvT* 12 (1952–53) 303.

14. W. Marxsen, *The Lord's Supper as a Christological Problem*, trans. L. Nieting (Philadelphia, 1970). Critique in Patsch 50–58.

15. The Hallel was followed by a fourth cup (*Pesah.* X, 7). This might have been omitted for the same reason for which the lamb or bitter herbs were omitted (see Patsch 225, n. 40).

16. In the minds of the evangelists this "preparation for the Passover meal" could have referred to the first Christian Supper as well as to the Jewish Passover meal. On this question see below, 192–193.

17. See *Ber.* 46a; Dalman 133f.; Billerbeck IV, 616; Jeremias 173ff.

18. Jeremias 49 and 84 (nn. 4–5).

19. Schürmann, "Das Weiterleben der Sache Jesu im nachösterlichen Herrenmahl," in *Jesu Abendmahlshandlung als Zeichen für die Welt* (Leipzig, 1970), 71 (= *BZ* 3). Likewise Neuenzeit 69f. and Merklein 93.

20. With Schürmann, *BZ.*, 6, against Dalman 153 and Jeremias 69–70.

21. Unless it be regarded as an historicization of 1 Cor 10:16, which speaks of *the* "cup of blessing"; but the latter text is from a branch of the cultic tradition, and this makes the hypothesis unlikely.

22. Schürmann, *BZ* 6f. For the opposite view, Jeremias 218–37.

23. See Jeremias 15–88; see below, 306–308.

24. Except for Patsch 34–36. The usual main objection to this entire view is that it is practically impossible to distinguish the Passover meal of Jesus' day from a solemn Jewish meal (see Neuenzeit 69f. or Merklein 93).

25. According to Jeremias 223 the red color of the wine symbolizes the blood of Jesus. A few Old Testament passages do compare wine and blood, but they are not supported by any valid rabbinical text.

26. See above, 159–160. The pages that follow correspond pretty much to what I say in *Face à la mort*, 105–08. I think it necessary to present in a rounded way what the historian might say regarding the thinking of Jesus; readers already familiar with this material can simply skip to page 168.

27. See Is 25:6; Mt 8:11; 22:1–10; Rev 3:20; see above, 37–38.

28. Schürmann, *Recit* 26f.

29. See above, 87–89.

30. This interpretation is not based on the dubious hypothesis that Jesus took part in a Jewish Passover meal (see below, 306–308). It also rules out that of Jeremias who attributes to Jesus an "avowal of abstinence" (see below, Chapter XIII, n. 4).

31. Jn 13–17. This discourse belongs, of course, to the testamentary genre.

32. Lk 22:21–38; see below, 236–243.

33. Thus W. G. Kümmel, "Jesus und die Anfänge der Kirche" (1953), in his *Heilsgeschehen und Geschichte* (Marburg, 1965), 289–309.

34. B. Rigaux, "Die 'Zwölf' in Geschichte und Kerygma," in H. Ristow and K. Matthiae (eds.), *Der historische Jesus und der kerygmatische Christus* (Berlin, 1962), 468–88. See below, 232.

35. See above, Chapter VII.

36. Some critics are of the opinion that the phrase about the multitude migrated from the words over the bread and became attached to the words over the cup. Thus, e.g., Merklein, "Überlieferungsgeschichte," 236. Following Schürmann, "Weiterleben," 13, 15f., 22f., and Patsch 151–225, Merklein thinks that the conceptual scheme of expiation was current in the period of Jesus and that there is nothing against its attribution to him. In his view, the words over the bread contained the reference to the "multitude," but the reasons he gives do not require this inference.

37. See above, 120–123.

38. In *Face à la mort*, 29–171 (especially 109–13 and 168–71).

39. See *Les miracles de Jésus selon le Nouveau Testament* (Paris, 1977), 346, 361f.

40. Because the blood signified life it belonged to God. See above, 143.

41. Lk 22:27. See the pages on this subject in my essay, "Jésus devant sa mort à la lumière des textes de l'institution eucharistique" (above, n. 2), 163–67, or in *Face à la mort*, 94–96.

42. See above, 85–90.

43. Some manuscripts of Lk 22:19f. have only Lk 22:19a: "This is my body," without the addition of "which [is] given for you," and without the command of remembrance and the words over the cup. Today, however, the critics as a body regard the long

text as sure; see Schürmann, "Lk 22, 19b–20 als ursprüngliche Textüberlieferung," *Bib* 32 (1951) 364–92, 522–41, and II, 35f. See also the extensive treatment in Jeremias 139–59. But even if the short text is not authentic, it calls for historical explanation.

44. The situation here is comparable to that which I have described in speaking of the various terminologies in which faith in the saving value of Christ's death is expressed: see *Face à la mort*, passim.

45. See above, 99.

46. See above, Chapters III and VI.

47. See above, 72.

48. P. Benoit, "Le récit de la Cène dans Lc XXII, 15–20," *RB* 48 (1959) 389 (= his *Exégèse et Théologie* I, 195).

49. The list of proponents of authenticity or non-authenticity is given in Schürmann II, 123–29. See also Betz 23f.; Neuenzeit 111–16; Jeremias 168, 238; Hahn, "Motive," 341f.; Patsch 79; Merklein 99.

50. Thus Hahn, "Motive," 341, and "Zum Stand der Erforschung des urchristlichen Herrenmahles," *EvT* 35 (1975) 559; Merklein 237f. The way was prepared for this reconstruction by S. Dockx, "Le récit du repas pascal: Marc 14, 17–26," *Bib* 46 (1965) 445–53, whose views are repeated, without reference, by Schenk, *Passionsbericht*, 189–93; D. Dormeyer, *Die Passion Jesu als Verhaltensmodell* (Münster, 1974), 100–10; Schenke, *Studien* 290–92. See E. Hirsch, *Frühgeschichte des Evangeliums* I (1941), 153f.

51. According to J. M. Hanssens, *Institutiones liturgicae. De ritibus orientalibus* II/1 (Rome, 1930), 79–88 (nos. 139–41), this custom is attested in *Acta Joannis* (2d cent.), ch. 72, 85, 106–10; *Acta Thomae* (ca. 200), ch. 26–29, 49–50, 133; *Acta Petri* (3d cent.), ch. 5; *Ps. Clement.* (4th cent.), *Hom.* 14. It would ordinarily be thought that these attestations were insufficient to prove the existence of such a eucharistic practice under one species; but proponents also cite scriptural texts that allude to such a possible practice: Lk 22:20 (short text); Jn 6:32–35; Lk 24:35; Acts 2:42, 46; 20:7, 11; 27:35, all of which speak only of bread in the context of the Eucharist. I refer the reader to specialists in liturgical history.

52. See above, 55.

53. *Maranatha:* 1 Cor 16:22; Rev 22:20; *Did.* 10, 6. See B. Sandvik, *Das Kommen des Herrn beim Abendmahl im Neuen Testament* (Zurich, 1970), 13–36.

54. I need not emphasize the point that the foregoing recon-

struction is hypothetical. H. Merklein has made a comparable attempt, but with one important difference from mine: he attributes the expiatory scheme to Jesus.

Notes for part III

INTRODUCTION

1. H. I. Marrou, *The Meaning of History*, trans. R. J. Olsen (Baltimore, 1966), 125.

2. Thus in his recent critical essay, "Überlieferungsgeschichte," H. Merklein looks for a "common *Ursprungsform* (not an *Urform*!)" (p. 82), solely for the words spoken at the Supper.

3. With G. Theissen I have tried to show how to establish the structure of a New Testament miracle story; this structure makes it possible to explain the "generation" of the texts as we have them; see X. Léon-Dufour (ed.), *Les Miracles de Jésus selon le Nouveau Testament* (Paris, 1977), 291–353.

X. THE MESSAGE OF MARK

1. TOB, *Nouveau Testament*, 172.

2. E. Schweizer, *The Good News according to Mark*, trans. D. H. Madvig (Richmond, 1971), 299.

3. R. Pesch, *Das Abendmahl und Jesu Todesverständnis* Freiburg/Br., 1978), 112.

4. K. Kertelge, "Das Abendmahl Jesu im Markusevangelium," in *Mélanges H. Zimmermann* (Bonn, 1980), 67–80.

5. Mk 6:31; 6:35f; 8:14.

6. This is one aspect of the theology which Mark systematizes in "the messianic secret": the divine glory that seeks manifestation in the works of Jesus must be as it were restrained so long as the mystery of the Son of Man—his passion and resurrection—cannot be proclaimed with complete openness. It was a condition of revelation that Jesus could not say openly what he was until by his death he had shown the meaning of his "titles."

7. Mk 14:32. See my *Face à la mort*, 113–43.

8. The present participle *ekchynnomenon* does not necessarily have a future meaning; the tense must depend on the meaning of the sentence. See below, Chapter XII, n. 10.

9. Mk 14:2, 12–16, 26; 15:6; 16:1.

10. Therefore the name "feast of Unleavened Bread" (Ex 12:15–20). Unleavened bread (Greek: *azymoi*, without yeast) was

regarded as purer than leavened bread (Ex 34:25; 1 Cor 5:7f.). Beginning in the seventh century B.C. this feast was identified with the feast of Passover.

11. Jer 31:2–21; Is 40:3–5.

12. Is 65:17–25; 11:1–9.

13. The translation is by M. McNamara and M. Maher in A. Diez Macho (ed.), *Neophyti 1. Targum Palestinense. Ms de la Biblioteca Vaticana* II. *Exodo* (Madrid-Barcelona, 1970), 441–42. [I have altered the translation slightly at two points to make it agree with the French translation of R. Le Deaut, which the author is using and which likewise appears in the Diez Macho volume and again in SC, no. 256 (1978) 96 and 98: in its opening sentence the translation of McNamara and Maher has "It is a night *reserved*," and in paragraph five ("The fourth night") it has "When the world reaches its end to be *redeemed*."—Tr.] The phrase "Book of Memorials" is explained further on in the text.

14. The letter to the Hebrews makes reference to this: "By faith Abraham, when he was tested, offered up Isaac. . . . He considered that God was able to raise men even from the dead; hence he did receive him back and this was a symbol" (11:17, 19).

15. I developed this point above, in Chapter VI, Sections I and II.

16. V. Taylor showed this a long time ago in his *The Gospel according to St. Mark* (London, 1952), 536. See D. Dormeyer, *Die Passion Jesu als Verhaltensmodell* (Münster, 1974), 91–94.

17. See above.

18. The remark, "after having sung psalms *(hymnēsantes)*," does not necessarily refer to the Passover ritual.

19. See R. Feneberg, *Christliche Paschafeier und Abendmahl* (Munich, 1971).

20. See 1 Cor 5:7; Ex 12:5, 13; 1 Pet 1:19; Acts 8:32; Rev 5:6, 12. This is independent of whether or not a lamb was eaten at the last meal of Jesus. In any case, once the community was scattered after the fall of Jerusalem, it was no longer possible to obtain lambs that had been immolated in the temple.

21. In connecting the account of the Supper with the Christian feast of Easter Mark is not in any way objecting to the custom of frequent eucharistic celebration (Acts 2:42–46; 1 Cor 11:21–33). He is simply making clear the paschal atmosphere that should characterize the eucharistic liturgy.

22. By "dialogical" I do not mean that there is an exchange of words but rather that the situation is a relational one: here Jesus

is in a reciprocal relation with his disciples. See above, Chapter III, Section III.

23. Thus W. Marxsen, *The Lord's Supper as a Christological Problem*, trans. L. Nieting (Philadelphia, 1970).

24. In keeping with its regular meaning in Greek the verb *lambanō* could be translated "Receive!".

25. It was "not customary for the head of the house expressly to invite his guests to eat the bread that was offered," according to A. Wünsche, *Neue Beiträge zur Erläuterung der Evangelien aus Talmud und Midrasch* (Göttingen, 1878), 331, who is cited in Jeremias 166, n. 4. See Dalman 133ff. Such formulas were, however, used in connection with the cup: Jeremias 166, n.3.

26. See above, Chapter IV.

27. In Mt the imperative "Take!" is followed by another: "Eat!" In the case of the cup, the formula is "Drink of it, all of you." The two imperatives are not simply echoes of a liturgy but signify that the disciples must actively receive the gift given 'em by Jesus.

28. A covenant "for the multitude" says equivalently what Paul says when he speaks of Christ as the new Adam.

29. Mt adds "for the forgiveness of sins," probably with reference to Is 53:10; see above.

30. See above.

31. See E. Lohmeyer, *Das Evangelium des Markus* (Göttingen, 1957), 306–07.

32. See K. Kertelge (n. 4), 74.

33. This is suggested by J. Gnilka, *Das Evangelium nach Markus* II (Neukirchen, 1979), 249.

34. I showed this to be the case in Chapter IV, above.

35. When this is the sense the Greek word used for "new" is *neos*, as in Mk 2:22, where it describes a wine of recent vintage.

XI. PAUL AND THE LORD'S SUPPER

1. Rom 6:1–11; Gal 3:27; see Col 2:12; Tit 3:5. See R. Schnackenburg, *Das Heilsgeschehen bei der Taufe nach dem Apostel Paulus* (Munich, 1950). The author qualified some of his statements in *MTZ* 6 (1955) 32–53.

2. The first letter to the Corinthians, which was written at Ephesus in about 56, was intended for a Christian community in a cosmopolitan city of notoriously dissolute morals. The cult of Aphrodite flourished there. Paul had stayed in Corinth for almost

eighteen months in 51–52. See F. J. De Waele, *Les antiquités de Grèce: Corinthe et saint Paul* (Paris, 1961), 50f., 91–96.

3. 1 Cor 1:18–25.

4. The formula, "Concerning [what you have written to me about] . . . " (see 7:1; 8:1; 12:1; 16:1), marks the transition from each development to the next. There are also allusions to Paul's first visit (11:2, 23; 15:1) and to what he has heard said of the community (15:1, 9).

5. On the various interpretations of 1 Cor 10 see Neuenzeit 44–66, 201–19. On 1 Cor 11:17–34 see C. Perrot, "L'eau, le pain et la confession du Seigneur crucifié," in J. Doré (ed.), *Sacrements de Jésus-Christ* (Paris, 1982).

6. See A. J. Festugière, *Le monde romain au temps de Notre-Seigneur* II. *Le milieu sprituel* (Paris, 1935), 92: "One of Herondas' *Mimes* tells of the prayer, sacrifice, and votive offering made by two women of Cos who come to thank Asclepius for a healing received. The final words of the prayer invite the god to the meal they are presenting to him. The sacrifice takes the form of a meal, but a light one. Cynno would have liked to bring an ox or a fat sow; she can only afford a cock. The servant gives the cock to the sacristan. While the women are in the temple admiring the works of art that adorn it, the sacristan immolates the victim on the altar in front of the god's house. He returns to say that everything has gone off splendidly and that the sacrifice augurs well. . . . Of the animal whose throat has been cut one part goes to the god; another, the thigh, to the sacristan; the remainder (which is in the proper sense of the word an idolothyte or food sacrificed to an idol) will be eaten by the pious women."

7. See *ibid.*, 46, n. 7: "A sacrifice is often followed by a public meal in which the other portions of the victim are divided among the faithful. . . . The parts left for the faithful are generally eaten on the spot. . . . If some flesh of the victims is left after the distribution, the priest has the right to sell it."—And on 96: "In the Roman period the practice of sacrifices followed by meals is constant. St Paul devotes an entire chapter of the first letter to the Corinthians to the question of idolothytes, that is, the flesh of victims; it happened every day that a large part of the butcher's meat came from sacrifices to pagan gods, where the flesh was eaten in the temple or sold in the market."

8. 1 Cor 8:13, which concludes the discussion in 8:7–13.

9. 1 Cor 9:1–23. Even if this digression can be placed only artificially in the context of the idolothytes, the text as a whole seems to require this location.

10. 1 Cor 10:23, which anticipates the discussion in 10:27–33.

11. 1 Cor 8:7. This translation from TOB gives the sense of a text that, taken literally, is very difficult: "still accustomed to idols." Another manuscript has "with the consciousness they still have of idols," i.e., of taking part in idolatry.

12. 1 Cor 9:24–27.

13. 1 Cor 10:12, which draws conclusions from the discussion in 10:1–13.

14. Deut 32. This great text is probably still present in Paul's mind when, further on (11:30), he reminds his readers—in a way that strikes us as strange—of the punishments awaiting those who do not respect the demands of Christian cult (see below, 218).

15. 1 Cor 10:18; see Ex 32:6; Lev 7:6, 15; Deut 12:11f.; 18:1, 4.—By "altar" in this context Jews understood God himself.

16. On Pauline demonology see H. Schlier, *Principalities and Powers in the New Testament* (Quaestiones Disputatae 3; New York, 1961).

17. The terms *koinōnia* has been the subject of many studies: see H. Seesemann, *Der Begriff KOINONIA im Neuen Testament* (Giessen, 1933); F. Hauck, "Koinōnia," *TDNT* 3 (original = 1938) 789–809; G. V. Jourdan, *JBL* 67 (1948) 111–24; H. Sieben, in *DSp* 8 (1974) 1743–45; J. M. McDermott, *BZ* 19 (1975) 64–77, 219–33; R. Schnackenburg, in R. Schnackenburg, F. Hahn, and K. Kertelge (eds.), *Einheit in der Kirche* (Freiburg, 1979) 52–93; G. Panikulam, *Koinonia*, 123ss.

18. In about 110 A.D. Plutarch says that "what impels us to a complete communion *(koinōnia)* at our meetings is that we converse together . . . together we enjoy *(metechomen)* listening to the lyre-player or flute-players . . . I much prefer the banquets described by Pindar, which often brought the heroes together around a noble table in perfect fellowship" *(Table Talk* II, 10, 1, 643B–E).

19. Rom 15:26; 2 Cor 8:4; 9:13 (with preposition *eis*).

20. Phlm 6 (with the thing shared in the genitive case).

21. Eph 5:11 (with the dative).

22. Phil 1:5 (with preposition *eis*).

23. 2 Cor 1:7; Phil 3:10 (with the genitive).

24. Rom 12:13; Phil 4:14 (with the dative).

25. Phil 2:1 (with "spirit" in the genitive).

26. There is no known example of secular Greek using the genitive to express communion with a person.

27. 1 Cor 1:9. Provided the Holy Spirit be regarded as a "per-

son," it is appropriate here to recall the "communion in the Holy Spirit" with which Paul ends his second letter to the Corinthians (2 Cor 13:13).

28. See G. Bornkamm, "Lord's Supper and Church in Paul" (1956), in his *Early Christian Experience,* trans. P. L. Hammer (New York, 1969) 139.

29. A. J. Festugière, *L'idéal religieux des Grecs et de l'Evangile* (Paris, 1932), 321, n. 7, has collected surprising formulas from some magical papyri, though these are admittedly somewhat late (4th–5th cent. A.D.): "You are I, and I am you"; "I know you, Hermes, and you know me. I am you and you are I" (*Papyri graeci magici,* ed. Preisendanz, VIII, pp. 36–38, 49). Festugière points out that the encounter with the god is not an end but a means of acquiring further magical power; the goal therefore is not a transformation of the person but a greater power.

30. Rom 6:8; Col 2:20.

31. Rom 6:6; Gal 2:19.

32. 2 Cor 4:14.

33. Rom 6:8; 2 Cor 13:4; Col 2:13; 1 Thess 5:10.

34. Phil 1:23; Col 3:3f.; 1 Thess 4:17.

35. This is Neuenzeit's explanation, 201–06.

36. This would be true even if the genitive *Christou* in the phrase "body of Christ" were epexegetic, so that the translation would read: "communion with the body which is Christ." But the hypothesis is a shaky one, since it clearly cannot be carried over to the phrase "blood of Christ."

37. For example, Neuenzeit 213f.

38. See J. De Fraine, *Adam and the Family of Man,* trans. D. Raible (Staten Island, N.Y., 1965).

39. The verb *phagein* seems to be reserved here for the Lord's Supper; it is the verb used in "when the eating begins" (v. 21) and "when you gather to eat" (33), as distinct from the kind of "eating and drinking" (*esthiein kai pinein*) that is done in any and every context, whether religious (vv. 25, 26, 27, 28, 29) or secular (vv. 22, 34).

40. Paul is in agreement here with a pagan writer of his time, Plutarch, who cites the opinion of one of his guests: "Where each guest has his own private portion (*to idion*), companionship (*to koinon*) fails" (*Table Talk* II, 10, 1). G. Theissen, who cites this passage, notes that in antiquity the adjectives *idios* and *kyriakos* described types of property, thus *kyriakos logos* and *idios logos* designated imperial and private treasuries respectively; see his

"Social Integration and Sacramental Activity: An Analysis of 1 Cor. 11:17–34" (1974), in his *The Social Setting of Pauline Christianity: Essays on Corinth*, trans. J. H. Schütz (Philadelphia, 1982), 145–74 at 148. But (150) he assimilates *idion* to *ek tōn idiōn* (wrongly, in my opinion), so that (in his view) the "private" meals of 1 Cor 11 were contributed by well-off believers.

41. According to some authors, the Lord's Supper followed the order seen in the Antiochene tradition (Paul): words over the bread, meal, words over the cup. The hypothesis is quite shaky, since the poor who arrived late would then have been deprived of the Eucharist; would Paul not have come down even harder on such an abuse? Most critics (e.g., Bornkamm, "Lord's Supper . . ." [n. 28], 128) therefore think that the Eucharist came at the end of the meal. This hypothesis supposes that the actions over the bread and the cup came in direct succession, as in the Markan tradition. Finally, according to Theissen (151ff.) it is not possible to determine the organization of the liturgy: there was simply a meal which was known as the "Lord's Supper" because the bread was broken and the cup given in the name of the Lord.

42. Beginning in the second century this word designated meals, shared by Christians, which were not cultic as the Eucharist was, but which nonetheless had a certain liturgical cast. See W. D. Hauschild, "Agape I," *Theologische Realenzyklopädie* I (Berlin 1977), 748–53.

43. See above, Chapter I, n. 28

44. On these meals see C. Perrot, *MD* no. 137 (1979) 110f.; and see Theissen 155–62.

45. As I pointed out earlier; see above, 35.

46. See above, 19–20, and Reicke, *Diakonie*, 32f.; 151ff. (esp. 153–64).

47. This is the most interesting aspect of Theissen's work.

48. Acts 2:44f.; 4:32–35.

49. Theissen 146–51.

50. In the last part of the passage (11:28–34) Paul waxes rhetorical in a way that is readily visible in Greek where he plays on words having the same root *(krin-)* but different meanings: "recognize," "examine," "judge," "be judged," and "be condemned," to which are added, in v. 27, other terms from the juridical language of that age: "be guilty" and "unworthily."

51. See above, n. 14, of this chapter. When Paul connects death with an unworthy participation in the sacrament, he probably has in mind those who as a result will not live until the par-

ousia (1 Thess 4:13). Bornkamm, "Lord's Supper . . . " (n. 28) correctly points out that Paul's statement cannot be converted: he does not say that those who receive the body of Christ worthily will be preserved from dying (150).

52. The word *sōma* ("body"), which is the object of the required recognition, may of course refer to that body of the Lord of which Paul has just been speaking; on the other hand, there is nothing in the context that would justify making it mean "the ecclesial body" (see Betz 107). In my opinion, the reference is simply to the "thing" the person does: the "recognition" *(diekrinōn)* in 11:29 has its counterpart in the self-examination *(diekrinomen)* of 11:31. See above, Chapter VII, n. 7.

53. For example, according to Neuenzeit 87, Paul wants to restore a form of celebration that corresponds to what Jesus did. It is true, of course, that Neuenzeit supposes the tradition cited by Paul to be entirely Pre-Pauline.

54. Gal 2:20, Phil 3:10–12; Rom 5:9; see Eph 1:7; 2:13; Col 1:20.

55. 1 Cor 1:18. One reason why Paul had formerly persecuted Christians was the curse attached to death by crucifixion (Gal 3:13).

56. 1 Cor 15:4, 13, 20, 55.

57. Rom 6:3.

58. Rom 6:5. The translation given is a close reproduction of the Greek.

59. See above, Chapter V. On this point I disagree with Neuenzeit who is overly confident that literary criticism can take us back to some *Urbericht* or "original account."

60. 1 Cor 11:23. Does this indication of time belong to the primitive account or is it a Pauline summary? The arguments for each position do not generate conviction.

61. The Western variant in 11:24 reads: "This is my body broken *(klōmenon)* for you." According to J. Duplacy (in a conference at the Congress of the ACFEB in Tarbes, 1981) this reading possesses high value; he thinks it underscores the death of Christ and thus clarifies still further the thrust of the Pauline presentation.

62. 2 Cor 3:6; 5:17; Rom 6:4; 7:6.

63. Note that the verb "to drink" is not in the future tense but in the present subjunctive with an introductory *ean* ("if"): "each time you may drink."

64. The exhortation to remember would be readily understood by Greeks, accustomed as they were to funeral banquets held in memory of the deceased (see also Jer 16:7). See W. von Meding, *EvT* 35 (1975) 544–54.

65. See below, n. 72.

66. See above, 43–44.

67. Schürmann goes into the question in detail (II, 33f.); see also Neuenzeit 132f.

68. The Greek word for "proclaim" belongs to the family of words whose root is *aggel-*; these are part of a vocabulary that turned profane forms of behavior into sacral forms. Just as nowadays officials solemnly proclaim the opening of the Olympic Games, so in the ancient cult of the emperors a "herald" would proclaim the "good news" *(eu-aggelia)* of the birth of an emperor, for example, Augustus. Like these heralds, the "evangelists" were messengers of a good news.—Allowing for the nuance of extension or diffusion in time that is added by the preposition *kata*, Paul's word for "proclaim," *kataggelō*, corresponds pretty closely to the verb *kēryssō* (which the New Testament uses for the primitive Christian preaching), as can be seen from the use of the two verbs as equivalents in a passage of the letter to the Philippians: "to preach Christ" *(kēryssein)* in 1:15 and "to proclaim Christ" *(kataggelein)* in 1:18.

69. As in Acts 26:23. In other passages the object of the proclaiming is a person (Acts 17:3; Phil 1:17; Col 1:28) or a thing (Acts 13:5; 15:36; 17:23; 1 Cor 2:1; 9:14; 1 Thess 1:5).

70. See above, 23, 26–27; and C. Perrot, *MD* no. 137 (1970) 124.

71. As I said earlier, it seems useless to try to recover the formula used. Furthermore, the account of the Supper is already a statement rooted in history, and this keeps it from fantasy.

72. The "for" *(gar)* which introduces v. 26 suggests that the verb be taken as an indicative, not an imperative. See Schürmann II, 32, n. 129, for a list of authors who interpret it as an imperative.

73. On the symbolisms Paul uses in this area see my *Face à la mort*, 182–97.

74. See *ibid.*, 262–70.

75. *Ibid.*, 211. Some medical experts have told me that they would prefer *sclerosis* as being a more active term than *necrosis*, which means the change that takes place in a tissue as a result of

the death of its cells. See *Face à la mort*, 264, n. 16. I am not sure, however, that their remarks are accurate, at least if one sticks to the definition of the word: on the death of its cells a tissue undergoes an active change. At the end of the process the tissue is entirely necrotized.

XII. THE TESTAMENT OF JESUS ACCORDING TO LUKE

1. The references in the table are to the Greek *Testament of Naphtali*, trans. H. C. Kee in J. H. Charlesworth (ed.), *the Old Testament Pseudepigrapha 1. Apocalyptic Literature and Testaments* (New York, 1983), 810–14.—I am pleased to find that Bo Reicke has already called attention to the parallel in his *Diakonie*, 143.

2. The numbers used here are those given earlier in Chapter IV, Section II, where I listed the major themes in the testamentary genre.

3. In Luke the Greek verb *pathein* can refer to suffering in general (Lk 17:25) but, when applied to Christ, it means in most instances suffering that leads to death (24:26, 46; Acts 1:3; 3:18; 17:3). The same meaning is frequently found elsewhere as well (Heb 2:18; 5:7–9; 13:12; 1 Pet 2:21). Consequently, Christ's "suffering" includes both his passion and his death.

4. Jeremias 208 thinks the translation should be: "I would very gladly have eaten this passover lamb with you before my death," because the verb *epithymein* usually means a desire that cannot be satisfied, at least in Luke (15:16; 16:21; 17:22). Such an interpretation is not impossible, but neither is it required, especially since there is question here of a pre-Lukan tradition and since in Heb 6:11 the word surely means simply "desire." Jeremias claims that the only way to understand v. 17 is to see it as already reflecting the reason why, contrary to custom, Jesus does not share the cup (209), this reason being that he has decided to abstain from the bread and wine of the Passover meal in order to intercede for Israel (thus providing a basis for the Quartadeciman fast at Passover). But, although Jeremias increasingly refines his position in the successive editions of his book, he does not succeed in showing that there is really an "avowal of abstinence" at work here (H. Patsch accepts Jeremias' interpretation).

5. See above, 188–191.

6. In keeping with classical biblical usage the passive voice of the verb (*plerōthei* = be fulfilled) indicates that the agent is God himself.

7. The Greek word *basileia* can be translated as "kingdom" if the context is spatial, and as "reign" if the context is temporal (as in Lk 11:20).

8. The expression "eat the passover" means to celebrate the feast mentioned in Lk 22:16 and not necessarily to "eat the passover lamb" (contrary to Jeremias 208).

9. On the question of whether this meal did or did not follow the Passover ritual see the Appendix (section II), below.

10. Greek participles in the present tense are too often translated as referring to the proximate future, when they can and sometimes should be translated as present tenses in English. The meaning here is: "This is my body which *is being given*, my blood which *is being shed*." See above, Chapter X, n. 8.

11. See above, 36, and L. Goppelt, "Trapeza," *TDNT* 8 (original = 1966) 212; D. Gill, "A Neglected Aspect of Greek Sacrifice," *HTR* 67 (1974) 117–37.

12. Jn 13:30.

13. See 1 Cor 11:27.

14. See Heb 6:4–6, 10:29. See Schürmann, *Récit*, 78f., for an excellent discussion of the ecclesial dimension of the Lukan text.

15. Astounding though this dispute may seem in such a setting, it acquires some historical probability from the problems of precedence that arose at banquets (see above, 216–217).

16. Mk 10:35–45 = Mt 20:20–28. This pericope contains the same contrast between the prediction of the death/resurrection and the dispute among the disciples.

17. The person of Jesus is at the center of this final discourse; if he gives, and gives himself, it is because the Father has arranged everything with a view to him and because it is in him, thanks to his utterly selfless service, that the covenant is sealed.

18. In the words which he addresses to Peter in John's gospel Jesus intends to convey by his action that the disciple "has part in him" (Jn 13:8), a purpose which is the same as that of the eucharistic gift (see 1 Cor 10:16). But "to have part in Jesus" immediately implies that one is ready to let the example of Jesus act within oneself and produce fruits of fraternal service (Jn 13:15). On this passage see below, Chapter XIII, Section 1.

19. The order of Jesus to his disciples that they should distribute the multiplied loaves ("You give them something to eat": Lk 9:13) is sometimes interpreted as meaning that the twelve are being commissioned to feed the other members of the Church; in

fact, however, the crowd in the text is not distinguished into believers and non-believers.

20. See the discussion in Schürmann, *Récit*, 71–73.

21. See above, 92.

22. See O. de Dinechin, "KATHŌS. La similitude dans l'évangile selon saint Jean," *RSR* 58 (1970) 195–236. See below, 249–250.

23. Mt 19:28 records the same words in a different context in which the promise refers to "the new age" *(en te paliggenesia)*, that is, to the parousia, and consists in a collegial participation by the twelve in the judging of Israel. See J. Dupont, "Le logion des douze trônes," *Bib* 45 (1964) 355–92.

24. The verb "confer" (or "appoint") translates the Greek verb *dia-tithēmi*, which is from the same root as *dia-thēkē*, "covenant."

25. "Peter said to him: 'Lord, I am ready to go with you even to prison, even to death.' Jesus said: 'I tell you, Peter, the cock shall not crow today until you have three times denied knowing me'" (Lk 22:33f.; see Mk 14:29–31 = Mt 26:32–35). Luke does not record the announcement of the scattering: "You will all fall away; for it is written, 'I will strike the shepherd, and the sheep will be scattered'" (Mk 14:27 = Mt 26:31).

26. Lk 10:18; 11:18; 13:16. Luke attributes the temptation of Jesus to the "devil" (4:2f., 6) who "departs from him until the appointed time" (4:13). In Luke Peter is never called "Satan" (see Mk 8:33 = Mt 16:23).

27. Lk 22:3, see Jn 13:27.

28. See Mk 14:50 = Mt 16:56: "And they all forsook him and fled."

29. See Mk 14:28 = Mt 26:32: "After I am raised up, I will go before you to Galilee."

30. "The Lord has risen indeed, and has appeared to Simon" (Lk 24:34); note the recurrence of the name "Simon." See 1 Cor 15:5; Jn 21:15–17.

31. Simon is here called Peter, this being the name that suggests a solid foundation. On the possibility of the fall of leaders see 1 Cor 9:27; Gal 6:1; James 3:1f; and Schürmann, *Récit*, 80–84.

32. "Do not think that I have come to bring peace on earth; I have not come to bring peace, but a sword" (Mt 10:34).

33. "Put your sword back into its place; for all who take the sword will perish by the sword. Do you think that I cannot appeal to my Father, and he will at once send me more than twelve

legions of angels? But how then should the scriptures be fulfilled, that it must be so?" (Mt 26:52–54).

34. See Lk 21:17 "You will be hated by all for my name's sake."

35. In 22:37 Luke is citing Is 53:12.

36. Lk 9:3; 10:4; 12:29–31.

37. Mk 14:8 = Mt 26:12.

XIII. THE EUCHARIST ACCORDING TO JOHN

1. Jn 3:5; 6:51b–58; 19:34. See R. Bultmann, *Theology of the New Testament,* trans. K. Grobel (2 vols.; New York, 1951, 1955), I, 139, 142, 147.

2. E. Schweizer, "Das johanneische Zeugnis vom Herrenmahl" (1953) and "Das Herrenmahl im Neuen Testament" (1954), reprinted in his *Neotestamentica* (Zürich-Stuttgart, 1963), 379–94 and 367–70. H. Strathmann, *Das Evangelium nach Johannes* (Göttingen, 1963), 126.

3. O. Cullmann, *Early Christian Worship,* trans. A. Stewart Todd and J. B. Torrance (SBT 10; London, 1953), 37–119. This essay dates from 1951.

4. W. Michaelis, *Die Sakramente im Johannesevangelium* (Bern, 1946).

5. E. Hoskyns, *The Fourth Gospel,* ed. F. N. Davey (London, 1947); A. Corell, *Consummatum est. Eschatology and Church in the Gospel of St. John* (London, 1958); B. Vawter, "The Johannine Sacramentary," *TS* 17 (1956) 151–66; P. E. Niewalda, *Sakramentssymbolik im Johannesevangelium* (Limburg, 1958).

6. Ignatius of Antioch, *Eph.* 20, 2, speaks of the Eucharist as "medicine for immortality."

7. As Niewalda does.

8. R. Schnackenburg, "Die Sakramente im Johannesevangelium," in *Sacra Pagina* II (Paris-Gembloux, 1959), 235–54; R. E. Brown, "The Johannine Sacramentary Revisited" (1962), in his *New Testament Essays* (Milwaukee, 1965), 51–76; idem, *The Gospel according to John* (2 vols.; Anchor Bible 29–30; New York, 1966 and 1970), 1:cix–cxiv.

9. Many, however, give these chapters the title, "Discourse after the Supper," without adverting to the fact that in the context there is no question of a eucharistic meal but simply of Jesus' farewell. The discourse admittedly begins only in 13:33, but by reason of the introduction in 13:1 it is inseparable from the washing of

the feet, which is a key part (namely, the establishment of the community) of the testament of Jesus.

10. See above, Chapters IV and XII.

11. The washing of the feet symbolizes the gift of service to the very end (13:3–11). The symbolism is discussed again in the perspective of Jesus' "example" (13:12–20).

12. See O. de Dinechin, "KATHŌS. La similitude dans l'évangile selon saint jean," *RSR* 58 (1970) 208–13.

13. See above, Chapter XII.

14. On the testamentary form see above, Chapter IV.

15. 13:2.

16. 13:15–17.

17. 13:34f.

18. 15:18—16:4.

19. 14:15–28; 15:26; 16:5–22.

20. 14:13f.; 16:23–26.

21. It is clear that the Church in which John lived practiced the eucharistic rite. As a result critics generally think that John is deliberately taking a position in regard to it. For other explanations of the absence of the account of institution see R. Schnackenburg, *The Gospel According to John* III, trans. D. Smith and G. A. Kon (New York, 1982), 42–47.

22. See X. Léon-Dufour, "Et là, Jésus baptisait (Jn 3, 22)," in *Mélanges E. Tisserant* (Vatican City, 1964), I, 295–309.

23. The following discussion is based on my technical study of the discourse: "Le mystère du Pain de vie (Jn VI)," *RSR* 46 (1958) 481–523.

24. Thus in the conversation with Nicodemus, after a first, summary revelation (3:3) a twofold objection leads into a twofold discussion: "How can one be born again? Is such a thing possible?" (3:4). Jesus begins by answering the second part of the objection: It is indeed possible by the power of the Spirit and water (3:5–8). Nicodemus then repeats the first part of the objection, which has to do with the means required (3:9), and Jesus gives his answer (3:10–15). The mysterious words of Jesus in 3:3 thus give rise to a twofold objection and lead to a twofold development of the thought. If this is indeed the case—and other examples could be given in confirmation—then the evangelist's intention is to group the various statements of Christ *around* these fundamental objections, and the latter cannot serve as starting points.

25. In vv. 37 and 39 it is the Father who gives to the Son; this is a different theme from the one to which I am referring here.

26. Instead of looking for a "better order" among the verses (M.-J. Lagrange), it is possible to show that vv. 36–40 form a coherent entity. A chiasmus links them closely together. V. 40b recalls vv. 35f., both positively by mentioning eternal life and the last day, and negatively by the expression "see and believe," which is contrasted with "those who see and do not believe." Vv. 39b and 37 both speak of what the Father gives and of the theme of not rejecting, of losing nothing.

27. V. 48, which repeats v. 35 ("The bread of life is myself"), might be taken either as introducing the second development (49–58) or as concluding the first by repeating the same sentence. It seems preferable to make it the beginning of the second part, because then the endings of the two parts correspond nicely:

Truly, truly, I tell you, whoever believes has eternal life (47)	Whoever eats this bread will live for ever (58)

28. The unity of the discourse has also been defended by B. Gartner, *John 6 and the Jewish Passover* (Uppsala, 1959); P. Borgen, "The Unity of the Discourse in Jn 6," *ZNW* 50 (1959) 277f., and *Bread from Heaven* (Leiden, 1965); J.-N. Aletti, "Le discours sur le pain de vie (Jn 6). Problèmes de composition et fonction des citations de l'Ancien Testament," *RSR* 62 (1974) 169–87.

29. This was proposed almost simultaneously by J. Bonsirven, "*Hoc est corpus meum.* Recherches sur l'original araméen," *Bib* 29 (1948) 205–19, and J. Jeremias, "Zur Exegese der Abendmahlsworte Jesu," *EvT* 7 (1947) 60; see also Jeremias, *Eucharistic Words*, 198–201. This reconstruction is challenged today.

30. See A. Feuillet, "The Principal Biblical Themes in the Discourse on the Bread of Life" (1960), in his *Johannine Studies*, trans. T. E. Crane (Staten Island, N.Y., 1965), 53–128.

31. See also Is 65:11–13; Sir 24:19–22.

32. Feuillet (n. 30), 73.

33. See Hos 2:25; Jer 31:33; Cant 2:16.

34. M.-J. Lagrange, *L'Evangile selon saint Jean* (Gabalda, 1925, 1936⁵), 195f.

35. J. Wellhausen (1908), 32; F. Spitta (1910), 156; E. von Dobschütz (1929), 163; R. Bultmann, *The Gospel of John*, trans. G. R. Beasley-Murray, R. W. N. Hoare, and J. K. Riches (Philadelphia, 1971; original = 1941), 218–33; idem, *Theology of the New*

Testament (original = 1948–51), I, 147; E. Schweizer (1939), 155; J. Jeremias, *Die Abendmahlsworte Jesu* (1941), 43–46, and (1949²), 59.

36. E. Ruckstuhl, *Die literarische Einheit des Johannes-Evangeliums* (Freiburg, 1951), 265f.; J. Jeremias, *ZNW* 43 (1952–53) 255f.

37. *The Jerusalem Bible* (New York, 1966), *New Testament*, 157, n. *d*: "Some interpreters hold that a discourse about the Eucharist (6:51–58: Jesus nourishing the soul with his flesh and blood, cf. 6:51 +) has been inserted into the narrative-discourse which may be summarized as follows: the Jews ask for a 'sign' like that of the manna, vv. 30–31; cf. 1:21 +; Jesus tells them, 'The Father's message, which I pass on to man, (cf. 3:11 +) makes of me man's true bread, a nourishment that only those with faith can receive,' vv. 32f; the Jews do not understand, vv. 60–66; only Peter and the disciples believe, vv. 67–71." [*The New Jerusalem Bible* (New York, 1985) repeats this information, but adds that vv. 31–58 are more probably "one integral sermon" (p. 1757, n. *d*).—Tr.]

38. *L'Evangile et les Epîtres de saint Jean* (Paris, 1973), 118, n. *b*.

39. Osty makes no reference to it; the TOB is satisfied to say simply: "Section devoted explicitly to the sacrament of the Eucharist; there is general acknowledgment of the Johannine character of the passage" (307, n. *o*): " . . . themes which here take on a eucharistic coloring" (n. *r*).

40. R. Schnackenburg, *The Gospel according to John* I, trans. K. Smyth (New York, 1968), 215.

41. Symbolism here becomes allegory. Heracleon (second century), the first commentator on the fourth gospel, is already an allegorist of the most extreme kind: thus he describes the husband of the Samaritan woman as "fellow from the pleroma" (fr. 18) and interprets the two days which the Savior spends in Samaria as "the present Aeon and the future one in marriage" (fr. 38) (translations from *Gnosticism. A Source Book of Heretical Writings from the Early Christian Period*, ed. R. M. Grant [New York, 1961], 200 and 204). This use of the text serves to justify his own gnostic system. Allegorization is a danger that constantly threatens a reader of John, but the danger should not keep us from holding to the authentic symbolism in the gospel; see H. de Lubac, *Histoire et Esprit. L'intelligence de l'Ecriture d'après Origène* (Paris, 1950).

42. See my *Les Evangiles et l'Histoire de Jésus*, 125–34 (ET:93–98).

43. Lalande, *Vocabulaire technique et critique de la philosophie* (Paris, 1947³), 1058. The pages that follow here draw upon a paper which I read at Toronto in August of 1980 and published under the title, "Towards a Symbolic Reading of the Fourth Gospel," *NTS* 27 (1980–81) 439–56.

44. Life: Ez 47:1–12; Rev 22:1, 17; Jn 7:37f.; purifying waters: Ez 16:4–9; 36:24–27; Mt 3:11; 1 Cor 6:11; terrifying waters: Gen 6–8; Job 12:15; 40:23; Ez 26:19f.; Rev 12:15; see above, 127–128.

45. As I pointed out above, 35. The symbolism occurs in various sayings of Jesus, as, for example, when he says (citing Deuteronomy): "Human beings do not live on bread alone but on every word from the mouth of God" (Mt 4:4 par. = Deut 8:3), or when he tells his disciples that his "food" is to do the Father's will (Jn 4:34).

46. X. Léon-Dufour, "Le signe du Temple selon saint Jean," *RSR* 39–40 (1951–52) 155–75.

47. *Ibid.*, 156, 173–75; see *Les Evangiles et l'histoire de Jésus*, 115–25 (ET:86–93).

48. "Towards a Symbolic Reading" (n. 43), 443–45. [The two unidentified quotations that follow in this and the second-next paragraphs are from this essay, 443–44 and 445 respectively. - Tr.]

49. Thus Jn 7:38f; 11:50–52; 12:16; 12:32f.

50. At least beginning in v. 53. Schürmann has shown that 6:51c ("And the bread that I shall give is my flesh for the life of the world") refers directly not to the eucharistic sacrament but to the saving death of Jesus; see his "Joh. 6,51c—ein Schlüssel zur johanneischen Brotrede" (1958) and "Die Eucharistie als Repräsentation und Applikation des Heilsgeschehens nach John 6, 53–58" (1959) in his *Ursprung*, 151–66 and 167–87. I differ from Schürmann inasmuch as he regards vv. 53–58 as a kind of midrash on the eucharistic words in connection with the preceding revelation on the death of Jesus.

51. With one difference: the sacrifice of the cross, which is implied in the image of the "raising up" of the Son of Man, acquires an independent value here under the symbol of eating, while in the conclusion of the discourse the raising up (i.e., the "ascending") refers only to the ascension.

52. Jn 10:11, 15; 11:50–52; 13:37f.; 15:13; 17:19; 18:14.

Admittedly, all these texts have the verb *tithēmi* or *apothanein* and *hagiazō* instead of *dounai;* to justify the choice of *dounai* it is enough to recall its recurrence in 6:11, 27, 31, 32, 34 (see Mt 20:28 par.; Gal 1:4). See above, 121–122.

53. A. Schlatter, *Der Evangelist Johannes* (Stuttgart, 1948), 178.

54. See the recent commentaries on these various texts; e.g., Schnackenburg III (n. 21).

55. 6:11, 13; 3:34 and 4:14; 10:10.

56. *Adv. haer.* III, 11, 5 (SC 211:153). See R. E. Brown, *New Testament Essays* (n. 8), 69f., citing a reference of Niewalda to a catacomb.

57. Some critics (e.g., R. E. Brown, *The Gospel according to John* 2:951f.), having opted for a eucharistic interpretation of the Cana story, think that the sacraments of the Eucharist and baptism are symbolized by the blood and water that flow from the side of the crucified Jesus. For John says that from the side of the crucified Jesus "at once there came out *blood and water.* He who saw it has borne witness—his testimony is true, and he knows that he tells the truth—that you also may believe" (19:34f.). The blood flowing from the side bears witness to the reality of the personal sacrifice of Jesus. Can we also see in it "eucharistic blood"? Such an allusion is not impossible if one recalls that the word "blood" occurs elsewhere in John only in the discourse on the Bread of Life (6:53–56) and if one assumes a eucharistic dimension in the episode at Cana where Mary was present, and then observes that Mary is also at the foot of the cross. Finally, this passage should be compared with the passage in the first letter of John (5:8) which speaks of the three witnesses, especially since the water, coming as it does after the Spirit, symbolizes the sacrament of baptism.

58. In the Greek translation of Ps 79:9–16. See C. H. Dodd, *The Interpretation of the Fourth Gospel* (Cambridge, 1953), 410ff.

59. On the difficulties in a eucharistic interpretation of the passage see Brown, *The Gospel according to John* 2:1098–1100, who takes a favorable view of it. See also M. Kehl, *GL* 24 (1970) 105f., and A. Shaw, "The Breakfast by the Shore and the Mary Magdalene Encounter as Eucharistic Narratives," *JTS* 25 (1974) 12–26.

60. Jn 1:34; 1:51; 1:33; 3:34; 7:38; 10:36, 38 (see 14:10f., 20); 17:6, 26; 11:52; 17:23; 17:19; 14:23.

61. Jn 7:37; 4:20f.

62. See E. Malatesta, *Interiority and Covenant* (Rome, 1978), 27–36.

Notes for Part IV

XIV. OVERTURE

1. Readers desirous of seeing the spiritual conclusions that follow from this exegetical study are urged to read the writings of Karl Rahner. He suggests an authentic response for modern believers in such matters as adoration of the Blessed Sacrament, visits to the Blessed Sacrament, thanskgiving after Mass (which has nothing to do with the duration of the presence of the "species"), presentation of the Mass to the "young," and so on; see his *The Christian Commitment. Essays in Pastoral Theology,* trans. C. Hastings (New York, 1963), 136ff., 171ff. (in England = Mission and Grace, vol. 1) Further refinements can be found in the essays: "Word and Eucharist" and "The Presence of Christ in the Sacrament of the Lord's Supper," in *Theological Investigations* 4, trans. K. Smyth (Baltimore, 1966), 253–86 and 287–311.

2. See A. Malvy, "Lavement des pieds," *DTC* 9 (1926) 32–36.

3. On Pseudo-Dionysius and his posterity see R. Roques, *L'univers dionysien* (Paris, 1954), 245–302 (especially 256–71). See also M.-D. Chenu, *Nature, Man, and Society in the Twelfth Century,* ed. and trans. J. Taylor and L. K. Little (Chicago, 1968), 82–83 and 127.

4. See my *Resurrection and the Message of Easter,* trans. R. N. Wilson (New York, 1974), 242.

5. On the shift of mentality and on the entire question see H. de Lubac, *Corpus Mysticum. L'Eucharistie et l'Eglise au Moyen Age* (Paris, 1944); see also G. Martelet, *The Risen Christ and the Eucharistic World,* trans. R. Hague (New York, 1976), 122–46.

6. See my *Resurrection* (n. 4), 213–17.

7. Thus a pamphlet writer who aimed at being "pastoral" thought he could answer a difficulty by saying that Jesus is not "in" the host; but the answer was based on an inadequate theology of "signs" according to which signifiers are on the same plane as, but distinct from, what they signify. See L. Charlot, *Jésus est-il dans l'hostie?* (Angers, 1976); and see *DC* 74 (1977) 131–34.

8. The *koinōnia* achieved through eucharistic eating must be connected with *kathōs* which, as I pointed out (Chapter XIII at n. 12), refers to origination rather than exemplarity, that is, it is

Jesus himself who performs in his disciples the service that is to be their distinguishing mark. Such is the dynamism set in motion by the presence of the risen Lord, whether in the eucharistic rite or in the life of fraternal service.

9. To the extent that the disciples subsequently do what Jesus himself has done, the question arises whether the diversity of roles should not likewise find expression in the liturgical action. A "presidential" role should suggest the irreducible otherness of Jesus in relation to the disciples. The Church is indeed the body of Christ, but on the other hand the Church is not Christ himself; the images which Paul uses correct one another, for alongside the image of the Church as "body" there is the image of the Church as wife to Christ the husband. The New Testament does not, of course, undertake to determine the details of the liturgical action; nonetheless the duality Christ/Church calls for expression in the course of this action. This means that a "president" cannot be simply an appointee of the assembly, but must also be the "other" who stands over against the Church.—This last remark evidently does not in any way prejudge the question of who can fill the role of president.

The preceding observations have to do with the eucharistic liturgical action as a whole; they may however indirectly throw some light on the controversy about the role of the priest as one who acts "in the name of Christ" or "in the name of the Church"—an alternative which recent theoreticians regard as improper (see Y. Congar, Preface to B. D. Marliangeas, *Clés pour une théologie du ministère. In persona Christi. In persona Ecclesiae* [Paris, 1978]; along slightly different lines, C. Giraudo, *La struttura* . . . [Chapter II, n. 46], 361–66). My remarks do not necessarily support the definition (dating from the twelfth century) of the priest as one who has the "power" to consecrate; they reflect rather the Eastern tradition to which Y. Congar refers in citing A. Bloom: "As an icon, the priest must allow the message which he bears (without being identical with it) to shine through him. He must have the ability to be there without imposing his presence. He enters the sanctuary, behind the iconostasis, but this is neither his right nor his privilege, for Christ alone can be there in his own right. The priest stands in the sanctuary as an icon, *in persona Christi*" (Marliangeas 10). It can be said, then, that by reason of his function the president "symbolizes" the officiating Christ; it is clear, however, that the president also speaks in the name of the Church.

10. As H. de Lubac brilliantly showed in his *Corpus mysticum* (n. 5), *passim* and especially in the conclusion of the book: "When applied to the Eucharist *corpus mysticum* meant *corpus in mysterio* and was directly correlated with a *mysterium corporis*. Understandably, then, it seemed quite natural throughout a first period of time to distinguish the sacramental body from the historical, crucified body. . . . By stages which I have described, the designation *corpus mysticum* was shifted from the Eucharist to the Church; once again, in an analogous sense, there was a *mysterium corporis*, that is, the *corpus mysticum* was the mystery of the ecclesial body as signified by the sacrament, and the ecclesial body could properly be said, in this radical sense, to be 'contained' in the Eucharist. Then, in a new transition, there was a passage from *mysterium corporis* to *corpus in mysterio*, from signification to thing signified. The Church was now the mystical body of Christ; this meant, quite simply, that it is the body of Christ as signified by the sacrament. *Mysticum* is a contraction for *mystice significatum, mystice designatum*" (281).

11. Two remarks. The first is aimed at an historicist mentality: the eucharistic celebration cannot be reduced to an offering solely of the bread; even if it is possible that historically only the words over the bread go back to Jesus himself, and even if in the beginning there was here and there a celebration using only one species, it is certain the New Testament revelation requires a double liturgical action, using both the bread and the wine.

The second remark: It is not for exegetes to decide whether the Eucharist, in order to be worthy of the name, requires the particular matter which we call bread and wine. What is certain is that Jesus himself, as well as the early Christians, used bread and wine and that the meal celebrated in remembrance of Jesus should somehow reflect what was done then.

12. See the essays of A. Vergote, "Dimensions anthropologiques de l'eucharistie," in *L'Eucharistie, symbole et réalité* (Gembloux, 1970), 7–56, and L. M. Chauvet, "La dimension sacrificielle de l'Eucharistie," *MD* no. 123 (1975) 47–78.

13. See I. de la Potterie, *La Vérité dans saint Jean* (Rome, 1977), II, 758–83.

ENVOI

1. A. Néher, *L'Existence juive, Solitude et Affrontement* (Paris, 1962), 133–40.

APPENDIX

1. Dalman 106–84; Billerbeck IV, 41–76; Jeremias 84–88.

2. *Pesahim* X.

3. In addition to Billerbeck IV, 611–39 see especially G. Dix, *The Shape of the Liturgy* (Westminster, 1945), 50ff., summarized by L. Bouyer, *MD* no. 18 (1949) 34–46.

4. Dom A. Calmet, "Dissertation sur la dernière Pasque de Notre Seigneur Jésus-Christ," in *Dissertations qui peuvent servir de prolégomènes de l'Ecriture Sainte, revues, corrigées, considérablement augmentées, et mises dans un ordre méthodique* III (Paris, 1720), 280–94. This work reprints the introductions and prefaces of the great commentary which we now have only in a second edition: *Commentaire littéral sur tous les livres de l'ancien et du nouveau Testament. L'Evangile de Matthieu* (Paris, 1725²), cxlv–clxi. Calmet lists as proponents of his view Tertullian, Hilary the Deacon, and authors cited under the names of St. Clement of Alexandria and St. Peter of Alexandria, as well as some recent writers, among them M. Toynard and Father Lami. For this reason, Calmet says, "I am determined to maintain that in the last year of his life Jesus Christ did not celebrate the legal Passover, either at the same time as the other Jews or before them" (294).

5. "Ut tota Dissertatio in problema verteretur": p. 1 and 60B–62 of the Latin translation published by J. D. Mansi in 1760.

6. Jeremias remains the leader of those who argue that the Last Supper was a Passover meal. Recently, G. J. Bahr, "The Seder of Passover and the Eucharistic Words," *NT* 12 (1970) 181–202.

7. Thus Dix (n. 3); V. Taylor, *The Gospel according to St. Mark* (London, 1952), 664–67.

8. One of the first modern critics to argue that the meal did not follow the Passover ritual was T. Preiss, "Le dernier repas de Jésus fut-il un repas pascal?" *TZ* 4 (1948) 81–101, reprinted in his *Vie en Christ* (Neuchâtel, 1951), 115–31. L. Bouyer helped to popularize this opinion: *MD* no. 18 (1949) 34–46.

9. Jeremias 15–88.

10. Jeremias 88.

11. See above, Chapter X, Section III, "Jewish Passover and Passover of Jesus."

Index

Abstinence, 34, 164–166, 239, 307
Account: of institution of Eucharist, 161–162; liturgical, 82–85; Sinai, 144–145. *See also* Account of Lord's Supper
Account of Lord's Supper: and action of Jesus, 57–59; articulation of, 54–57; axes of, 55, 69–72; constitutive elements of, 50–51; extent of, 47, 50; historical elements in, 163–164; historical factor of, 84–85; liturgical factor of, 82–84; meal setting of, 52–53; meaning of, 73–75; in New Testament, 46; structure of, 72–73; synchronic reading of, 46–47, 76–77; and tradition, 176–179; and viewpoint of disciples, 65–69; and viewpoint of Jesus, 60–65; as whole, 53–54. *See also* Eucharistic texts
Actions of Jesus: and bread, 51, 57–59, 62–63; and Eucharist, 162–164; historical element of, 164; and memory, 105; and wine, 51, 57, 59
Acts of the Apostles: 2:46, 22–25; and community, 21; and eucharistic practice, 15; and pooling of possessions, 218
Agape, 89, 217. *See also* Lord's Supper

Anamnēsis, 72, 109–110, 114, 224
Anthropology, 9, 64, 108, 148, 212, 289
Antiochene tradition: and body, 120–123; and death of Jesus, 224–225; description of, 97–99, 101; and words of Jesus, 173; and words over bread, 117, 130, 179, 222; and words over cup, 137–139, 179
Apostles. *See* Acts of the Apostles; Apostolic teaching; Disciples
Apostolic teaching, 26–28
Appearance of risen Jesus: in Emmaus, 26; and Eucharist, 30, 39, 275, 293; and food, 33, 37; and Jewish rite, 22; outside of temple, 25; to Simon, 241
Aramaic, 97, 99–100, 119, 123
Assembly: Christian, 17, 22–29; and covenant, 225; inequality in, 217–220; Jewish, 18–19; and meal, 18, 35–38; and present salvation, 225; symbolism of, 35–38

Banquet: eschatological, 201; final, 38, 111; funerary, 110; heavenly, 72, 166; image of, 165; of kingdom, 54; on last day, 38; and Lord's Supper, 195–198
Baptism, 203, 218, 225–226, 252, 288

383